AF594096

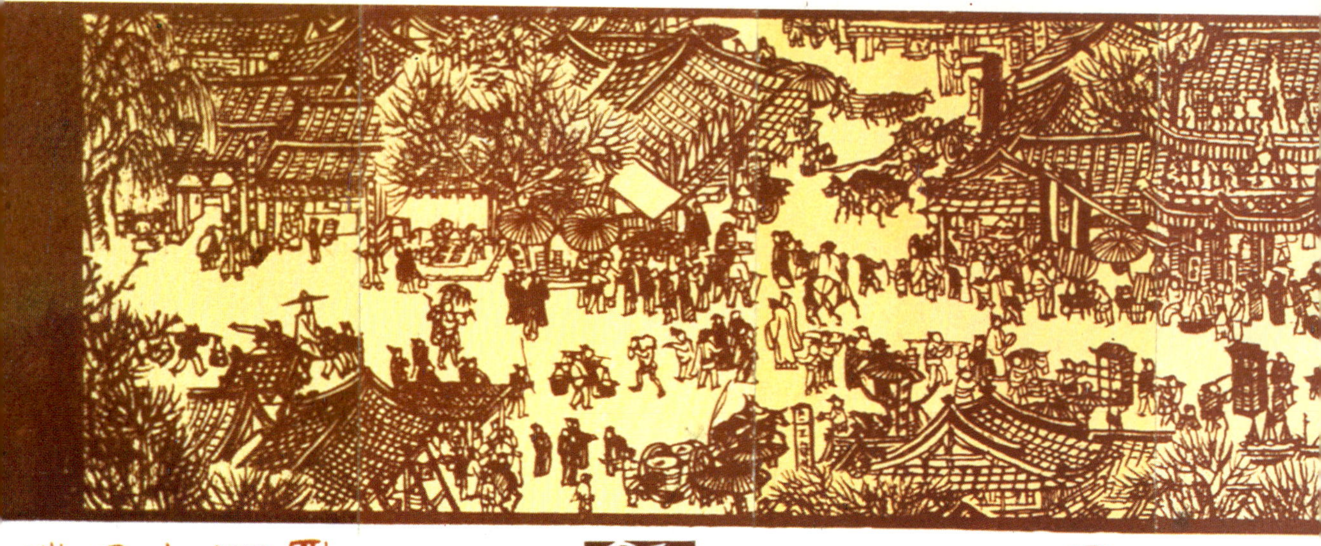

清明上河圖  清明上河圖

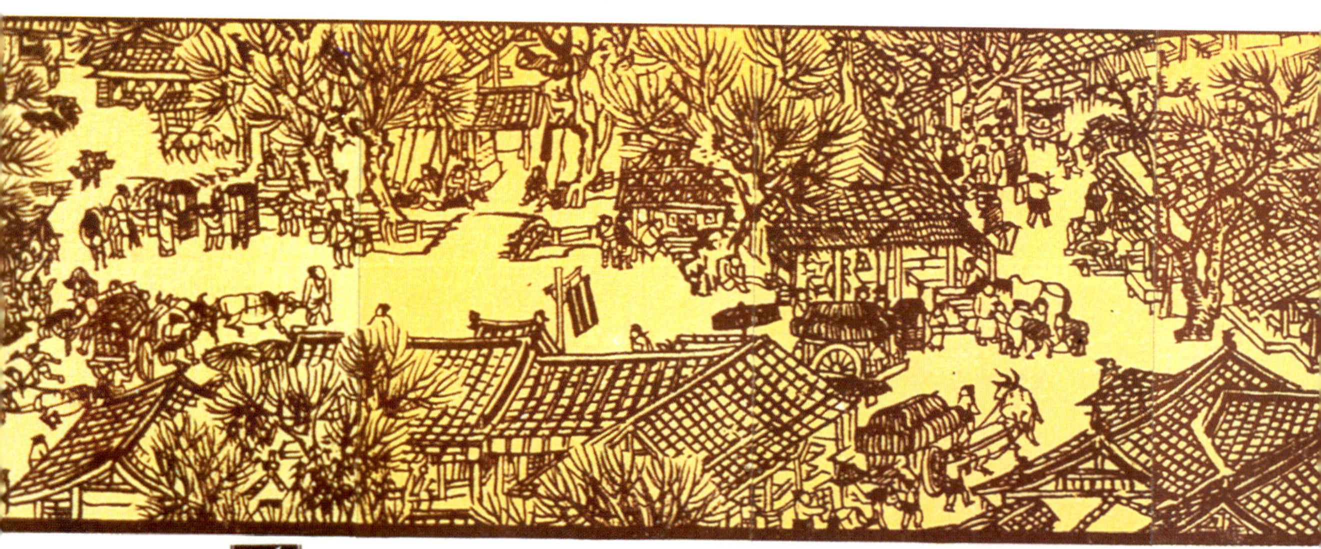

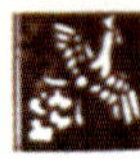 清明上河圖 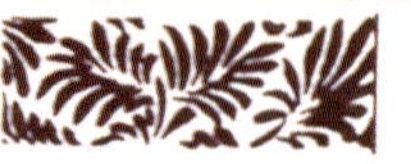 清明

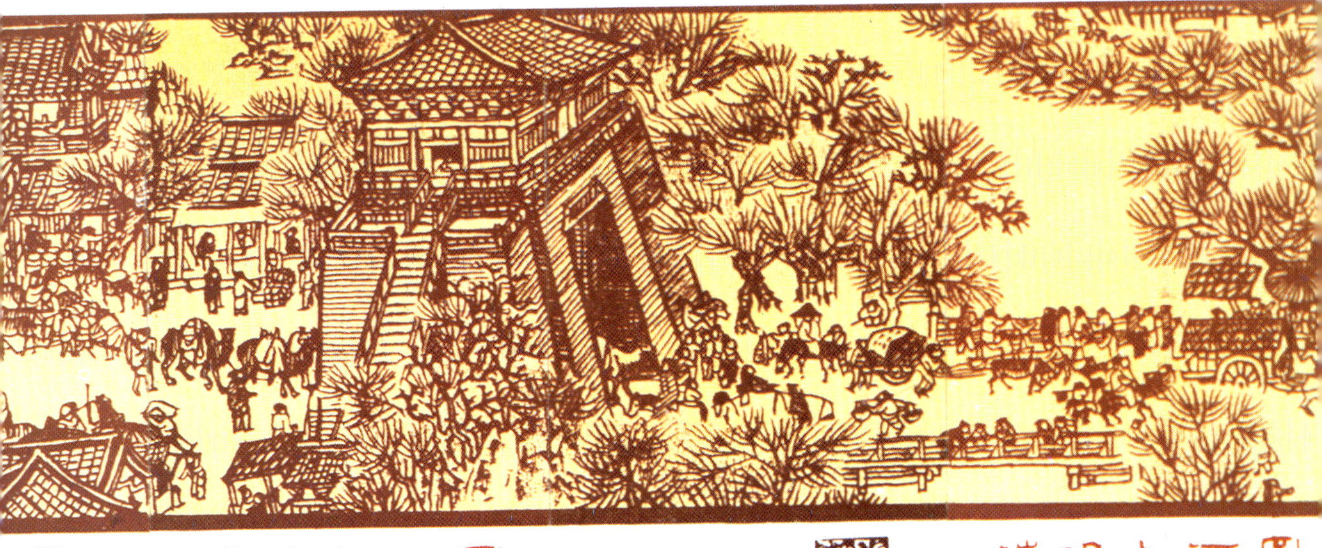

清明上河圖

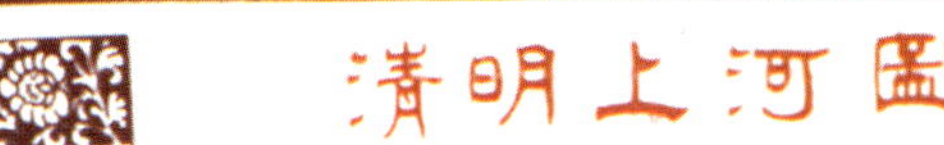

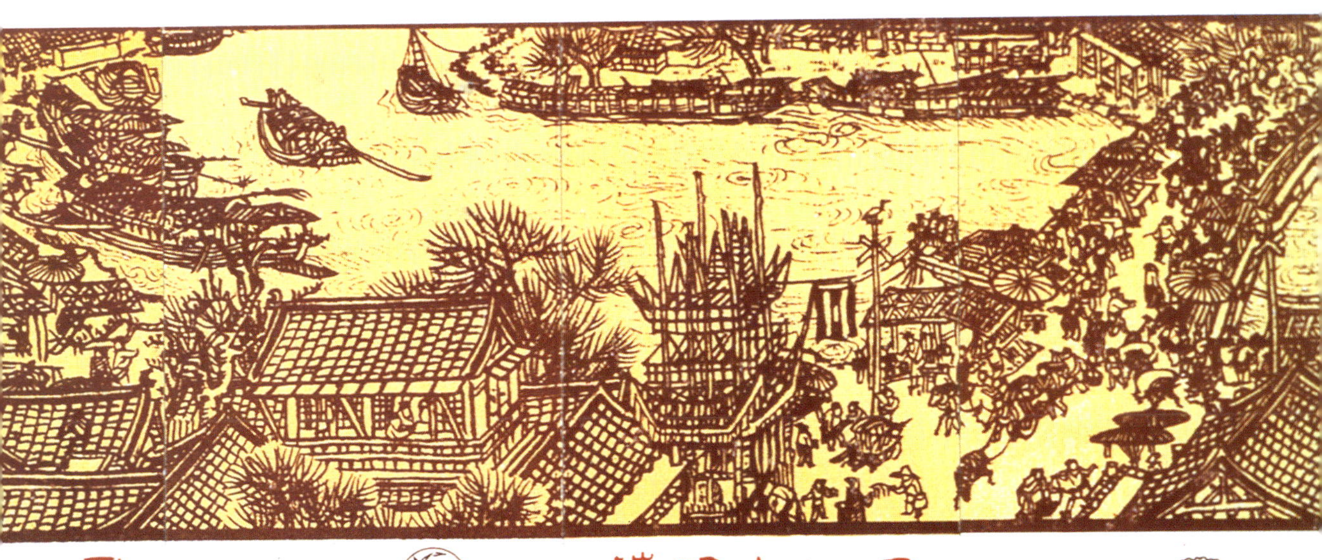

河圖

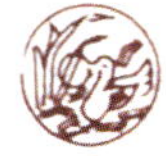

清明上河圖

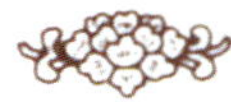

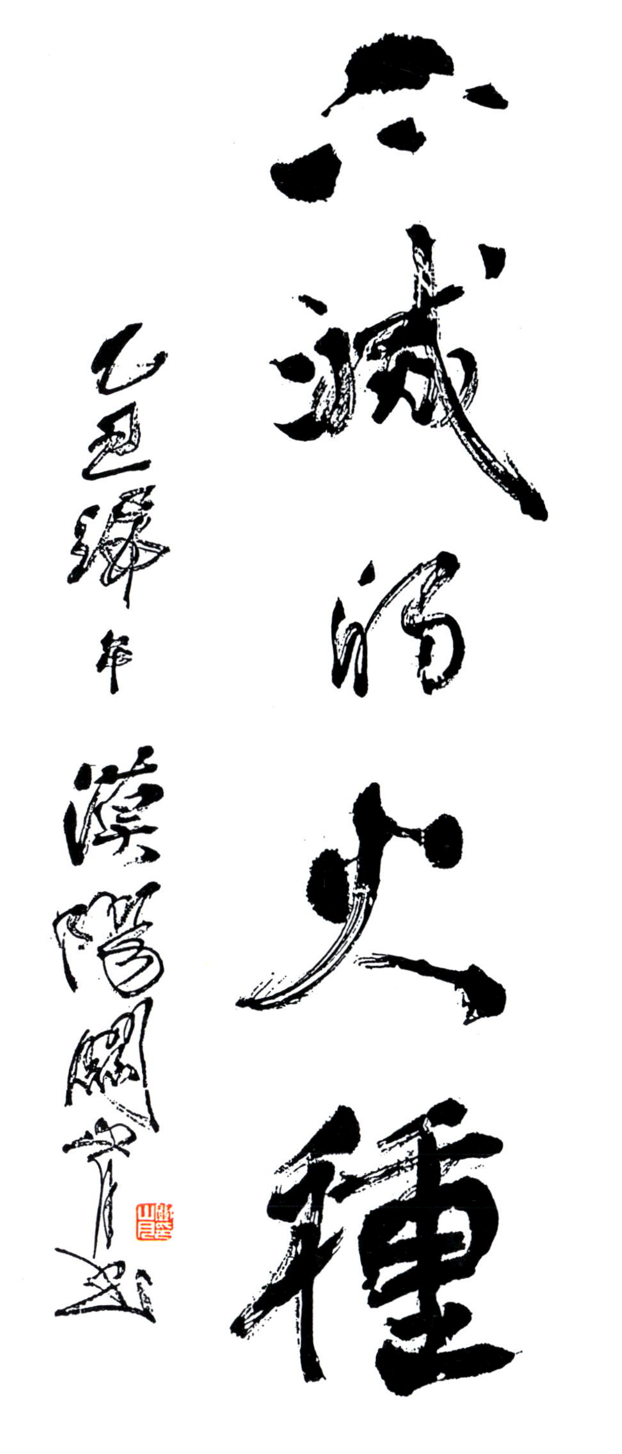

Unquenchable Spark
An inscription by Guan Shanyue

Chinese Matchbox Covers

Matchbox covers by courtesy of Ji Zhiguang
Edited by Zhou Daguang

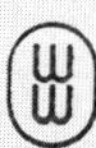

FOREIGN LANGUAGES PRESS BEIJING

First Edition 1989

ISBN 0-8351-2215-8 ISBN 7-119-00390-9

Published by Foreign Languages Press
24 Baiwanzhuang Road, Beijing, China

Distributed by China International Book Trading Corporation
(Guoji Shudian) P.O.Box 399, Beijing, China

Printed in the People's Republic of China

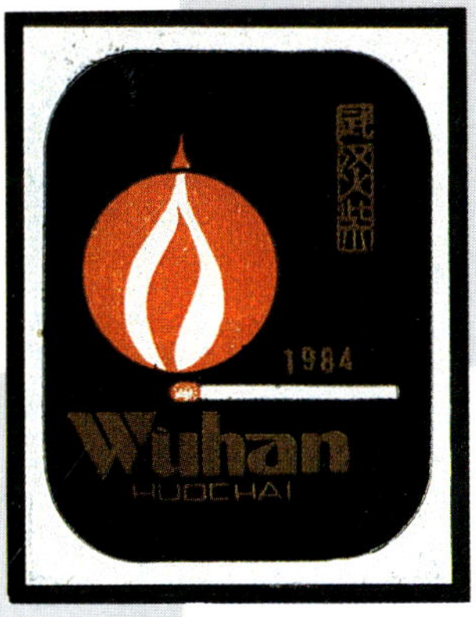

Contents

Looking at China Through Her Matchbox Covers

By Qin Mu*

Chinese Matchbox Covers opens a window through which foreigners can see China, offering fine illustrations of beautiful scenery as well as local conditions and customs.

Have you been in the following situation? In a dining hall or guestroom, a tourist casually picks up a box of matches, strikes one and lights his cigarettes. Just as he is about to put down the box, his attention is caught by the cover. He enjoys it, reflects on it, and then smiles. Finally he puts it away as a souvenir. In recent years, matchbox covers from all countries have been made more distinctive and colourful. People keep matchbox covers because they reflect the appearance and mood of a country. Many collectors in the world collect stamps, pictures and photos, clocks and ancient coins. Likewise, collecting matchbox covers is also popular among many people. This album shows how colourful and intriguing Chinese matchbox covers can be.

People strive to improve their lives by increasing the array of daily necessities. The use of fire is a case in point. In ancient times people got fire by drilling wood, then by striking flint, a method which was used for thousands of years. After the development of chemistry in the 18th century people placed a wooden stick coated with rich potassium chlorate against a sulphuric acid holder to produce fire. The 19th century scientific achievements led to the Swedish invention of the friction match in 1833. Use of this match gradually spread from Europe to various parts of the world. At first, matches' coating of yellow phosphorus caused safety problems because of its poisonous nature and low ignition point. During the next twenty years the safety match was developed by replacing yellow with red phosphorus. Over the last one hundred years the variety of matches has increased notably. Today one rarely sees people get fire produced by striking flint. The match and its successor, the lighter, are used throughout the world.

In the beginning the matchbox was simple. As time went on people gradually noticed that, even though it was a small box, thousands of people used it. The match is more frequently used than stamps, so people illustrated the covers with advertisement, scenery and other artistic pictures. Matchbox artistry became a specialty throughout Sweden, Japan, the United States, Czechoslovakia, the Soviet Union and Yugoslavia. Gradually, collectors of matchbox covers emerged.

Matchbox cover collecting has the same significance as collecting stamps and ancient money, costs less and has more extensive sources. So it is popular with many young people. History, local conditions and customs of a nation can be gleaned from matchbox covers. It is not overstatement to say that matchbox cover collection can form a small library or art gallery. Glancing over the covers can broaden one's knowledge and yield aesthetic pleasure. In recent years China has developed many associations of collectors of matchbox covers. The magazine *Chinese Matchbox Covers* and some journals provide a forum for exchange of information.

Although the technology of match production has been fully developed in contemporary China, China has not had the match for long, and many people are still inclined to call it the "foreign fire." The first Chinese match produced at the end of the Qing Dynasty (1644-1911) was packaged very simply. Portraits of the Empress Dowager Ci Xi and dragons, symbolic of the royal house, were printed on the box. These covers represent the first Chinese matchbox covers. Since only a few were published (most of the covers being printed with well-wishing words only), they are currently very precious and hard to get. With the overthrow of the Qing court came struggle among the warlords, domestic trouble and foreign invasion. The content of the matchbox covers changed accordingly, now portraying colourful local symbols, traditional auspicious designs, promotion of domestic goods as well as city life. But the design and printing were still of poor workmanship. Over the past thirty years, however, like stamps, the matchbox covers of New China boast a wide variety and content among the finest of the world.

This album displays a wide range of content: The evolution of Chinese history; historical and cultural relics; scenic spots and historical sites; unique animals and plants as well as literature and art. Readers from various countries will note the distinctive Chinese flavour of the style and content. With respect to cultural relics, the album shows three-thousand-year-old bronzeware, murals from ancient tombs, wooden or pottery figures of warriors and horses buried with the dead emperors, stone carvings and the time-honoured Painted Pottery Culture. With respect to history, one finds portraits of many well-known people in ancient China, including great thinkers such as Confucius in 500 B.C. and Wang Anshi in the 11th century, seismologist Zhang Heng, mathematician Zu Chongzhi, natural scientist Shen Kuo and medical scientist Li Shizhen.

China's four world-known inventions—paper-making, printing, compass and gunpowder are also illustrated. In addition to national heroes, there are men of letters, travellers and skillful craftsmen. With respect to scenic spots and historical sites, almost all the great sights of China are included: The Great Wall, the Forbidden City in Beijing, the historical sites in Nanjing, the sites of the Han and Tang dynasties in Xi'an, the Mansion and the Temple of Confucius in Shandong, the classical gardens in Suzhou and Hangzhou, the beautiful landscapes in Guilin and Yangshuo, the scenic Taishan and Huangshan mountains, and the Potala Palace in Tibet.

Giant pandas, golden monkeys, red-crowned cranes, goldfish, peonies, narcissi, plum blossoms and chrysanthemum are fully illustrated. Also shown are well-known paintings and calligraphies of the past, different types of theatrical makeup in operas, folk songs and dances, representative figures in the famous Chinese novels, fables and the contemporary daily life. All the covers are meticulously designed and printed. Many covers are arranged into series of three to ten covers in order to give vivid expression to different images. There are also high-quality tourist covers ranging from ten to a hundred in one set.

There is an old Chinese saying that by staying at home reading a book or enjoying a painting, one can travel. Modern TV now helps achieve this goal. However, this album is better than a TV set because TV leaves no room for reflection. This album does much better in that respect.

The album also can let collectors of various countries know how precious their collections of Chinese matchbox covers are. It can convey some ideas about China to those abroad who have never visited this country or who are learning Chinese. The book also serves to console homesickness in overseas Chinese.

Matchbox covers exhibited in this album are from the collection of Ji Zhiguang, a famous collector from Yangzhou of Jiangsu Province. Over the past thirty-some years he has collected 120,000 sets totalling 1.5 million covers. He also possesses a great number of covers from more than a hundred countries. He ranks first in the amount of his collection in China and third in the world, thereby winning the title of "the king of Chinese matchbox covers." He is on the board of directors in the China Collectors' Association.

---

*Qin Mu is a council member of the Chinese Writers' Association, Vice-President of the Federation of Writers and Artists of Guangdong Province, and Vice-President of the Chinese Writers' Association, Guangdong Branch.

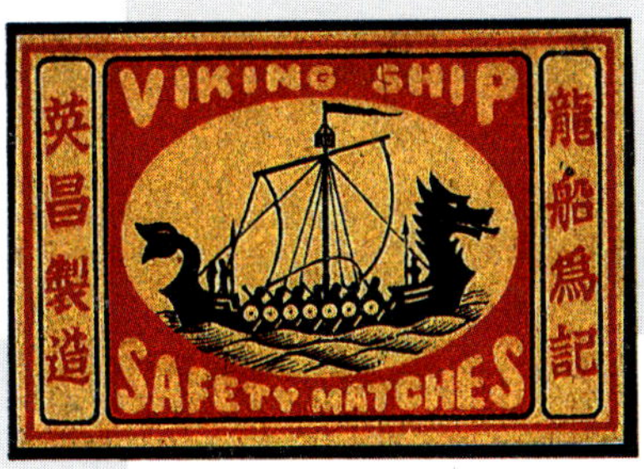

MATCHBOX COVERS BEFORE 1949

Matchboxes appeared in China less than one hundred years ago. In the mid-19th century, when China was reduced to a semi-feudal and semi-colonial country, matches and other goods were introduced into China from the West. They were called yanghuo(foreign fire). Only the rich could afford to use them at that time since they were still hard to find in China. Ordinary people kept live cinders or struck flints to start a new fire. By the end of the 19th century after foreign capitalists had founded match factories in China, match factories were also set up by Chinese capitalists. As match output increased, rural as well as urban people used them. To attract more customers, the matchbox covers, known as matchbox pictures in Chinese, were produced with increasingly exquisite printing and versatility of style and content. Their artistic value also increased. Looking at them today, we may find that their content quite dated. But they are rare and valuable because they reflect historical events, social features, customs and even people's longing for a better life.

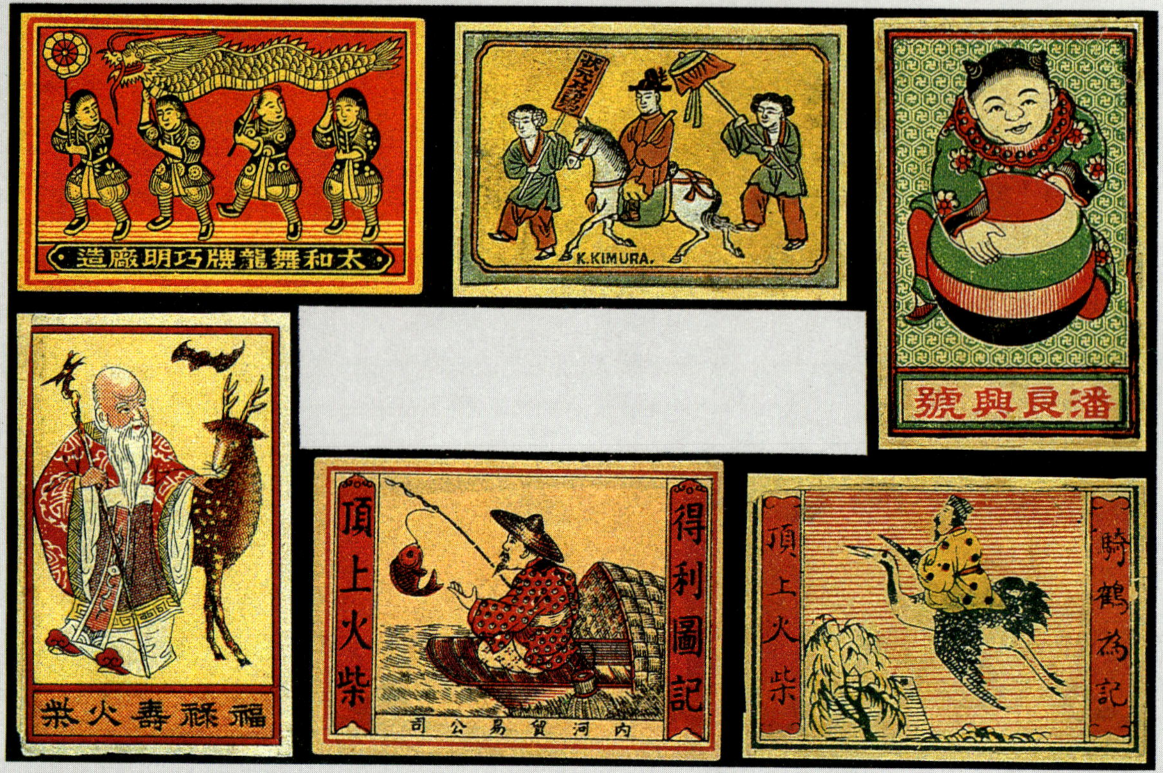

The Earliest Chinese Matchbox Covers

Printed in about the early 19th century, this group of matchbox covers tells of Chinese folklore and daily life. The dragon dance on the upper left is believed to be the first matchbox cover in China, although its date is unknown. The one on the lower left has a bat, a sika deer and God of Age, each representing happiness, wealthiness and longevity. (The Chinese characters for bat, deer and age are homonymous with those for happiness, wealthiness and longevity.) Becoming the No.1 Scholar, Old Angler and Riding the Crane to Yangzhou show people's wish to be rich, famous and immortal.

Made in Guangdong

55 mm x 36 mm

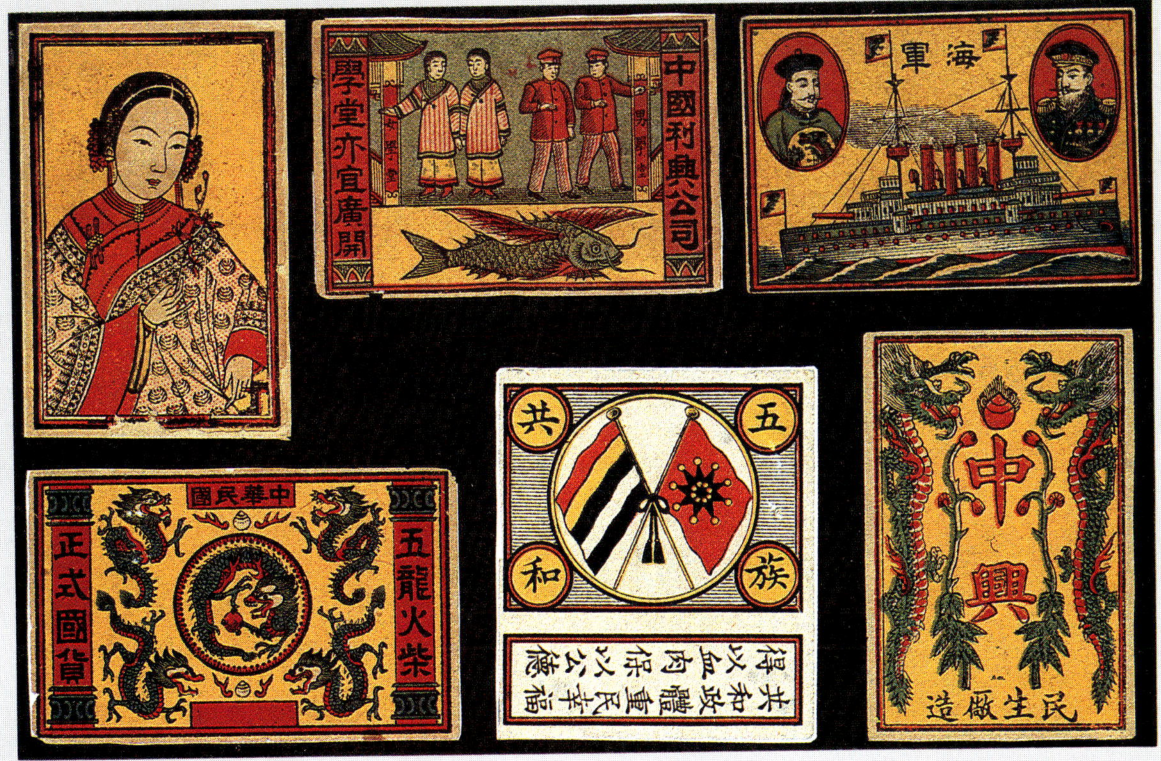

Historical Events

This precious set was printed in about the end of the 19th century and the early 20th century. From the upper left: the Portrait of the Empress Dowager Ci Xi, designed specially for the celebration of her 60th birthday in 1894; Opening All Kinds of Schools, designed in 1898 for the promotion of modern schools in China; The Navy, printed in memory of the Sino-Japanese War of 1894-95, the portrait on the upper left corner being that of Ding Ruchang, Commander-in-Chief of the Northern Navy of the Qing Dynasty. From lower left: Five Dragons, printed in 1912 when Yuan Shikai (1859-1916) usurped the state power; Republic of the Five Nationalities, printed in the mid 1920s when Li Yuanhong (1864-1928) became president of the Republic, the five colours on the flags representing the five nationalities of Han, Manchu, Mongolian, Hui and Tibetan.

Made in Guangdong

55 mm x 36 mm

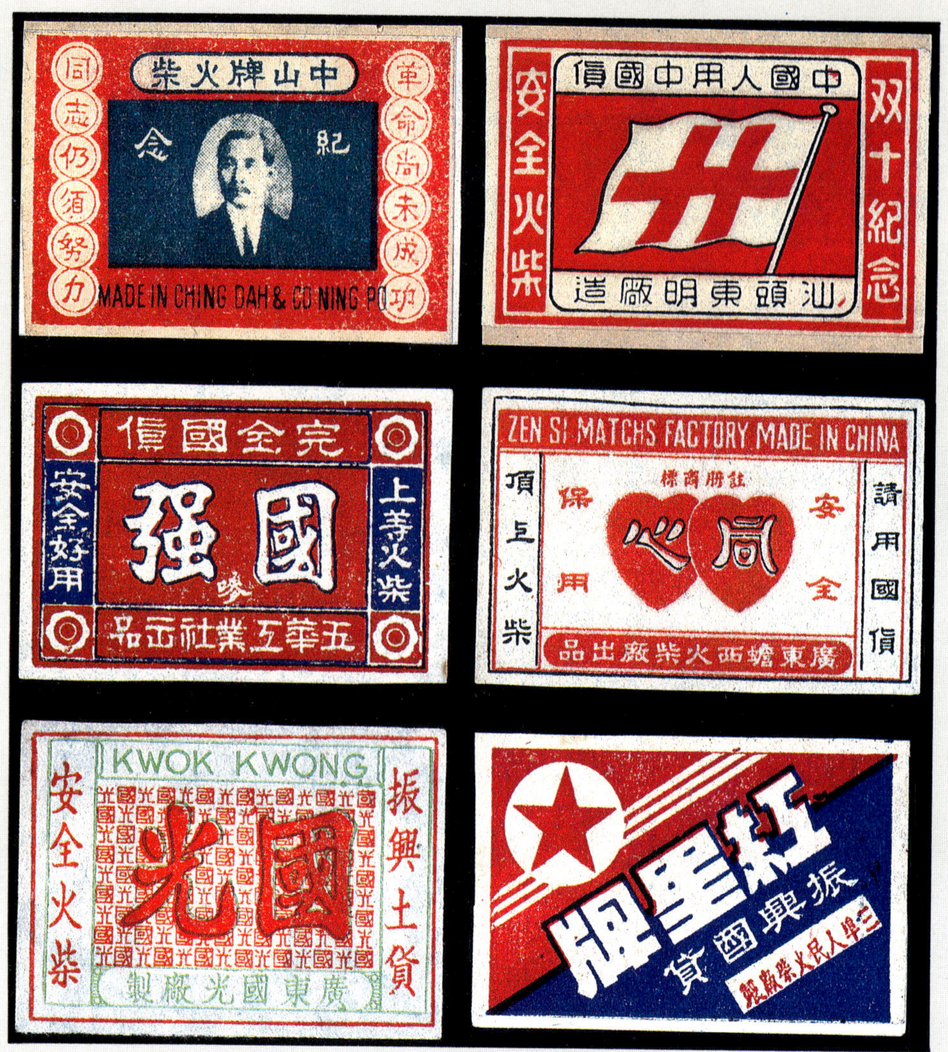

In Memory of the National Revolution

This group of matchbox covers portrays the National Revolution of 1911 when Dr. Sun Yat-sen(1866-1925), pioneer of the Chinese revolution, instigated an armed uprising to overthrow the Qing Dynasty and founded the Republic of China. The first and second covers from the upper left were painted to mark the revolution led by Dr. Sun Yat-sen. The remaining four, designed to promote Chinese products, show the Chinese people's resentment against foreign goods flowing into the Chinese market, hindering the emerging national industry.

Made in Guangdong
55 mm x 38 mm

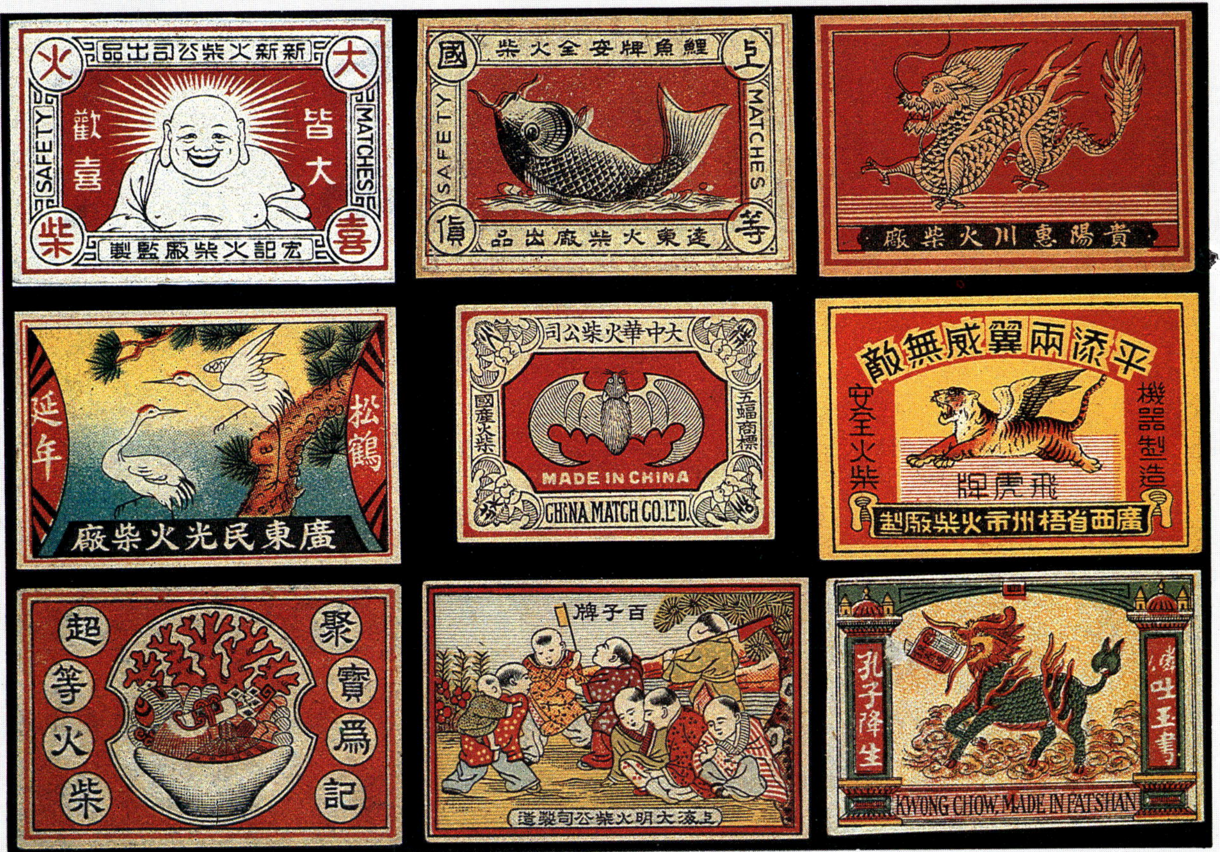

Matchbox Covers of Good Luck

This group of works of the 1920s expresses people's longing for happiness and good luck. Among them, the Great Buddha signifies happiness for all; the carp stands for success; the dragon symbolizes soaring high; the cranes and the pine represent longevity; the bats imply happiness; the winged tiger means invincibility; the treasure bowl indicates constant wealth; the group of children symbolizes having many sons; and the unicorn throwing up books signifies the birth of gifted scholars.

Made in Shanghai, Guangdong, Guangxi and Guizhou

53 mm x 36 mm

Scenery Covers

These covers feature mainly rivers and traditional pavilions, embellished with aeroplanes, trains and ships, expressing people's wish to develop industry, revitalize the nation and strive for a bright future.

Made in Guangdong and Shanghai

53 mm x 35 mm

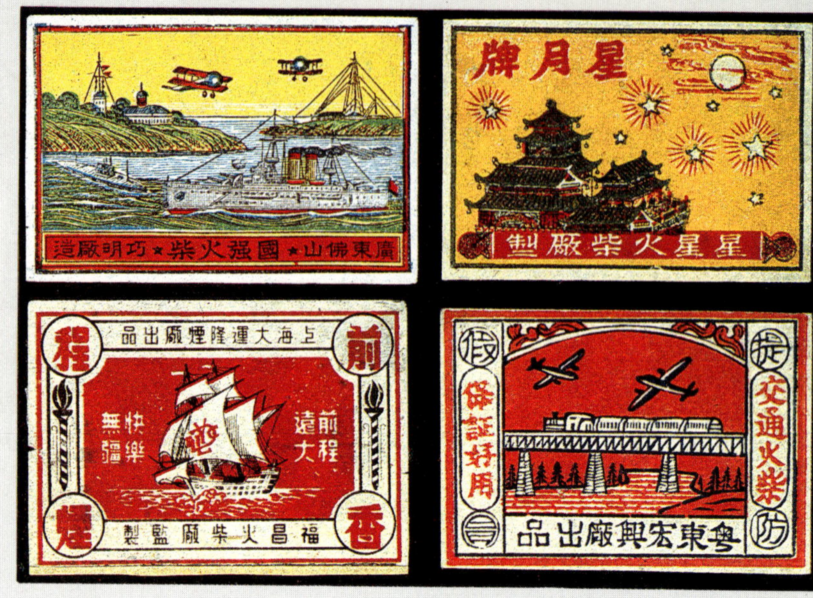

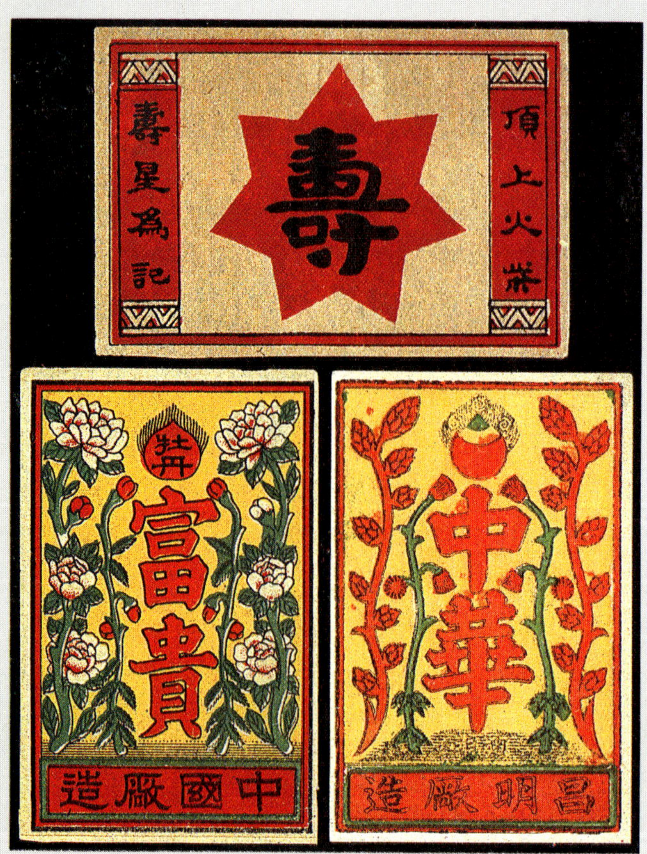

Happy Announcement

On happy occasions and celebration days, Chinese like to put up happy announcements on lintels or on screen walls. The Lucky Star Shines is usually the blessing to an elderly man on his birthday.

Made in Guangdong

54 mm x 37 mm

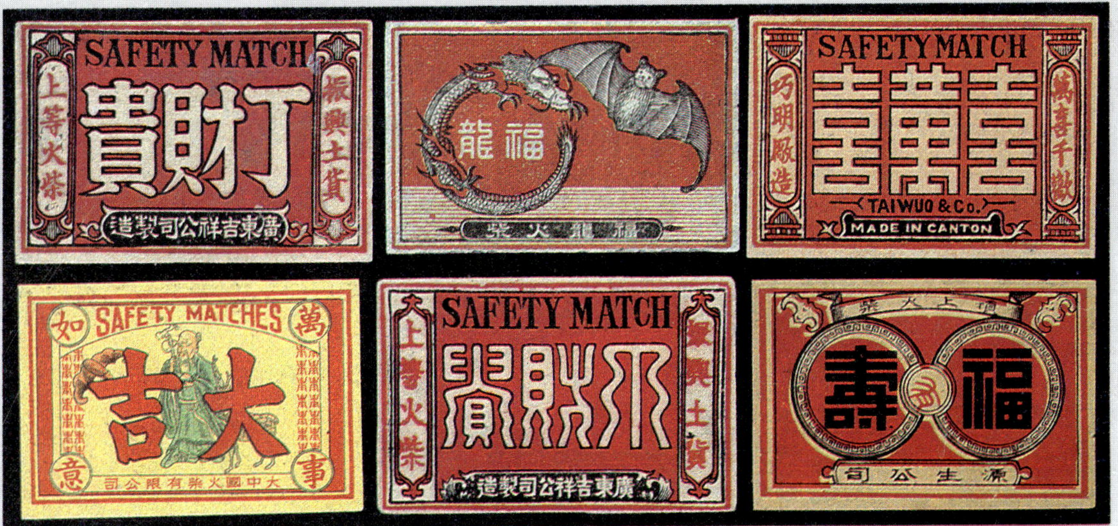

Lucky Words

The common Chinese name, Ding Caigui, on the first cover from the upper left and the second cover from the lower left, literally means having a growing family, rich financial resources and thus, flourishing wealth. The lucky words reflect the thinking and taste of the ordinary Chinese folk at the time.

Made in Guangdong

56 mm x 37 mm

Covers with City Names

Due to the imbalance of economic development in old China, people treasured products made in the few industrially developed big cities. City names like Beijing or Shanghai in this group are very eye-catching and attention-getting.

Made in Beijing, Shanghai, Guangdong, Shandong and Datong

53 mm x 35 mm

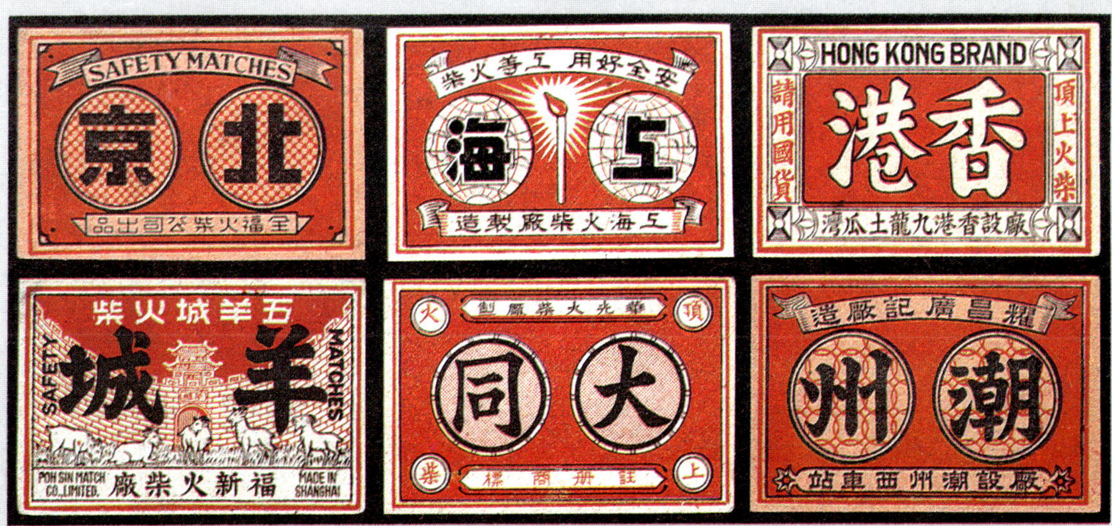

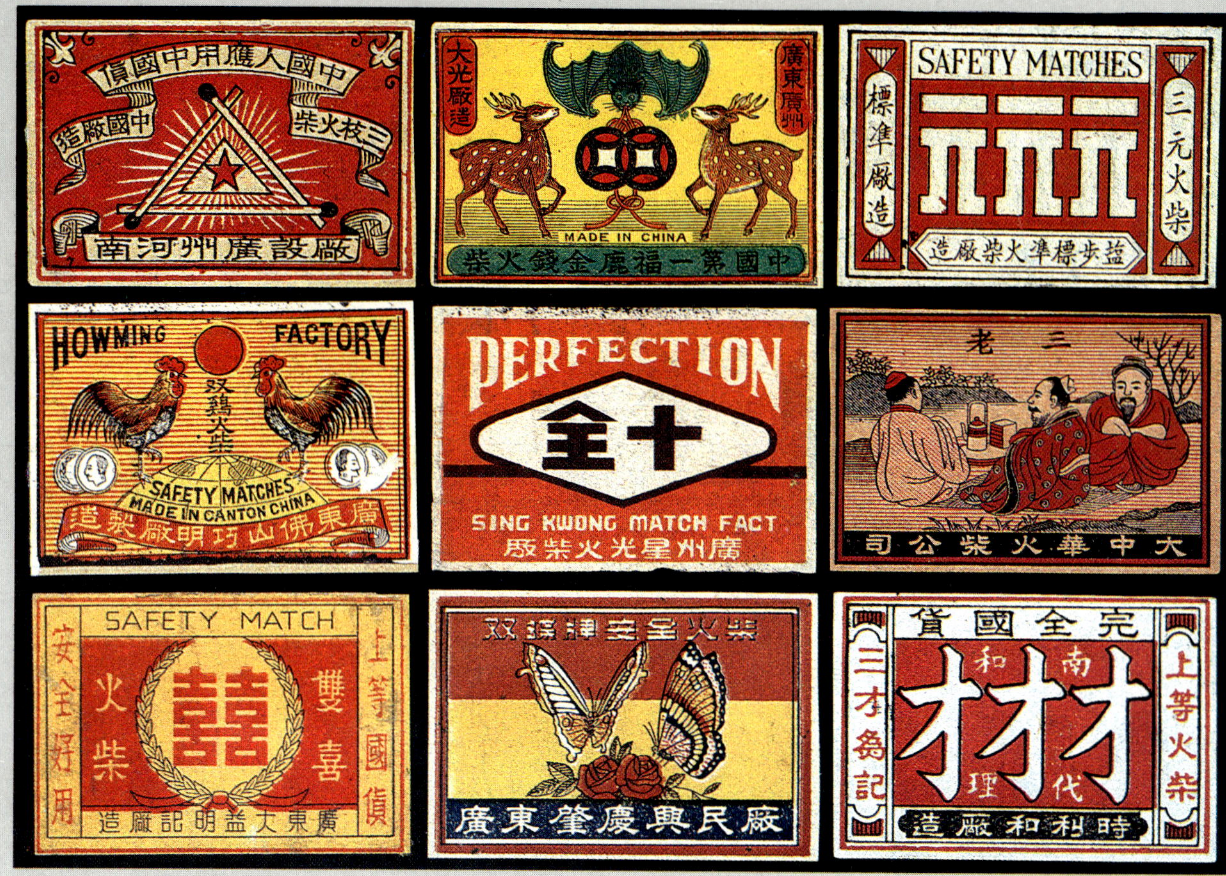

Covers with Chinese Characters

Using double or triple Chinese characters, these covers reflect the traditional belief of the Chinese that good things come in two or three. The double characters are therefore a lucky sign. The triple characters generally mean multitude, implying lots of good luck or achievement of many gains by only one action. Made before the 1940s, they reveal the customs and the way of thinking of ordinary people then.

Made in Guangdong
54 mm x 36 mm

Folklore Covers

This group shows the characters and events in popular Chinese folklore. Nezha, on the first cover from the upper left, is a legendary little hero; Sui Renshi, on the third from the upper left, is said to be the first who made fire by drilling wood, thus bringing light to people and making cooked food possible. The Cowherd and the Weaving Maid on the left in the second row, tells of an affectionate couple who, separated by the Heavenly River created by the Heavenly Emperor, could meet only once a year.

Made in Shanghai; and Ningbo, Zhejiang Province

53 mm x 36 mm

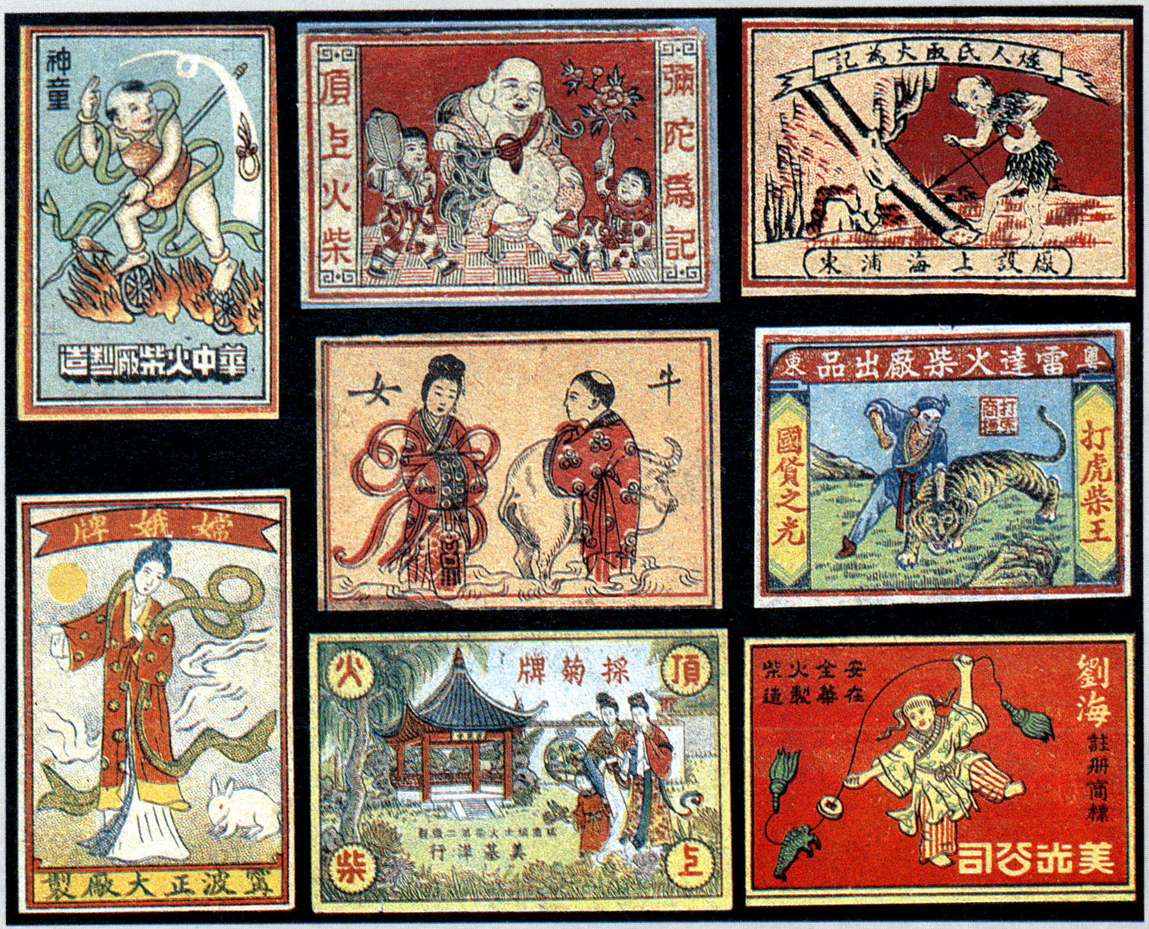

Scenes of Daily Life

Printed in the 1940s, this set shows the people farming, fishing, gathering firewood, reading and picking lotus and mulberry. With a strong local flavour, they are among the rare excellent specimens of their time.

Made in Guangdong; Fuzhou, Fujian Province; and Ningbo, Zhejiang Province

53 mm x 35 mm

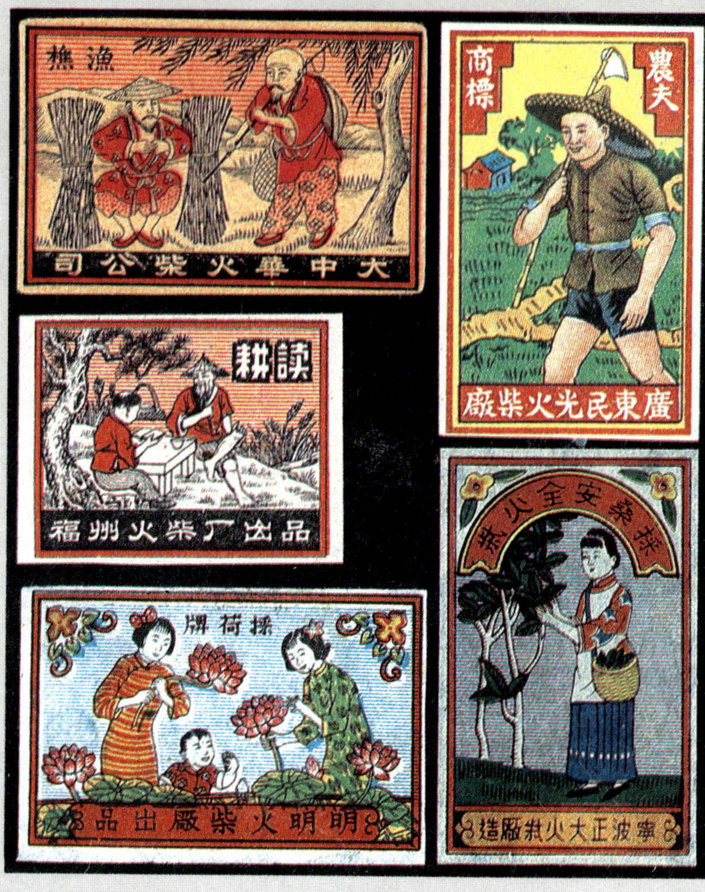

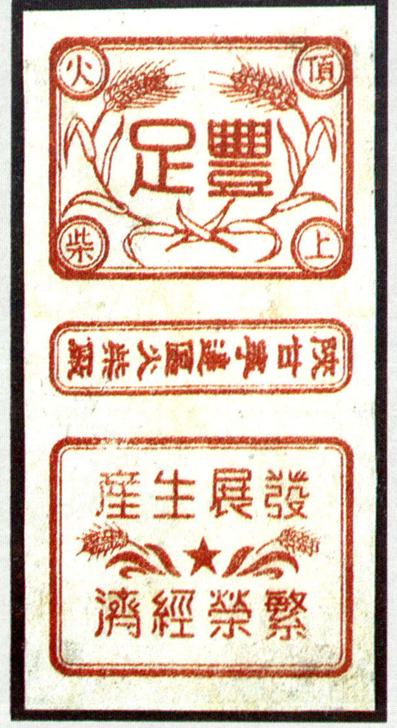

The Great Production Movement

In order to fight against the attacks by Japanese invaders and the blockade by the domestic reactionary forces in the later stage of World War II, the Chinese Communist Party started a vigorous production movement in the Shaanxi-Gansu-Ningxia Border Region. They called on the army and the people to "develop production" and make a "flourishing economy." A rare historical object, this cover reflects through the simple characters what happened at that time.

Made in Yan'an, Shaanxi Province

84 mm x 43 mm

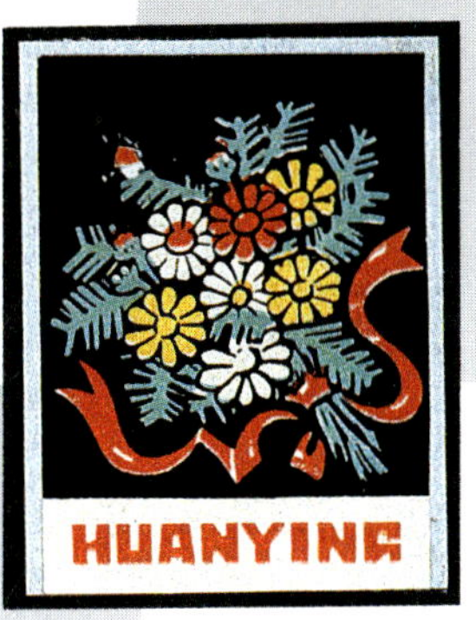

MATCHBOX COVERS AFTER 1949

After the founding of New China in 1949, the match industry, like other industries, developed rapidly. The match then came into use by every Chinese family, although lighters and electric cooking utensils were also being used.

The development of the match industry also led to progress in the design of matchbox covers. The increase in quality not only meant more customers and sales promotion but also was intended to spread knowledge and enhance the aesthetic appeal of the matchbox covers. To further develop the cover designing art, a national association of matchbox covers and local branches were set up so that designers and fans can share their collections.

Varied both in theme and content, this part, composed of nine categories including landscape, figures, cultural relics and flowers, gives a general idea of contemporary Chinese matchbox covers.

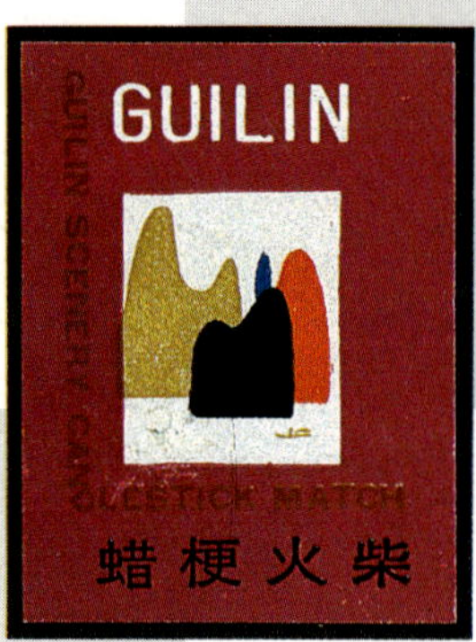

Magnificent Landscape

China is a country with long civilization, vast territory, beautiful landscape and numerous historical sites.

Through vivid pictures, this section shows China's famous mountains, great rivers, scenic spots, cultural relics and modern scenes.

It also exhibits the exquisite printing and various styles by the talented designers. This section leads the viewer to many places in China and thus promotes a better knowledge of the country.

The Great Wall

Stretching for 6,700 kilometres from the west at Jiayu Pass, Gansu Province, to the east at Shanhai Pass, Hebei Province, the Great Wall was first built separately by the northern princely states to resist the attack of enemies in the 5th century B.C. After the unification of China in 221 B.C. by Qin Shi Huang(First Emperor of the Qin Dynasty), all the sections were connected into what is now known as the Great Wall, one of the world's oldest and most magnificent architectural structures.

This group of matchbox covers shows the spring, summer, autumn and winter scenes at the Badaling section, one of the best-preserved of the Great Wall to the north of Beijing.

Made in Beijing

102 mm x 56 mm

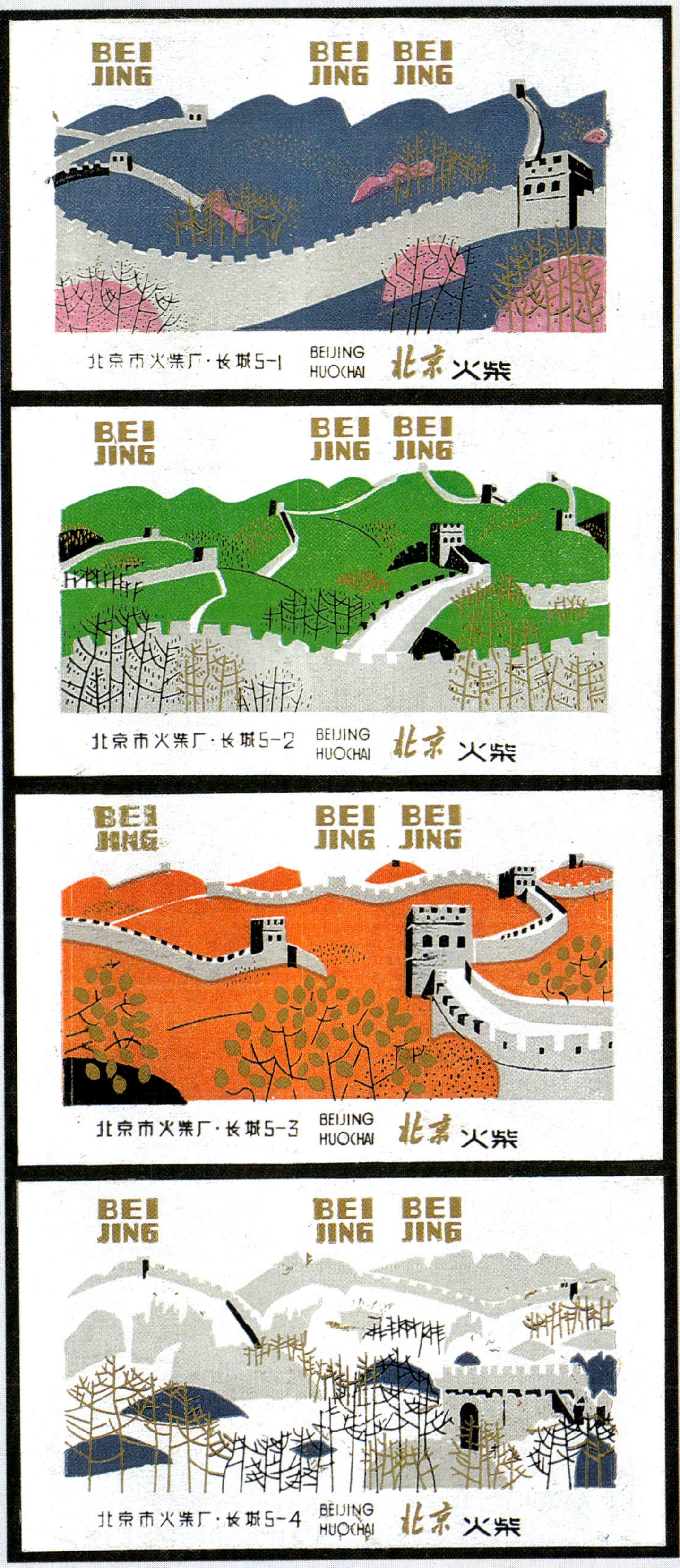

中山公园原是明清封建帝王祭祀土地神的社稷坛。汉白玉砌成的社稷坛上以南红、西白、北黑、东青、中黄五个方位铺着五种颜色的土，名“五色土”。北面的“拜殿”1928年改为中山堂。唐花坞与水榭隔水相望，水榭三面环水，湖中是四宜轩小岛，西岸是杜鹃山，如同画境。

北京市火柴厂

北京 BEIJING 12-1

中山公园

故宫是明清两代的皇宫。这组表现中国古典建筑传统和独特风格的庞大建筑，始建于明永乐四年（1406年），总面积七十二万多平方米，宫室九千多间。殿宇巍峨，宫阙重叠，画栋雕梁。三大殿中的太和殿俗称“金銮殿”，是故宫最堂皇的建筑。历代艺术陈列馆中陈列各朝代的珍贵艺术品。

北京市火柴厂

北京 BEIJING 12-2

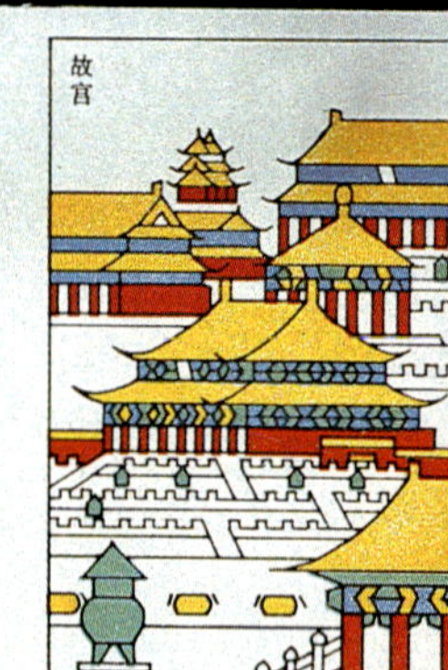

北海，中国现存最完整的古代园林之一。公元九世纪，辽代在此建瑶屿行宫，后经历代多次修建。一六五一年在广寒殿废墟上建白塔。琼岛是全园中心，白塔高耸，亭、台、殿、阁，交相辉映。水面广阔，备有游船。若湖上荡桨，欣赏水面倒映的美丽白塔及绿树红墙，令人心旷神怡。

北京市火柴厂

北京 BEIJING 12-4

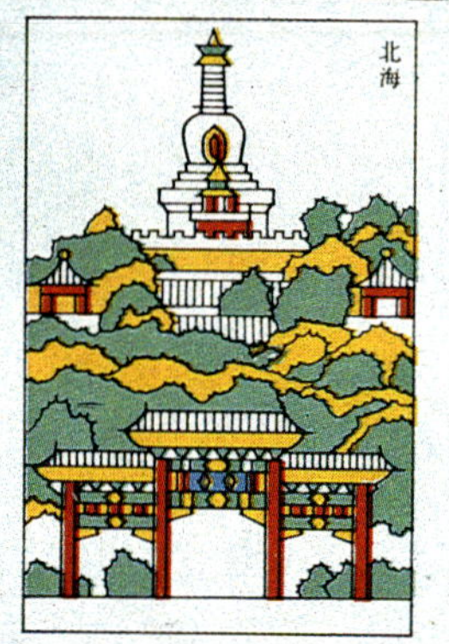

天坛，明清两代皇帝祭天的地方。明永乐十八年（1420年）建成。建筑艺术高超，布局精美，是中国古典建筑艺术结晶。祈年殿纯砖木结构，彩画精美，皇穹宇院内有著名的“回音壁”，“三音石”。圜丘坛是封建帝王祭天和祈雨的地方，站在石坛中心喊话，能听到很大的回音。

北京市火柴厂

北京 BEIJING 12-5

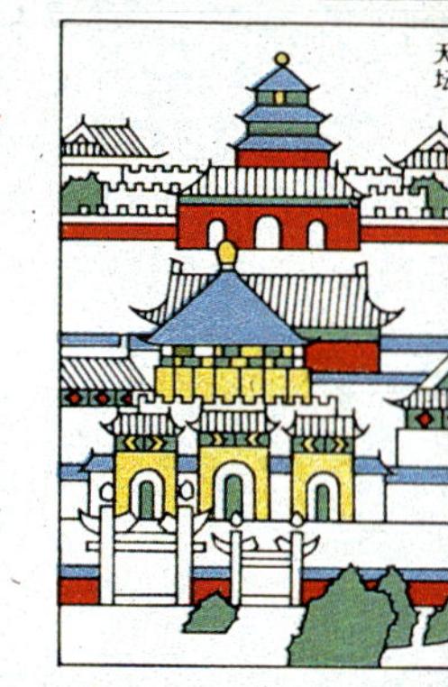

颐和园，总面积四千三百五十亩，水域占四分之三，是在国内外享有盛誉的古典园林。湖光山色间，殿堂、楼、阁、廊、榭、亭、桥，拥山抱水，绚丽多姿。万寿山前山是以佛香阁为中心的巨大建筑群，山下七百二十八米长廊蜿蜒曲折，十七孔桥连接南湖岛，后山后湖一番江南景色。

北京市火柴厂

北京 BEIJING 12-7

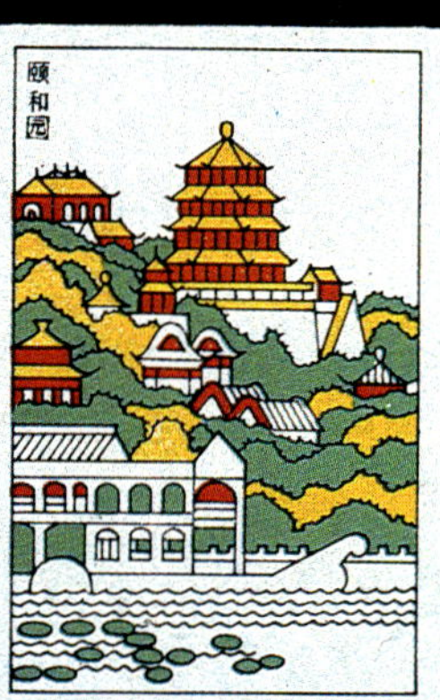

香山，自然风光优美。地势高，林木密。夏季清凉，是避暑胜地；最著名的是香山秋色，霜秋时，遍山黄栌树，叶焕丹红，如火似锦；建筑名胜北路有昭庙、琉璃塔、见心斋、眼镜湖；中路有芙蓉馆、玉华山庄、多云亭、西山晴雪；南路有森玉笏、阆风亭、半山亭、香山寺、双清等。

北京市火柴厂

北京 BEIJING 12-8

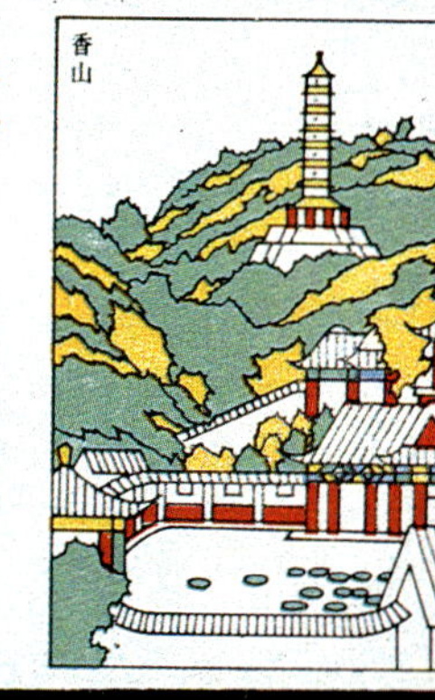

灵光寺·八大处是西山东麓间的八大古刹的总称。二处灵光寺，最早叫龙泉寺，明成化十四年（1478年）改称灵光寺。殿后的大金鱼池中的金鱼是一八五一年以前放养的。池东有巨大辽塔塔基。一九五九年，中国佛教协会为安放佛教遗物在寺内重建佛牙塔；塔高五十多米，砖木结构。

北京市火柴厂

北京 BEIJING 12-10

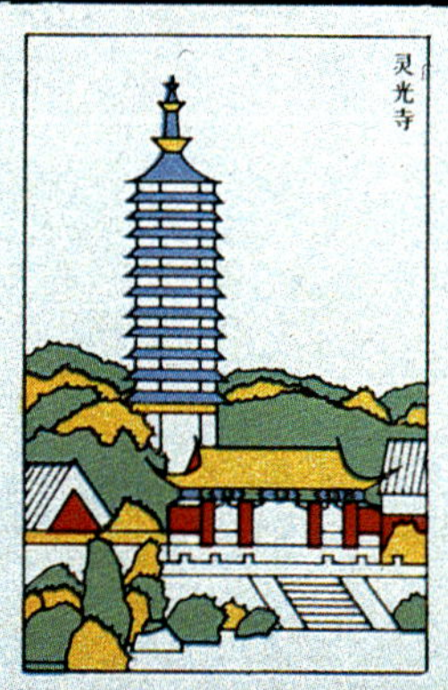

长陵·十三陵是明朝十三个皇帝的坟墓，在约四十平方公里的陵区内，分布着长陵、献陵、景陵、裕陵、茂陵、泰陵、康陵、永陵、昭陵、定陵、庆陵、德陵、思陵，统称明十三陵。长陵规模最大，棱恩殿宏伟壮丽。地下宫殿定陵规模浩大，建筑豪华，经发掘整理，辟为定陵博物馆。

北京市火柴厂

北京 BEIJING 12-11

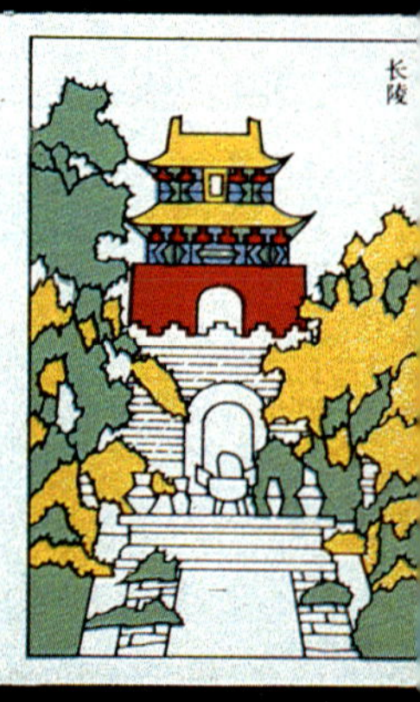

景山，在故宫北，元代称做"青山"，明代称做"煤山"，清代改名景山。山四周有路可登升。五座山峰，峰峰有亭，中峰万春亭，观妙亭、辑芳亭、周赏亭、富览亭四亭左右对称排列，逐次降低。万春亭是北京内城中心和过去北京城内的最高点。登上景山，可俯视北京全城的壮丽景色。

北京市火柴厂

北京㊟ BEIJING 12-3

景山

陶然亭公园在北京城西南隅，康熙三十四年（1695年）有人在此建亭，取唐代诗人白居易"更待菊黄家酿熟，与君一醉一陶然"的诗句，名陶然亭。湖岸有振云庵，山石树木，环湖成荫，自然意趣盎然。

北京市火柴厂

北京㊟ BEIJING 12-6

陶然亭

碧云寺，西山风景区中最雄伟的古老寺院。创建于元代（1331年），清乾隆十三年（1748年）大规模扩建。解放后，重建了孙中山纪念堂。寺院布局层层封闭，从山门直达寺顶共六层，回旋串连，引人入胜。罗汉堂，五百罗汉环室陈列，形态不一。汉白玉金刚宝座塔，布满精致的浮雕。

北京市火柴厂

北京㊟ BEIJING 12-9

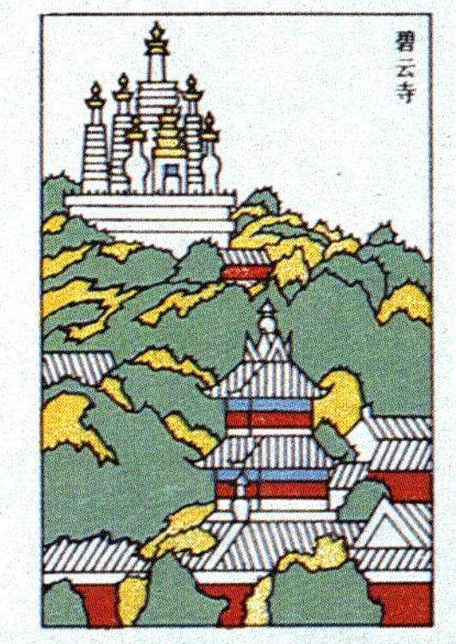

八达岭·万里长城是中华民族勤劳智慧的结晶，是我国古代劳动人民创造的一个世界奇迹。长城东起山海关，西到嘉峪关，横跨七省、市、自治区，绵延起伏一万二千七百多里，故称万里长城。北京西北的八达岭关城，明代建筑，登上八达岭高峰，万里长城如长龙翻山越岭，不见首尾。

北京市火柴厂

北京㊟ BEIJING 12-12

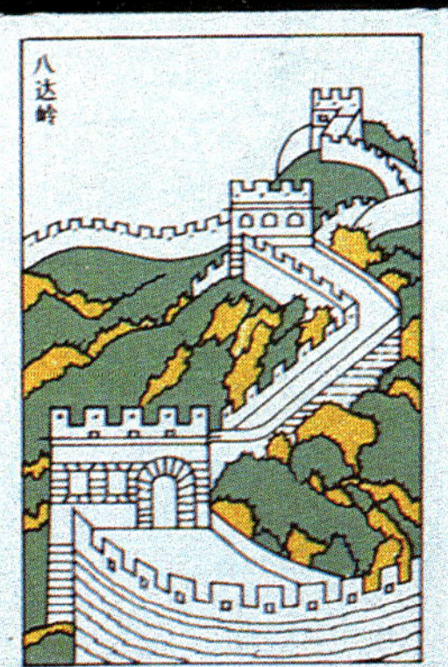

Beijing Scenery

A well-known cultural city, Beijing has been the capital of China for many dynasties and is now the capital of the People's Republic of China. The city therefore abounds in cultural relics and historical sites. From top left, this group shows twelve scenic spots including the Zhongshan Park, Forbidden City, Jingshan Park, Beihai Park, Temple of Heaven, Taoranting Park, Summer Palace, Fragrant Hill, Azure Cloud Temple, Divine Light Temple, the Mausoleum of the Ming Emperor Zhu Di, and Badaling.

Made in Beijing

89 mm x 53 mm

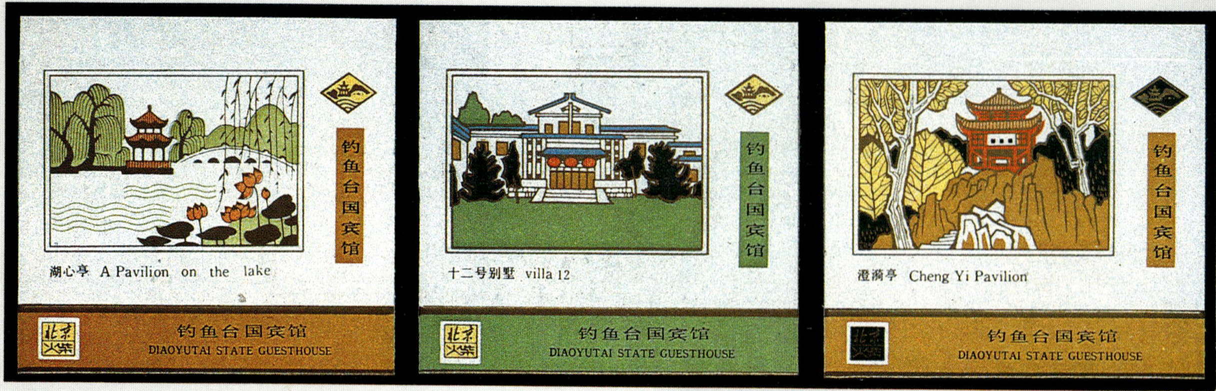

Scenes of the Diaoyutai State Guesthouse

With quiet and beautiful surroundings, Diaoyutai(Angling Terrace) is located in the west suburbs of Beijing. According to historical records, Emperor Wanyan Jing(1168-1208) of the Kin Dynasty, used to fish here. Later it became a scenic spot. Since 1949, it has been a state guesthouse for the heads of foreign states and other distinguished guests visiting China.

From left to right: Mid Lake Pavilion, No.12 Villa, and Clear Ripple Pavilion.

Made in Beijing

96 mm x 56 mm

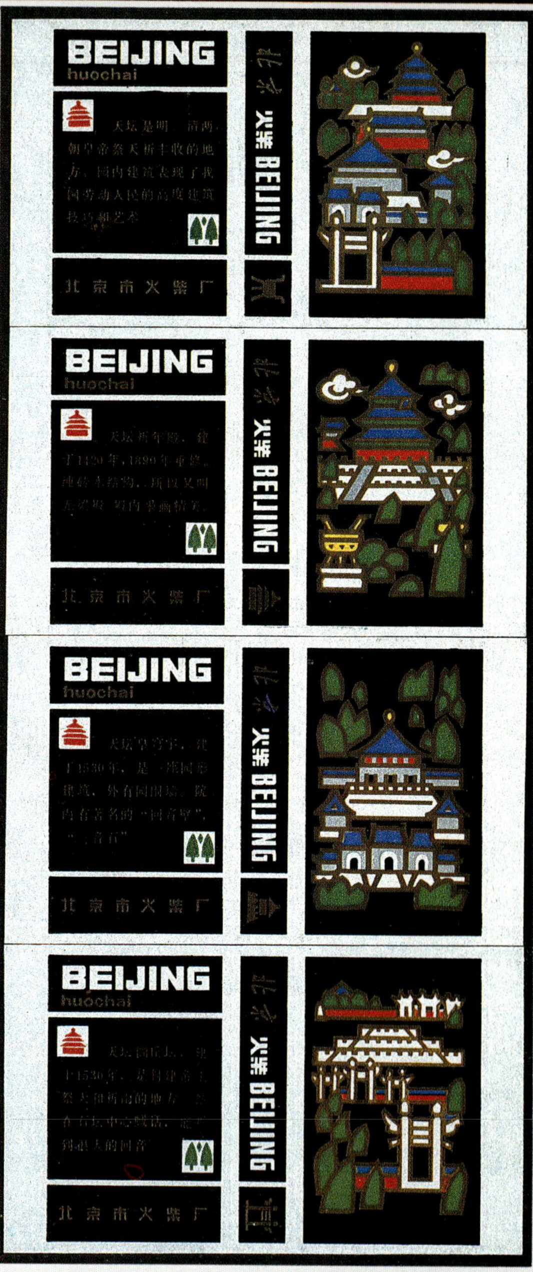

The Temple of Heaven

First built in the early 14th century in the south of Beijing, the Temple of Heaven used to be the place where the emperors of the Ming and Qing dynasties came to pray for good harvests. Many buildings here have extraordinary vaulted ceilings as the ancient Chinese believed that the sky was round.

From top to bottom: Bird's-eye View of the Temple of Heaven, Hall of Prayer for Good Harvests, Imperial Vault, and Circular Mound.

Made in Beijing

96 mm x 56 mm

Heilongjiang Landscapes

With fertile land and dense forest, Heilongjiang in the northernmost part of China abounds in grain, timber and oil.

Made in Hulan, Heilongjiang Province

86 mm x 46 mm

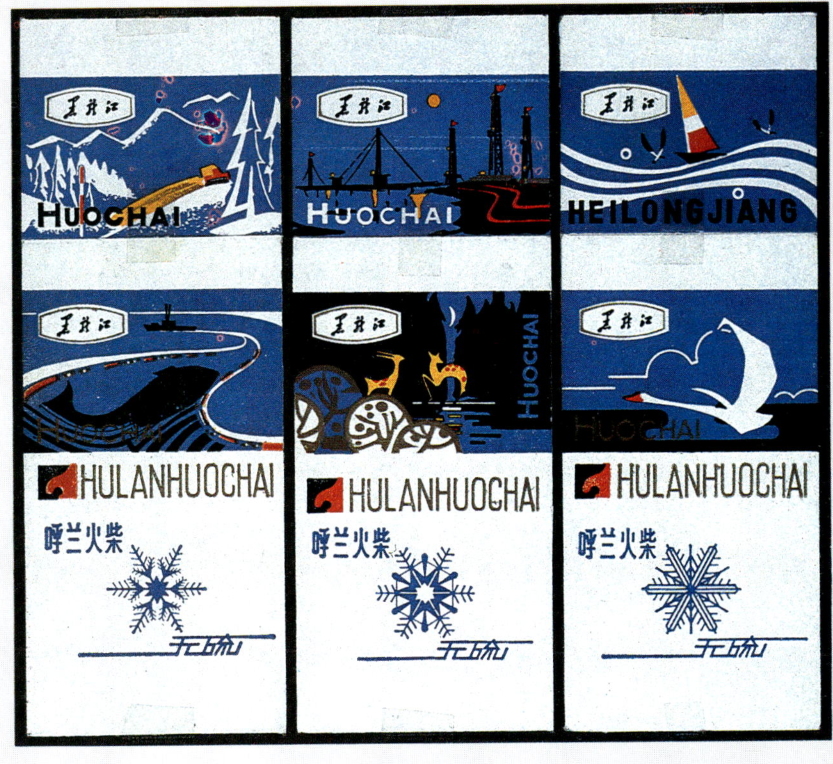

Ice Sculptures

Winter in Harbin, capital city of Heilongjiang Province, is long and has much snow, conditions which are ideal for ice sculpturing. Every year, ice cubes are ground and carved into many kinds of figures, animals and buildings. The sculptures are lit up with colourful lights, creating the feeling that one has come to a crystal fairyland. This group shows the ice-carved pagodas, gates and pavilions.

Made in Hulan, Heilongjiang Province

92 mm x 46 mm

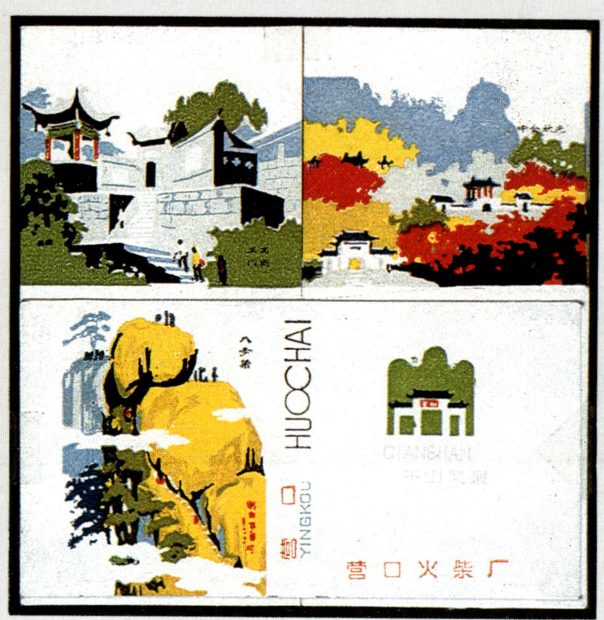

Yingkou City

Situated by the Liaodong Bay, Yingkou is a port city of Liaoning Province with a relatively developed industry and agriculture. This group shows the main scenic spots in Yingkou.

Made in Yingkou, Liaoning Province
102 mm x 52 mm

Dalian City

Surrounded on three sides by sea at the south tip of the Liaodong Peninsula, Dalian is one of China's well-known port cities and summer resorts. Its beautiful scenery has attracted tens of thousands of tourists from home and abroad every year. This group shows landscapes of Bangchui(Wooden Club) Islet off the Dalian coast.

Made in Yingkou, Liaoning Province
98 mm x 54 mm

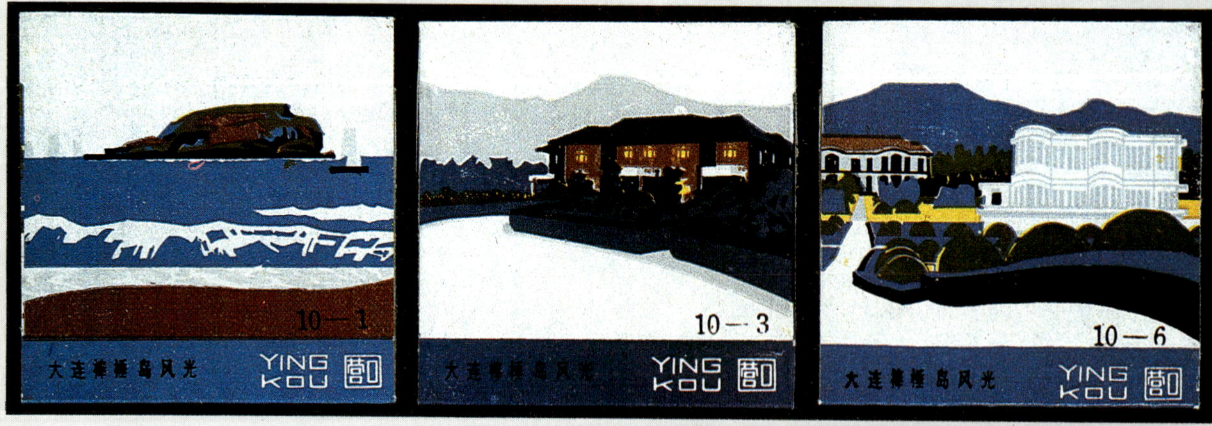

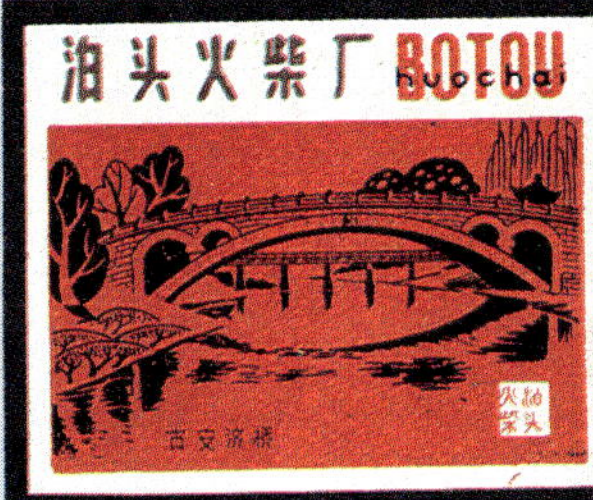

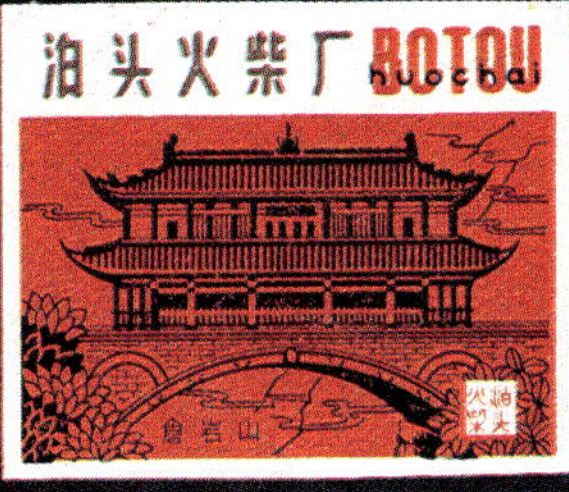

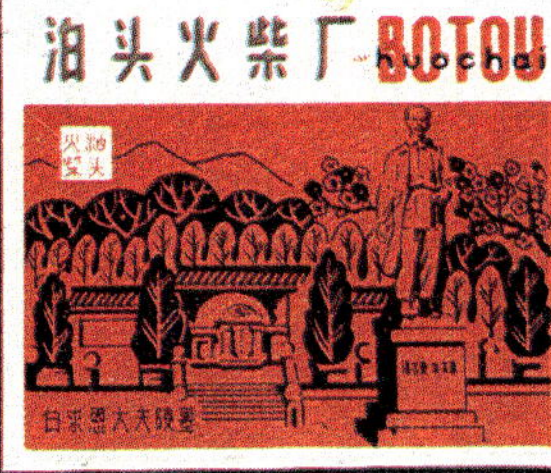

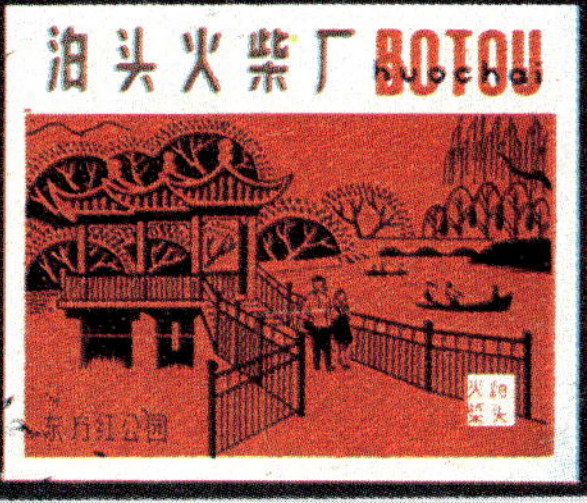

Hebei Province

With the Bohai Bay to its east and the Taihang Mountains to its west, Hebei Province is situated on the North China Plain and has numerous historical sites.

The Anji Bridge on the first cover was built in the early 7th century. With a length of 50.82 metres and a width of 9.6 metres, it spans over the Xiaohe River in Zhaoxian County.

The Green Cliff Mountain on the second cover is studded with many temples situated atop steep cliffs and strange stones. The single-arch bridge in front of the Fuqing Temple extends across the deep valley and has pavilions built on it.

The third one shows the tomb of Dr. Norman Bethune; and the fourth one, the Dongfanghong Park.

Made in Botou, Hebei Province

44 mm x 34 mm

Qinhuangdao City

Situated in the east of Hebei Province, Qinhuangdao is a well-known natural harbour in north China. The Beidaihe Beach there with soft sand and calm water is a natural bathing beach. As the Great Wall ends here, Shanhai Pass served in the past as a place of strategic importance. Clockwise: the harbour, beach, Shanhai Pass gate-tower, and sailing boats.

Made in Qinhuangdao, Hebei Province

92 mm x 56 mm

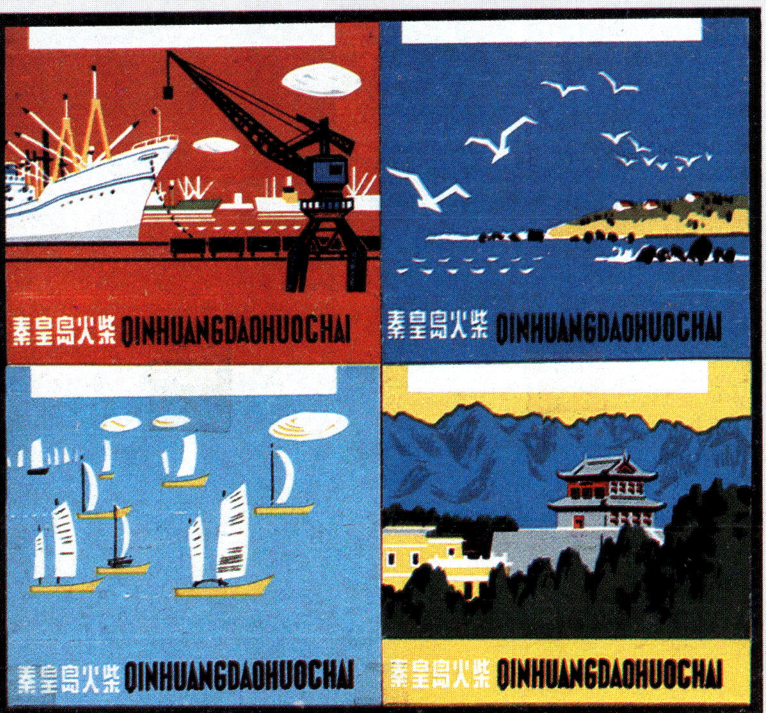

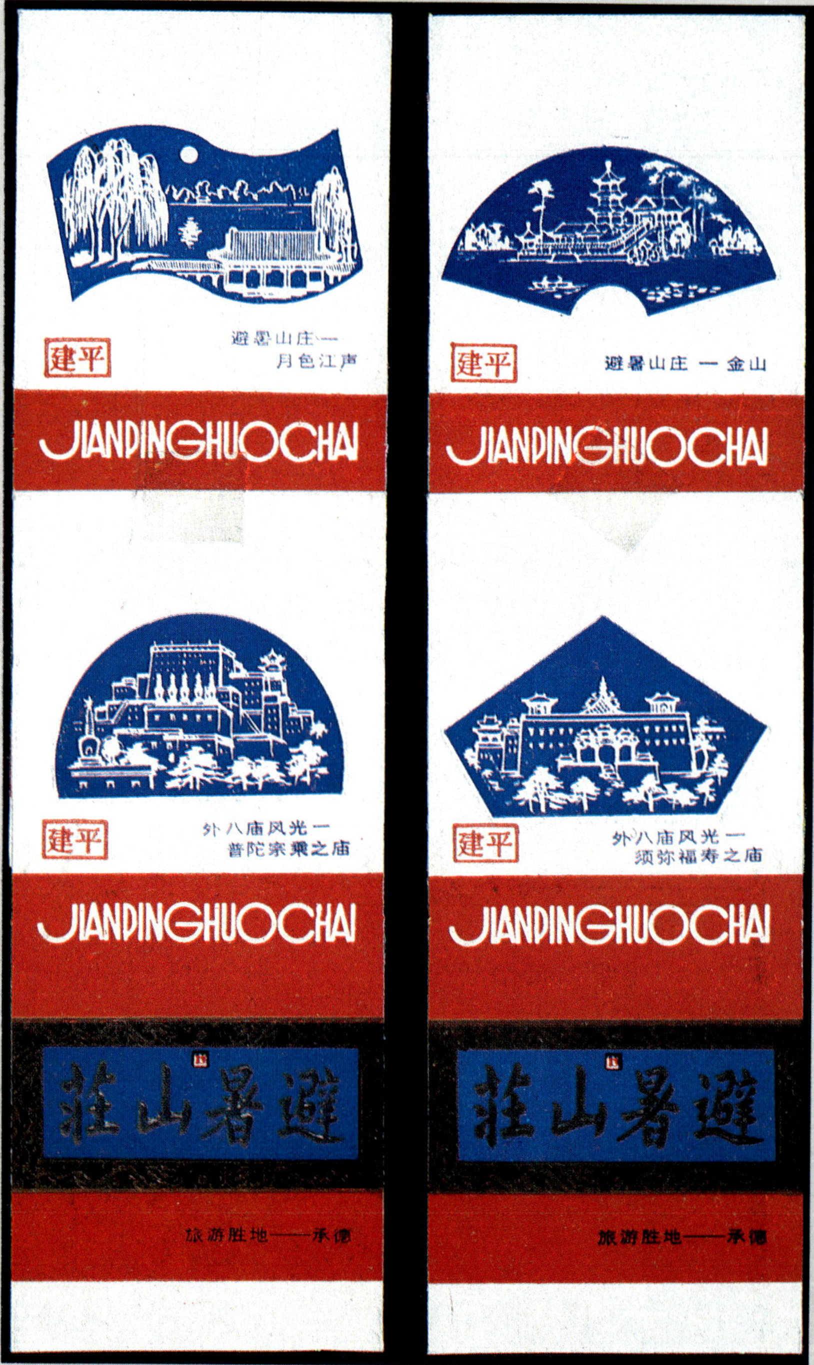

Chengde Summer Resort

Built in 1703, the Summer Resort in Chengde, Hebei Province, was formerly the temporary residence for the Qing emperors when away from the capital. Many buildings and gardens there were modelled on those in famous scenic spots in other parts of the country. The architecture in "The Moonlight over the Lake" on the top left is shown in the style of a Beijing courtyard, and the Golden Hill on the top right is a copy of the Golden Hill Temple in Zhenjiang of Jiangsu Province. The Putuozongcheng Temple, known as Lesser Potala Palace, and the Sumeru Happiness Temple on the bottom were built in the style of Tibetan temples.

Made in Chengde, Hebei Province

103 mm x 46 mm

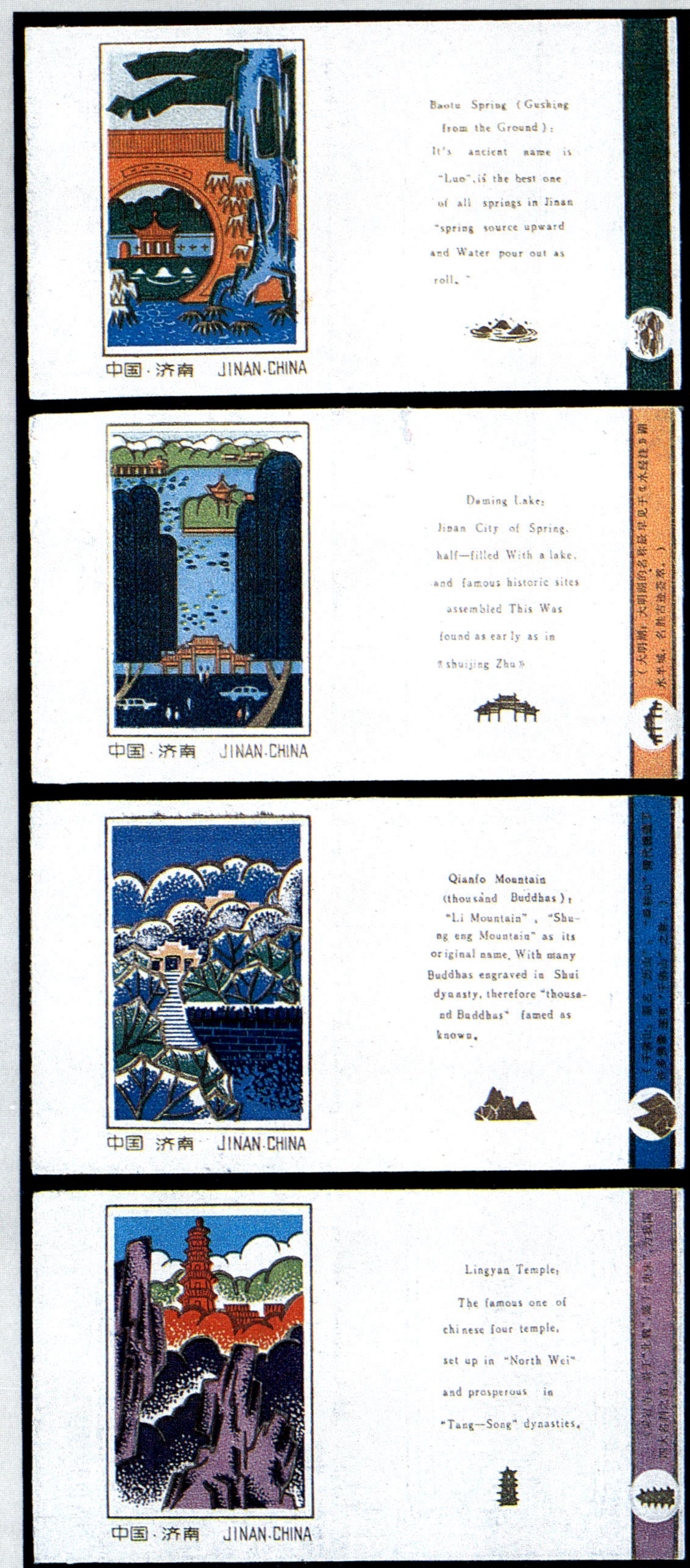

Jinan, "City of Springs"

Provincial capital of Shandong, Jinan is also known as a "city of springs." From top to bottom: Baotu Spring, the first of the seventy-two springs in the city; Daming Lake in the north of the city, the end point of all the springs and streams; Thousand-Buddha Hill, covered by hundreds of Buddhist images carved since the 6th century; and the magnificent Lingyan Temple situated in quiet and beautiful surroundings.

Made in Jinan, Shandong Province

104 mm x 57 mm

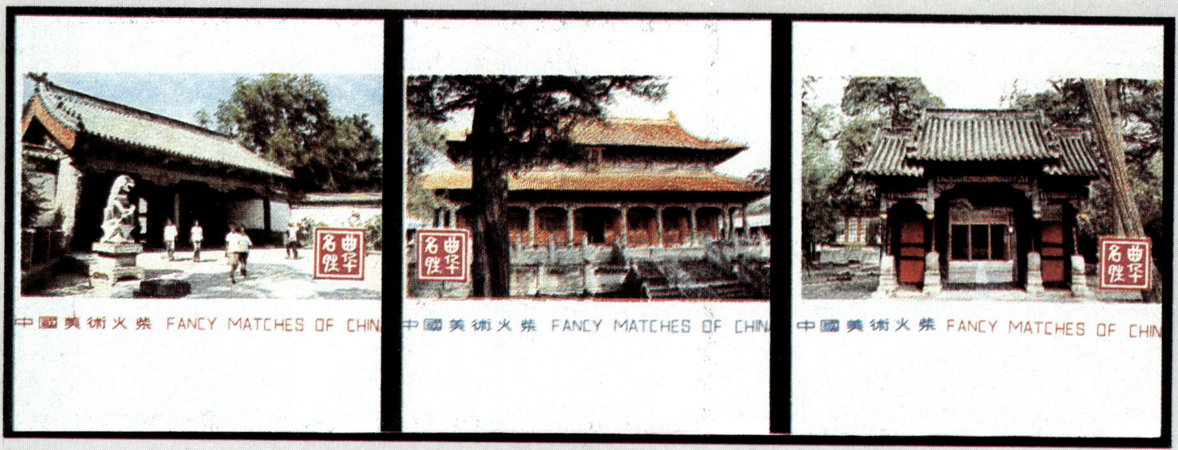

Qufu, Hometown of Confucius

Qufu in southwest Shandong Province is the hometown of Confucius, the great philosopher of Chinese history. The three famous historical sites—Confucius Temple, Confucius Mansion and Confucius Forest are all found here.

From left to right: Gate of Confucius Mansion, Hall of Great Perfection, and Double Light Gate.

Made in Jinan, Shandong Province

91 mm x 48 mm

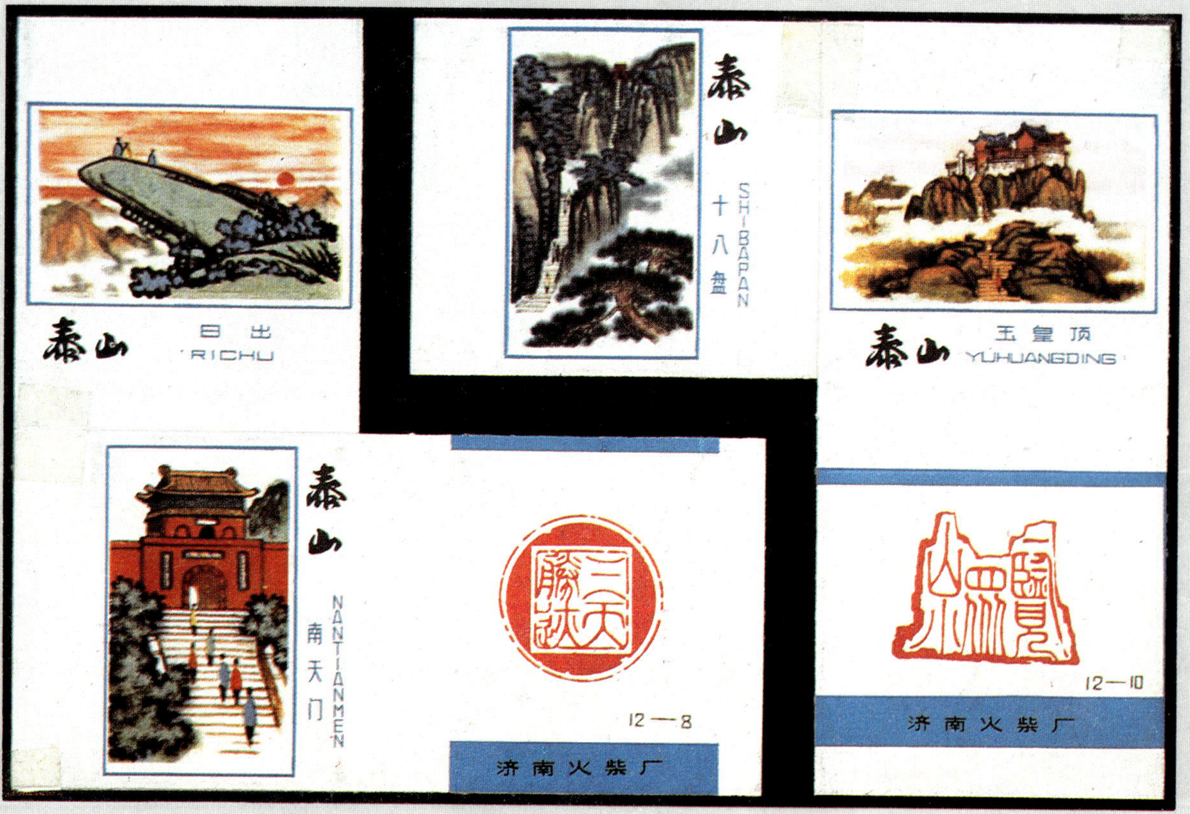

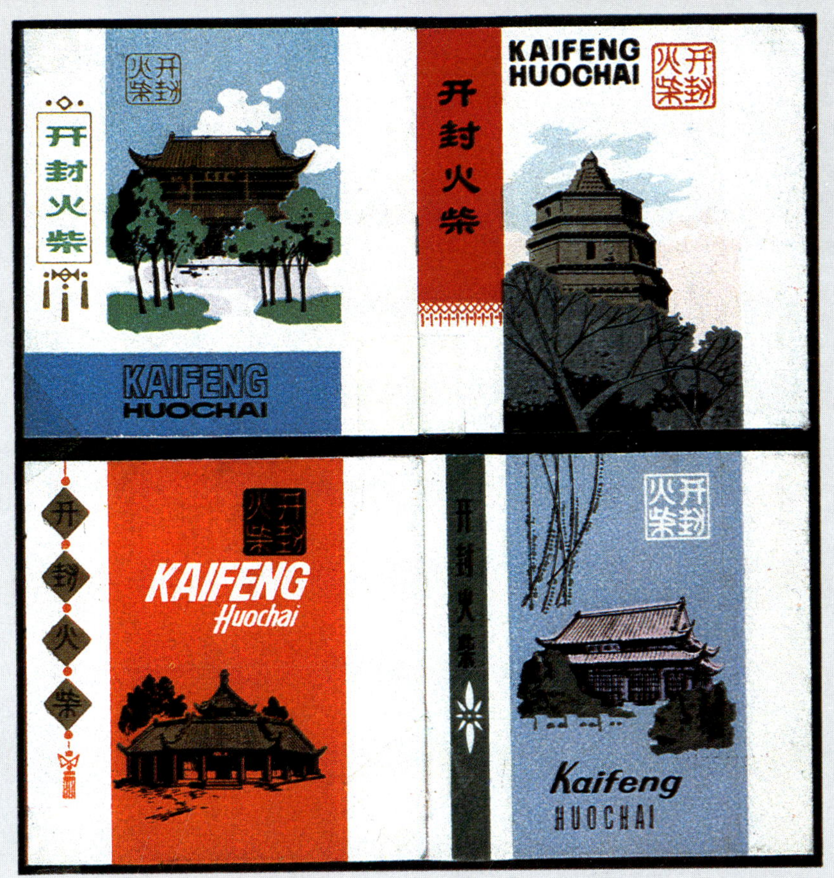

Kaifeng, an Ancient Capital

One of the six ancient capitals of China, Kaifeng of Henan Province has the remains of numerous cultural and historical treasures such as the old streets and lanes, palaces, pavilions, temples and pagodas.

Clockwise: Guchui Terrace, Fanta Pagoda, Great Hall of Dragon Pavilion, and Octagonal Glazed Palace.

Made in Kaifeng, Henan Province

94 mm x 47 mm

Scenic Mt. Tai

Situated in Tai'an County of Shandong Province, Mt. Tai is also known as Mount of the East among the five famous mountains in China. The stone steps lead visitors past gurgling streams, flying waterfalls and precipitous cliffs to the 1,545-metre main peak, where they can enjoy the fantastic sunrise over the East China Sea.

From top left: Sunrise, Eighteen-Bend Mountain Path, and Jade Emperor Peak; bottom: South Heavenly Gate.

Made in Jinan, Shandong Province

101 mm x 47 mm

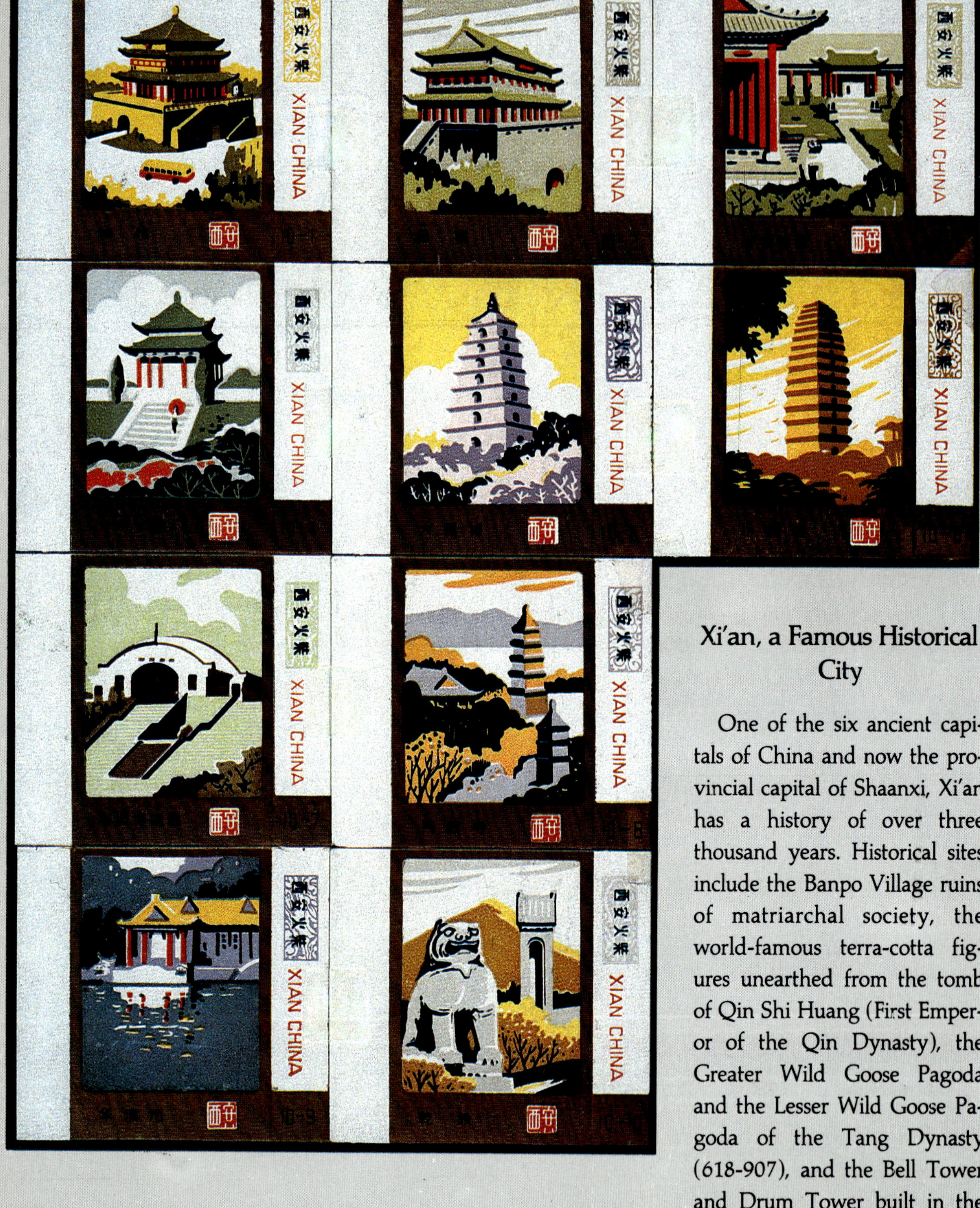

Xi'an, a Famous Historical City

One of the six ancient capitals of China and now the provincial capital of Shaanxi, Xi'an has a history of over three thousand years. Historical sites include the Banpo Village ruins of matriarchal society, the world-famous terra-cotta figures unearthed from the tomb of Qin Shi Huang (First Emperor of the Qin Dynasty), the Greater Wild Goose Pagoda and the Lesser Wild Goose Pagoda of the Tang Dynasty (618-907), and the Bell Tower and Drum Tower built in the Ming Dynasty (1368-1644).

The numerous cultural relics both above and underground show the brilliant civilization of ancient China.

From left, top to bottom: Bell Tower, Drum Tower, Shaanxi Museum, Xingqing Park, Greater Wild Goose Pagoda, Lesser Wild Goose Pagoda, Banpo Museum, Xingjiao Temple, Huaqing Pool, and the Qianling Mausoleum of Emperor Gaozong and Empress Wu Zetian of the Tang Dynasty.

Made in Xi'an, Shaanxi Province

107 mm x 53 mm

Yan'an, Cradle of the Chinese Revolution

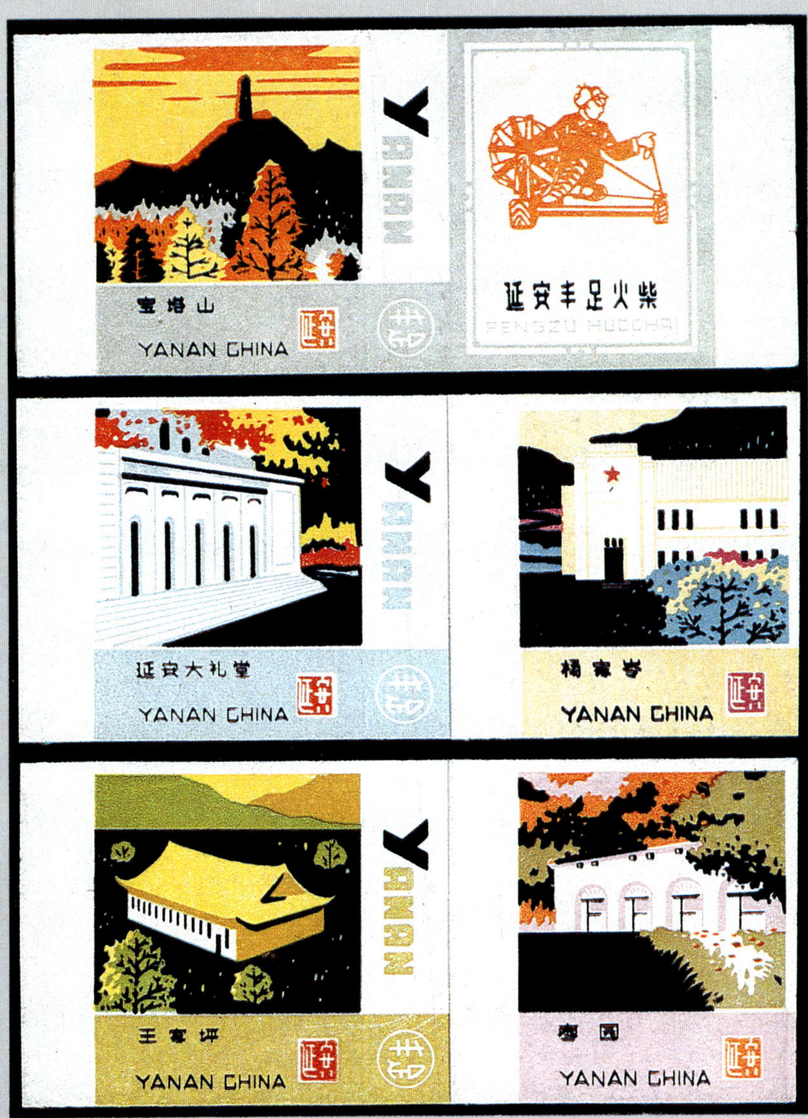

A venerated place of the Chinese revolution, Yan'an in north Shaanxi is the place where, between 1937 and 1947, the Central Committee of the Communist Party of China led the Chinese people in their war against Japan and the War of Liberation.

This group of covers commemorates the various revolutionary sites in Yan'an. First row: Yan'an Pagoda, built in the Ming Dynasty (1368-1644), the symbol of revolution for progressive young people since 1937 when the Central Committee of CPC moved to Yan'an; from left, second row: Yan'an Auditorium, where the 7th National Congress of the CPC was held, and Yangjialing, seat of the Party Central Committee before 1943; from left, bottom row: Wangjiaping, site of the Central Military Commission of the Communist Party of China, and Date Garden, site of the Secretariat of the CPC Central Committee.

Made in Yan'an, Shaanxi Province

107 mm x 46 mm

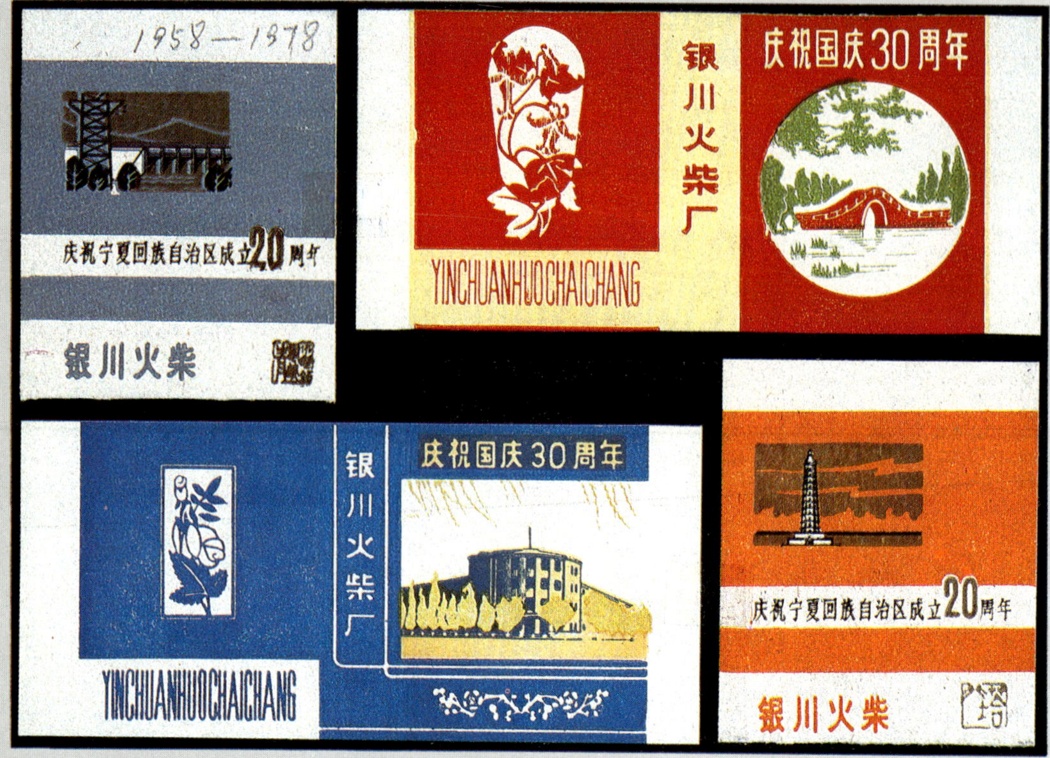

Ningxia Hui Autonomous Region

With Yinchuan as its capital city, Ningxia, situated to the west of the Hetao Plain in the Yellow River valley, is inhabited by the Hui, Han and Manchu peoples.

Once the capital of the Western Xia regime (1038-1227), Yinchuan has been a famous city since the ancient times and boasts many historical sites. Ningxia has always been a west-east hub of transportation and communication in north China.

One of the two sets of matchbox covers shown here was designed in 1978 for the 20th anniversary of the Ningxia Hui Autonomous Region. The other, in 1979, for the 30th birthday of the People's Republic of China.

Made in Yinchuan, Ningxia Hui Autonomous Region

101 mm x 46 mm

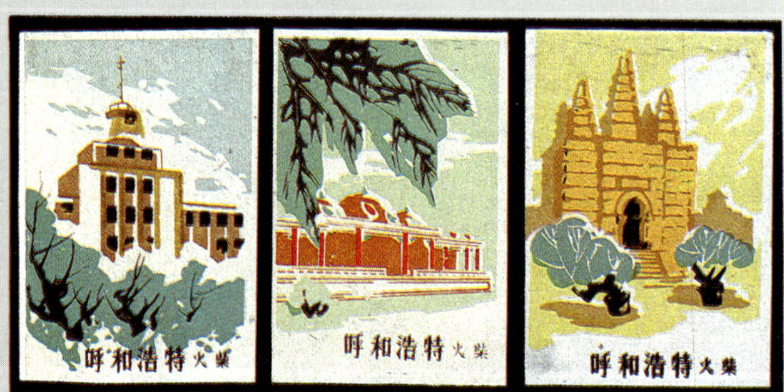

Huhhot City

The city on a prairie, Huhhot, meaning the city of green in the Mongolian language, is the capital of the Inner Mongolia Autonomous Region. This set of covers introduces both old and

Xinjiang Uygur Autonomous Region

With high snowy mountains, flat basins and vast deserts, Xinjiang in northwest China covers an area of over 1.6 million square kilometres and has its capital in Urumqi, in the north of the region. This set of covers shows the landscape and constructions in Xinjiang. From left, bottom: the ancient pagoda in Kashi Mosque, and the Urumqi Airport.

Made in Urumqi, Xinjiang Uygur Autonomous Region

91 mm x 45 mm

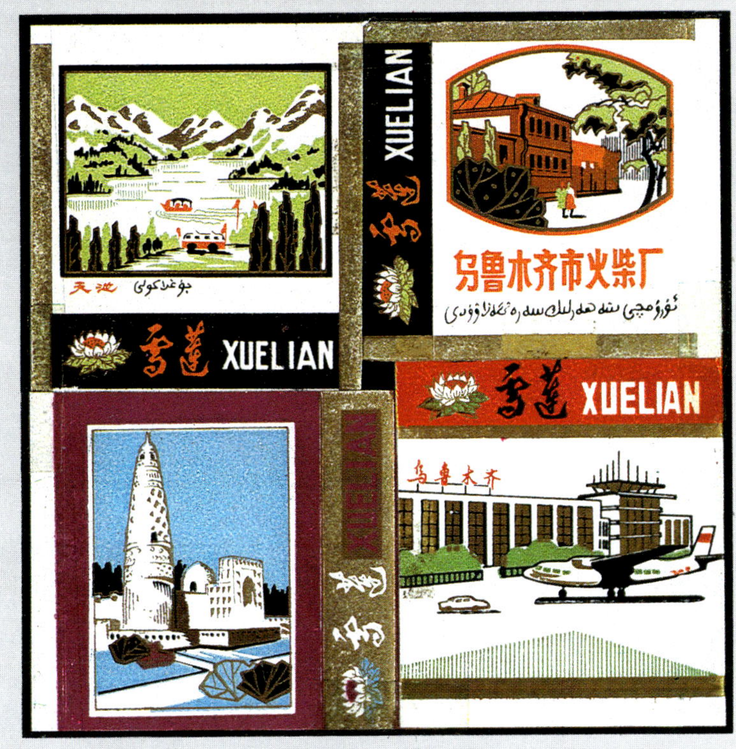

Tibet Autonomous Region

With an average elevation of four thousand metres, Tibet on the Qinghai-Tibet Plateau southwest of China is also known as the "roof of the world." The temperature here is low and the air very thin. But there is abundant sunshine, snow mountains, roaring rivers, dense forests and evergreen pastures. Lhasa is the region's capital. From left to right: the Potala Palace in Lhasa and the Yarlungzangbo River.

Made in Lhasa, Tibet Autonomous Region

41 mm x 33 mm

new constructions in Huhhot. From left, TV Station Race Course, and Five Pagoda Temple of the 13th century. top: The Stadium

Made in Huhhot, Inner Mongolia Autonomous Region

52 mm x 36 mm

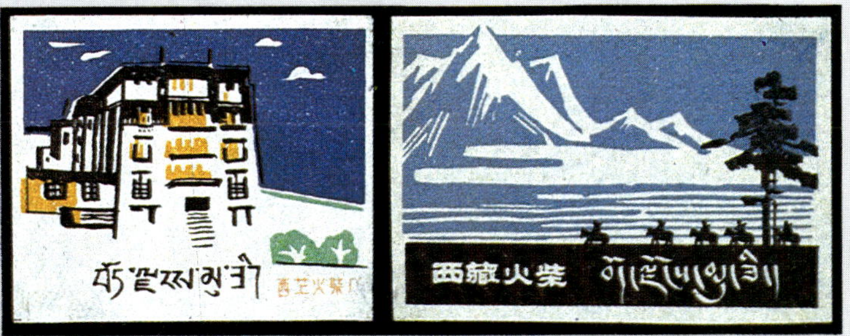

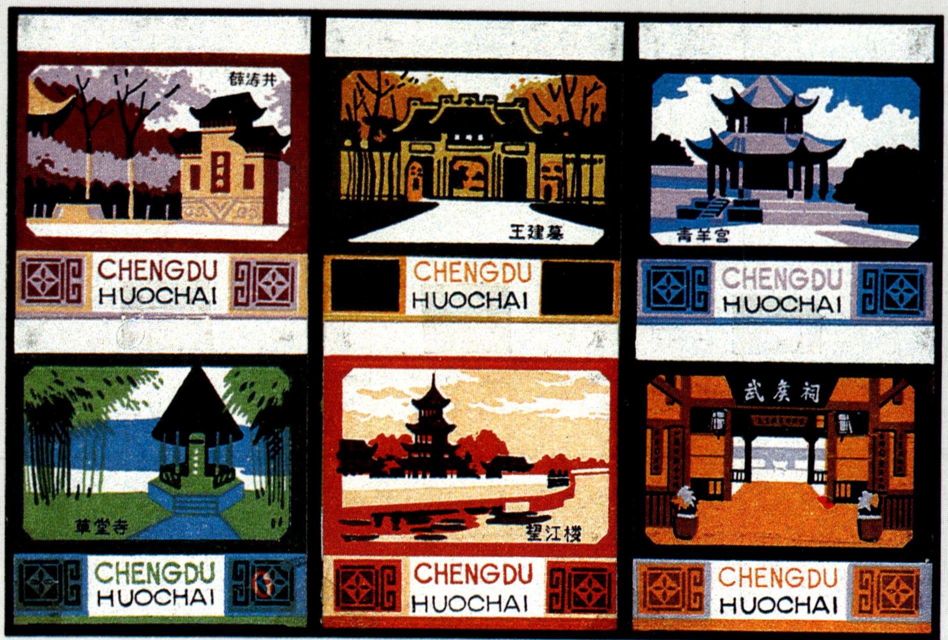

Chengdu City

Chengdu, the capital of Sichuan Province, "the land of plenty," has a history of over two thousand years and abundant historical sites. The weather here is humid. Its products are numerous since it has a fairly developed industry and commerce. This set of covers shows some of the city's historical sites (clockwise): Xue Tao Well, Wang Jian Tomb, Black Goat Palace, Wu Hou Temple, Riverside Tower and Du Fu Thatched Hut.

Made in Chengdu, Sichuan Province

77 mm x 43 mm

Scenic Mt. Emei

One of the four well-known Buddhist mountains in China, Mt. Emei, with its main peak of 3,099 metres above sea level, is situated in Emei County, Sichuan Province. Its beautiful sceneries, numerous cultural relics and historical sites have attracted thousands of tourists. This group shows ten tourist sites. From top to bottom, left column: Lucky Light at the Golden Summit, Early Morning Mist at Hongchun, Twin Bridges at Qingyin Pavilion, Evening Chime at the Sacred Temple, and Autumn Breeze and Clear Water; from top to bottom, right column: Moonlight over the Elephant Bathing Pond, House of the Nine Immortals, Green Cliff, Clouds Around Luofeng Peak, and Sunshine After Snow at Daping.

Made in Leshan, Sichuan Province

90 mm x 46 mm

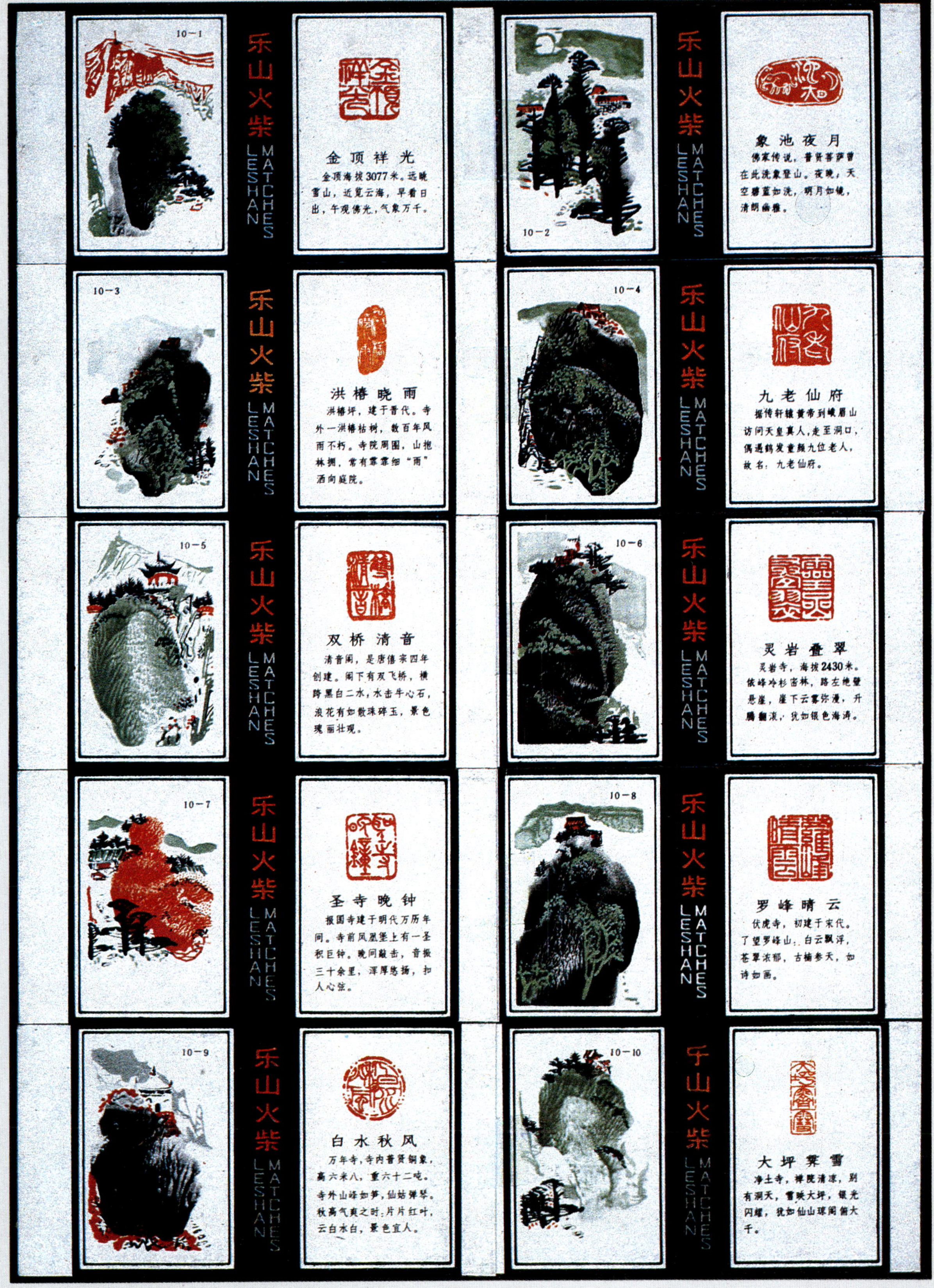
10-1
乐山火柴
LESHAN MATCHES
金顶祥光
金顶海拔3077米。远眺雪山，近览云海，早看日出，午观佛光，气象万千。
10-2
乐山火柴
LESHAN MATCHES
象池夜月
佛家传说，普贤菩萨曾在此洗象登山。夜晚，天空碧蓝如洗，明月如镜，清朗幽雅。
10-3
乐山火柴
LESHAN MATCHES
洪椿晓雨
洪椿坪，建于晋代。寺外一洪椿枯树，数百年风雨不朽。寺院周围，山抱林拥，常有霏霏细“雨”洒向庭院。
10-4
乐山火柴
LESHAN MATCHES
九老仙府
据传轩辕黄帝到峨眉山访问天皇真人，走至洞口，偶遇鹤发童颜九位老人，故名：九老仙府。
10-5
乐山火柴
LESHAN MATCHES
双桥清音
清音阁，是唐僖宗四年创建。阁下有双飞桥，横跨黑白二水，水击牛心石，浪花有如散珠碎玉，景色瑰丽壮观。
10-6
乐山火柴
LESHAN MATCHES
灵岩叠翠
灵岩寺，海拔2430米。依峰冷杉密林，路左绝壁悬崖，崖下云雾弥漫，升腾翻滚，犹如银色海涛。
10-7
乐山火柴
LESHAN MATCHES
圣寺晚钟
报国寺建于明代万历年间。寺前凤凰堡上有一圣积巨钟。晚间敲击，音振三十余里，浑厚悠扬，扣人心弦。
10-8
乐山火柴
LESHAN MATCHES
罗峰晴云
伏虎寺，初建于宋代。了望罗峰山，白云飘浮，苍翠浓郁，古楠参天，如诗如画。
10-9
乐山火柴
LESHAN MATCHES
白水秋风
万年寺，寺内普贤铜象，高六米八，重六十二吨。寺外山峰如笋，仙姑弹琴。秋高气爽之时，片片红叶，云白水白，景色宜人。
10-10
乐山火柴
LESHAN MATCHES
大坪霁雪
净土寺，禅院清凉，别有洞天，雪映大坪，银光闪耀，犹如仙山琼阁偷大千。

Kunming, "City of Spring"

Provincial capital of Yunnan, Kunming has a springlike weather all year round and is a place of strategic importance in southwest China. West Hill and Dianchi Lake are the two famous tourist sites in Kunming.

The four covers above show the beauty of Dianchi Lake, and the centre one below, Dragon Gate on West Hill.

Made in Kunming, Yunnan Province

88 mm x 42 mm

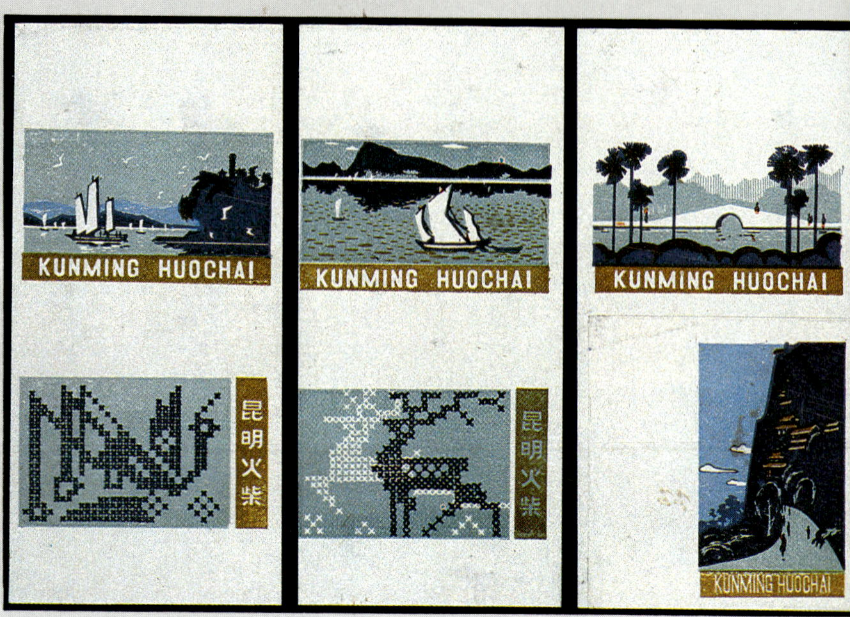

Fantastic Stone Forest

With an area of 26,000 hectares, the Stone Forest is situated in the Lunan Yi Autonomous County in Yunnan Province. Covered with grotesque crags and bizarre pinnacles, it looks like a huge forest at a distance and like a precipice at close range.

Clockwise: Suspension Penholder, Peak of Glossy Ganoderma of Ten Thousand Years, Elephant at Stone Terrace, Phoenix Combing Its Wing, and Gate of the Stone Forest.

Made in Kunming, Yunnan Province

99 mm x 51 mm

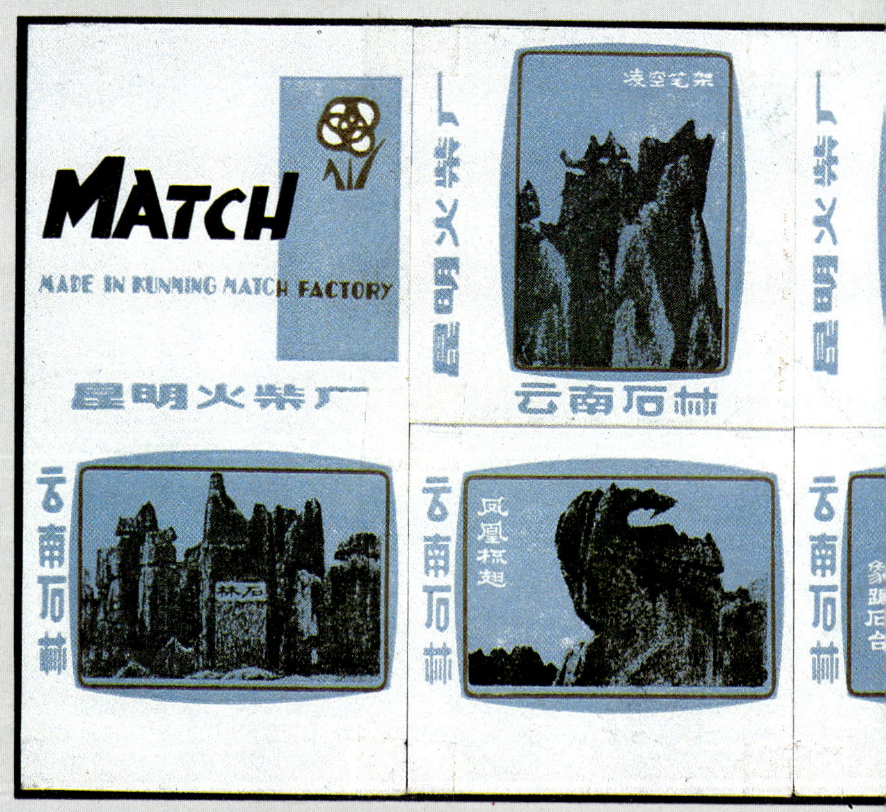

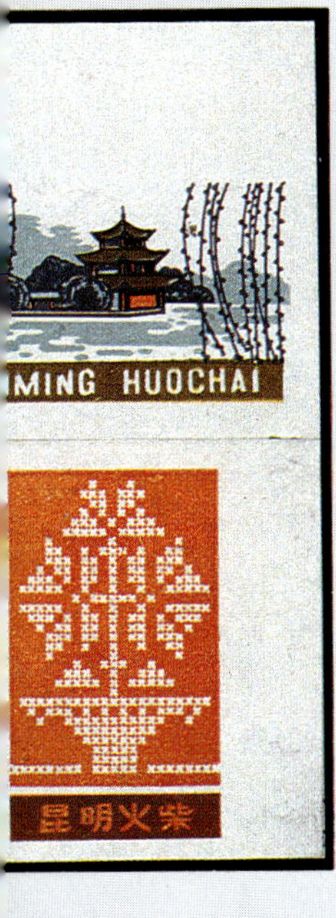

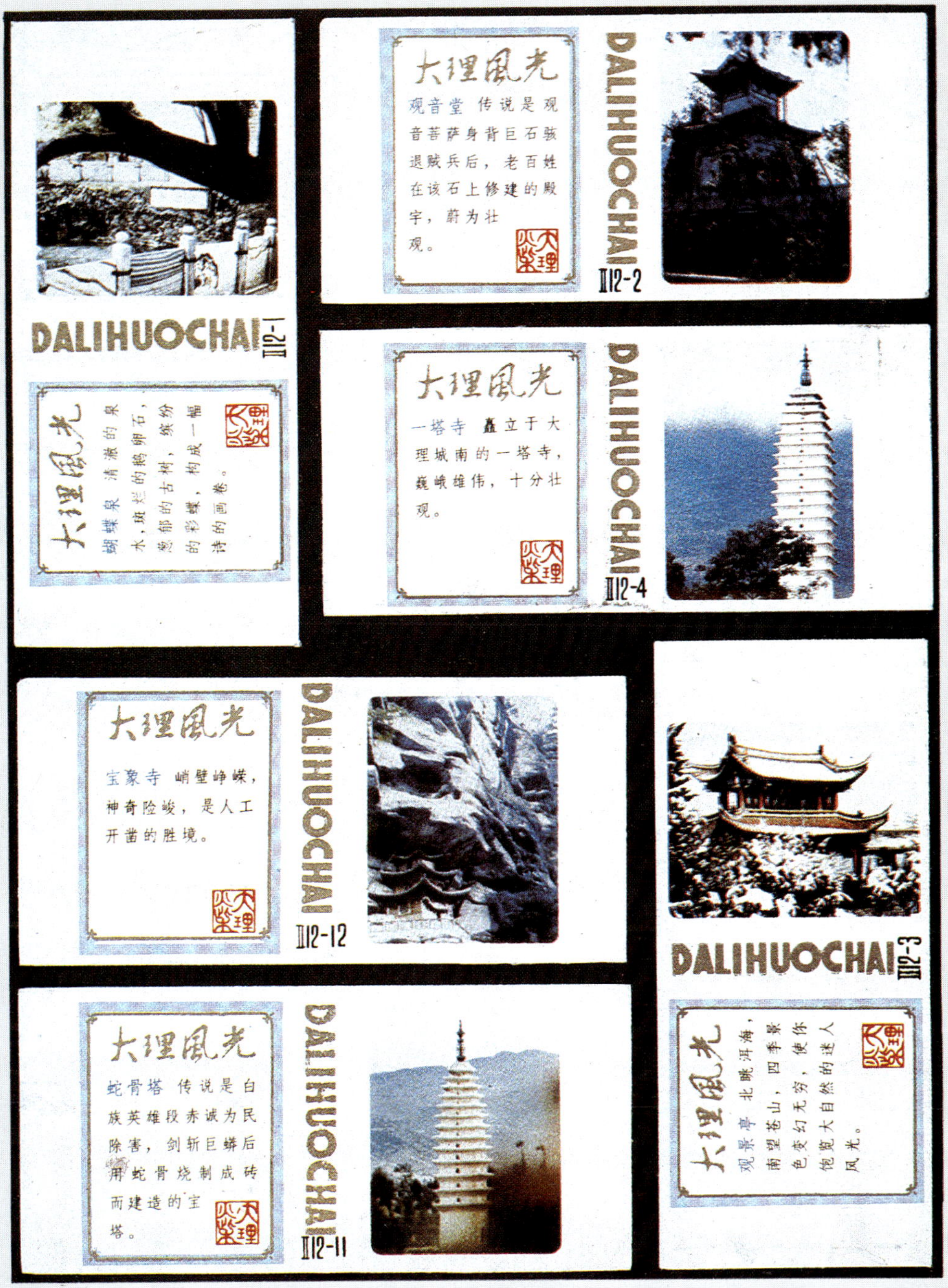

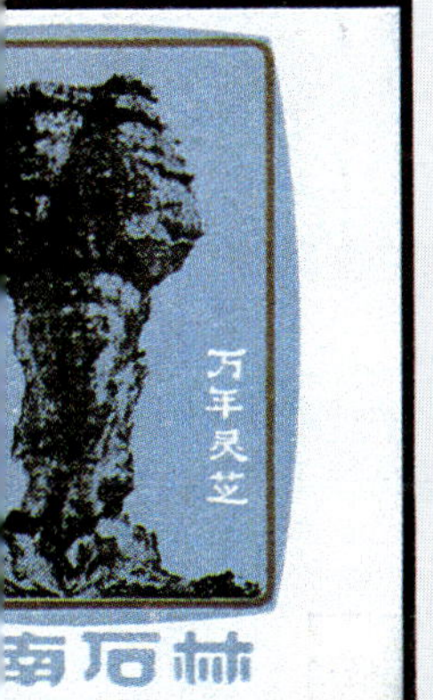

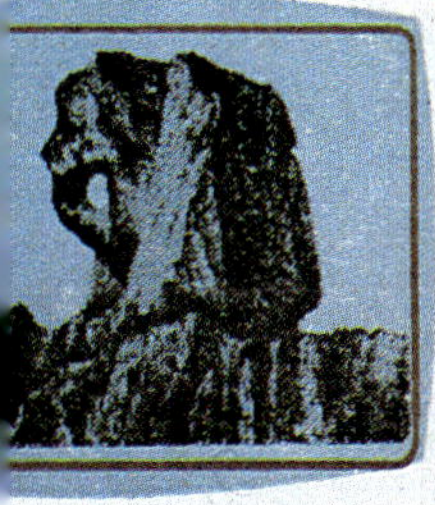

Dali Vignettes

Situated to the west of Kunming, Dali is one of the tourist resorts in Yunnan Province. Cangshan Mountain and Erhai Lake make a beautiful landscape on the plateau.

From left, top to bottom: Butterfly Spring, Goddess of Mercy Hall, Treasure Elephant Temple, Single Pagoda Temple, Snake Bone Pagoda, and Viewing Pavilion.

Made in Dali, Yunnan Province

97 mm x 44 mm

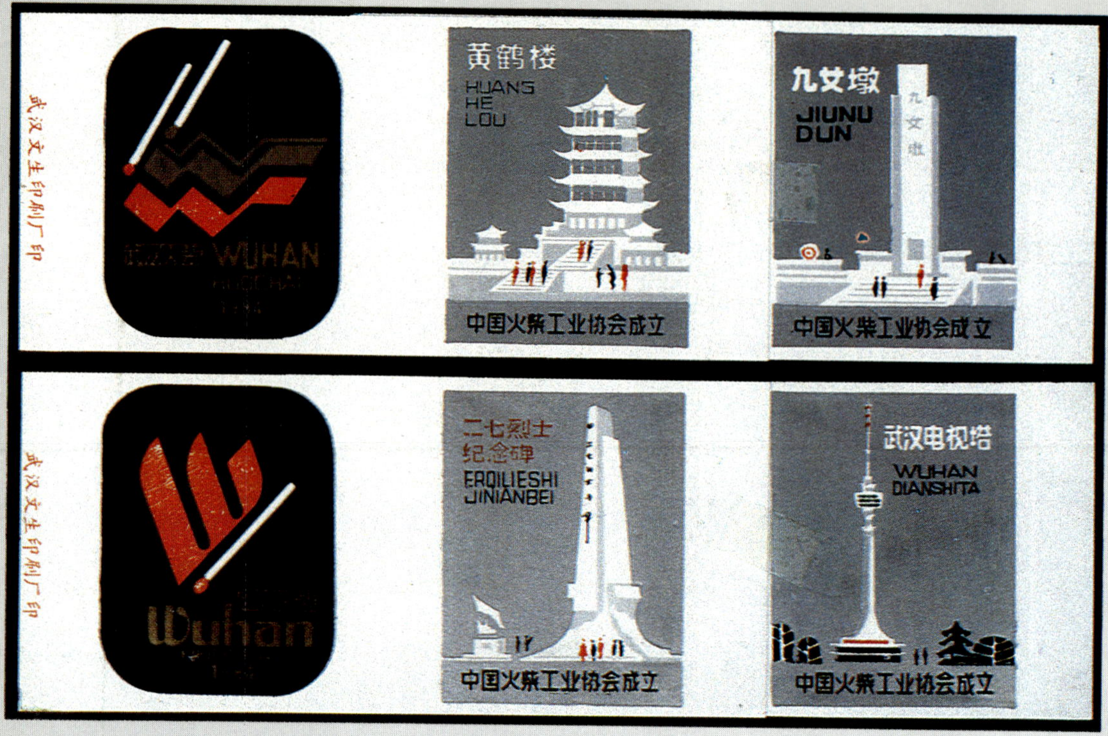

Wuhan City

Situated at the confluence of the Yangtze and Hanshui rivers, Wuhan, provincial capital of Hubei, has been a hub of land and water transport since ancient times. Also a city of historical importance, it is quite developed both culturally and economically.

This group shows the constructions in Wuhan, old and new (clockwise): Yellow Crane Pavilion, Monument to the Nine Heroines, Wuhan TV Station, and Monument to the Martyrs of the Great Strike of February 7, 1923.

Made in Wuhan, Hubei Province

101 mm x 44 mm

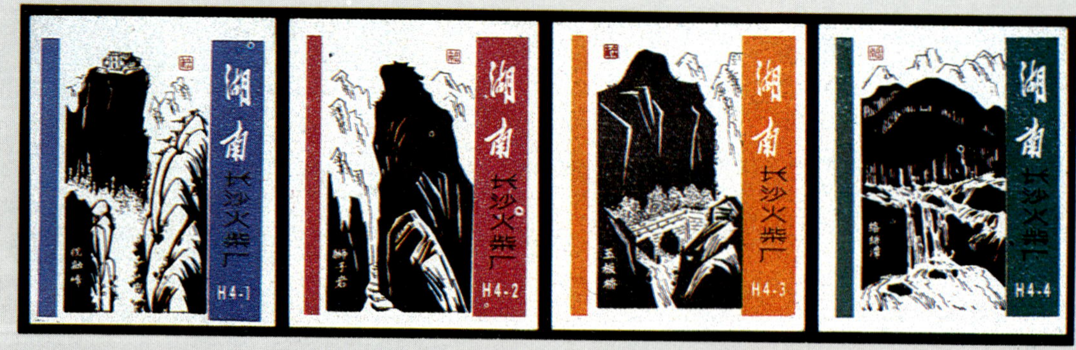

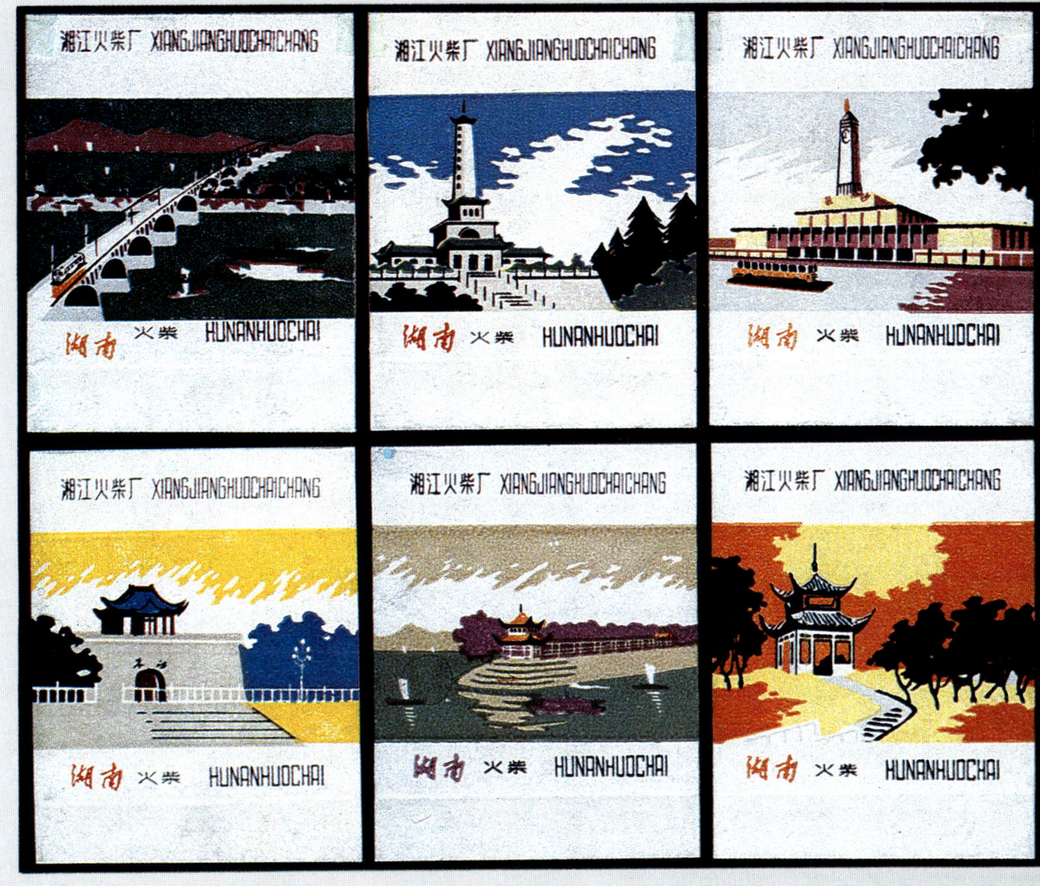

Changsha City

Changsha, provincial capital of Hunan, is another city of historical importance and a tourist attraction, flanked by the Beijing-Guangzhou Railway on its left and the Xiangjiang River on its right. The Yuelu and Miaogao mountains stand on each side of the Xiangjiang River.

Orange Islet (lower middle), and Aiwan Pavilion (lower right) on Yuelu Mountain are musts for tourists in Changsha.

Made in Changsha, Hunan Province
103 mm x 46 mm

Scenic Mt. Hengshan

Known as "Mountain in the South," Mt. Hengshan in the south of Hunan is one of the five famous mountains in China. Of the 72 peaks, Zhurong of 1,290 metres above the sea level is the highest. Hengshan is also scattered with temples and historical sites.

From left to right: Zhurong Peak, Lion Cliff, Jade Landing Bridge, and Luosi Crossing.

Made in Changsha, Hunan Province
42 mm x 35 mm

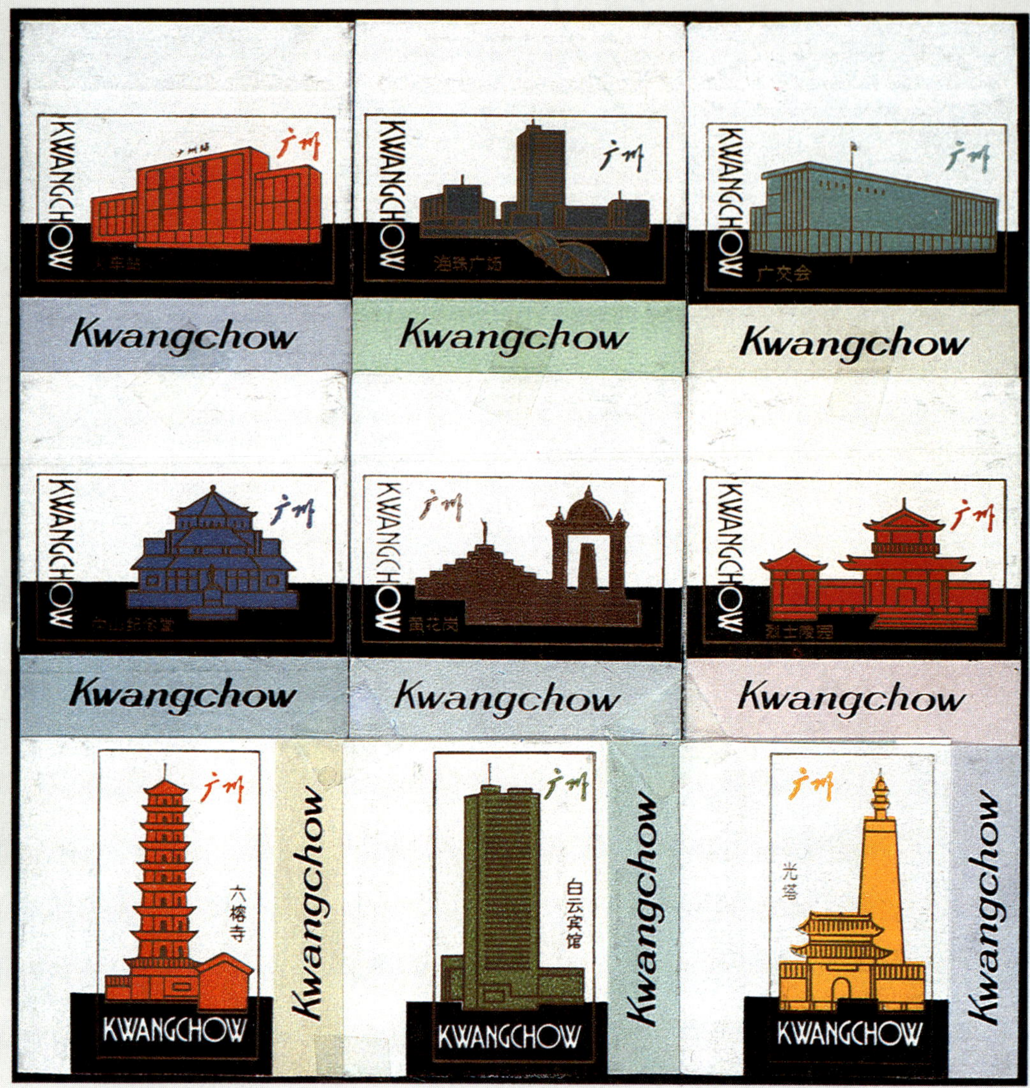

Guangzhou, "Gate of the South"

Guangzhou, the provincial capital of Guangdong, has a well developed industry, commerce and shipping business. The people of Guangzhou have a history of resistance against foreign invaders and armed uprisings, and thus there are also a lot of historical sites. The city, with its warm weather, numerous products and beautiful scenery, is a nice place for tourists. From left, top to bottom: Guangzhou Railway Station, Haizhu Square, Guangzhou Export Commodity Fair Centre, Sun Yat-sen Memorial Hall, Huanghuagang Cemetery of Seventy-Two Revolutionary Martyrs, Revolutionary Martyrs' Cemetery, Six Banyans Temple, Baiyun Hotel, and the Brightness Pagoda.

Made in Guangzhou, Guangdong Province

85 mm x 47 mm

Nanhai County

Nanhai in Guangdong Province is situated at the Pearl River Delta, its flat fertile land crisscrossed by waterways. Xijian Mountain in its southwest is a tourist site.

From left, top to bottom: Jade Lake Garden, Guifeng Pagoda, Gongkeng Sparrow Garden, Homebound Fishing Boats, Spring Wave at Yamen Gate, Long Bridge over Jade Lake, Chishi Temple, Glittering Pearl at Gudou, Ciyuan Palace, and Birds' Paradise.

Made in Nanhai, Guangdong Province

93 mm x 44 mm

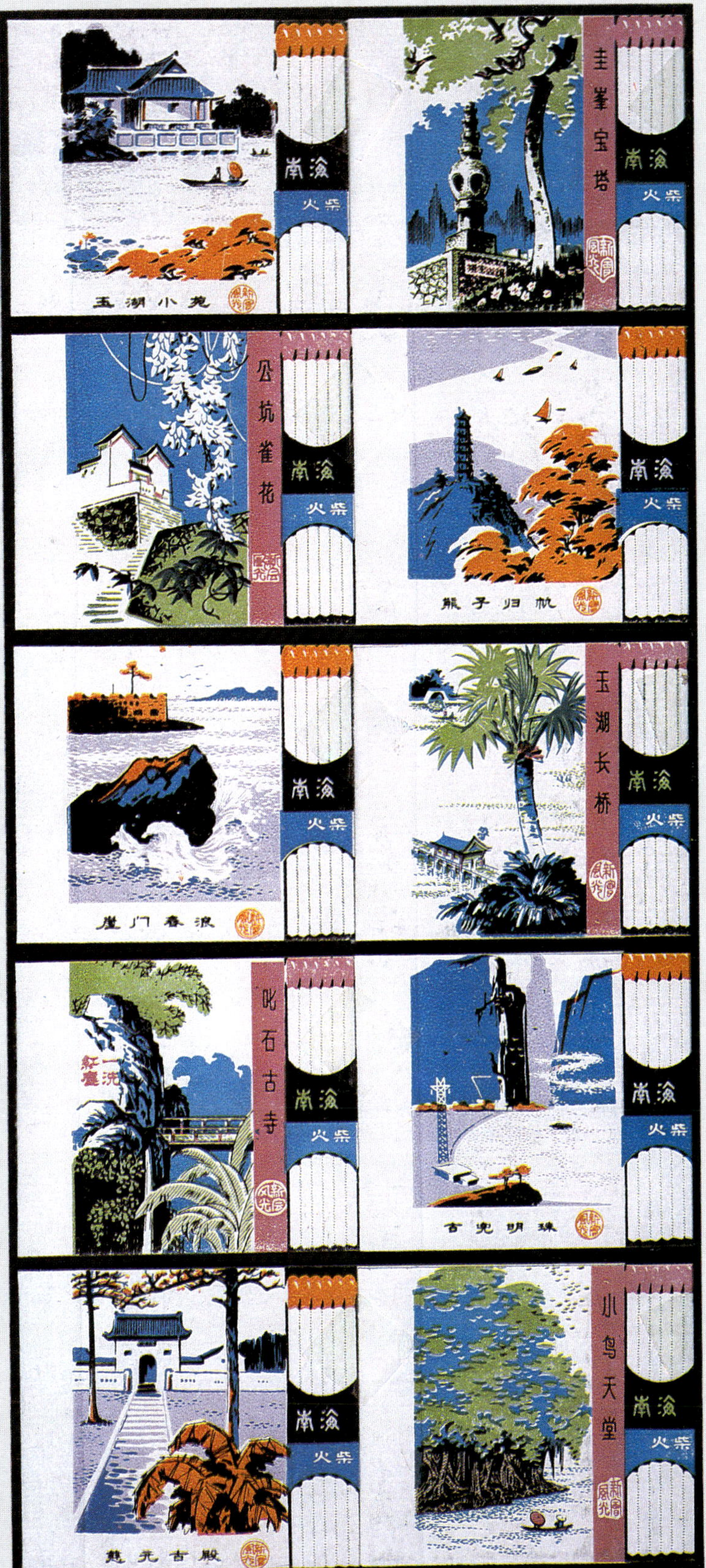

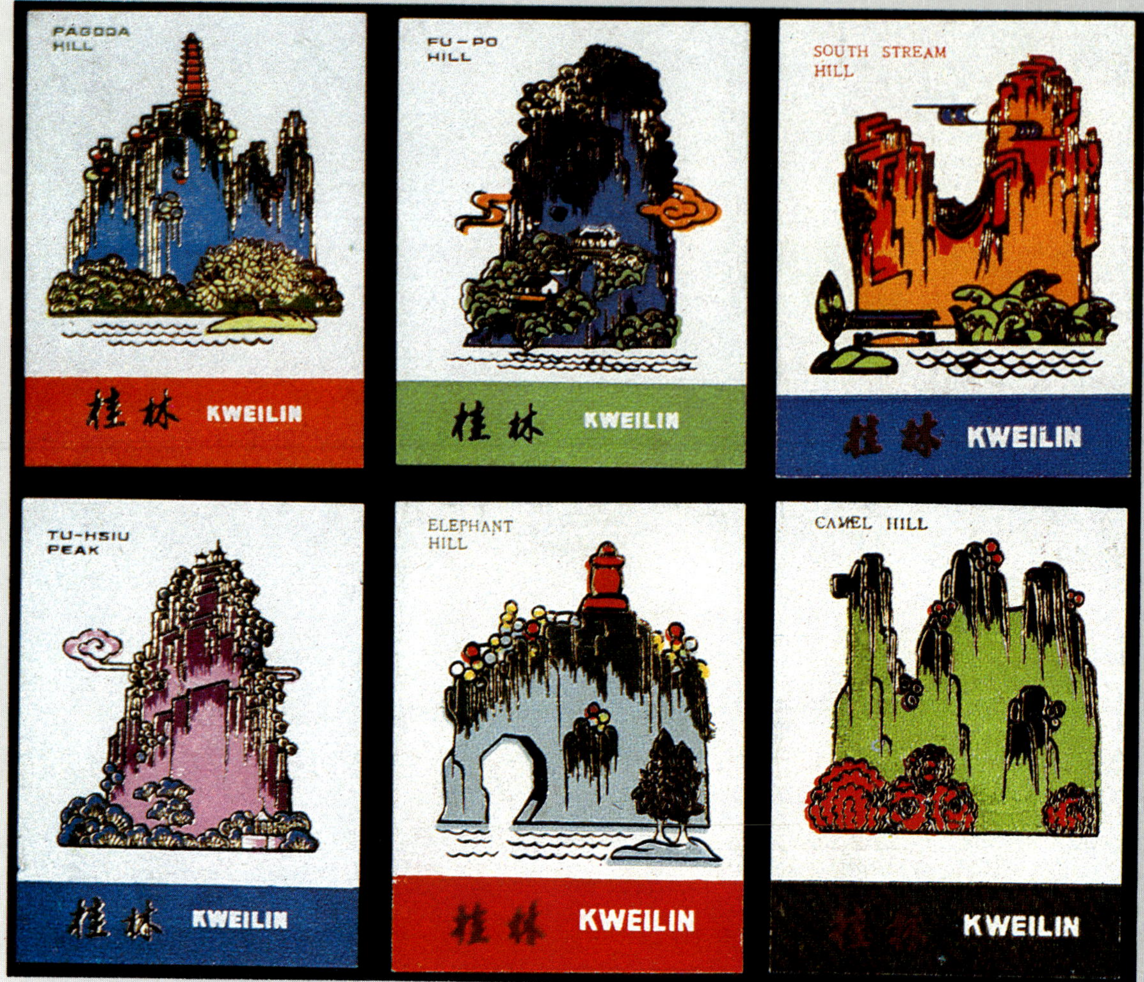

The Scenic Wonders of Guilin

Guilin, situated in the northeast of Guangxi Zhuang Autonomous Region, is surrounded by oddly shaped mountains and clear water. The scenery is said to be the finest under heaven. Shown here are the picturesque landscapes of Guilin (clockwise): Pagoda Hill, Wave Curbing Hill, South Stream Hill, Camel Hill, Elephant Trunk Hill, and Solitary Beauty Hill.

Made in Guilin, Guangxi Zhuang Autonomous Region

43 mm x 34 mm

Scenic Mt. Huangshan

Mt. Huangshan, located in the south of Anhui Province, is famous for its bizzare stones, peculiar pines, sea of clouds and hot springs. From top to bottom, left column: Hot Spring, Greeting Guests Pine, Celestial Capital Peak, and Begin-to-Believe Peak; from top to bottom, right column: Jade Screen Tower, Monkey Enjoying the Sea View, Jade Screen Steps, and Hundred-Thousand-Foot Waterfall.

Made in Wuhu, Anhui Province

101 mm x 53 mm

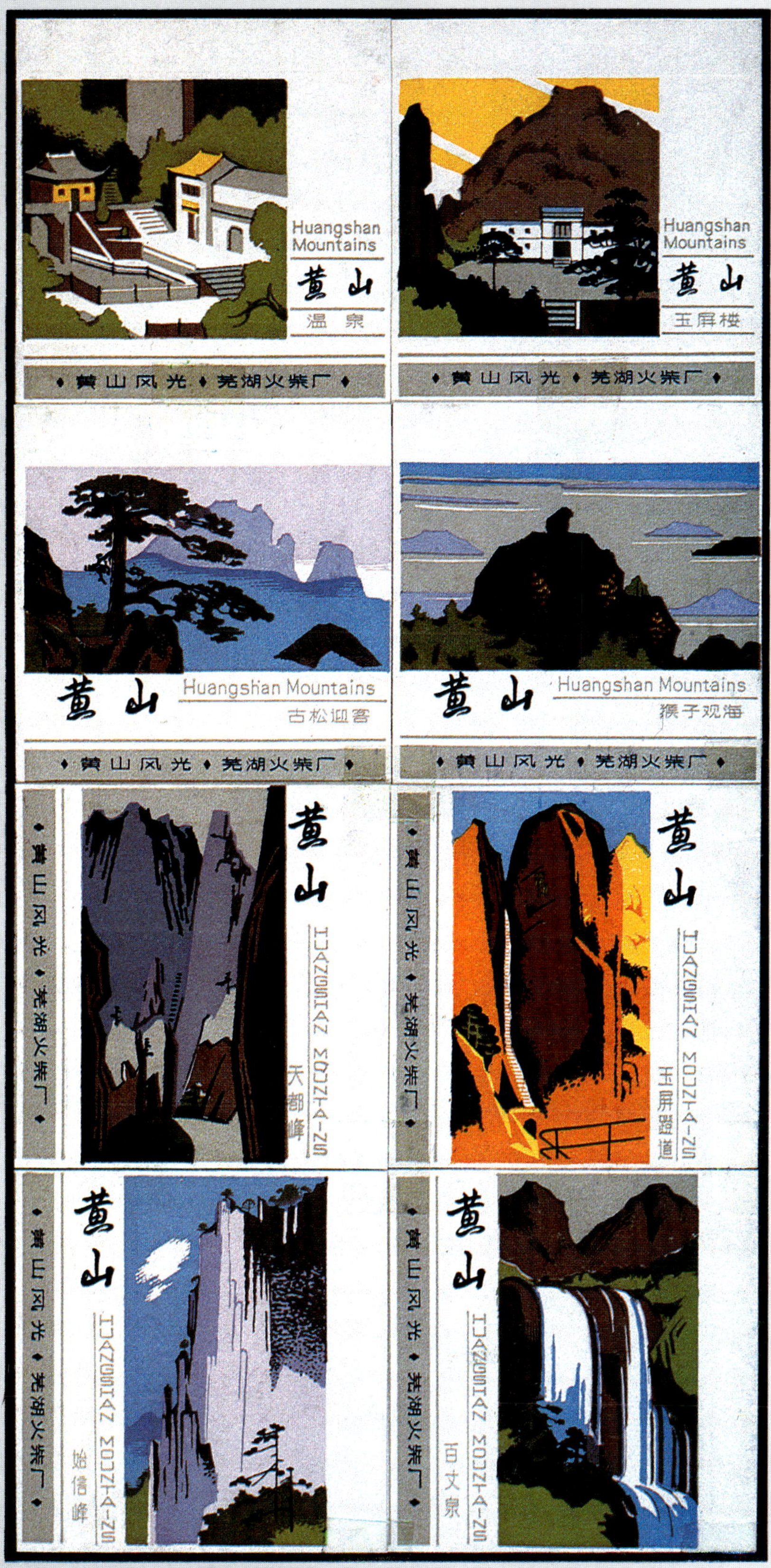

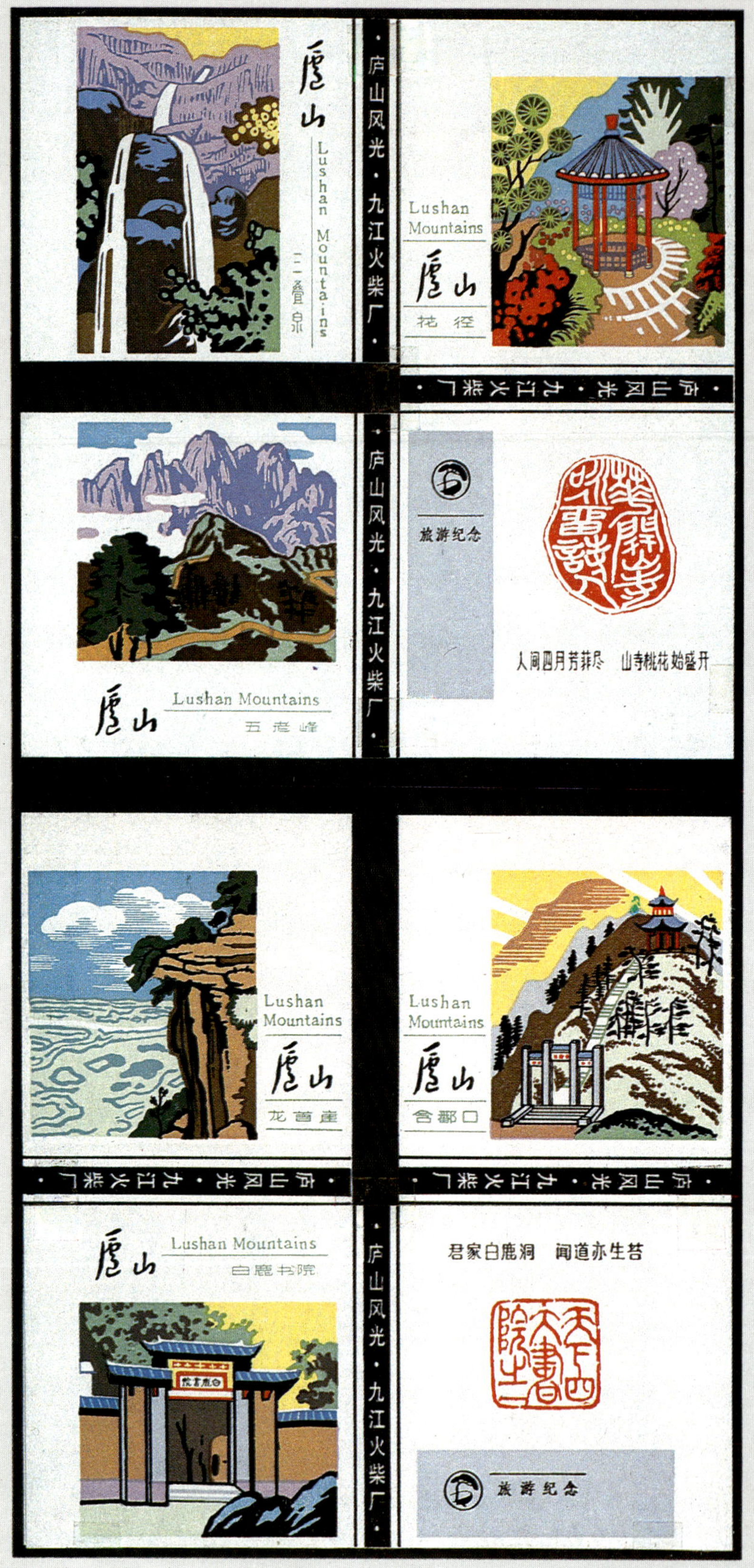

Scenic Mt. Lushan

Situated north of Jiangxi Province and west of Poyang Lake, Mt. Lushan stretches for twenty-five kilometres from east to west along the Yangtze River. As the mountain is forever shrouded in mist, tourists leave there without knowing the true features of Mt. Lushan. From left, top to bottom: Three-Step Spring, Flower Path, Five Oldsters Peak, Dragon Head Cliff, Hanpo Pass, and White Deer Academy.

Made in Jiujiang, Jiangxi Province

113 mm x 53 mm

Jiangxi Province

With its capital city in Nanchang, Jiangxi Province in the south of the middle-lower reaches of the Yangtze River is surrounded by mountains on three sides and borders on the Yangtze River in the north. An armed uprising launched by the Communist Party of China took place in Nanchang on August 1, 1927. The well-known Mt. Lushan lies in the north of the province. To the east of Mt. Lushan Poyang Lake finds its outlet to the Yangtze River. Here there is Stone Chime Hill, where one hears the waves pounding at the rocks as of many bells being sounded. On the bank of the Ganjiang River in Nanchang lie the ruins of Prince Teng's Pavilion, which was built in 653 and destroyed in 1926. Ganzhou and Ji'an are the two cities in the south of Jiangxi. Built in the Tang Dynasty, Yugu Terrace in the northwest of Ganzhou is 14 metres high and covers an area of 275 square metres.

Clockwise: Stone Chime Hill, Prince Teng's Pavilion, the Memorial Hall of the August 1 Nanchang Armed Uprising, and Yugu Terrace.

Made in Nanchang, Jiangxi Province
103 mm x 46 mm

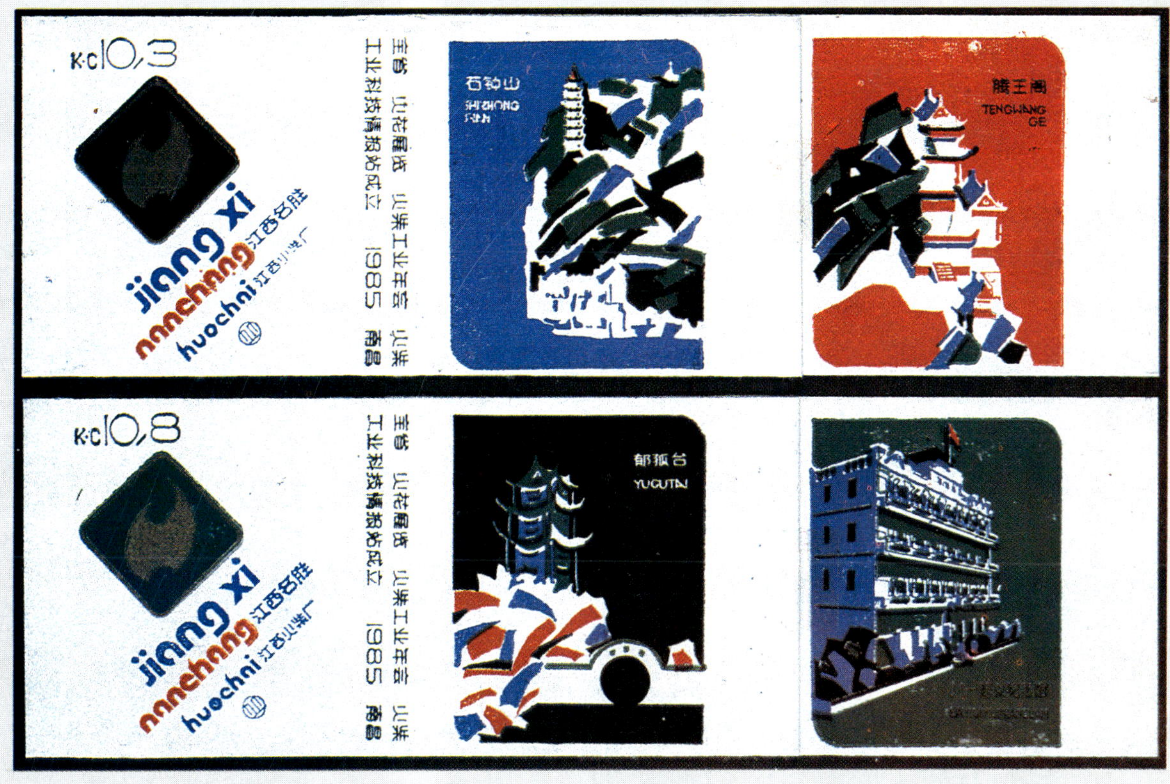

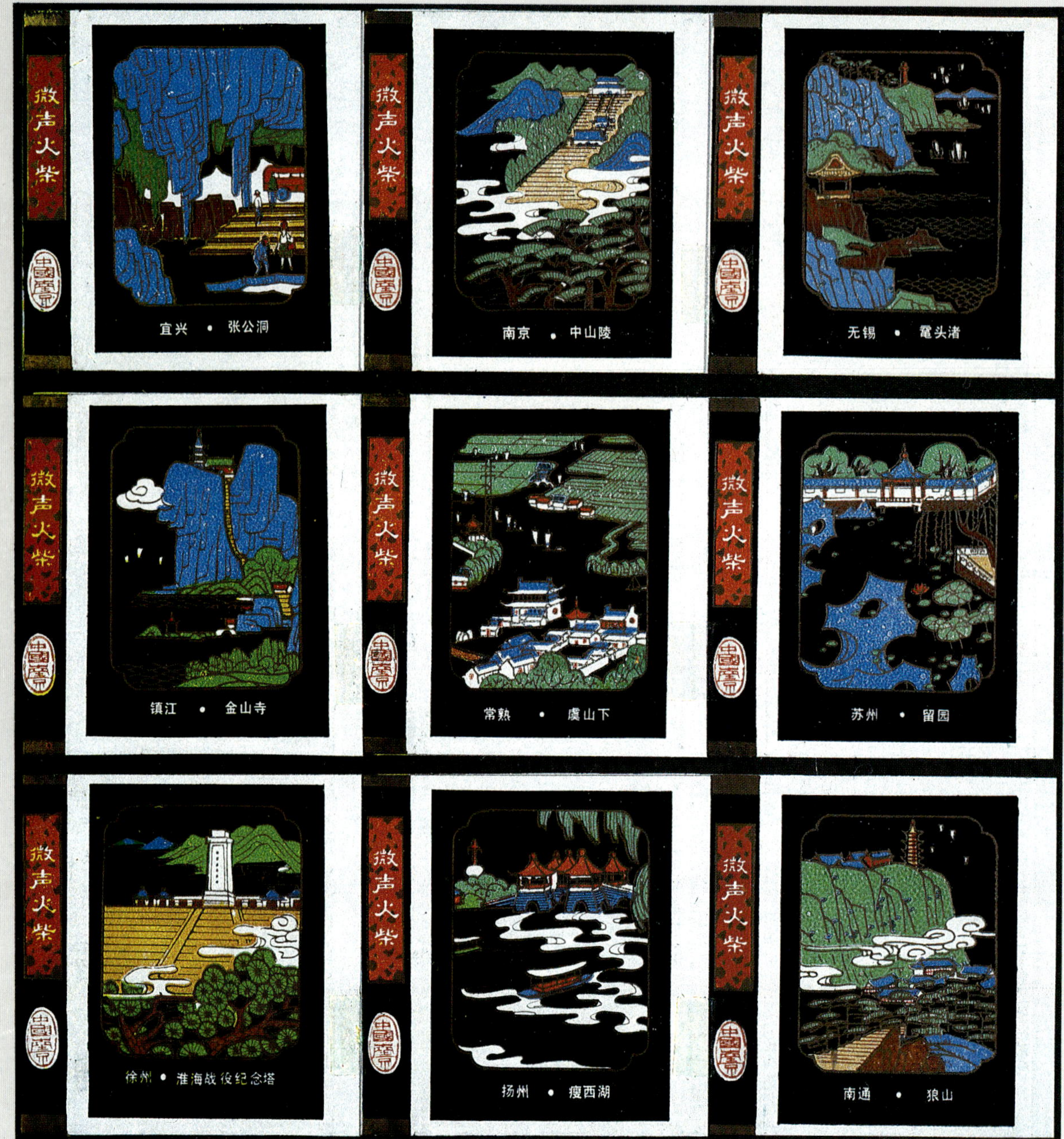

Jiangsu Province

Bordering the Yellow Sea in the east, Jiangsu Province is situated at the lower reaches of the Yangtze River. With plenty of rainfall, crisscrossing rivers and lakes, and picturesque sceneries, it is known as a land of fish and rice.

From left, top to bottom: Lord Zhang's Cave at Yixing, Sun Yat-sen Mausoleum at Nanjing, Turtle Head Islet at Wuxi, Golden Hill Temple at Zhenjiang, Yushan Hill at Changshu, Lingering Garden at Suzhou, Monument to the Huaihai Campaign at Xuzhou, Lesser West Lake at Yangzhou, and Wolf Hill at Nantong.

Made in Nanjing, Jiangsu Province

114 mm x 59 mm

Nanjing, an Ancient Capital

Also known as Jinling, Nanjing, the capital of Jiangsu Province, was the capital for ten different dynasties and replete with cultural relics and historical sites.

From left, top to bottom: Mausoleum of Ming Emperor Taizu, Sun Yat-sen Mausoleum, Drum Tower, Mochou (Not-to-Worry) Lake, Linggu Pagoda, and Chaotian Palace.

Made in Nanjing, Jiangsu Province

97 mm x 56 mm

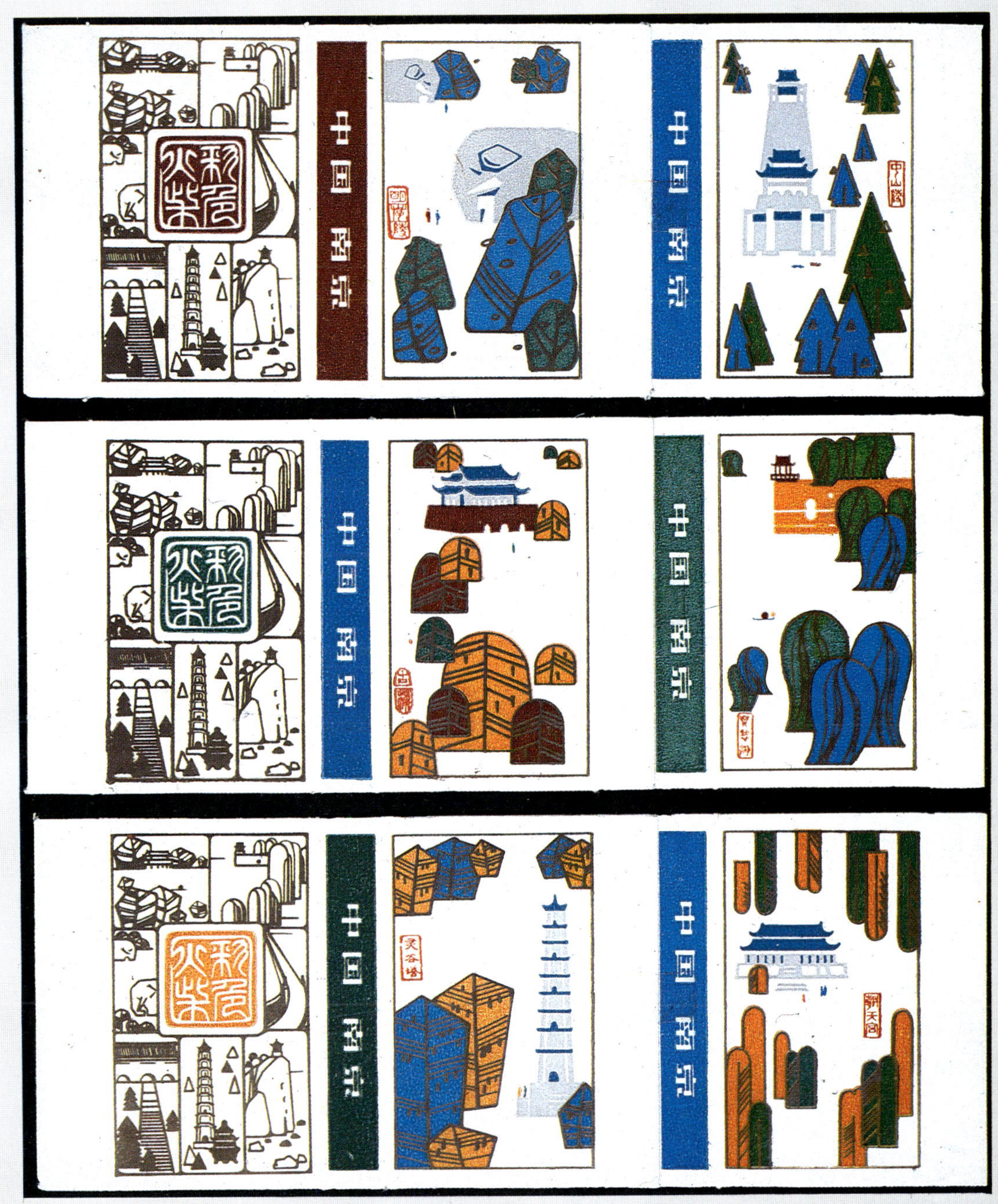

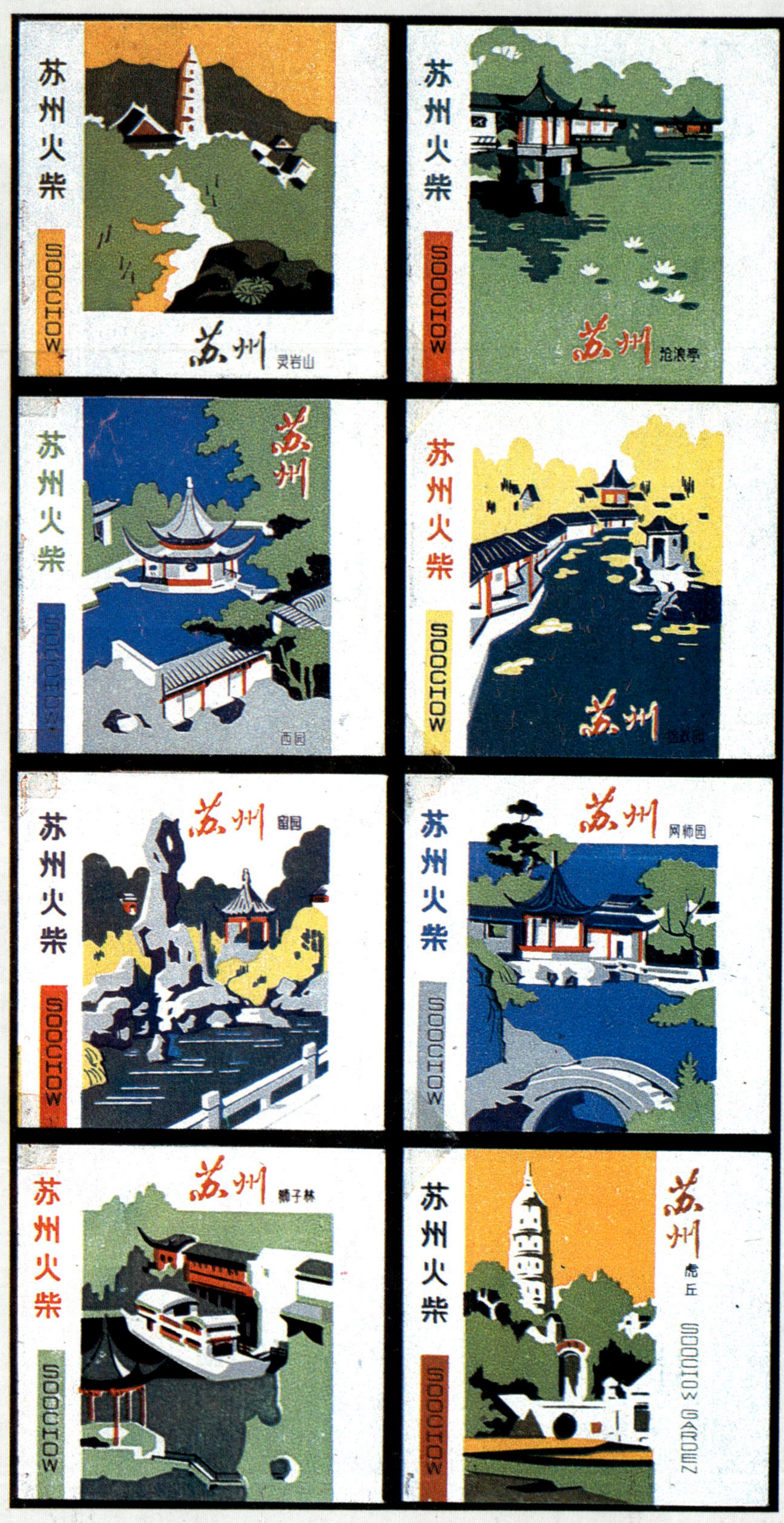

Suzhou Gardens

Known as the city of gardens, Suzhou in the south of Jiangsu has more than 170 gardens, big and small. Typical of Chinese design and style, these gardens are elegant and diversified.

From top to bottom, left and right columns: Lingyan Hill, West Garden, Lingering Garden, Lion Grove, Surging Wave Pavilion, Humble Administrator's Garden, Fisherman's Garden, and Tiger Hill.

Made in Suzhou, Jiangsu Province

104 mm x 53 mm

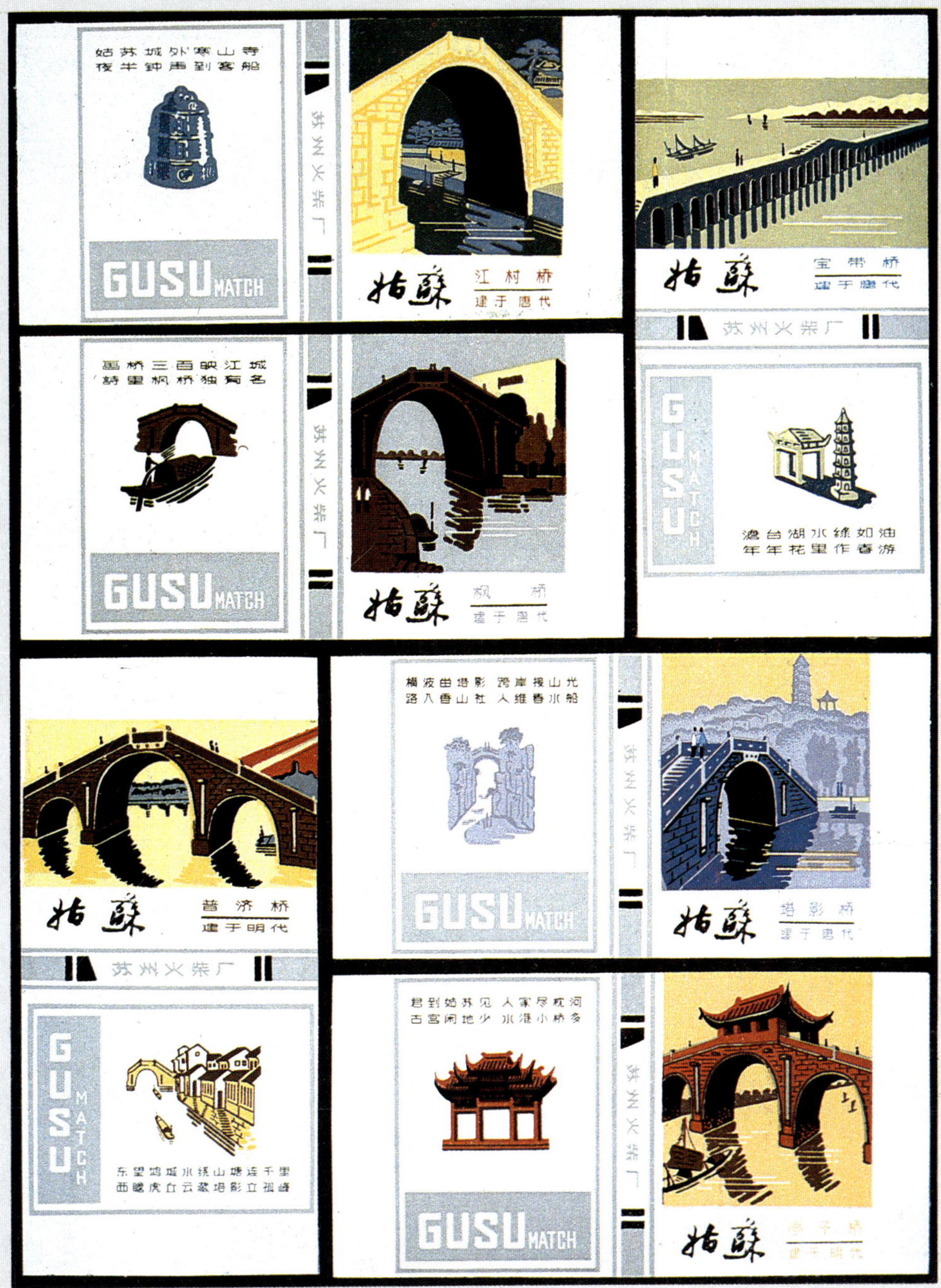

Ancient Bridges of Suzhou

Known as "Venice of the Orient," Suzhou has more than three hundred bridges, most of them stone arched ones, over the crisscrossing rivers.

The six bridges shown here are the most famous: Jiangcun Bridge (Tang Dynasty, upper left), Fengqiao Bridge (Tang Dynasty, middle left), Puji Bridge (Ming Dynasty, lower left), Baodai Bridge (Tang Dynasty, upper right), Taying Bridge (Tang Dynasty, middle right), and Tingzi Bridge (Ming Dynasty, lower right).

Made in Suzhou, Jiangsu Province

105 mm x 52 mm

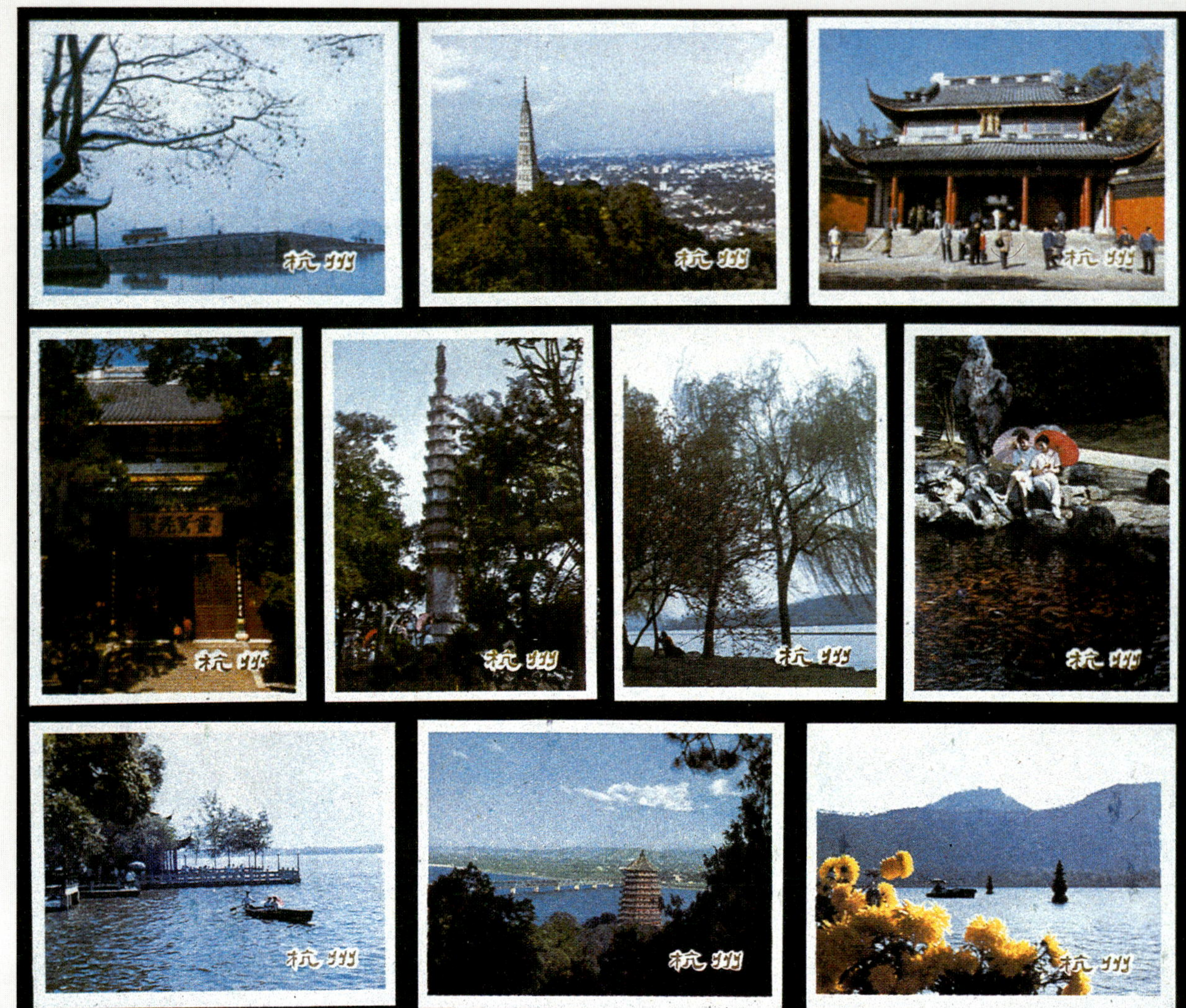

Picturesque West Lake

Vast and misty, West Lake is located in the western suburbs of Hangzhou, the provincial capital of Zhejiang. Beside the long causeways and on the islets stand green and luxuriant willows; scattered around the lake which is almost 50 square kilometres are the gardens and tourist areas, including over 40 scenic spots and more than 30 historical sites. Few people leave here without being impressed by the breathtaking sceneries of Hangzhou which, together with Suzhou, is believed to be the paradise on earth.

Shown here are the main scenic spots at West Lake (from left, top to bottom): Broken Bridge, Baochu Pagoda, Temple of Yue Fei, Monastery of the Spirits' Retreat, Xiling Seal-Engraving Society, Listening to Orioles Singing in the Willows, Viewing Fish at Flower Harbour, Autumn Moon on Calm Lake, Six Harmonies Pagoda, and Three Pools Mirroring the Moon.

Made in Hangzhou, Zhejiang Province
47 mm x 37 mm

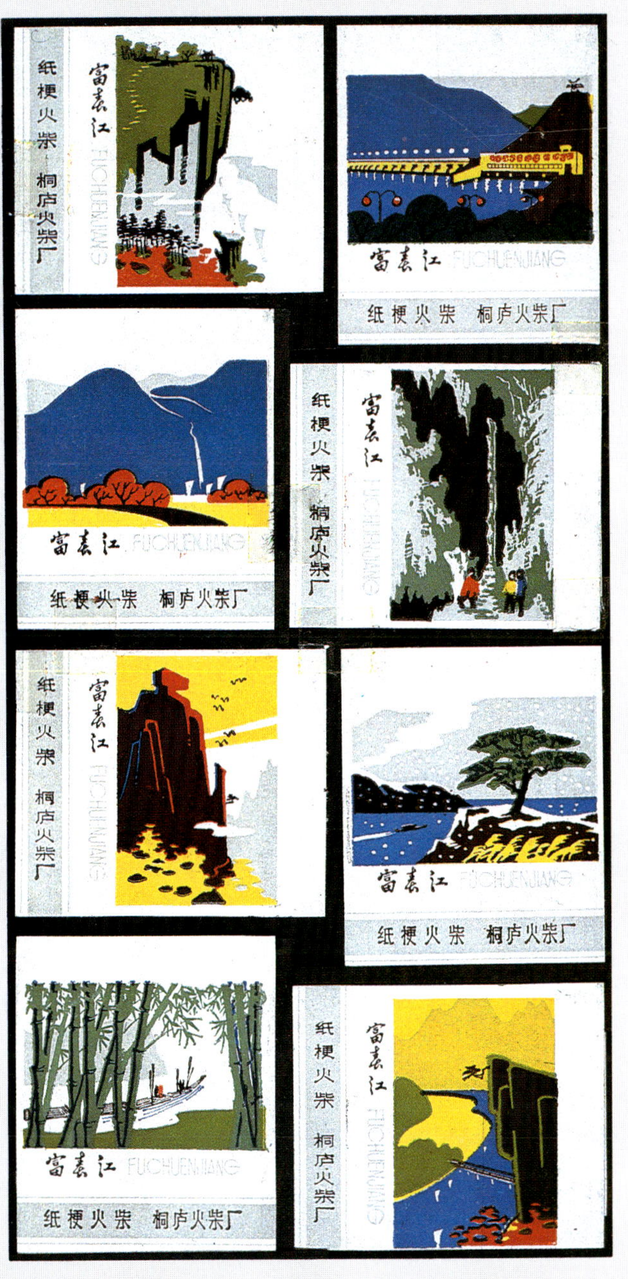

Beautiful Fuchun River

Flanked by green cliffs and bamboo trees, the Fuchun River in central Zhejiang Province is said to be matchless under heaven for its bizarre mountains and crystal-clear water.

From top to bottom, left column: Yan Ziling Fishing Terrace, Seven-*li* Ridge, Maling Hill, Tianmu Stream; from top to bottom, right column: Fuchun River Hydropower Station, Yaolin Cave, Luci Bay, and Tonglu Bridge.

Made in Tonglu, Zhejiang Province

96 mm x 45 mm

Scenic Mt. Putuo

One of the four Buddhist mountains in China, Mt. Putuo on Zhoushan Island in Zhejiang Province attracts thousands of tourists and pilgrims because of its beautiful sceneries and frequent Buddhist activities.

From left to right: Sunset at Putuo, Waves at Putuo, and Sunset at Pantuo.

Made in Ningbo, Zhejiang Province

101 mm x 53 mm

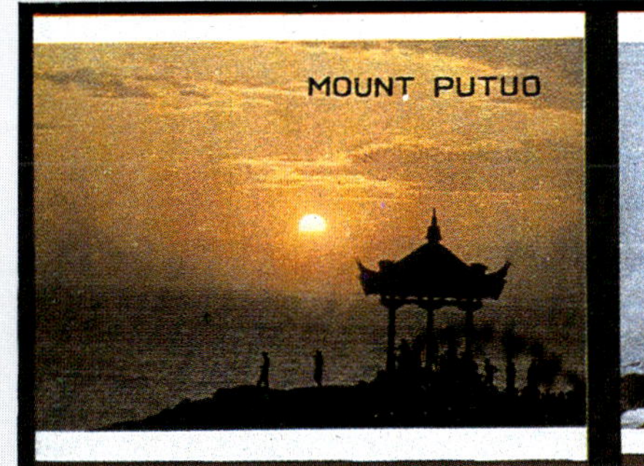

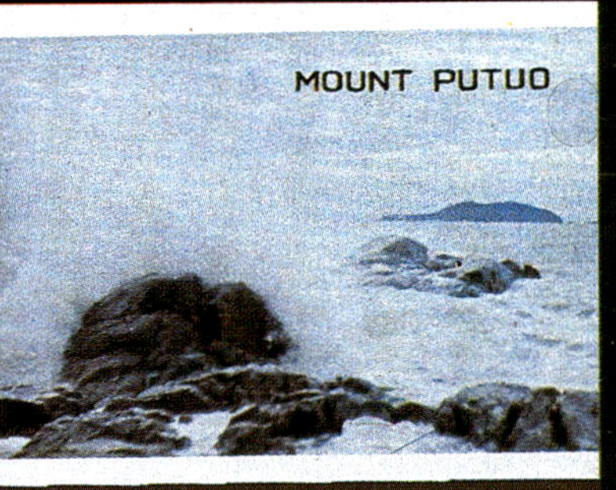

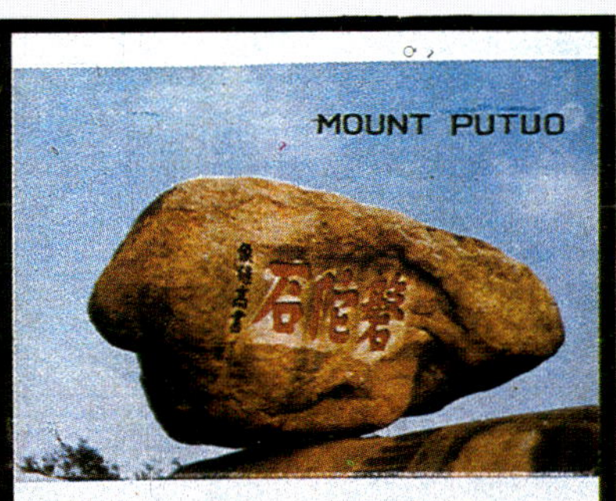

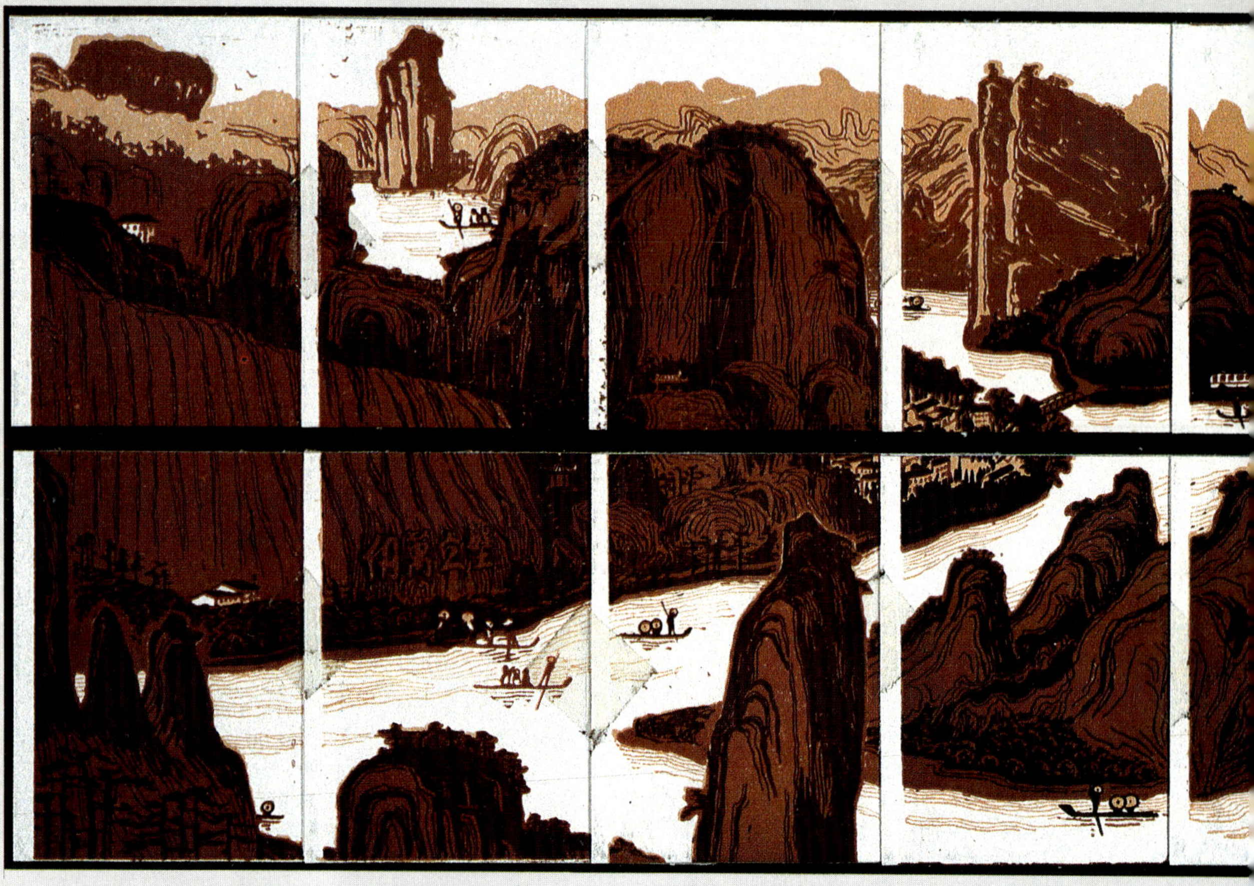

Wuyi Mountain Range

Situated at the border of Fujian and Jiangxi provinces, Wuyi Range stretches for about five hundred kilometres from north to south. The section in Chong'an County, Fujian Province, is extremely beautiful with its picturesque peaks, sea of clouds and zizagging streams.

Shown here is the scenery of the range on ten matchbox covers.

Made in Nanping, Fujian Province
91 mm x 52 mm

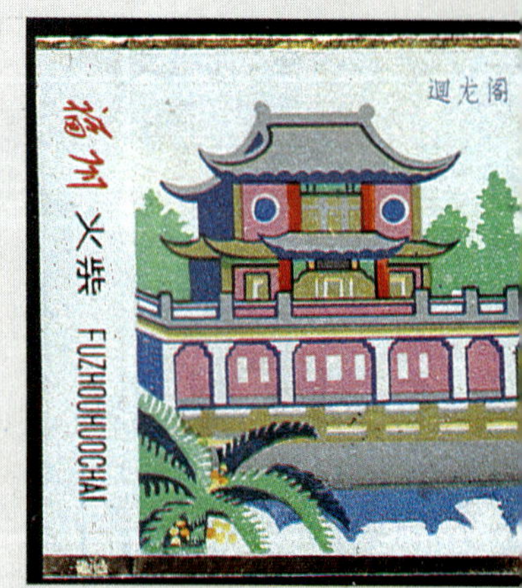

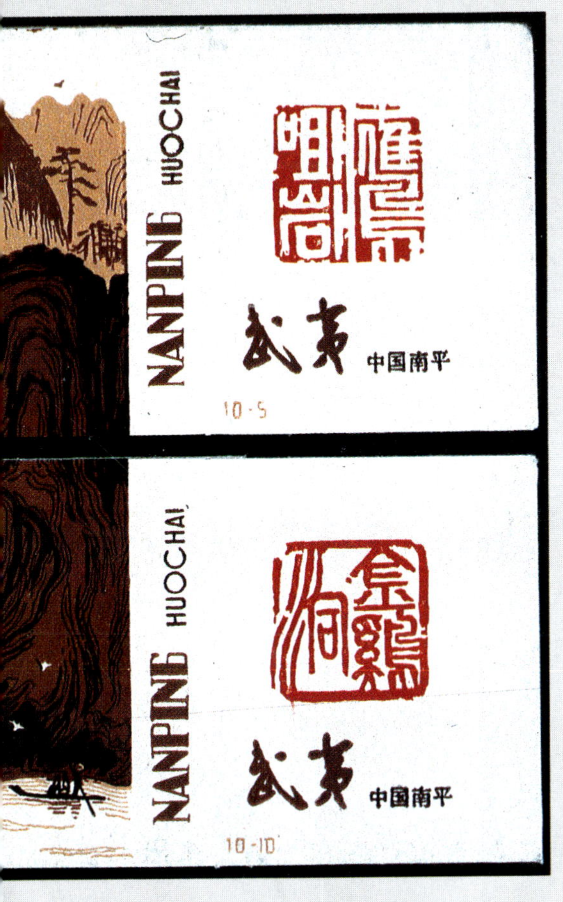

Fujian Province

With capital city in Fuzhou, Fujian is situated on the southeast coast of China with mountains in its west and small plains along the coast. Quanzhou and Xiamen in south Fujian are two well-known historical cities.

From left: Winding Dragon Pavilion at Fuzhou, Jade Maiden Peak at Wuyi Range, Gulang Islet at Xiamen, and East West Pagoda at Quanzhou.

Made in Fuzhou, Fujian Province

51 mm x 41 mm

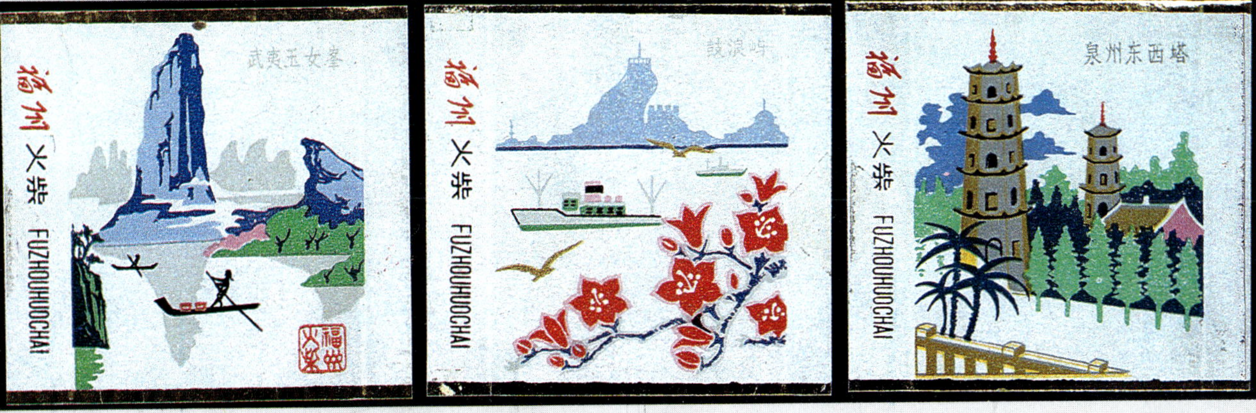

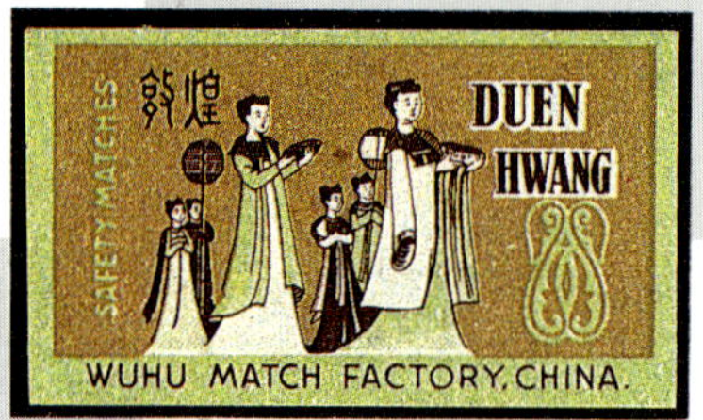

Eminent Figures

The match covers in this section of the album describe eminent persons, both Chinese and foreign, ancient and modern. They include famous statesmen, thinkers, military strategists, scientists, writers, artists and national heroes. Summaries of their lives and achievements are accompanied by vivid illustrations. As the covers in this section differ from one another in both form and content, so their artistic depictions also vary. For example, the illustrations Famous Buddhist Monks, Chinese and Foreign Scientists, and Ancient Chinese Philosophers are shown in different styles of painting with different colour applications. They all, however, are painted with meticulous care.

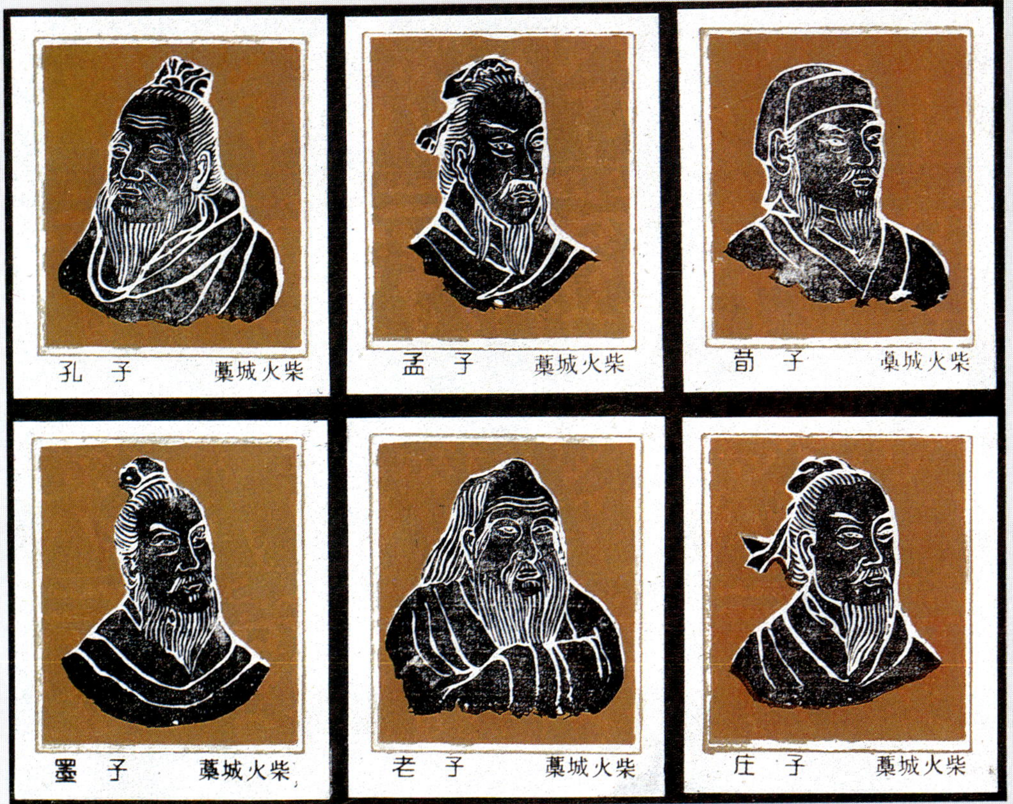

Ancient Chinese Thinkers

From left, top to bottom:

Confucius (551-479 B.C.), an outstanding thinker, educator and founder of the philosophy of Confucianism.

Mencius (372-289 B.C.), a thinker, statesman and educator of the Warring States Period, and a successor to Confucius' doctrine.

Xun Zi (313-238 B.C.), a thinker and educator, and prolific writer, who critically examined the academic schools of his time, contributing to the development of ancient materialism.

Mo Zi (468-376 B.C.), a thinker, statesman and founder of the Mohist School. Along with Confucianism, his theory was known as "doctrine of the famous schools." He strongly influenced the ideology of his time.

Lao Zi (722-647 B.C.), a thinker, founder of the Taoist School and author of the book *Laozi*. His doctrine had a very strong impact on the development of Chinese philosophy, so much so that his teachings were often quoted in support of the opposing materialist and idealistic schools.

Zhuang Zi (369-286 B.C.), a philosopher and author of the book *Zhuangzi*. Though his ideological system tended towards pessimism, his writings had a strong influence over the philosophy and literature of later generations.

Dong Zhongshu (179-104 B.C.), a philosopher who upheld Confucianism. Thanks to his promotion, Confucianism was endorsed by Emperor Wudi of the Han Dynasty and consequently established as ideological orthodoxy in Chinese feudal society for over two thousand

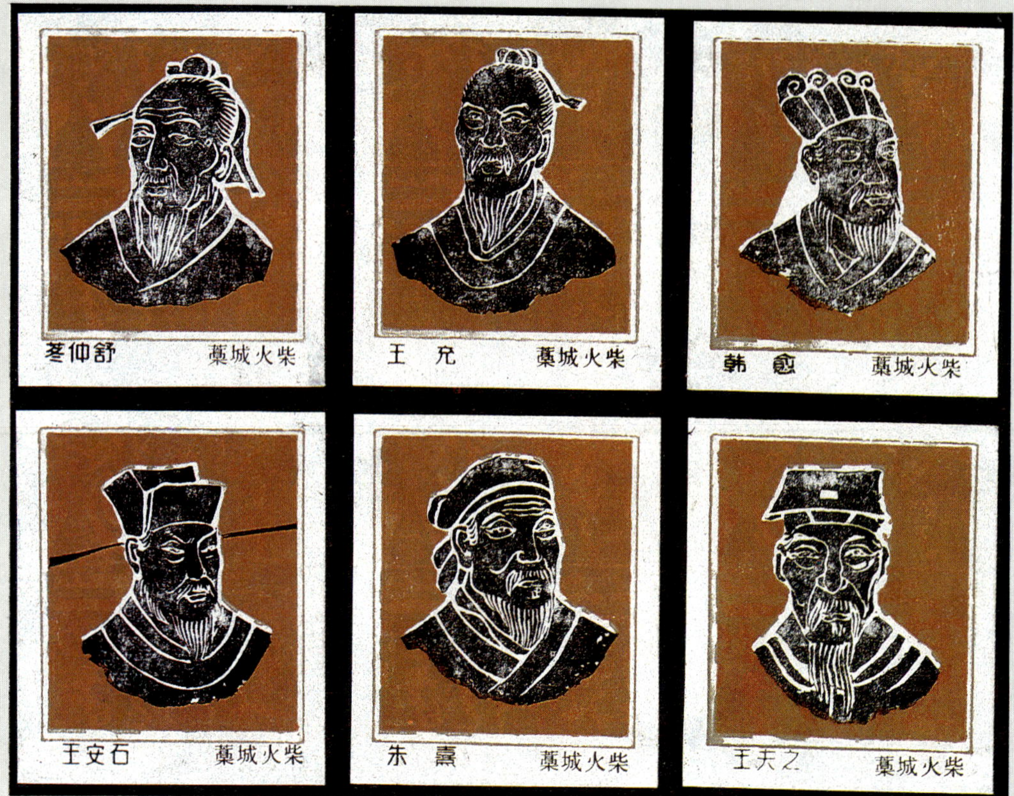

years.

Wang Chong (A.D.27-97), a philosopher of the Han Dynasty, who preached materialism and authored the book *Lun Heng* (*Discourses Weighed in the Balance*).

Han Yu (768-824), a writer and philosopher of the Tang Dynasty. He advocated Confucianism and rejected Buddhism. He held that literature should convey ideas and that the form of writing should suit the content.

Wang Anshi (1021-1086), a writer and statesman of the Song Dynasty. Throughout his life he advocated political reform and insisted on curtailing upper class privilege in an effort to boost economic development and increase the country's military strength. His poems and prose writings are pragmatic and realistic.

Zhu Xi (1130-1200), a philosopher and educator well versed in Confucian classics, history and literature, but chiefly remembered for his contribution to establishing of a system of objective idealism known as Neo-Confucianism.

Wang Fuzhi (1619-1692), a thinker in the late Ming Dynasty, who upheld patriotism and materialism, never changing his convictions even at the hour of his death.

Made in Gaocheng, Hebei Province
40 mm x 48 mm

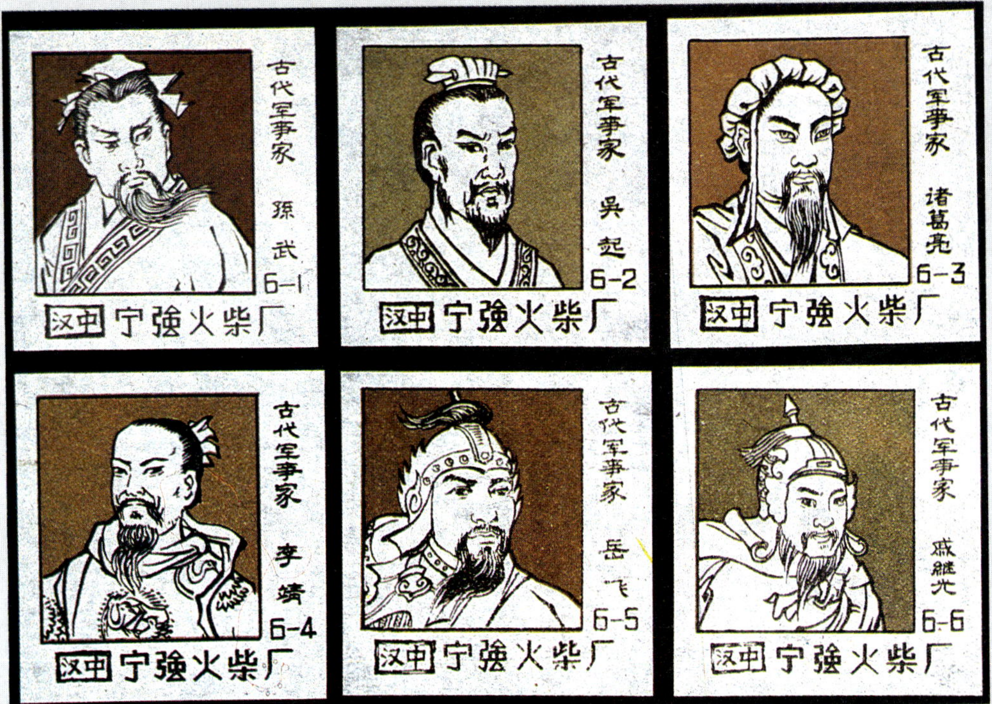

Ancient Chinese Military Scientists

From left, above:

Sun Wu, a military strategist who probably lived in the 5th century B.C. He was the author of the book *Master Sun's Art of War*.

Wu Qi (?-381 B.C.), a military martinet well versed in the art of war. He was also a protagonist of political reform.

Zhuge Liang (181-234), a military strategist and statesman of the Shu Kingdom during the Three Kingdoms Period. He was good in both military and administrative affairs.

From left, below:

Li Jing (571-649), a Tang Dynasty general who was well versed in the art of war and the employment of strategies. He wrote a book entitled *Duke Li's Art of War*.

Yue Fei (1103-1142), an anti-Kin hero of the Southern Song Dynasty who distinguished himself in war on many occasions. He was later executed on framed charges by treacherous officials in the Song court.

Qi Jiguang (1528-1587), a Ming Dynasty general known for his outstanding military service in the war against the Japanese sea pirates. He summarized his military experience in two books: *A Treatise on Efficiency* and *A Memoir on Training of Soldiers*.

Made in Hanzhong, Shaanxi Province

40 mm x 39 mm

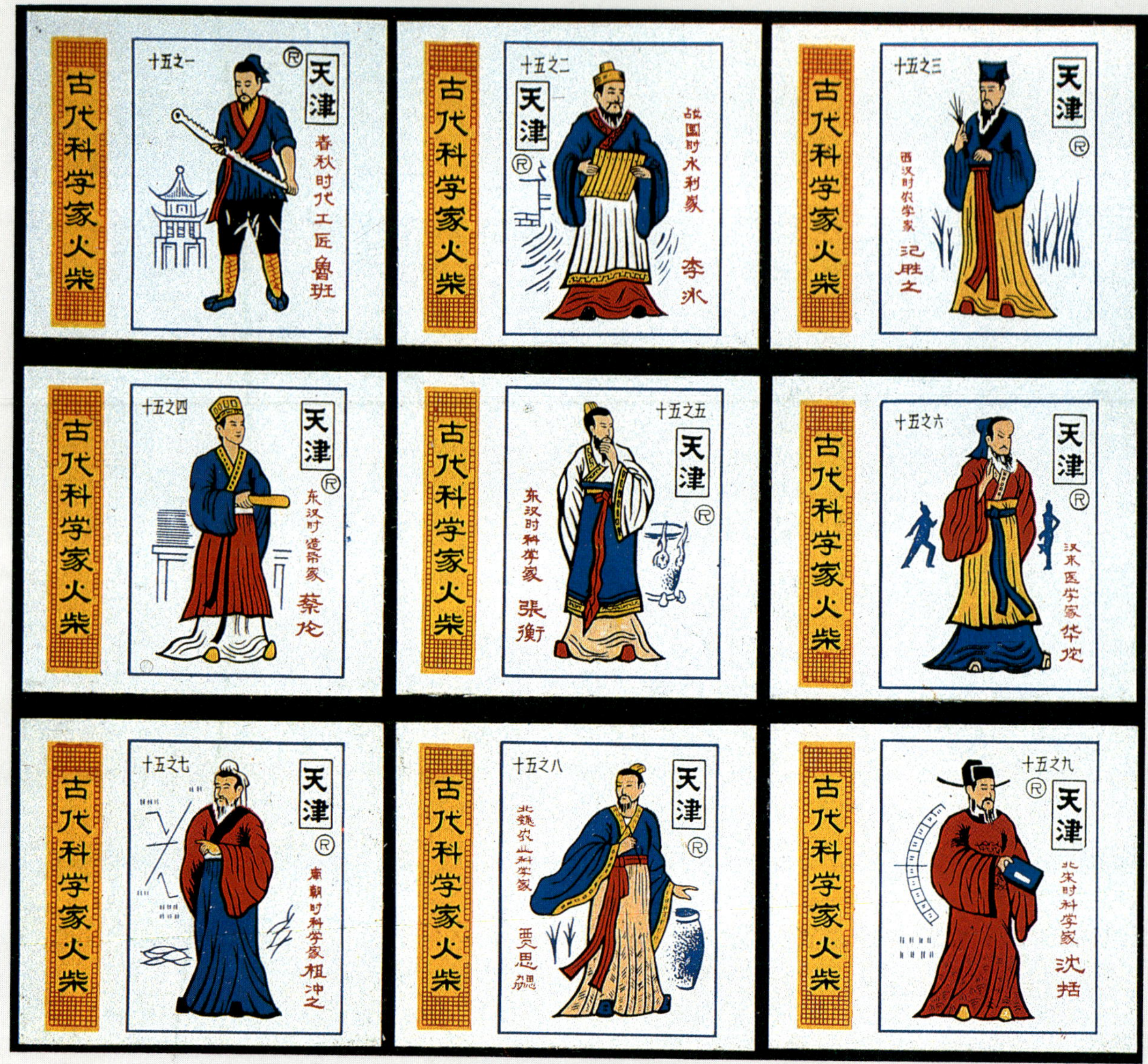

Ancient Chinese Scientists

From left, top row:

Lu Ban, a famous carpenter who lived in the 6th century B.C.

Li Bing, a water conservation expert in the 2nd century B.C., who supervised the construction of the Dujiang water conservation project in Sichuan Province.

Si Shengzhi, an agronomist of the 1st century B.C. and author of the *Book of Agriculture*.

From left, second row:

Cai Lun (?-121), an expert on paper making in the Eastern Han Dynasty.

Zhang Heng (78-139), an Eastern Han scientist who invented the armillary sphere and seismograph.

Hua Tuo (c.141-208), an Eastern Han medical scientist, who specialized in surgery.

From left, third row:

Zu Chongzhi (429-500), a mathematician of the Southern and Northern Dynasties, determined the famous quantity, π, between 3.1415926 and 3.1415927, the ratio of the

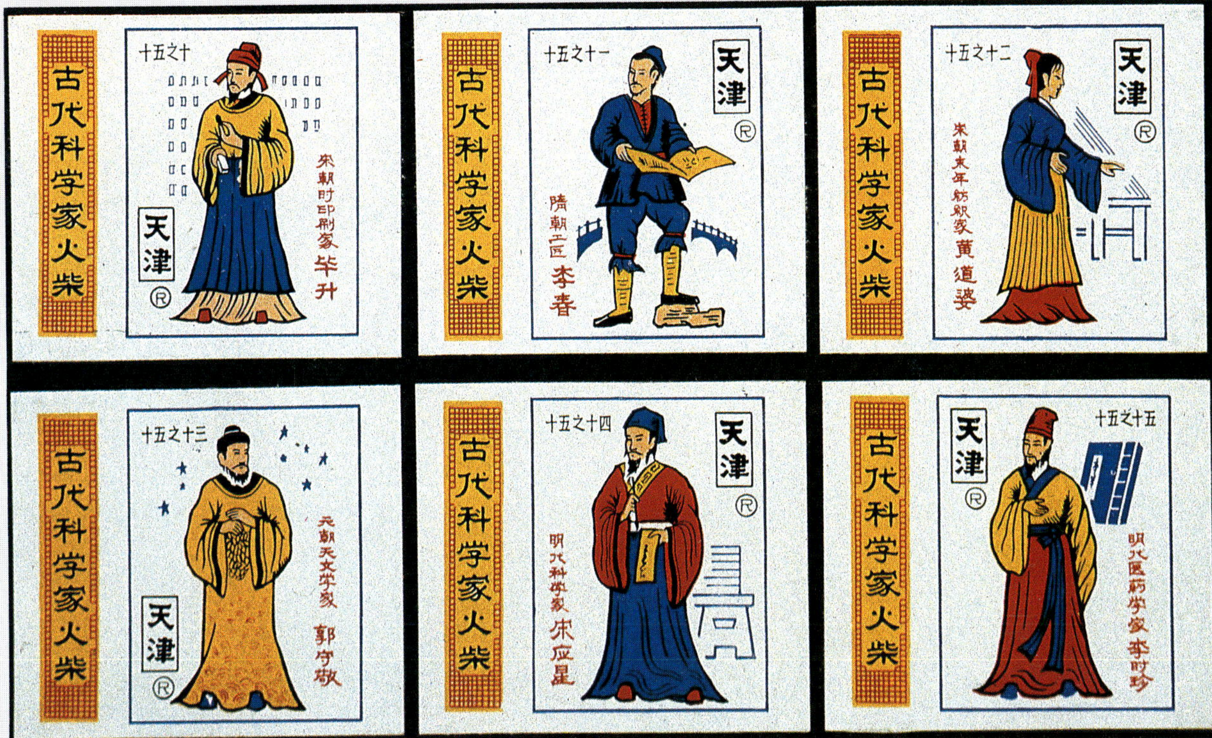

circumference of a circle to its diameter.

Jia Sixie, an agronomist of the Northern Wei Dynasty, who wrote *Important Arts for the People's Welfare.*

Shen Kuo (1031-1095), an eminent scientist of the Song Dynasty. He wrote a book entitled *Dream Stream Essays,* which included his observations on nature and his conclusions based on these observations.

From left, fourth row:

Bi Sheng (?-c.1051), a Song Dynasty inventor who devised movable type printing.

Li Chun, a 6th century architect who designed the Anji Bridge, an arch stone bridge which is known as the oldest surviving structure of its kind in the world.

Huang Daopo (1245-?), an innovator in textile techniques during the Yuan Dynasty, who was credited with the improvement of many tools for weaving and spinning.

From left, bottom row:

Guo Shoujing (1231-1316), a Yuan Dynasty astronomer who designed the Time-Telling Calendar.

Song Yingxing (c.1587-1661), a Ming Dynasty scientist and author of the book *Exploitation of the Works of Nature.*

Li Shizhen (1518-1593), a pharmacologist in the Ming Dynasty. He spent twenty-seven years on compiling his *Compendium of Materia Medica,* a comprehensive book on Chinese herbal medicine.

Made in Tianjin

53 mm x 46 mm

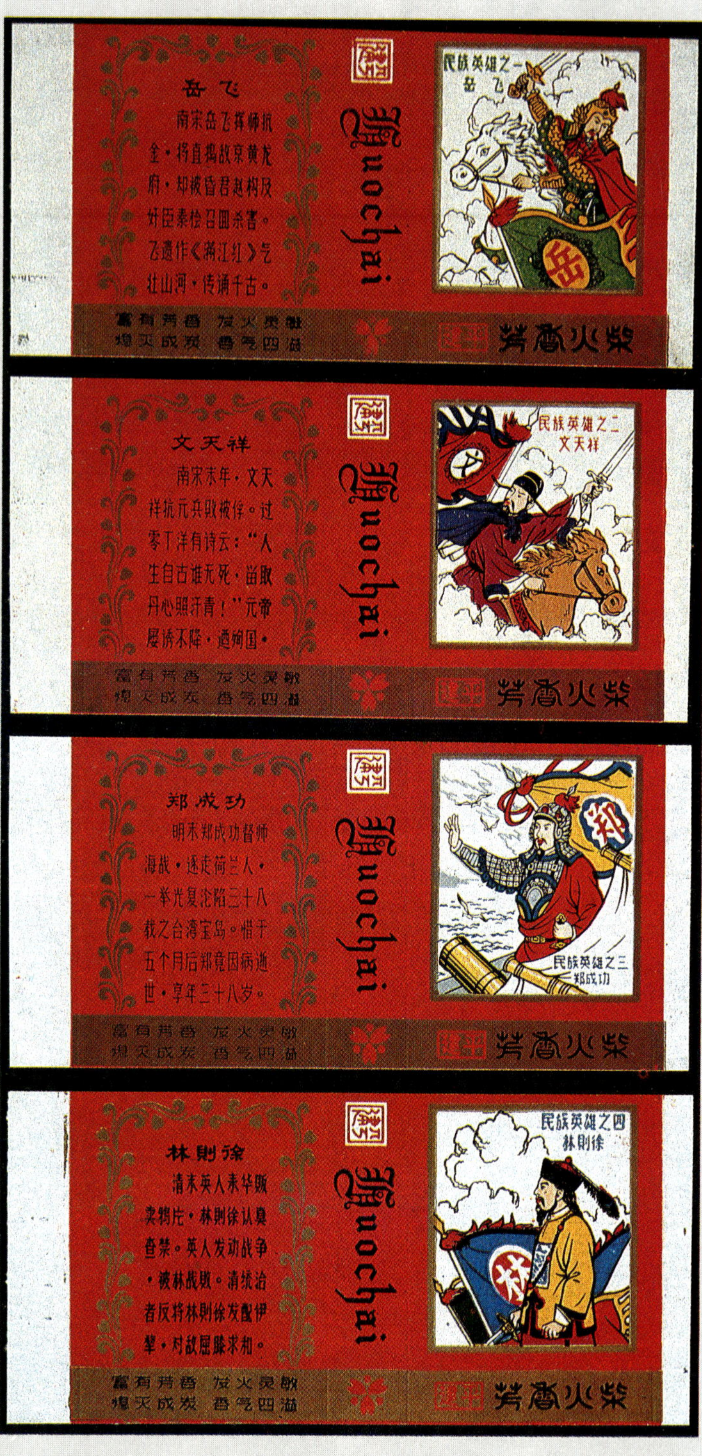

National Heroes in Ancient China

From top to bottom:

Yue Fei (1103-1142), an eminent general of the Southern Song Dynasty.

Wen Tianxiang (1236-1283), an anti-Mongol hero in the late Southern Song Dynasty. After his capture by the Mongols, he preferred death to surrender. In captivity he wrote a poem entitled the *Song of Justice*, which has been popular among the people ever since.

Zheng Chenggong (1624-1662), an eminent general in the late Ming Dynasty. He led his men in an eight-month-long battle against Dutch forces, and finally recovered China's Taiwan territory from them.

Lin Zexu (1785-1850), a statesman of the Qing Dynasty, was an official in Guangdong where he was highly acclaimed for his resistance against British aggression and his outlawing opium trade.

Made in Jianping, Hebei Province
97 mm x 45 mm

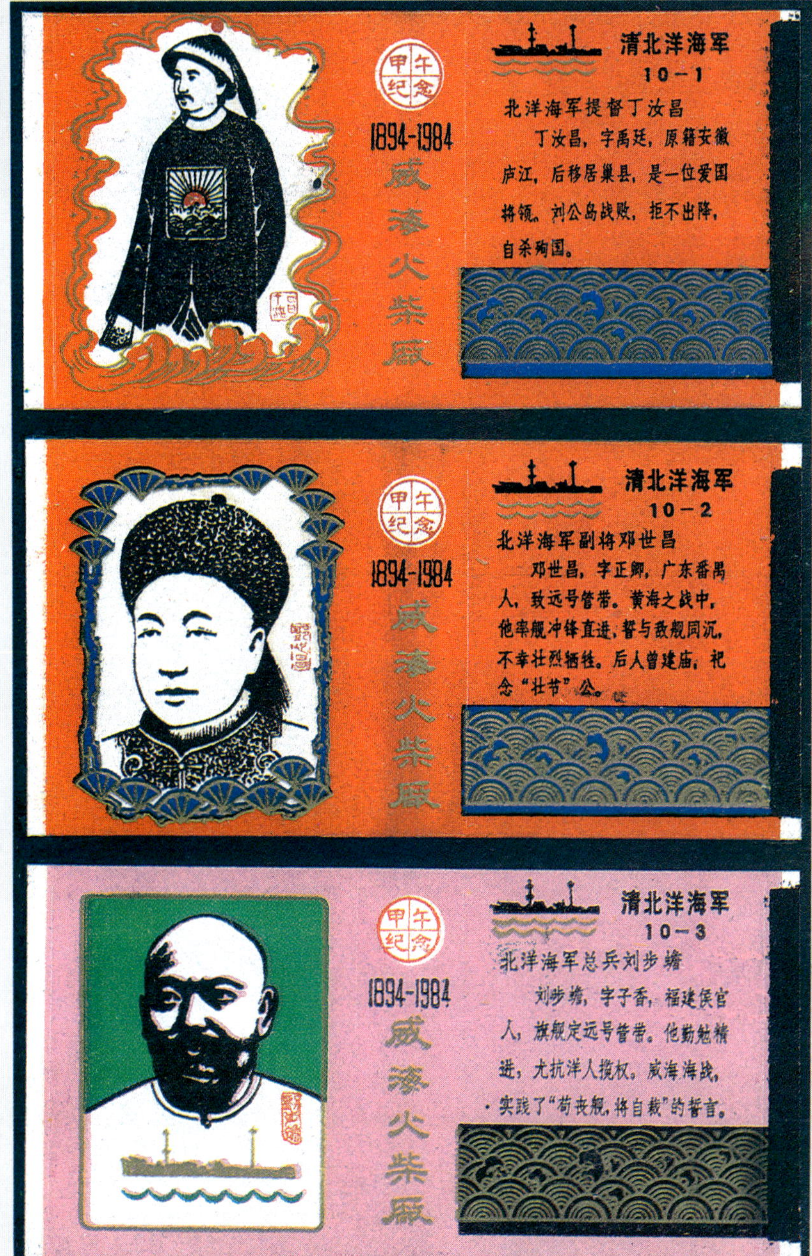

Chinese Generals in the Sino-Japanese War of 1894-95

The War began in August 1894. In February 1895, when Japanese troops attacked the military port of Weihaiwei, the soldiers and civilians there fought back bravely, many naval men and officers giving their lives in battle. In this set are the three famous naval commanders killed in action: (from top to bottom) Ding Ruchang, Deng Shichang and Liu Buchan.

Made in Weihai City, Shandong Province

88 mm x 46 mm

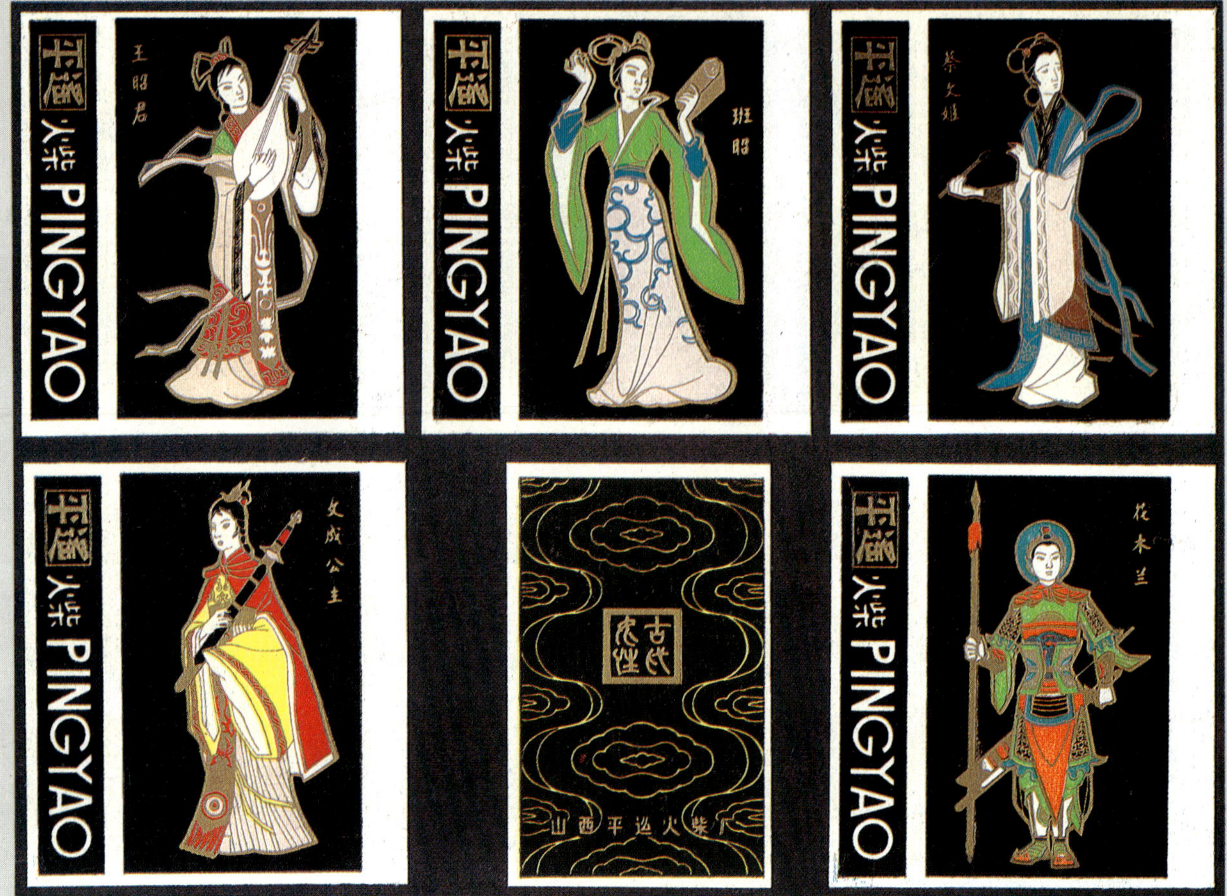

Women Celebrities in Chinese History

From left, top to bottom:

Wang Zhaojun, a palace serving maid of the Han Dynasty, helped develop good relations between the Han and the Xiongnus when she married the Xiongnu chieftain in 33 B.C.

Ban Zhao (c.49-120), a historian of the Eastern Han Dynasty and coauthor of *History of the Han Dynasty*.

Cai Wenji (A.D. 3rd century), an expert on musical temperament who authored a collection of poems entitled *Eighteen Airs for the Fife*.

Princess Wen Cheng (?-680), a scion of the Tang imperial family. When she was married to Songtsan Gambo, king of Tufan(now Tibet), she brought the civilization of the Han people with her and thus fostered friendly relations between the Han and Tibetan peoples.

Hua Mulan, a legendary folktale heroine popular between the fourth and sixth centuries. She disguised herself as a man to enlist in the army in place of her aging father and distinguished herself in battle.

Liang Hongyu, a woman general of the Southern Song Dynasty. In 1130, when her husband Han Shizhong resisted the Kin invaders at Huangtiandang, she assisted in battle by beating drums, thus proving herself to be a most courageous warrior.

Mu Guiying, a legendary figure of the Northern Song Dynasty, was popularly regarded as an intrepid and resourceful heroine who was extremely skilled in martial arts.

Li Qingzhao (1084-1151), a poet of the Song Dynasty, whose poems, composed in an elegant style, show high artistic quality.

Lin Heiniang, a leader of the Yi He Tuan (Boxers) Rebellion in the late 19th century. She organized the Red Lanterns Detachment in Tianjin to fight against the United Forces of the Eight Powers.

Hong Niangzi, a woman warrior in the late 17th century, who led peasants in rebellion and later joined the rebel forces under the command of Li Zicheng.

Made in Pingyao, Shanxi Province

56 mm x 98 mm

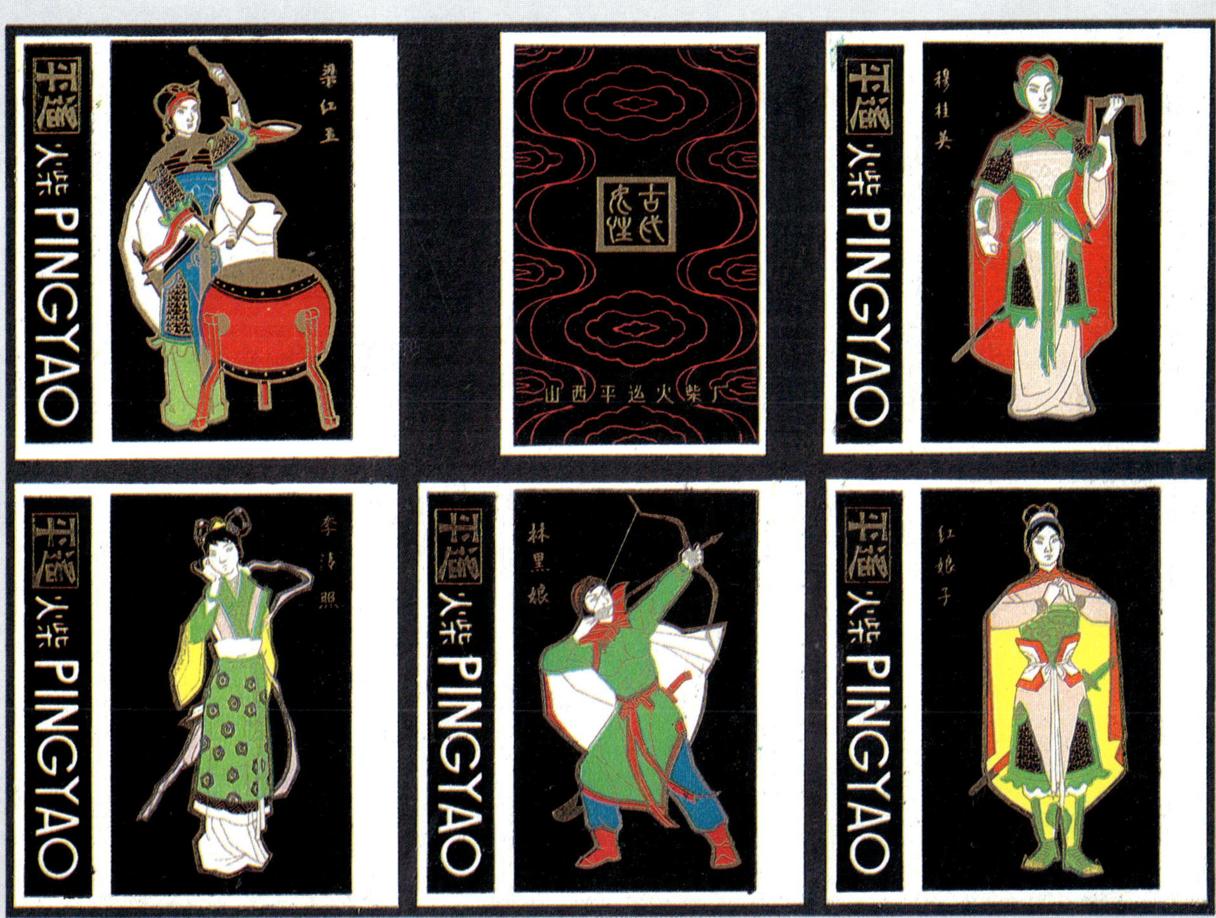

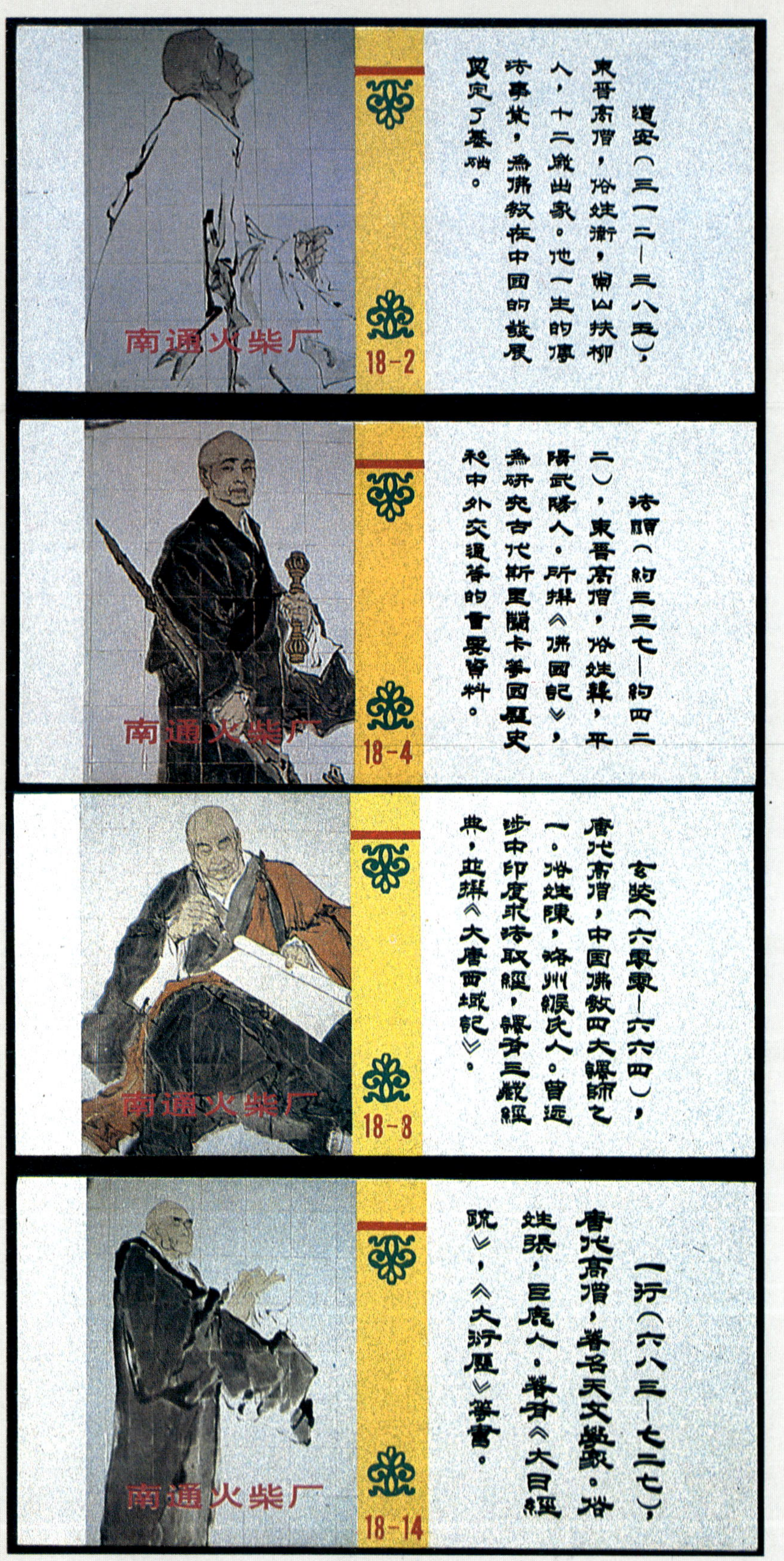

Eminent Buddhist Monks

From top to bottom: Dao An (312-385), who devoted all his life to the dissemination of Buddhist doctrine and laid the foundation for the development of Chinese Buddhism.

Fa Xian (c.337-422), author of the book *A Record of the Buddhist Countries.*

Xuan Zang (600-664), one of the four great translators of Buddhist sutras in China and author of the book *Records of Western Travels.*

Yi Xing (683-727), an astronomer as well as a monk who authored two books entitled *Annotations to the Mahavairocana-sutra* and *Dayan Calendar.*

Made in Nantong, Jiangsu Province

98 mm x 52 mm

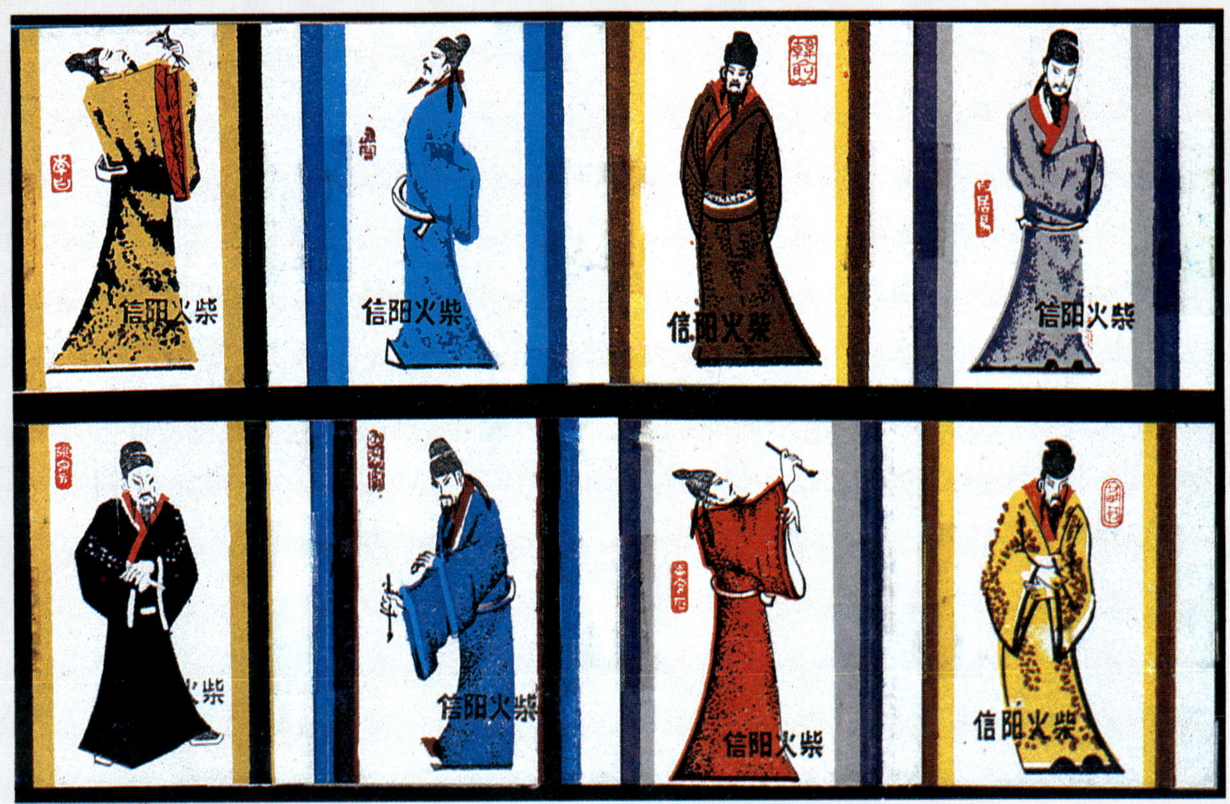

Men of Letters in the Tang and Song Dynasties

From left, above:

Li Bai (701-762), a poet of the romantic school in the Tang Dynasty. His poems were composed in a vivid and ebullient spirit, proving himself to be a poet of great talent.

Du Fu (712-770), a poet of the realistic school in the Tang Dynasty. Born into a time of turmoil, he was keenly aware of the ugliness of the society and the sufferings of the people, a sensibility which finds expressions in many of his poems.

Han Yu (768-824), a writer of the Tang Dynasty, claimed that literature should follow the traditional style of writing. His essays are known for their lucid exposition and coherence.

Bai Juyi (772-846), a Tang Dynasty poet who wrote in simple language. Sympathetic to the sufferings of the people, he claimed that poetry should mirror reality.

From left, below:

Liu Zongyuan (773-819), a writer of the Tang Dynasty. His poems and essays, which express his personal feelings, also reveal his progressive political and philosophical views.

Ouyang Xiu (1007-1072), a writer and historian of the Song Dynasty, made outstanding contributions in the field of history. He held that writings should serve a specific purpose and wrote his poems and essays in a forceful style.

Wang Anshi (1021-1086), a writer and statesman of the Song Dynasty, opposed bombastic writing and exposed the social evils of his time.

Su Shi (1036-1101), an erudite writer of the Song Dynasty, produced vivid and natural writings. His poems are both refined and unrestrained.

Made in Xinyang, Henan Province

87 mm x 43 mm

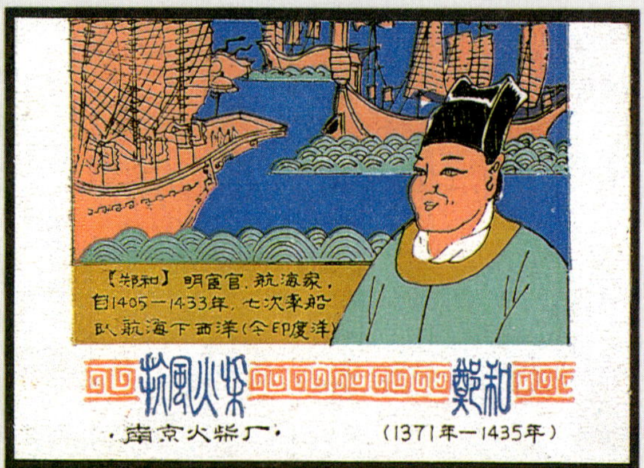

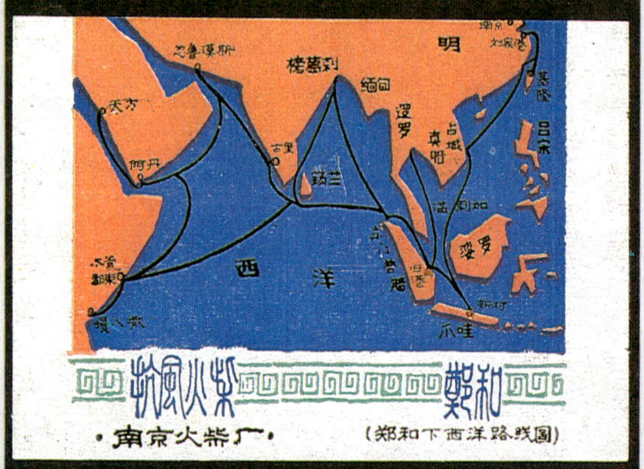

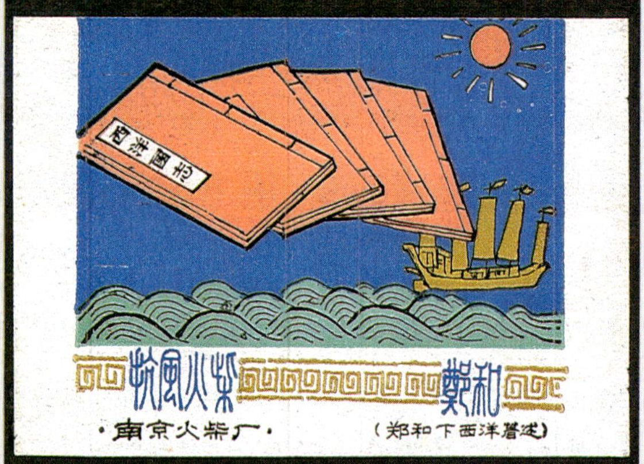

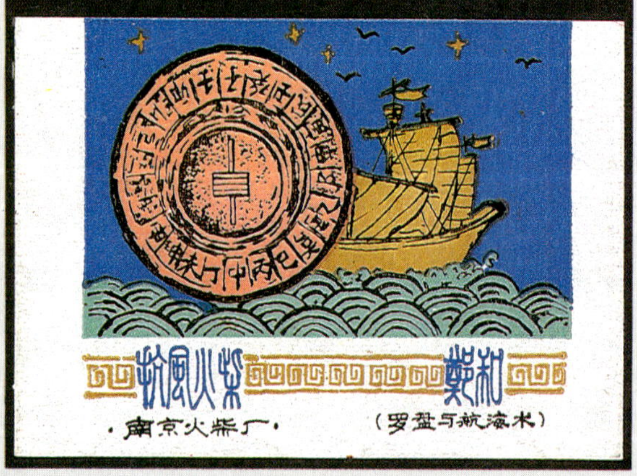

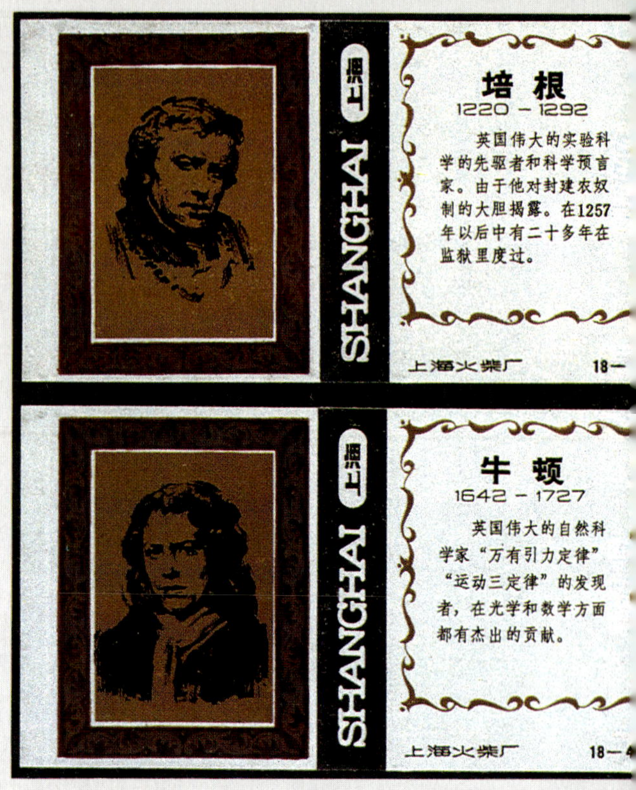

Zheng He, Great Navigator

Zheng He (1371-1435) was a palace official and navigator in the Ming Dynasty. Between 1405 and 1433, he made seven voyages to the Western Seas, in what are now the sea areas from Kalimantan to Africa. These voyages, some reaching as far as the eastern African coast and the outlet to the Red Sea, promoted economic and cultural exchanges between China and Afro-Asian countries. The largest of the ships used by Zheng He were 444 feet long and 180 feet wide and capable of holding 1,000 people. These voyages were more than half a century earlier than those made by Christopher Columbus and Vasco da Gama.

The covers in this set include a portrait of Zheng He, his voyage routes and his works.

Made in Nanjing, Jiangsu Province

83 mm x 48 mm

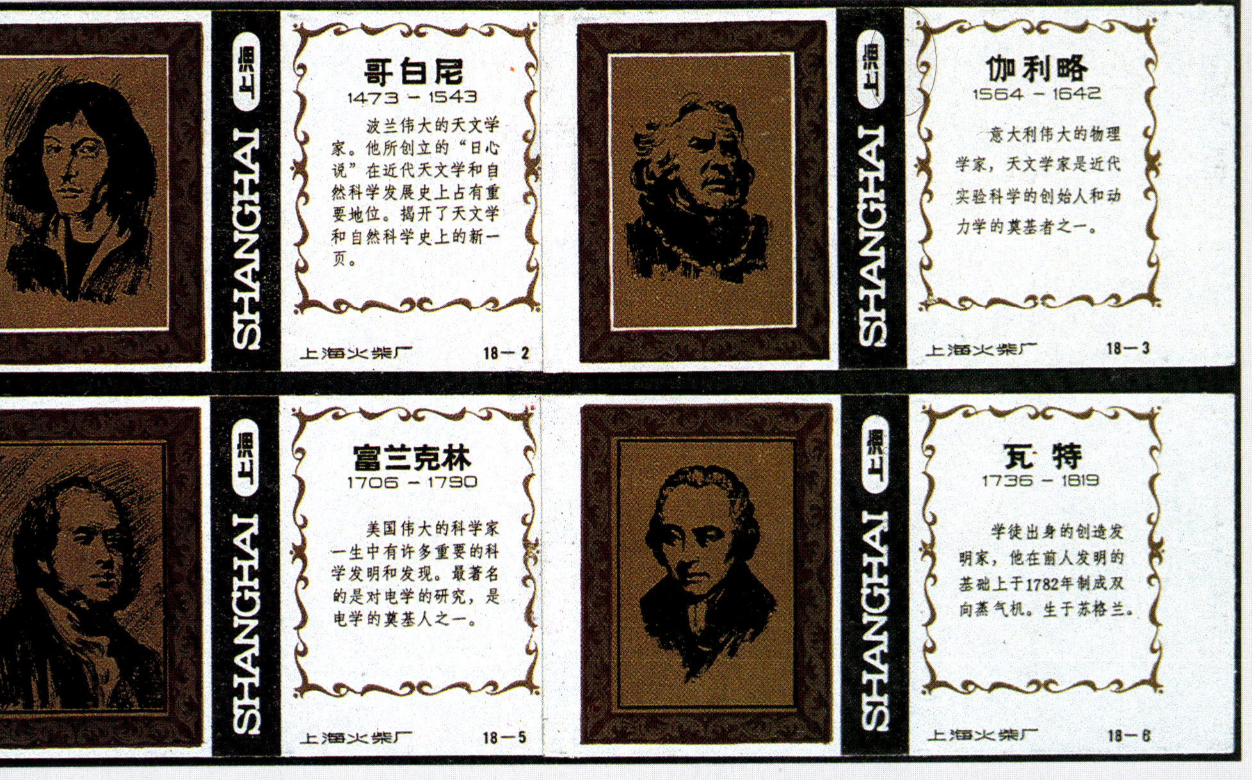

Foreign Scientists

From left, top row:

Roger Bacon (1220-1292), English philosopher and scientist who founded empirical science.

Nicolaus Copernicus (1473-1543), Polish astronomer, who advanced the idea that the earth and other planets revolve about the sun and that the earth is not the centre of the universe.

Galileo (1564-1642), Italian physicist and astronomer.

From left, second row:

Sir Isaac Newton (1642-1727), English physicist, who developed the law of universal gravitation and the three laws of motion.

Benjamin Franklin (1706-1790), American scientist, who developed a new theory on the nature of electricity.

James Watt (1736-1819), British inventor, who developed the double-acting steam engine in 1782.

From left, third row:

Alfred Bernhard Nobel (1833-1896), Swedish chemist, who established the Nobel Prizes with his fortunes.

Charles Darwin (1809-1882), British botanist, who developed the revolutionary theory of evolution by natural selection.

Thomas Edison (1847-1931), American inventor, a major contributor in electrotechnics, mining and chemical industries.

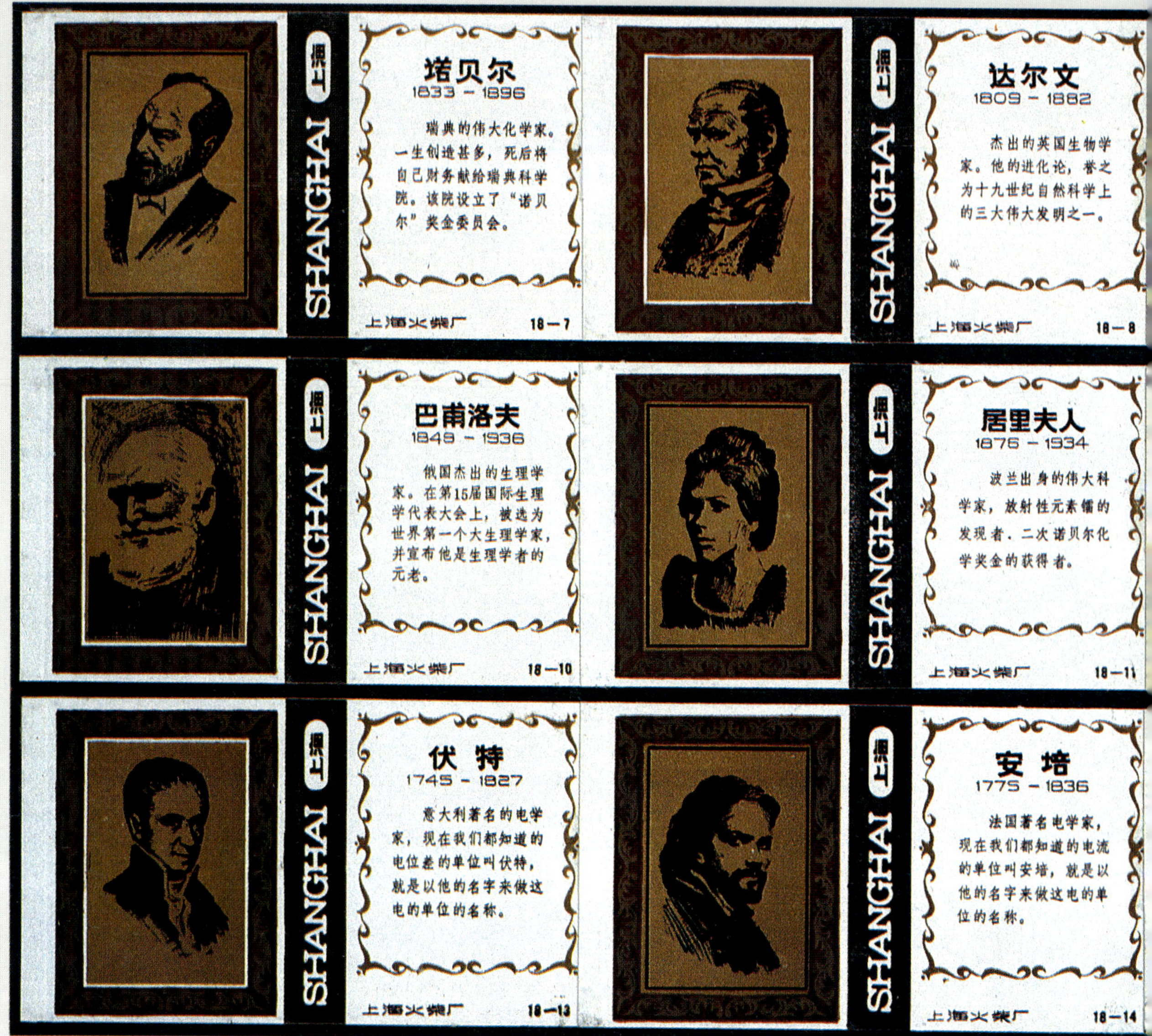

From left, fourth row:

Ivan Pavlov (1849-1936), Russian physiologist, a forerunner of physiological science.

Madame Curie (1867-1934), Polish-French scientist, who researched radioactivity and discovered radium.

Albert Einstein (1879-1955), German-American physicist, best known for his theory of relativity.

From left, bottom row:

Count Alessandro Volta(1745-1827), Italian physicist.

Andre Marie Ampere(1775-1836), French physicist.

Georg Simon Ohm(1789-1854), German physicist.

Made in Shanghai

101 mm x 51 mm

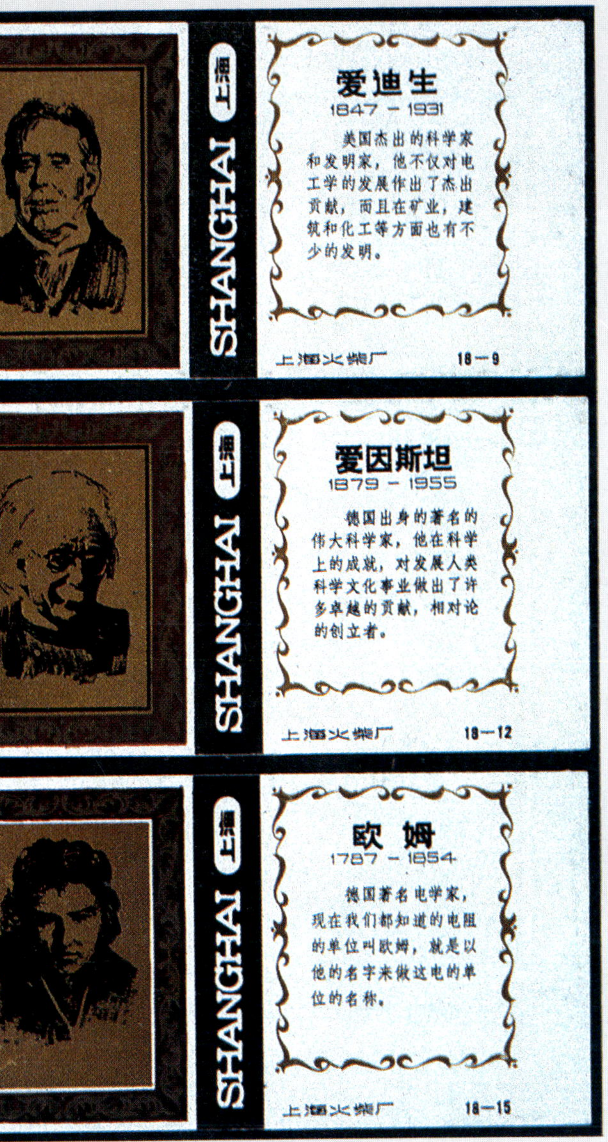
上海
SHANGHAI
爱迪生
1847 - 1931
美国杰出的科学家和发明家，他不仅对电工学的发展作出了杰出贡献，而且在矿业，建筑和化工等方面也有不少的发明。
上海火柴厂
18—9
上海
SHANGHAI
爱因斯坦
1879 - 1955
德国出身的著名的伟大科学家，他在科学上的成就，对发展人类科学文化事业做出了许多卓越的贡献，相对论的创立者。
上海火柴厂
18—12
上海
SHANGHAI
欧 姆
1787 - 1854
德国著名电学家，现在我们都知道的电阻的单位叫欧姆，就是以他的名字来做这电的单位的名称。
上海火柴厂
18—15

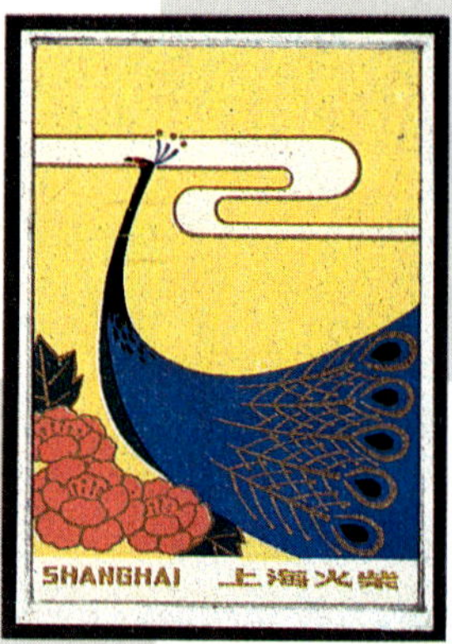

Fauna and Flora

The matchbox covers in this section comprise mainly plants and animals in the natural world. They are presented in a different way from traditional Chinese paintings, which generally express the artists' personal feelings and often have metaphorical meanings. These paintings, in contrast, put more emphasis on factual accuracy presented in an artistic manner.

It should also be mentioned that the "works" in this section employ both Chinese and Western painting techniques.

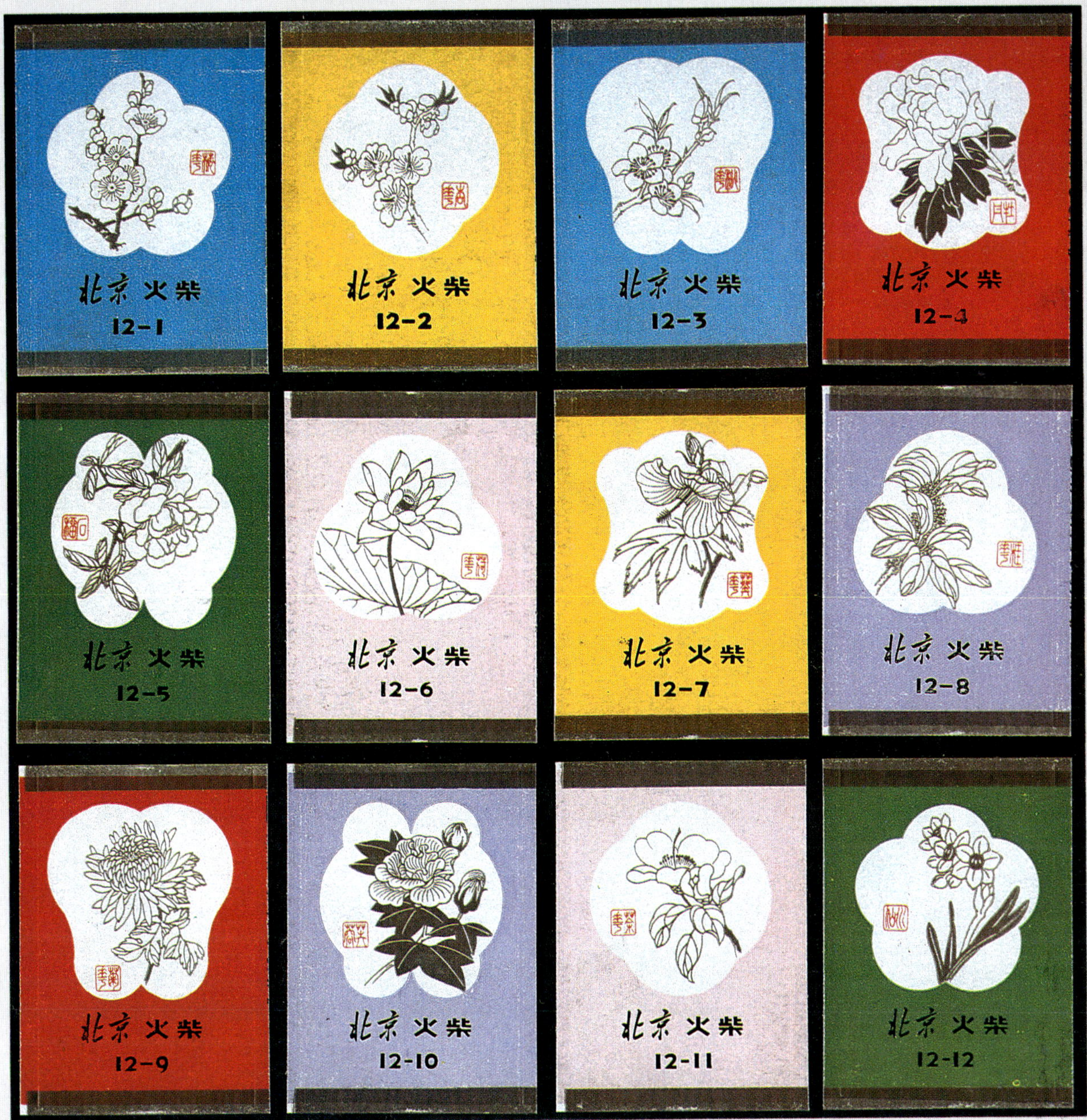

Flowers in Window Frames

The flowers in this group are painted with traditional contour techniques. Each flower is set against a backdrop of different garden window frames, while the name of the flower is marked with seal characters. All exhibit a strong national flavour touched by liveliness and classical elegance.

From left, top to bottom: plum blossom, apricot blossom, peach blossom, peony; pomegranate, lotus flower, sunflower, sweet-scented osmanthus; chrysanthemum, hibiscus, camellia,and narcissus.

Made in Beijing

104 mm x 56 mm

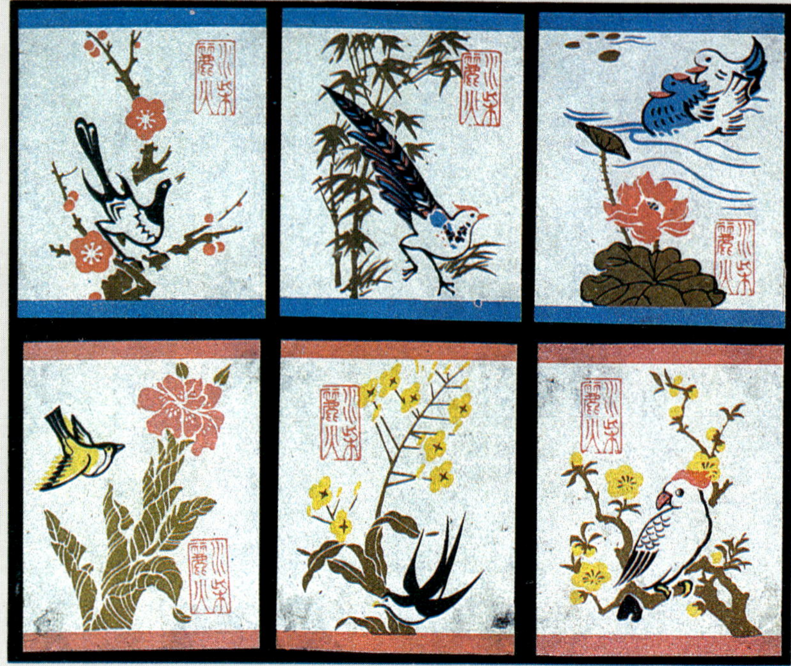

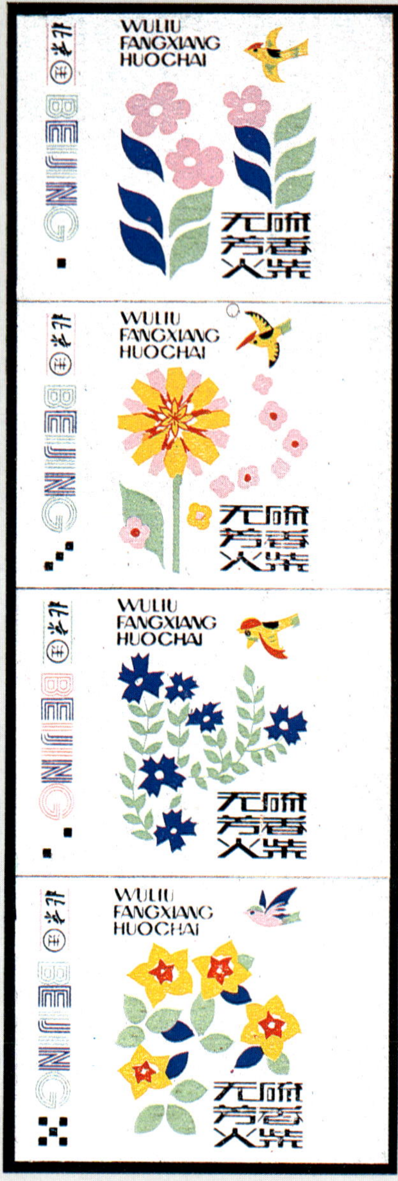

Flowers and Birds

In traditional Chinese paintings, flowers and birds belong to the same subject category. When flowers and birds are painted together, they please the eye all the more. This category is the most popular among the people. Though painted in different styles--some meticulous, others stylized--these three groups of covers are all characterized by the vivid artistic combination of motion and stillness and the ethereal and the substantial.

Made in Lishui, Zhejiang Province; Hangzhou, Zhejiang Province; and Beijing

42 mm x 35 mm, 48 mm x 36 mm, 106 mm x 44 mm

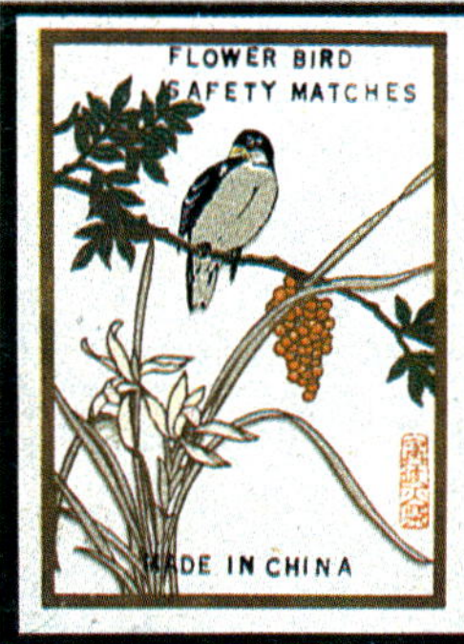

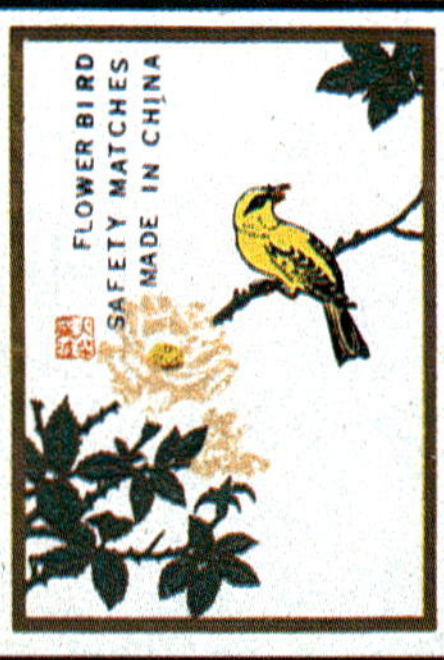

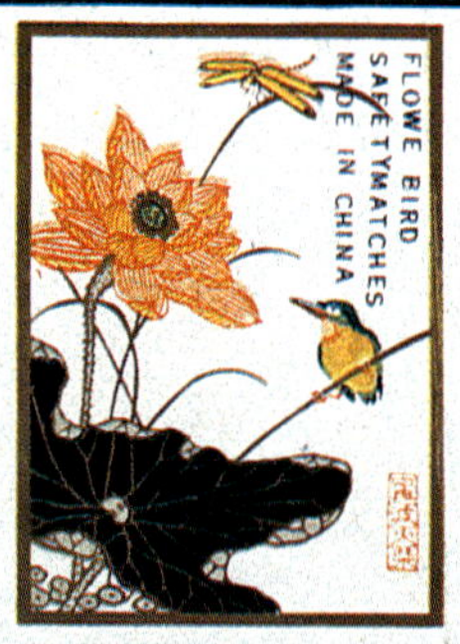

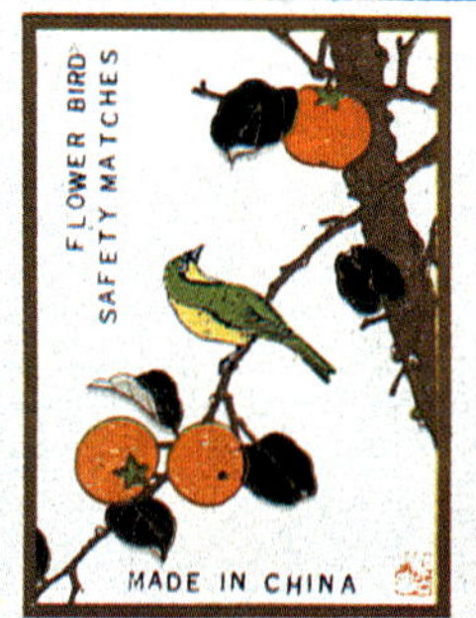

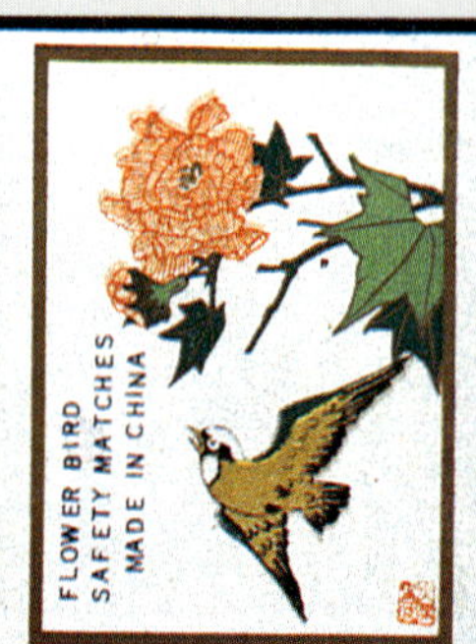

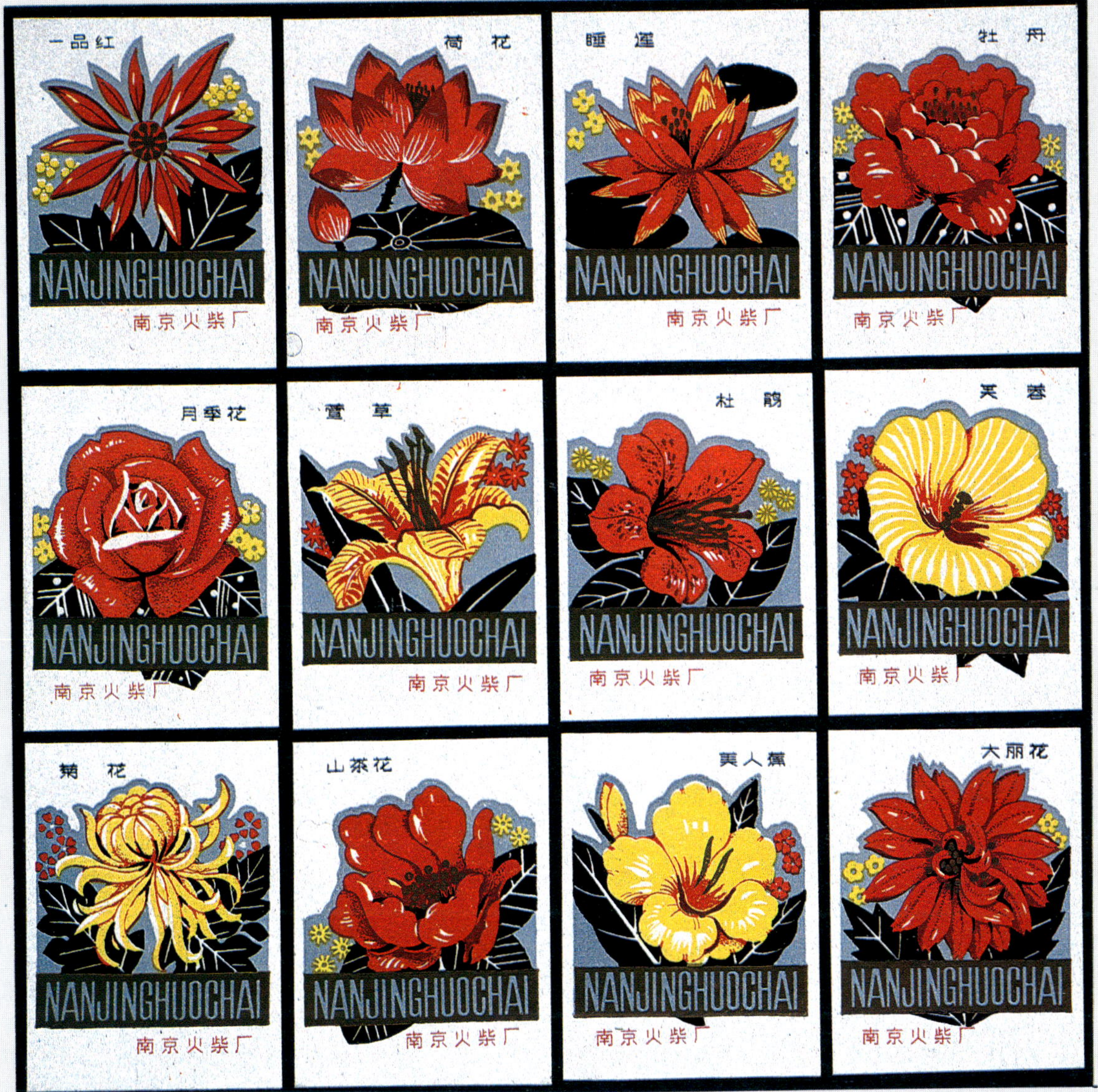

Flower Designs

These covers are all decorative flowers. The designer exaggerates the size of the blossoms, thereby giving prominence to the flowers' shape.

From left, top to bottom: poinsettia, lotus, water lily, peony; Chinese rose, tawny daylily, azalea, hibiscus; chrysanthemum, camellia, canna, and dahlia.

Made in Nanjing, Jiangsu Province

46 mm x 35 mm

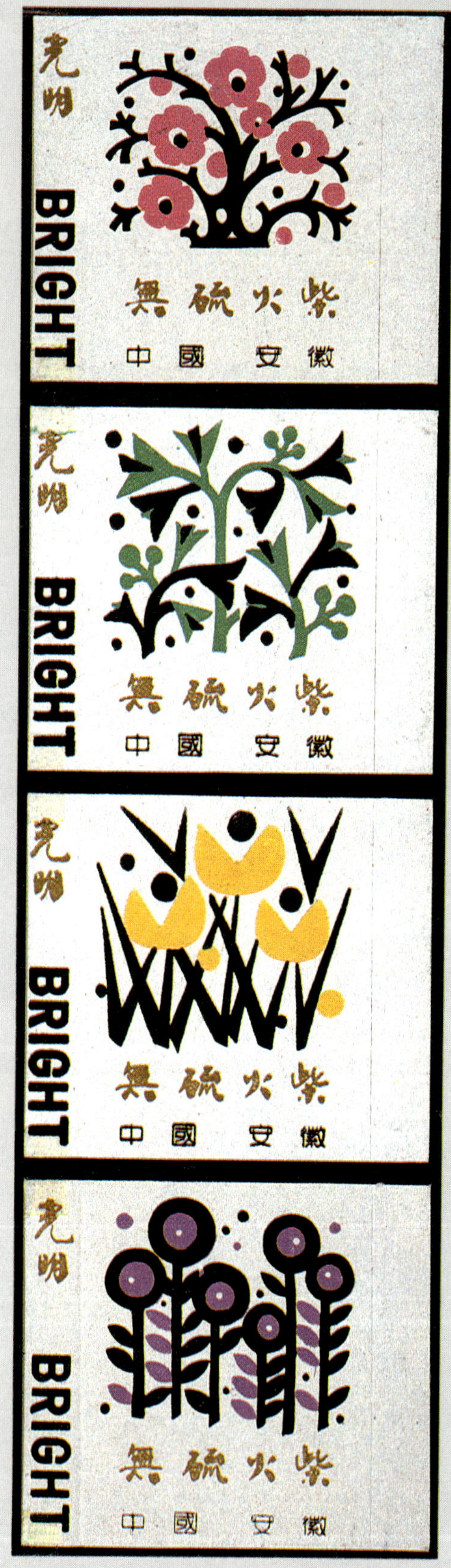
光明
BRIGHT
無硫火柴
中國 安徽

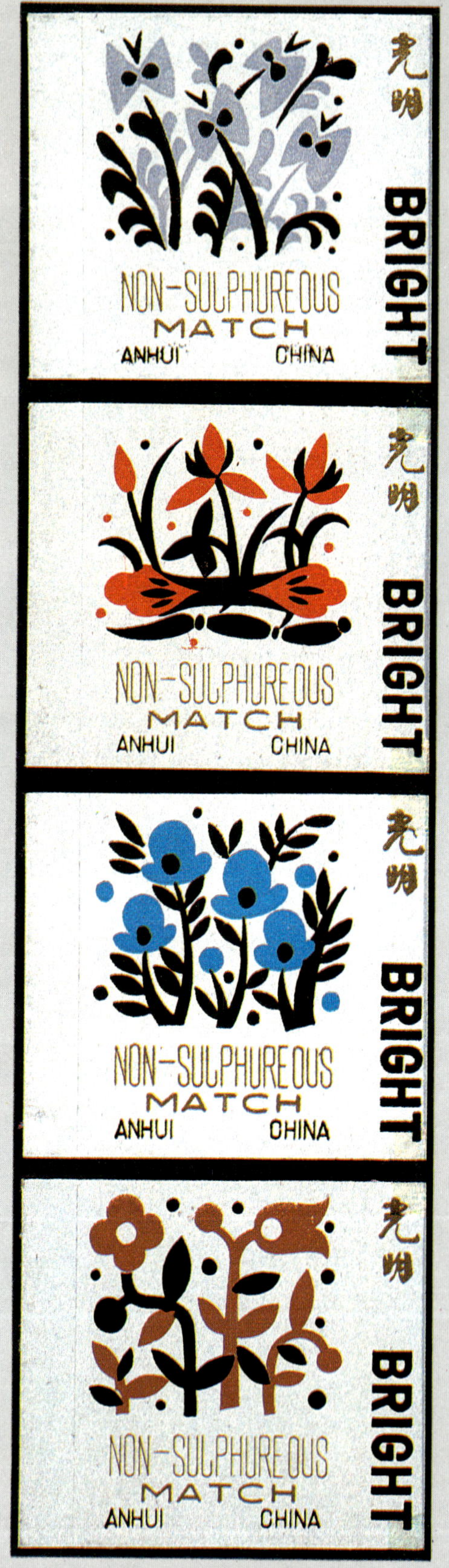
光明
BRIGHT
NON-SULPHUREOUS
MATCH
ANHUI CHINA

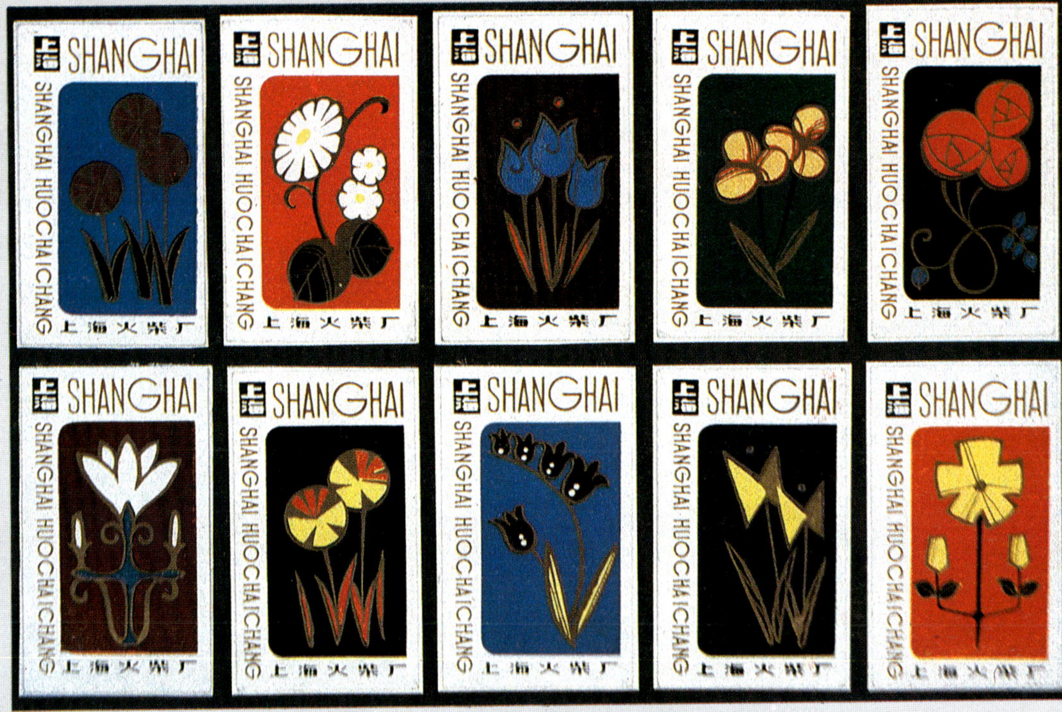

Stylized Flower Patterns

These three groups include flowers from different locales. All are treated so their shapes are metamorphosed, producing a most unusual effect. Moreover, each group of flowers is painted in a consistent style, thus creating a sense of grace and liveliness.

Made in Hefei, Anhui Province; Shanghai; and Zunyi, Guizhou Province

113 mm x 53 mm, 43 mm x 26 mm, 40 mm x 28 mm

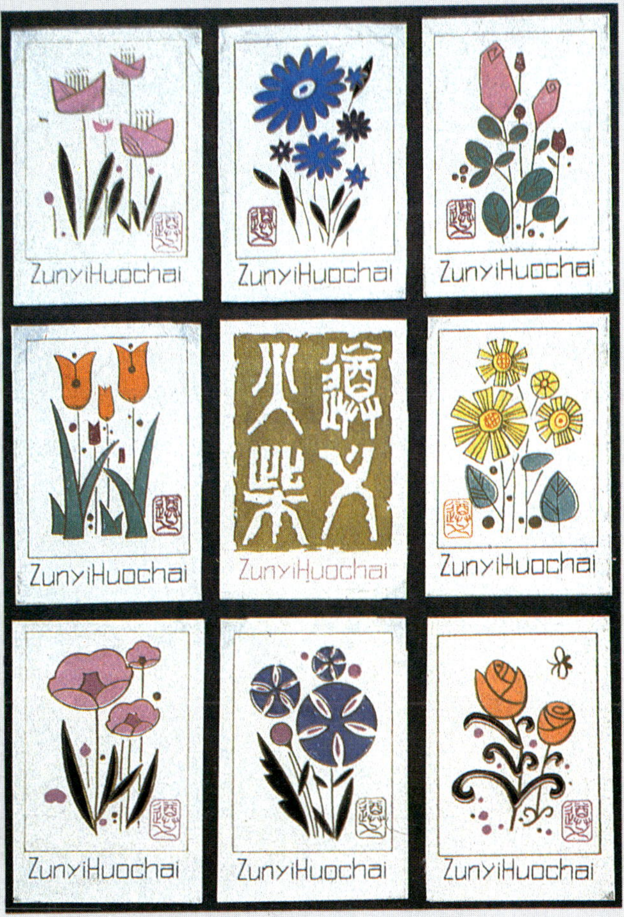

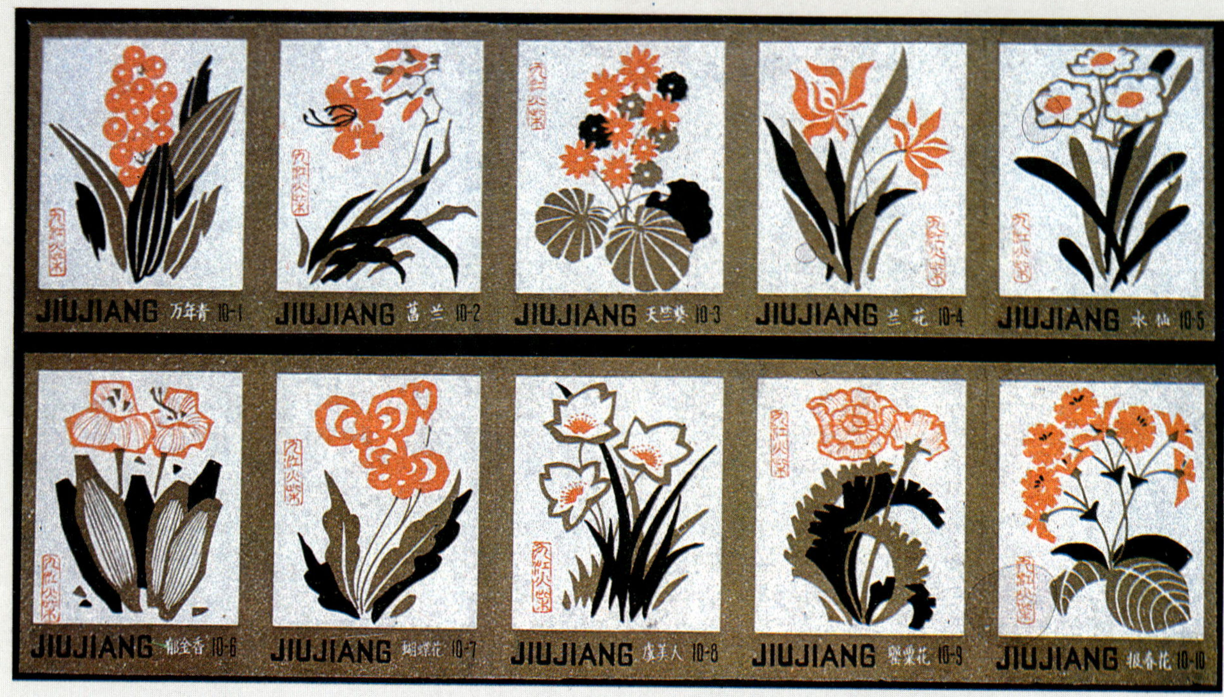

Coloured Flower Designs

The flowers in this group are executed in a rich variety of colours so the paintings look simultaneously fresh and varied.

Clockwise: evergreen, kudzuvine, fish pelargonium, orchid, narcissus, fairy primrose, poppy flower, corn poppy, fringed iris, and tulip.

Made in Jiujiang, Jiangxi Province

43 mm x 33 mm

Cactus

The cactus is classified as a perennial plant. Its peduncle, generally round or oval in shape, is fleshy and thorny, with occasional red, white or yellow blossoms. The cactus is a popular decorative plant.

Included in this set are the "nopalxochia," hedgehog cactus and "fuchsia."

Made in Qingdao, Shandong Province

43 mm x 34 mm

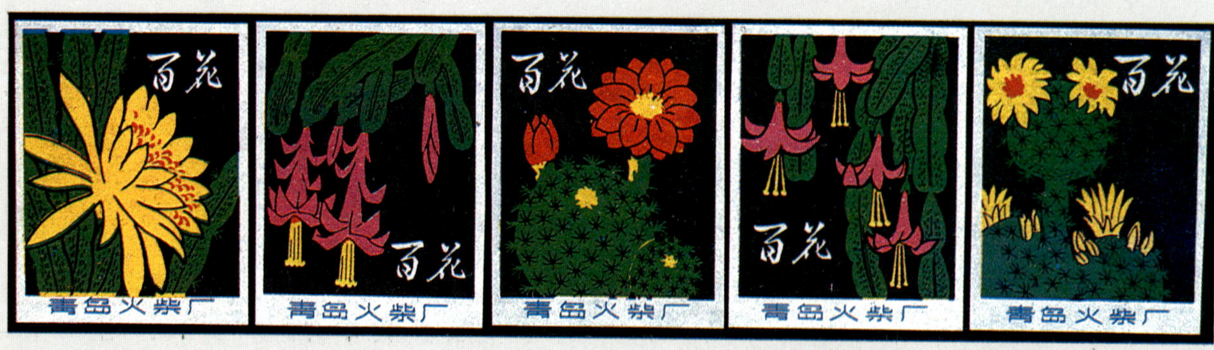

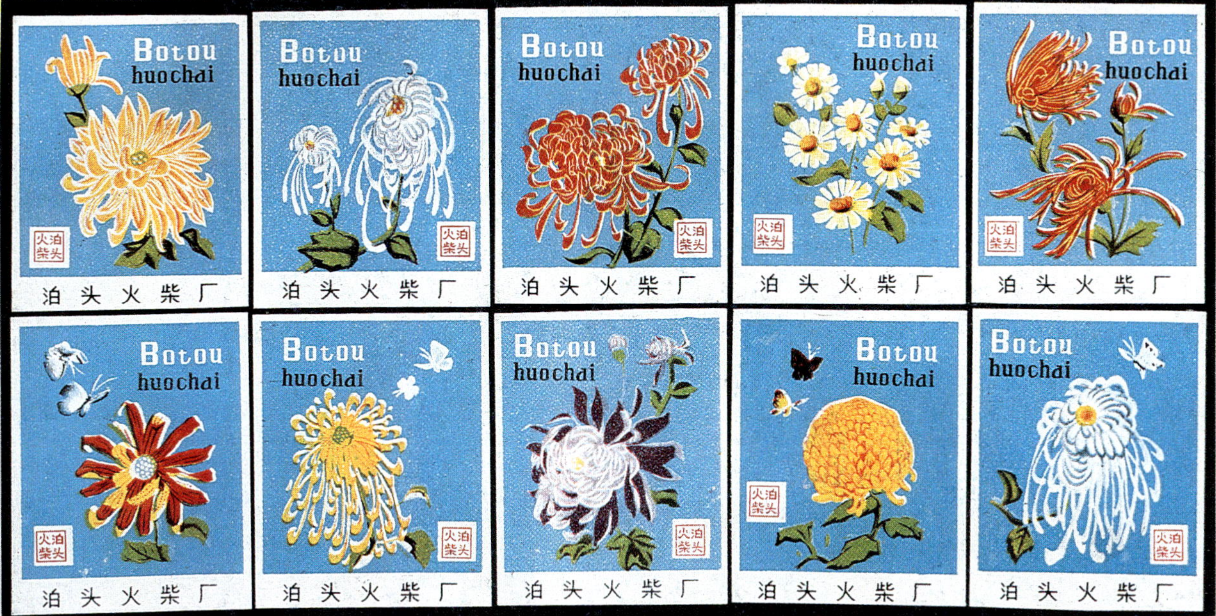

Chrysanthemums

Chrysanthemums grown in China include over three thousand varieties, which may serve either as decorative plants or as herbal medicine. As autumn sets in, chrysanthemums blossom in a rich array. Chrysanthemums are cold- and frost-resistant. Their hardy quality of "blossoming in spite of the frost" is highly regarded by the people of China.

Made in Botou, Hebei Province
44 mm x 35 mm

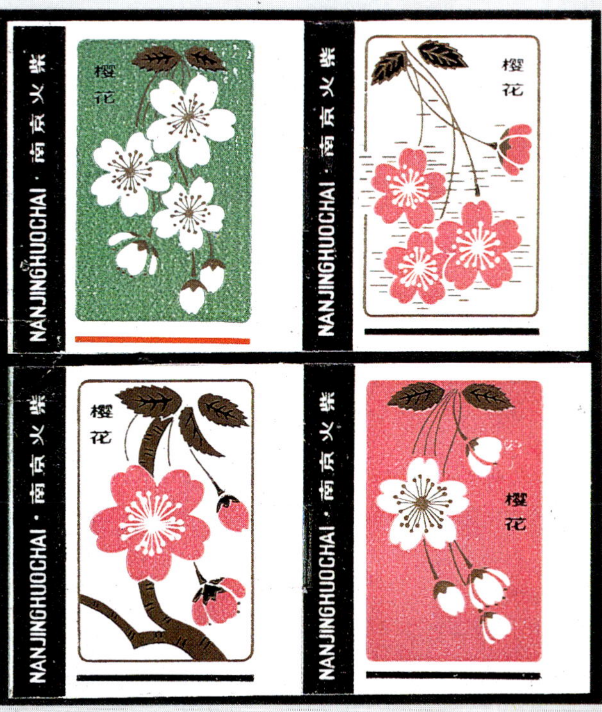

Oriental Cherries

Oriental cherries, which belong to the family of deciduous trees, grow mainly in Japan and China. The Tokyo cherry is the best known of all the cherries. Blossoming in spring each year, oriental cherries are popular decorative plants due to their delicate shape and bright colours.

Made in Nanjing, Jiangsu Province
84 mm x 50 mm

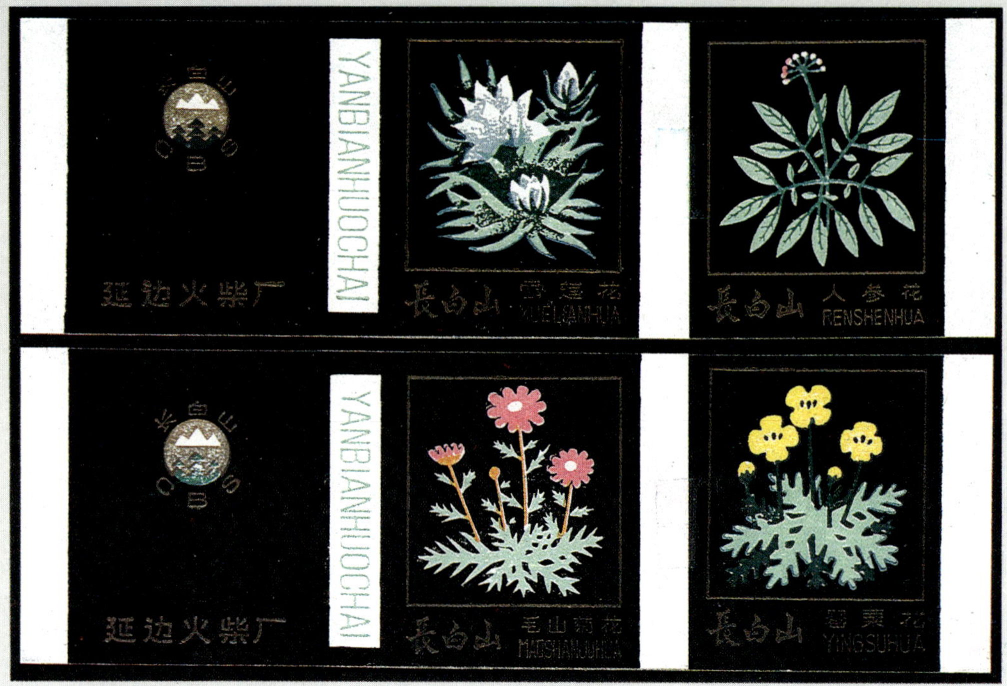

Plants of the Changbai Mountains

Stretching through the southeastern area of Jilin Province are the Changbai Mountains. Covered with dense forests, they boast a myriad of flowers and plants, some of which presented in this set of covers.

Clockwise: Snow lotus, ginseng flower,poppy flower and hairy dendranthema.

Made in Yanbian, Jilin Province

100 mm x 46 mm

Seasonal Flowers

These matchbox covers are seasonal flowers selected from different areas. Each has its distinctive features and charms which are represented by the different painting techniques.

Made in Xifeng, Shaanxi Province; Chongqing, Sichuan Province; Guangyuan, Sichuan Province; Dali, Yunnan Province; and Tengchong, Yunnan Province

51 mm x 36 mm, 43 mm x 35 mm

38 mm x 30 mm, 41 mm x 30 mm

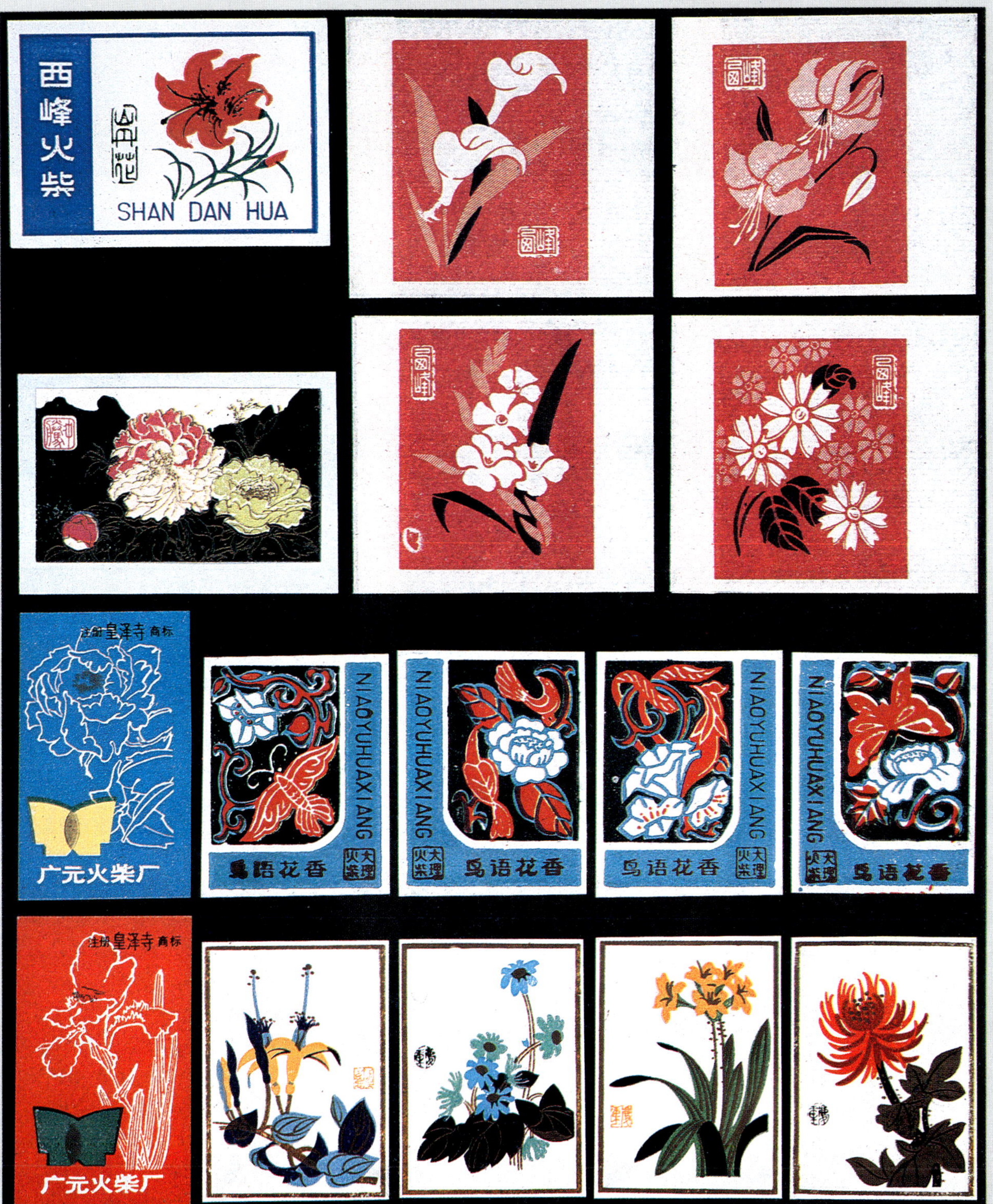
西峰火柴
SHAN DAN HUA
注册皇泽寺商标
广元火柴厂
NIAOYUHUAXIANG
鸟语花香
大理火柴
NIAOYUHUAXIANG
鸟语花香
大理火柴
NIAOYUHUAXIANG
鸟语花香
大理火柴
NIAOYUHUAXIANG
鸟语花香
大理火柴
注册皇泽寺商标
广元火柴厂

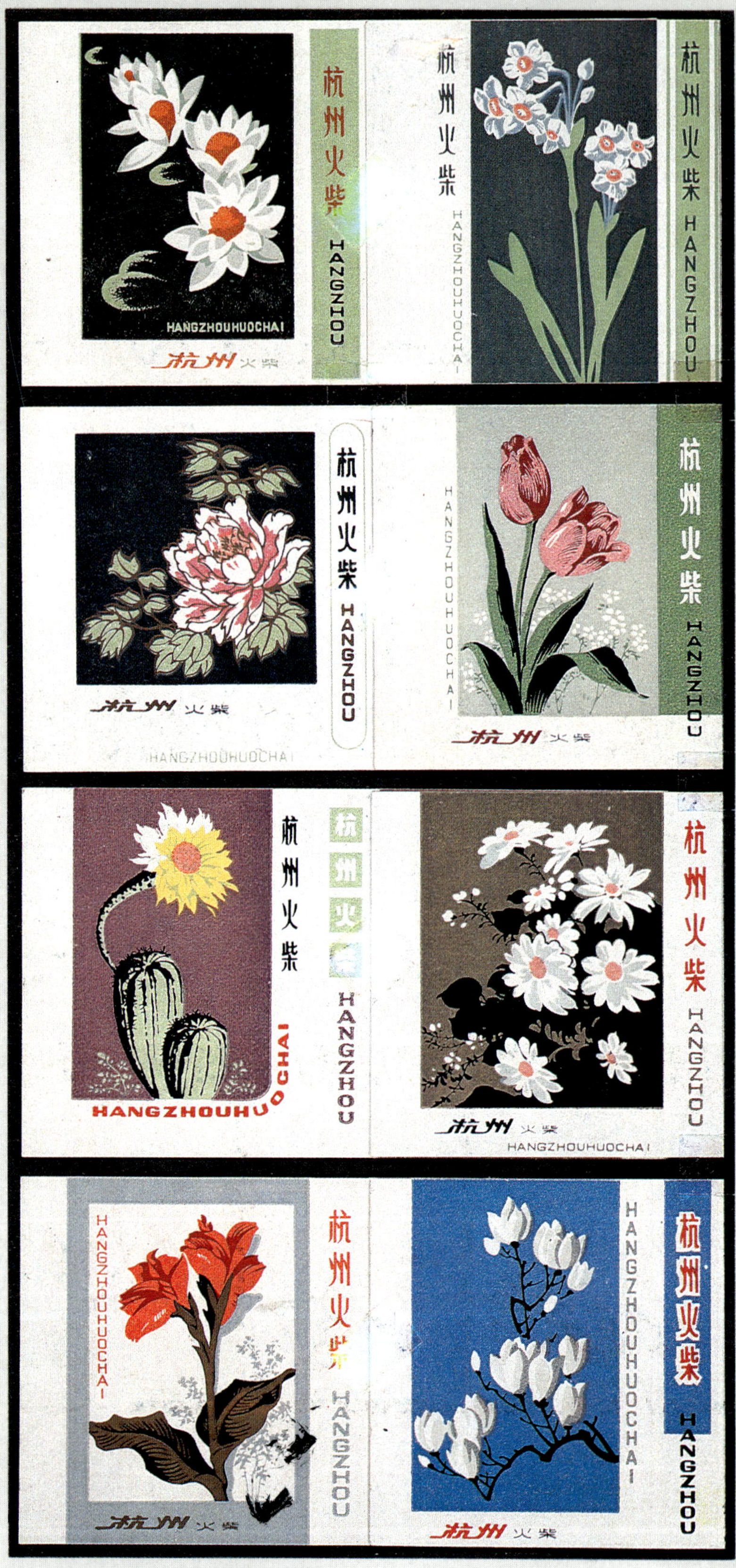

Flower Designs

This set of close-up flower designs combines the ethereal with the substantial. Rich colours accentuate the shapes of the flowers, enhancing the decorative effect.

From top to bottom, left column: water lily, peony, hedgehog cactus, canna; from top to bottom, right column: narcissus, tulip, chrysanthemum, and yulan magnolia.

Made in Hangzhou, Zhejiang Province

103 mm x 56 mm

Rare Animals

China is a vast territory with varied weather patterns which serves as home to many rare animals. Some of them are pictured here.

Top right: red-crowned crane;

From left, centre: white-lipped deer, Northeast China tiger, giant panda;

From left, bottom: golden monkey, Chinese alligator, and gibbon.

Made in Chongqing, Sichuan Province

44 mm x 31 mm

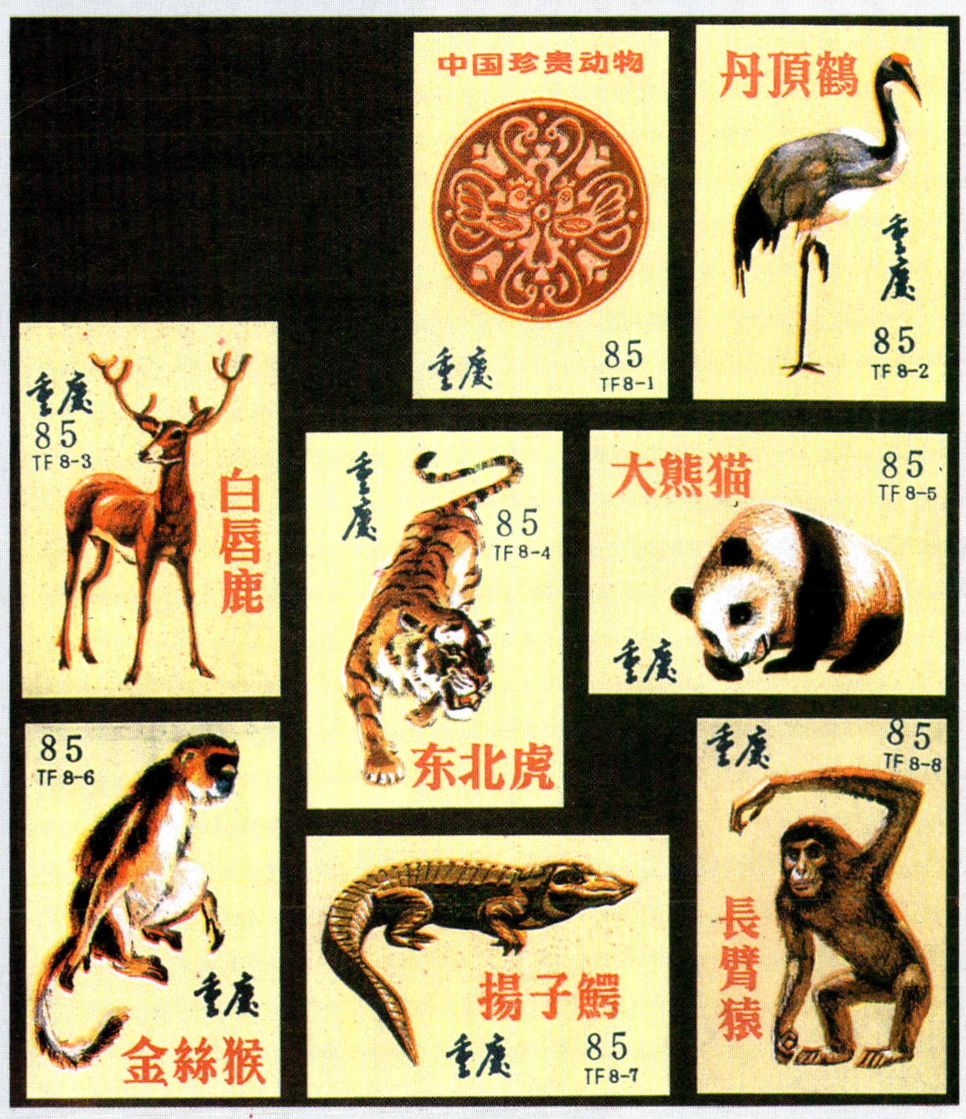

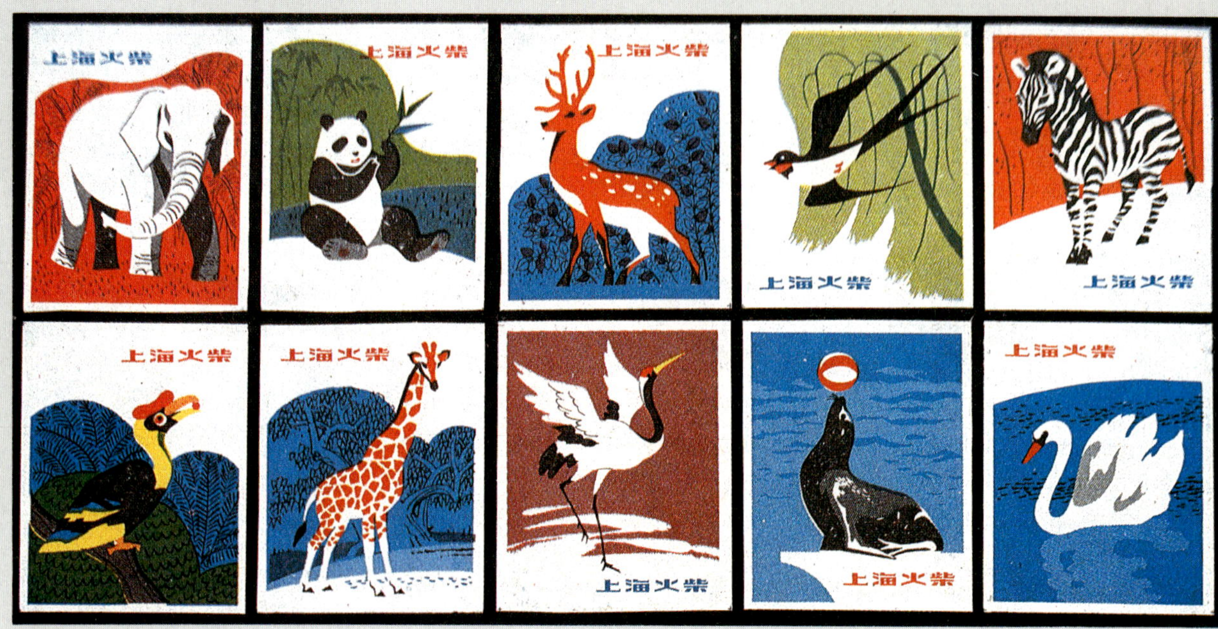
上海火柴
上海火柴
上海火柴
上海火柴
上海火柴
上海火柴
上海火柴
上海火柴
上海火柴
上海火柴

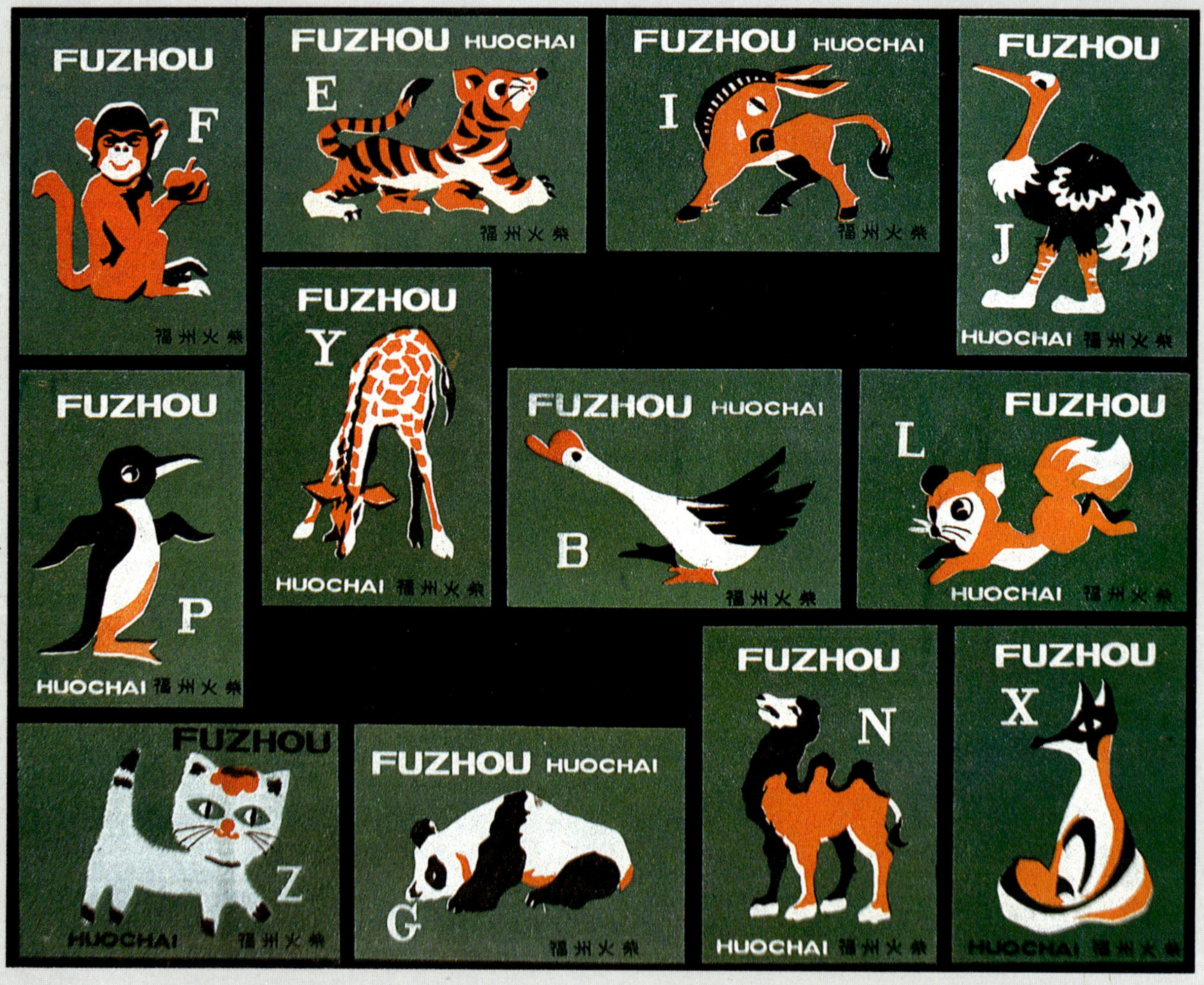

FUZHOU
F
福州火柴
FUZHOU HUOCHAI
E
福州火柴
FUZHOU HUOCHAI
I
福州火柴
FUZHOU
J
HUOCHAI 福州火柴
FUZHOU
Y
HUOCHAI 福州火柴
FUZHOU
P
HUOCHAI 福州火柴
FUZHOU HUOCHAI
B
福州火柴
FUZHOU
L
HUOCHAI 福州火柴
FUZHOU
N
HUOCHAI 福州火柴
FUZHOU
X
HUOCHAI 福州火柴
FUZHOU
Z
HUOCHAI 福州火柴
FUZHOU HUOCHAI
G
福州火柴

"Zoological Garden"

Each of these two sets has its own distinctive features in design. The covers above are painted in an exaggerated style producing an unaffected and decorative effect. Those below are painted in a more realist way, set in dramatic environments with sharply contrasting colours.

Made in Fuzhou, Fujian Province; and Shanghai

50 mm x 35 mm, 42 mm x 34 mm

Seal-Engraving Style Animals

The art of Chinese seal engraving has a long history and many forms have developed over the years, such as character and figure engraving. The imitations of figure engraving in this set have a unique style as seen in the concise and vigorous strokes cut in the tiny squares.

Made in Nanjing, Jiangsu Province

43 mm x 35 mm

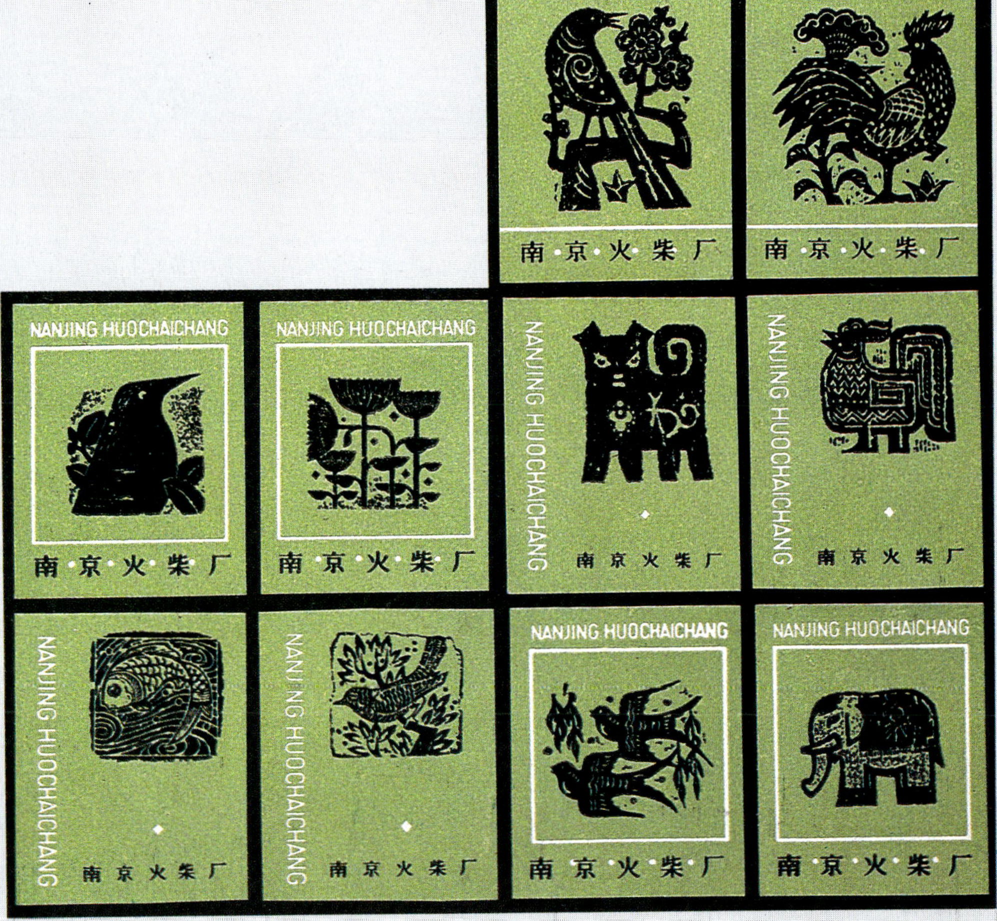

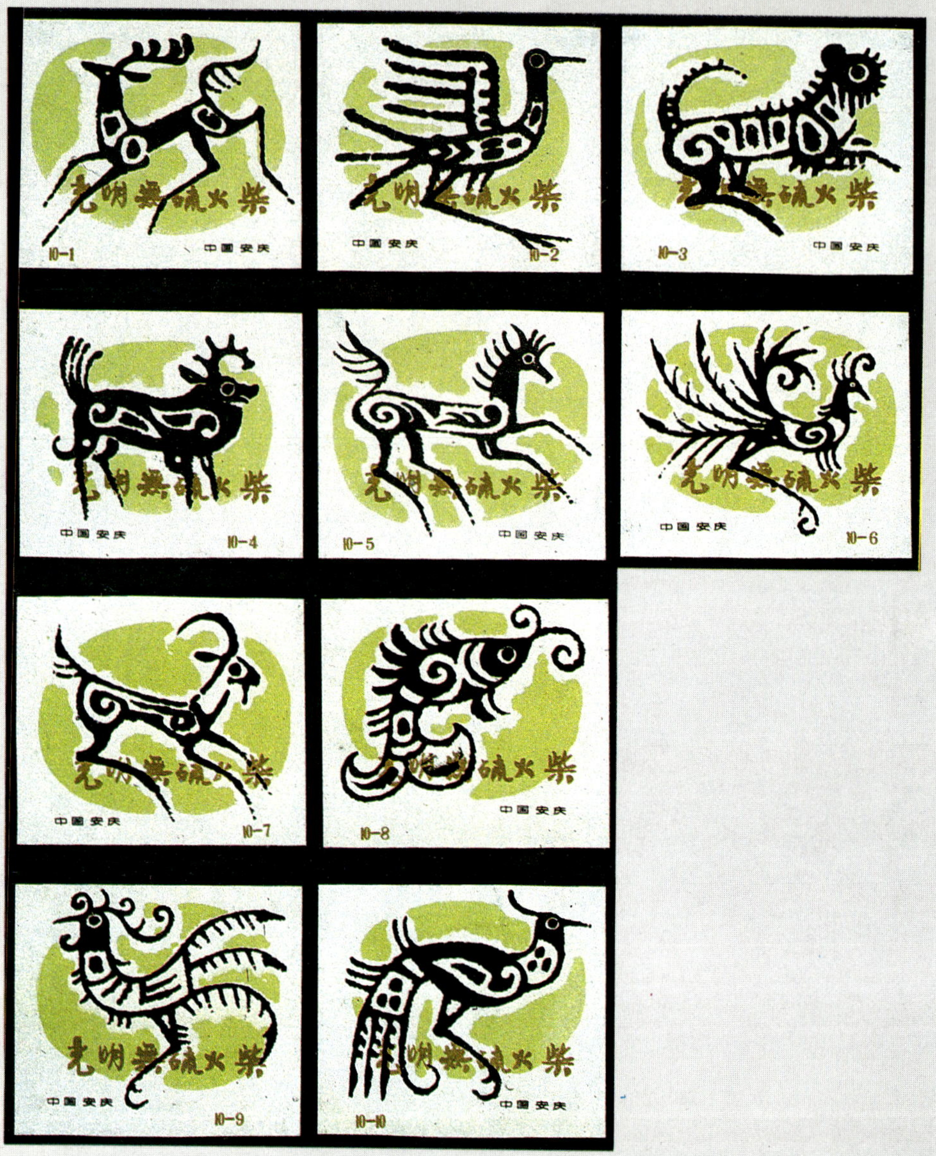

Animal Designs in the Rock Sculpture Style

The covers here are modelled after primitive rock sculptures with exaggerated strokes and pure colours. The varied animal paintings exhibit both classical and natural charms.

Made in Anqing, Anhui Province

41 mm x 34 mm

Stylized Animal Designs

Painted by Han Meilin, a famous Chinese painter of decorative animals, the animals in this set look charming and innocent, conveying a vitality and richness.

Lower left is Oriental ibis, a rare Chinese bird.

Made in Nanjing, Jiangsu Province

111 mm x 57 mm

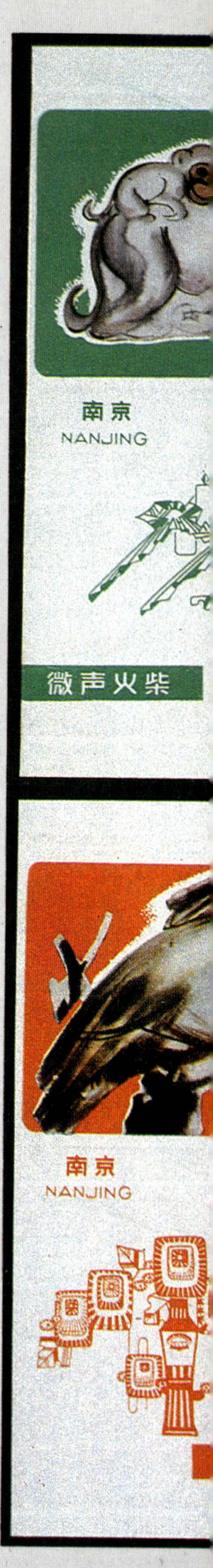

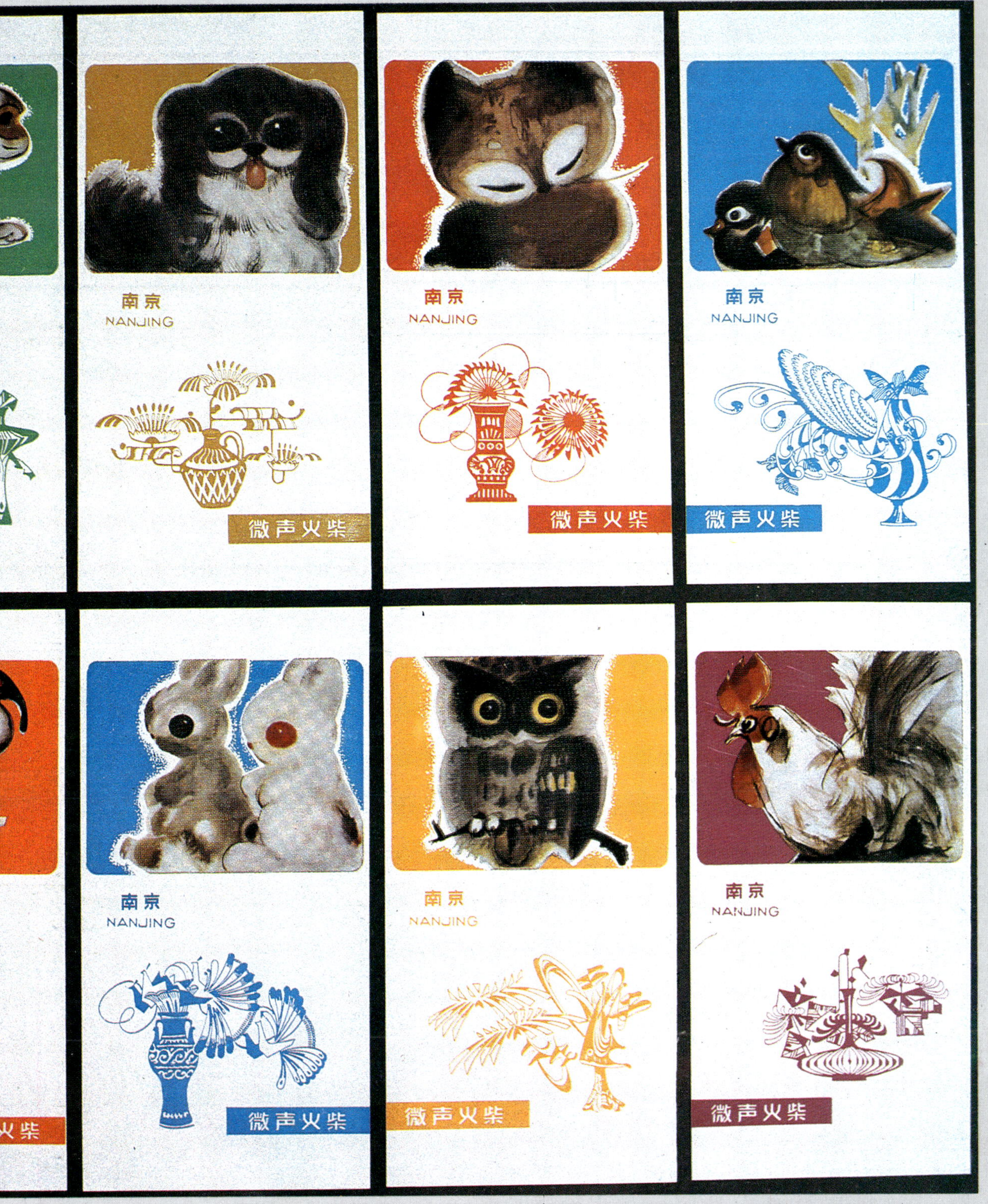
南京
NANJING
微声火柴
南京
NANJING
微声火柴
南京
NANJING
微声火柴
南京
NANJING
微声火柴
南京
NANJING
微声火柴
南京
NANJING
微声火柴
火柴

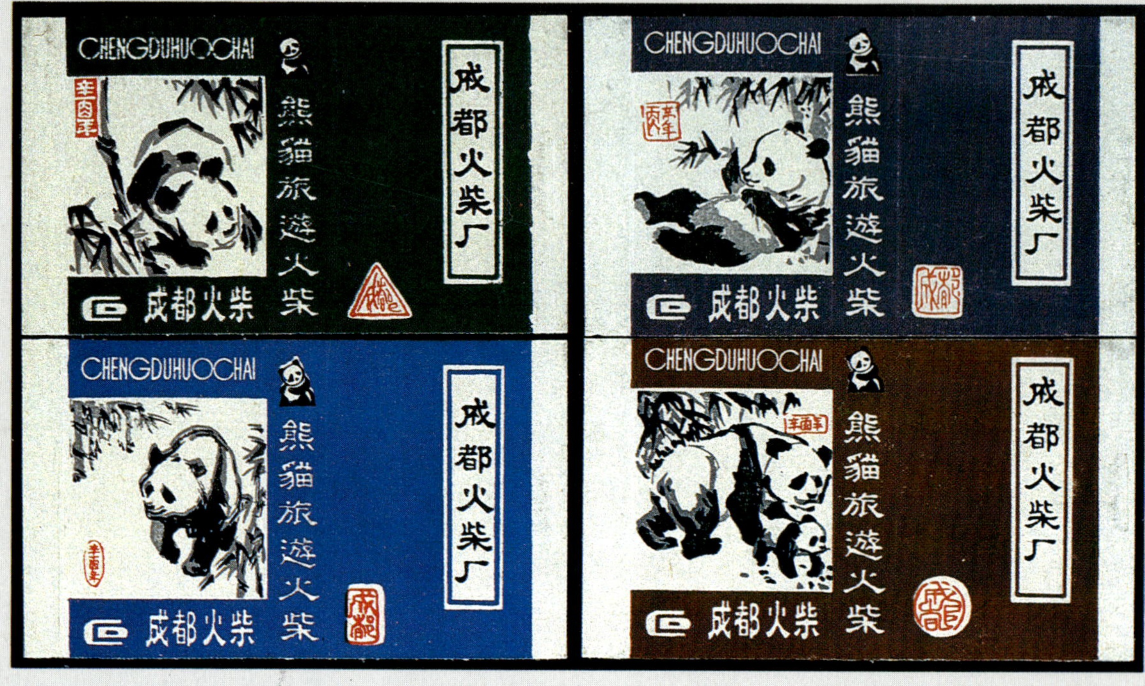

Pandas

Pandas inhabit primarily the three-thousand-metre-high mountains in China's Sichuan, Gansu and Shaanxi provinces. Nicknamed "living fossils," pandas are a rare animal species with only about a thousand members. Living on a bamboo diet, they are mild-tempered, charmingly naive and most lovable.

Made in Chengdu, Sichuan Province
77 mm x 43 mm, 44 mm x 25 mm

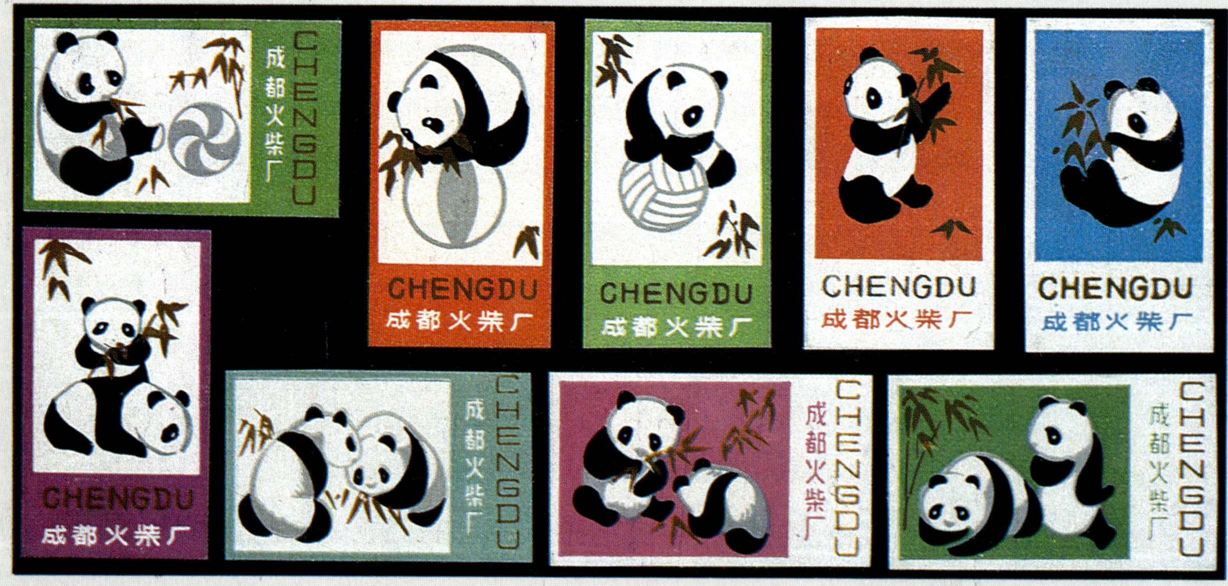

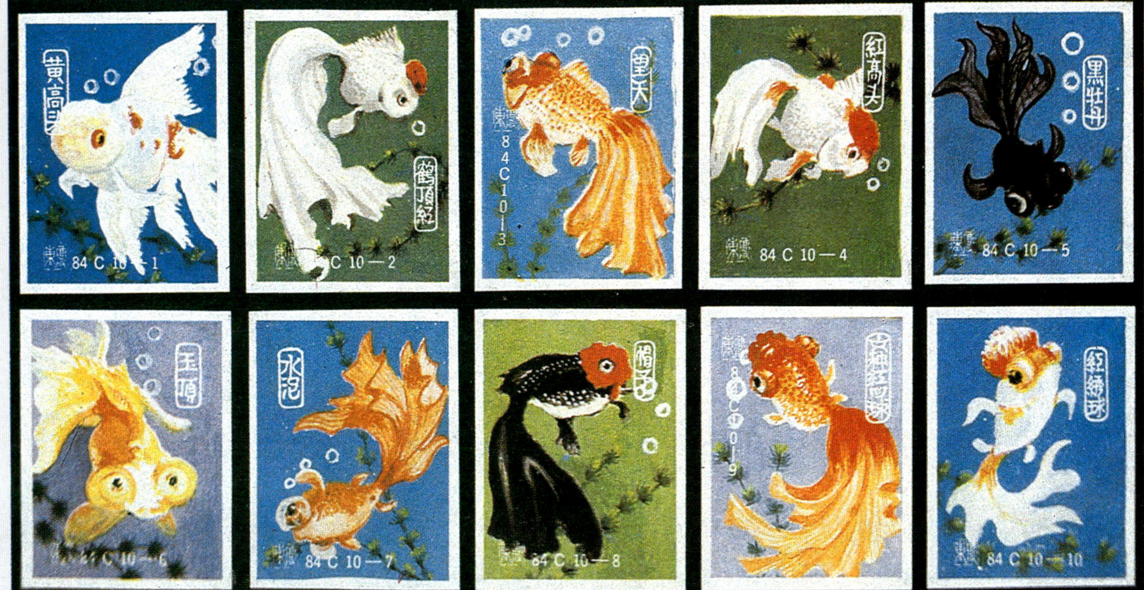

Goldfish

Goldfish were raised in China as far back as the 10th century. This fish species was developed for appreciation from the crucian carp. Gold fish have round and firm-fleshed bodies with bright colours. They have many varieties. Some of the more valuable varieties are yellow high head, red crane top, skygazing eyes, red high head, black peony (from left, above); jade top, bubbles, cap, four red balls, and red silk balls (from left, below).

Made in Chongqing, Sichuan Province; Pingjiang, Hunan Province

43 mm x 33 mm

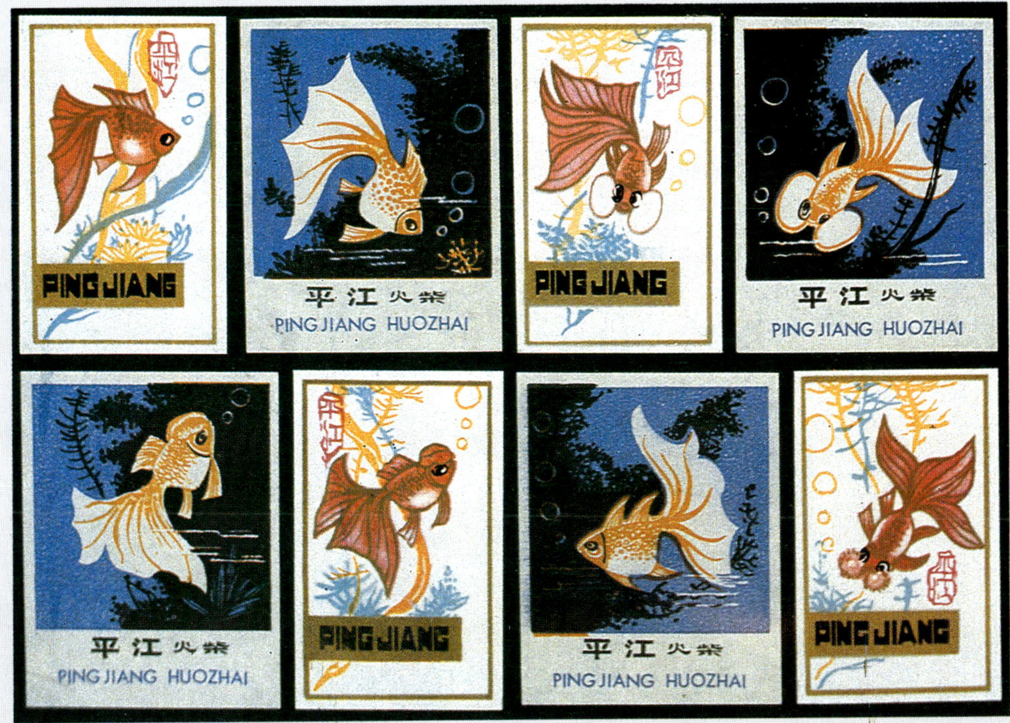

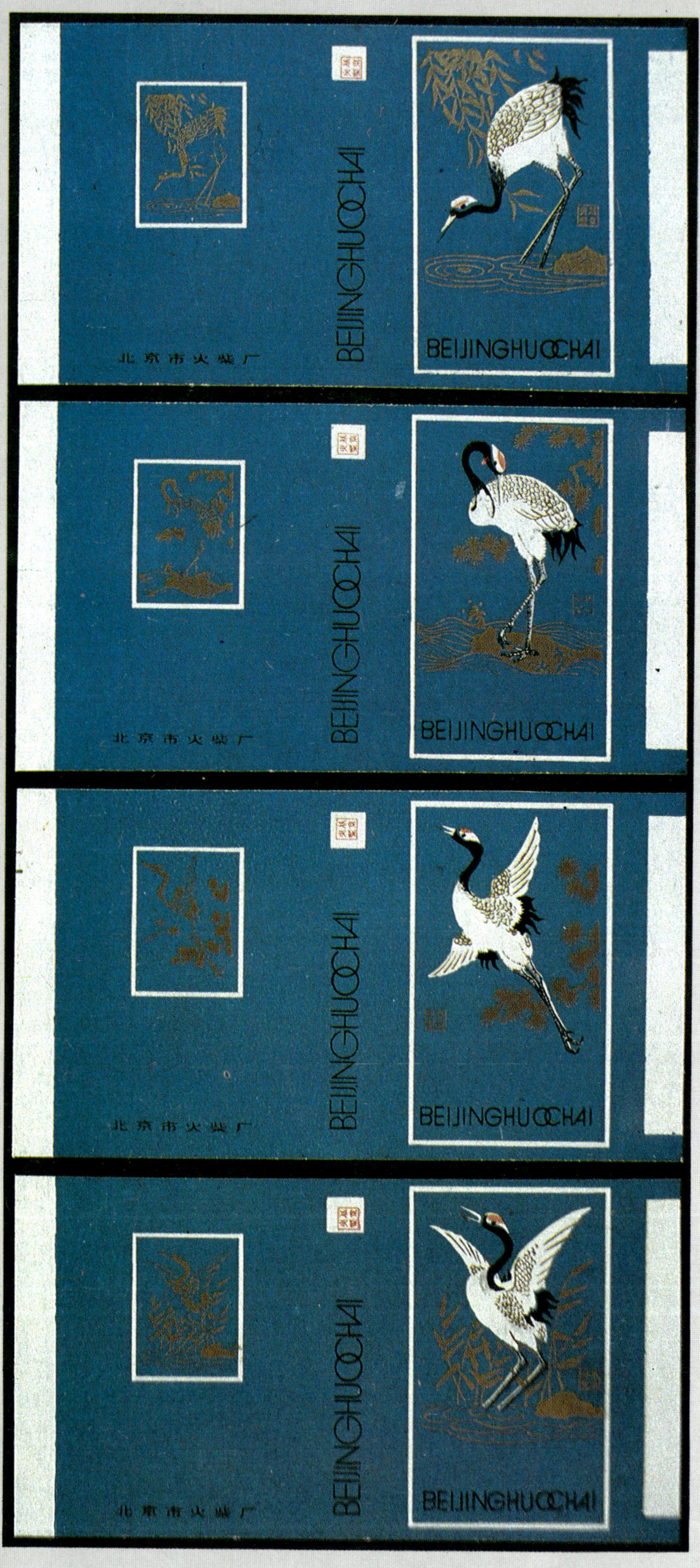

Red-crowned Cranes

Red-crowned cranes are a rare bird species which in China have been regarded as a symbol of longevity. With snow-white feathers and pure black wings and tails, red-crowned cranes inhabit the shallow shores in China's Heilongjiang and Jilin provinces. Sometimes they dance gracefully and warble sonorously.

Made in Beijing.

100 mm x 53 mm

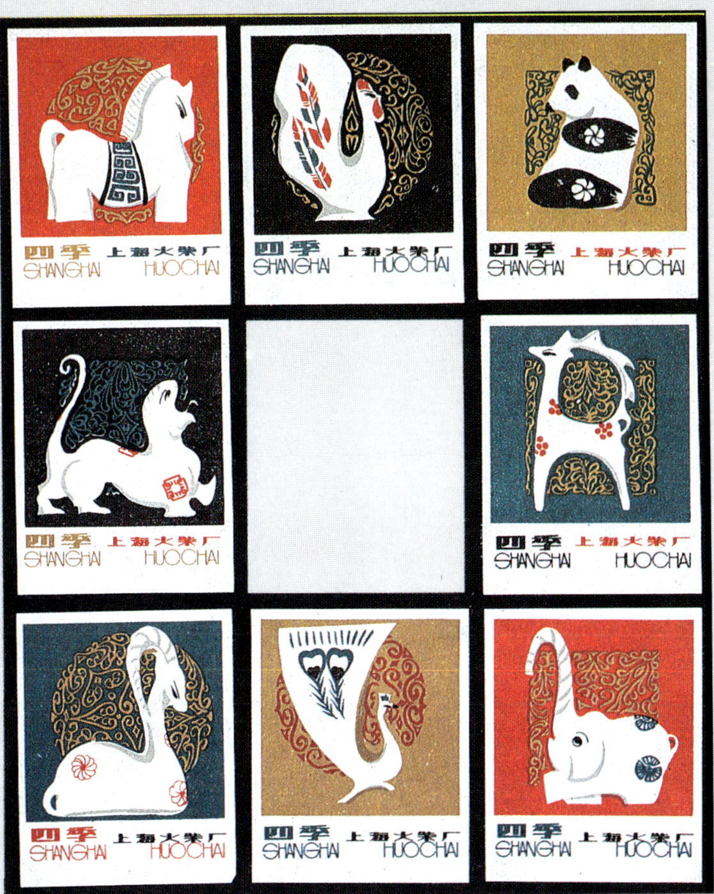

Clay Sculpture Animals

The animals in this set are painted sharply to resemble clay sculptures, the traditional Chinese folk handicraft.

Made in Shanghai

41 mm x 33 mm

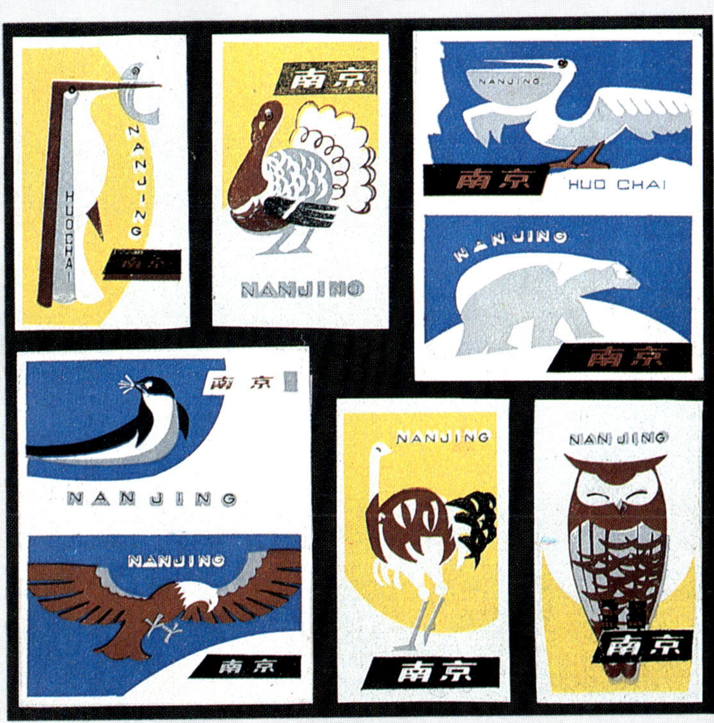

Animal Designs

The designs here are executed in a free and skillful style which strengthens their visual effect. All the animals bear a slight resemblance to human beings in one way or another, creating an impression at once lively and comical.

Made in Nanjing, Jiangsu Province

43 mm x 26 mm

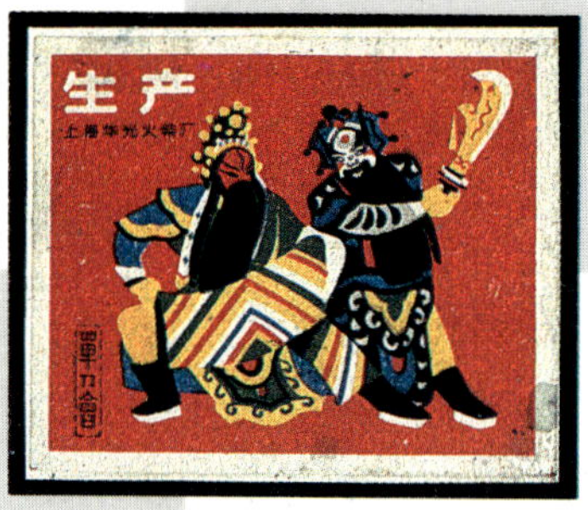

Art and Literature

Chinese art and literature have a long and varied history which has contributed enormously to the development of world civilization.

The covers in this section are based on ancient Chinese mythology, fables, novels, plays, musical compositions, paintings and calligraphic works. They illuminate the development of Chinese culture over thousands of years. The informative subject matter is taken from a wide range of original sources of high historical values.

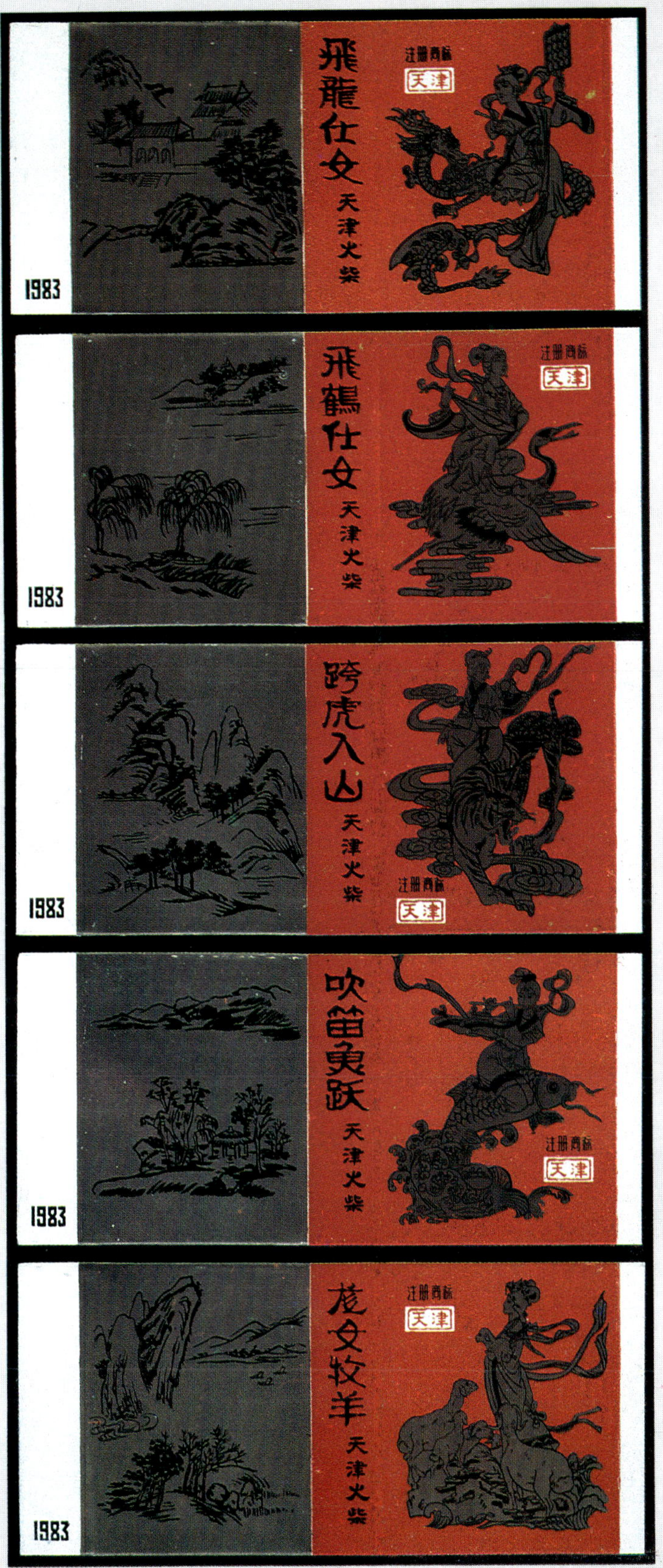

Fairy Tales

The covers in this set are based on ancient Chinese mythology.

From top to bottom: Fairy Goddess on a Flying Dragon, Fairy Goddess on a Flying Crane, Heading for the Mountains on Tiger Back, Playing the Flute to the Accompaniment of Dancing Fish, and Shepherdess.

Employing the line drawing technique of traditional Chinese painting, the designer creates exquisite images of beauty. Furthermore, the perspective enhances the aesthetic appeal of the design by bringing the distant hills and nearby waters into the proper proportions.

Made in Tianjin

102 mm x 46 mm

Eight Immortals Crossing the Sea

Eight Immortals Crossing the Sea is a popular Chinese folk tale about the eight immortals of the Taoist school having infinite magic power and the habit of practising charity. Each of them has different ways to cross the sea.

From left, top to bottom: Li Tieguai (Iron Crutch Li), Han Zhongli, Zhang Guolao, He Xiangu, Lan Caihe, Lü Dongbin, Han Xiangzi, and Cao Guojiu.

Made in Zhenjiang, Jiangsu Province

43 mm x 35 mm

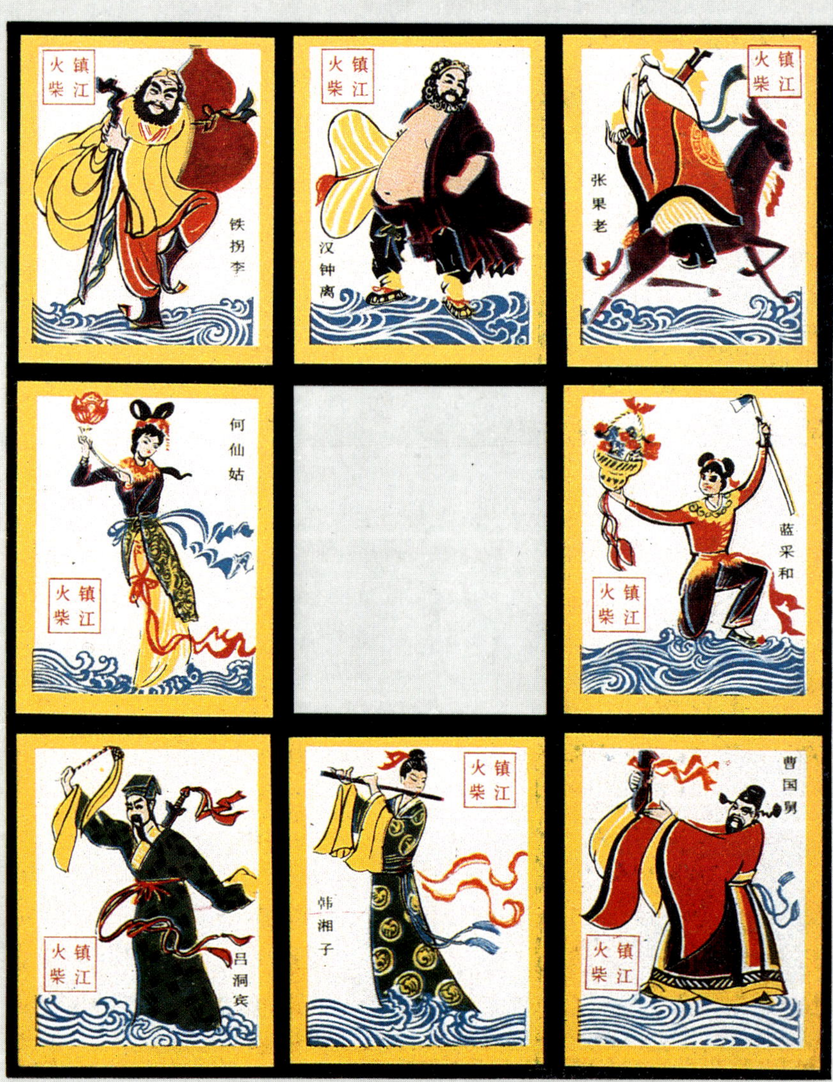

Fables

This group presents Chinese fables which illustrate a philosophical point.

From top to bottom:

The Fox Borrows the Terror of the Tiger. A fox tails after a tiger and avails himself of the terror caused by the tiger to scare away other wild beasts.

Donkey's Tricks. A tiger gets scared when he first sees the donkey, but on finding out that all that the donkey can do is bray or kick, he eats him up.

Dog and Rabbit Neither Comes to a Good End. A dog has chased after a rabbit for several days and nights. Finally, both of them die of exhaustion by the wayside where a farmer picks them up for a meal.

Snipe and Clam. A snipe grapples with a clam. The clam holds the beak of the snipe. Neither will let go of each other. A fisherman comes up and catches them both.

Made in Wuhu, Anhui Province

107 mm x 45 mm

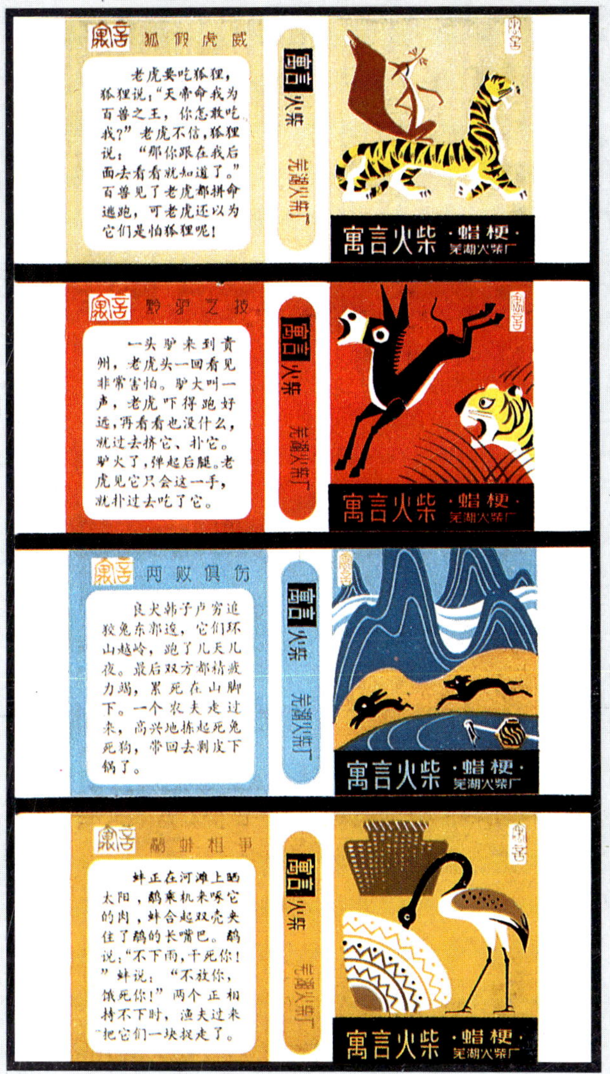

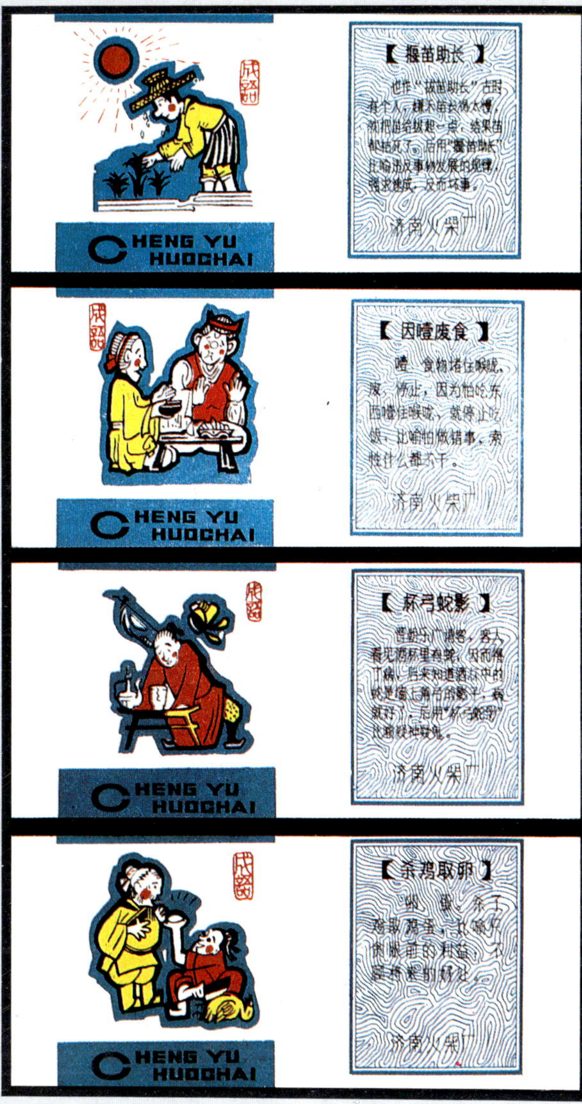

Proverbial Stories

This set includes four stories of Chinese proverbs. Each tells a moral tale.

From top to bottom:

Pulling the Shoots Up to Help Them Grow. A farmer thinks his shoots grow too slowly, so he pulls them upwards, only to cause the shoots to wither.

Giving Up Eating for Fear of Choking. A man chokes while eating and becomes so fearful that he decides to give up eating.

Mistaking the Reflection of a Bow in a Cup for a Snake. A man at a dinner party sees a snake in his wine cup. Seized by terror, he falls sick.

Killing the Hen to Get the Eggs. A man is anxious to have eggs, so he kills his hen in order to get eggs more quickly.

Made in Jinan, Shandong Province

106 mm x 46 mm

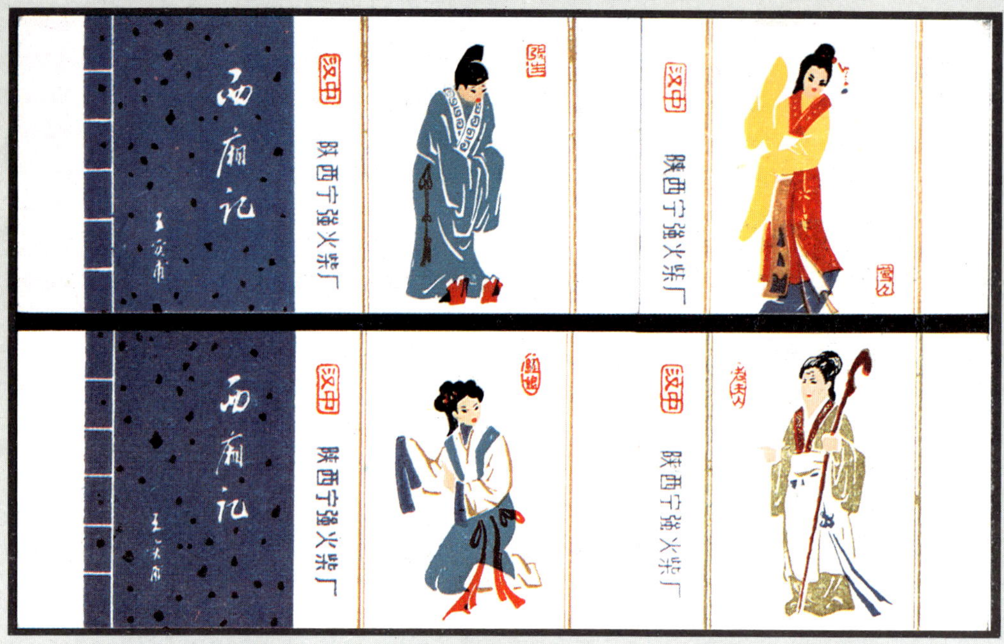

Characters in *Western Chamber*

Authored by the 13th century playwright Wang Shifu, *Western Chamber* is a play recounting the love story between the young scholar Zhang Junrui and Cui Yingying, daughter of a court official. This set presents the main protagonists in the play.

Made in Hanzhong, Shaanxi Province

107 mm x 50 mm

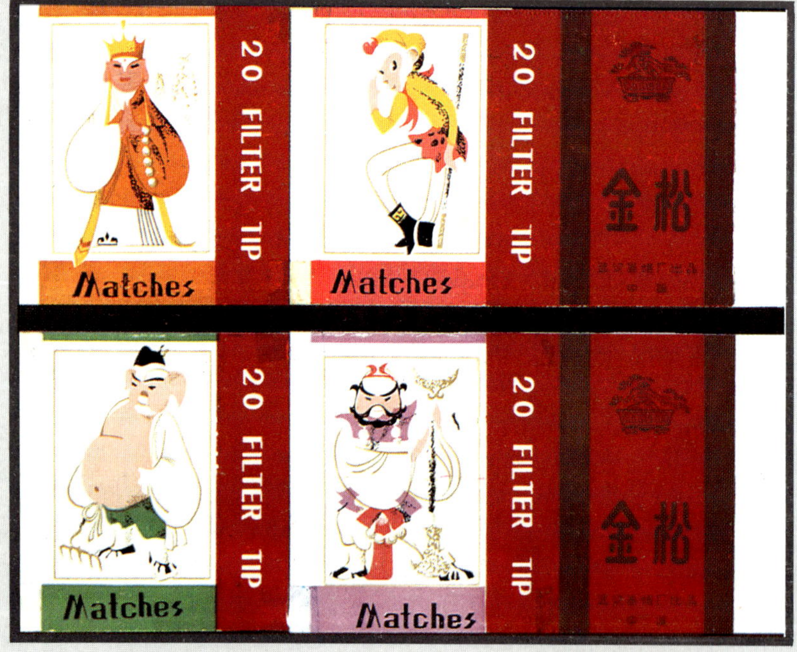

Characters in *Journey to the West*

Journey to the West, written by Wu Cheng'en (c. 1500—1582), is a mythological novel based on the historical fact and many relevant folk tales about the Tang Dynasty monk Xuan Zang's travel to India to fetch Buddhist sutras. The heroes of the novel include Xuan Zang, Monkey, Friar Sand and Pig (clockwise), all of whom have infinite magic powers.

Made in Wuhan, Hubei Province

77 mm x 44 mm

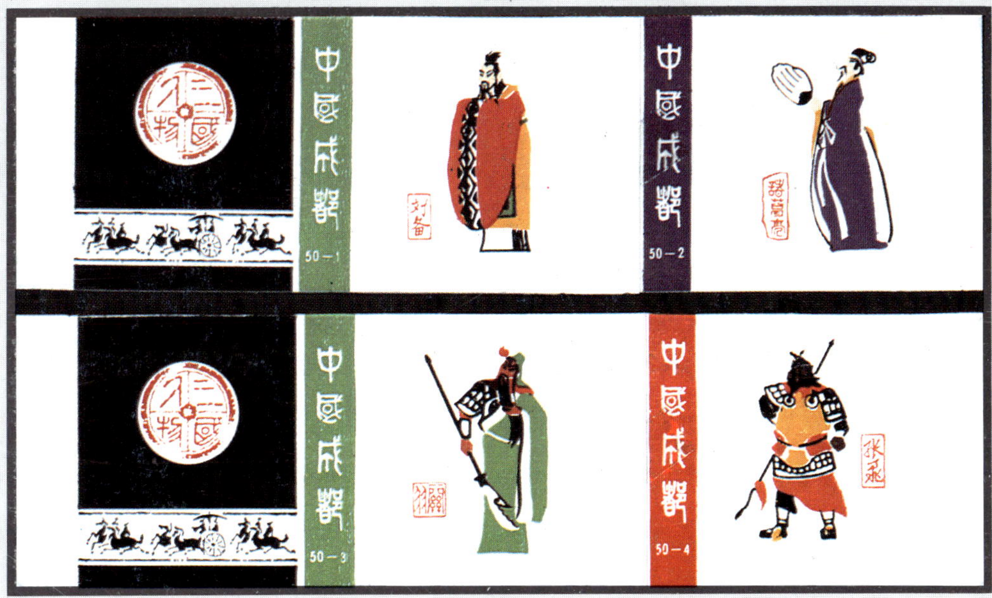

Characters in *Romance of the Three Kingdoms*

Written by Luo Guanzhong (c. 1330—1400) in the mid 14th century, *Romance of the Three Kingdoms* realistically describes the social turmoils of the late Han Dynasty (A.D. 3rd century). The high-quality novel also depicts the struggle for domination among the three separate kingdoms—Wei, Shu and Wu. This set illustrates the main characters from the Shu Kingdom (clockwise): Liu Bei, Zhuge Liang, Zhang Fei, and Guan Yu.

Made in Chengdu, Sichuan Province

106 mm x 46 mm

Characters in *Outlaws of the Marsh*

A famous novel authored by Shi Nai'an in the late 14th century, *Outlaws of the Marsh* portrays the peasant insurrection in the early 12th century. Representatives of the 108 peasant heroes described in the novel are shown (clockwise): Song Jiang, Wu Yong, Lin Chong, Lu Zhishen, Wu Song, and Li Kui.

Made in Heze, Shandong Province

46 mm x 33 mm

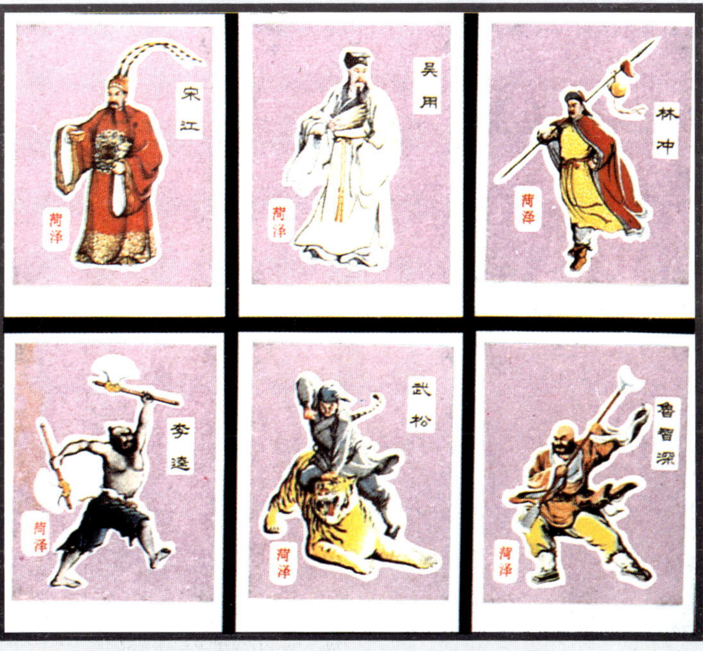

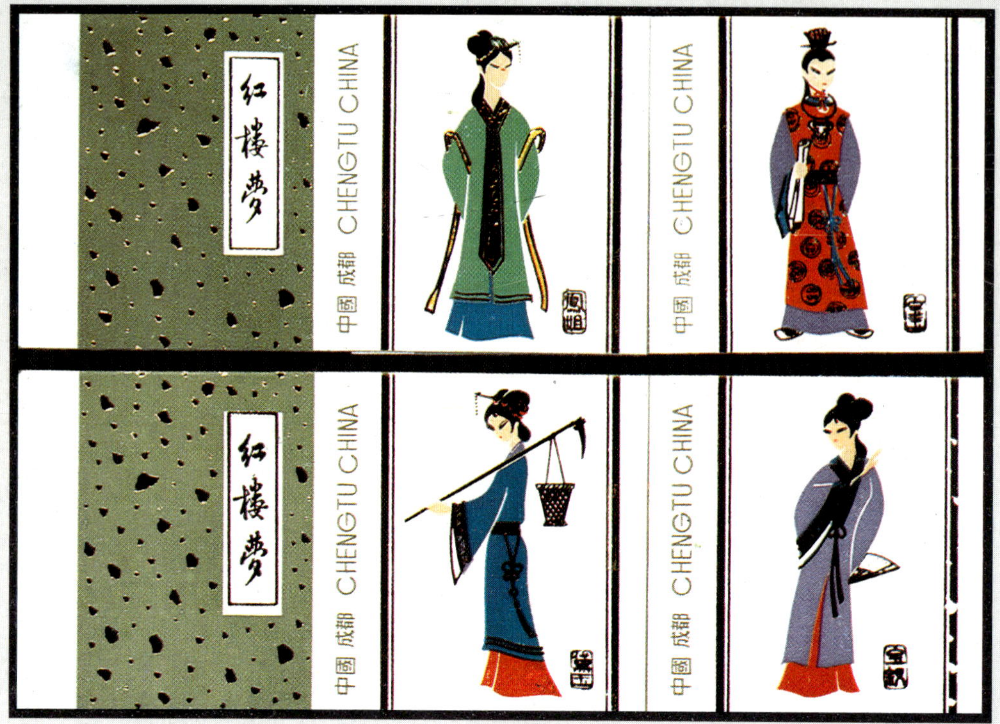

Characters in *A Dream of Red Mansions*

A Dream of Red Mansions, written by Cao Xueqin (?—1763) in the mid 18th century, takes as its central theme the tragic love between Jia Baoyu and Lin Daiyu. The novel lays bare the debauchery, corruption and internal strife of the feudal aristocracy and extols the rebellious spirit of the young people from the landlord and the lower social strata. The novel marks the peak artistic accomplishment in the development of the Chinese classical novel.

This set presents four of the main characters of the novel (clockwise): Wang Xifeng, Jia Baoyu, Xue Baochai, and Lin Daiyu.

Made in Chengdu, Sichuan Province

92 mm x 51 mm

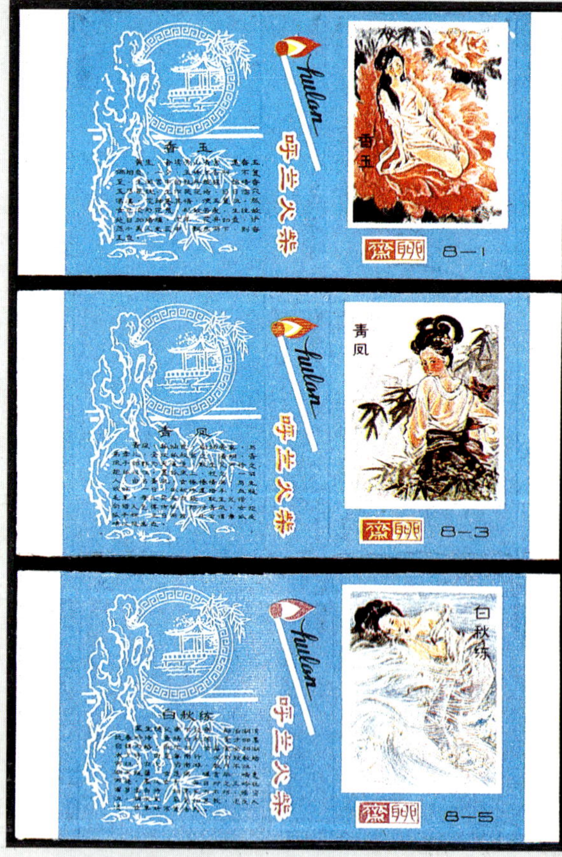

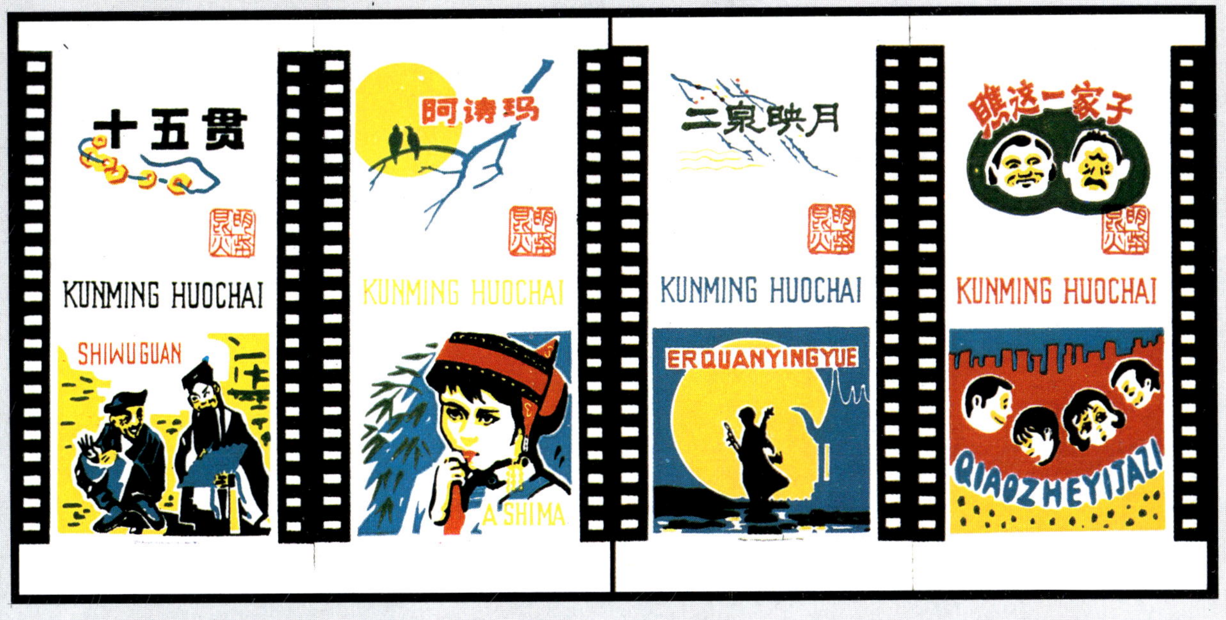

Movie Photos

The movie industry in China has witnessed a fairly rapid development in past years. Chinese movies have a distinctive national style rooted in Chinese folk art.

From left to right: *Fifteen Strings of Cash,* based on the stage production of a local opera; *Ashima,* a musical feature film based on mythological tales; *Two Strings Mirroring the Moon,* a musical feature film; and *Story About a Family,* a comic feature film.

Made in Kunming, Yunan Province

98 mm x 51 mm

Strange Tales of Liaozhai

Strange Tales of Liaozhai is a collection of short stories written by Pu Songling (1640—1715) in the late 17th century. In these four hundred stories, the author satirizes the evils of the society and attacks the feudal civil examination system and marriage system with tales about foxes and ghosts.

From top to bottom: Fragrant Jade, Green Phoenix, and Bai Qiulian.

Made in Hulan, Heilongjiang Province

94 mm x 45 mm

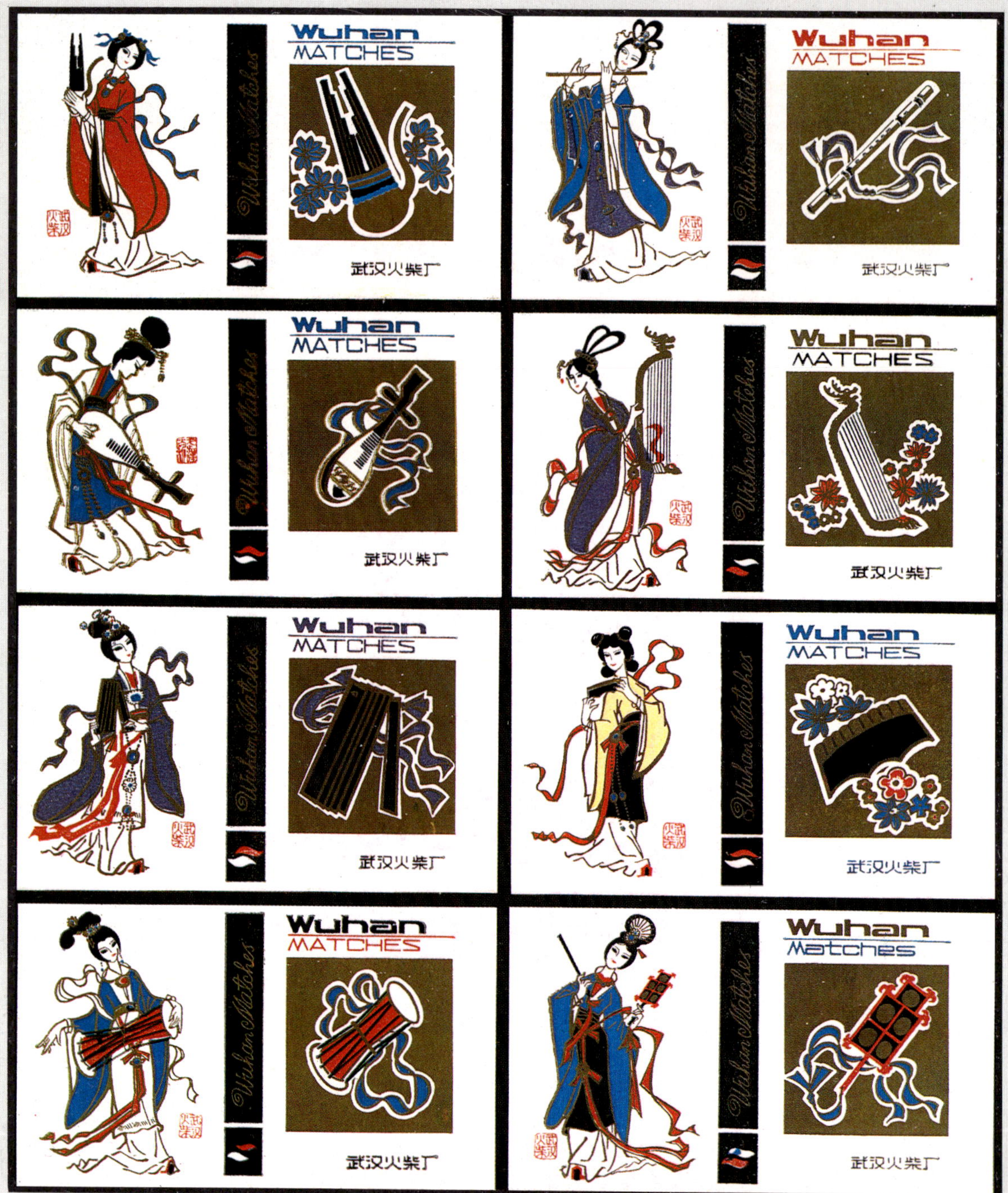

Ancient Musical Instruments

Chinese folk musical instruments may be classified into many types. They have served as witness to the cultural development of the various nationalities in China and as a vehicle of the cultural exchanges among these nationalities.

From top to bottom, left column: *sheng* (a reed pipe wind instrument), *pipa* (a plucked string instrument with a fretted fingerboard), castanets, slim-waist drum; from top to bottom, right column: *hengdi* (flute), *konghou* (an ancient plucked stringed instrument), *paidi* (flutes in series), and gong chimes.

Made in Wuhan, Hubei Province
90 mm x 51 mm

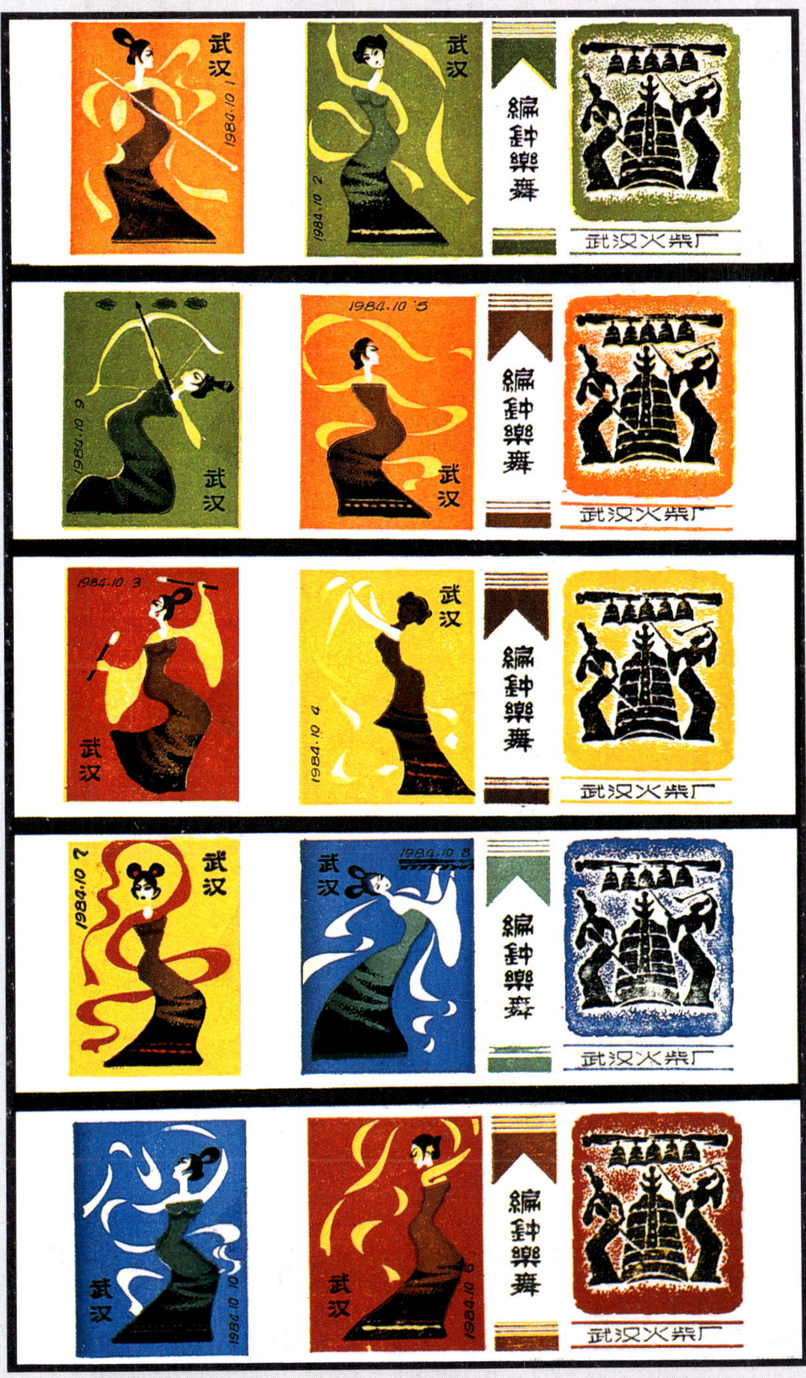

Bianzhong Bell Dance

Bianzhong bells are an ancient Chinese percussion instrument made of bronze. The bells, which vary in size, are hung on wooden supporters in a certain order to give forth melodious and sonorous sound when struck.

The *bianzhong* bell dance is choreographed in the ancient style and accompanied by *bianzhong* bells, reviving scenes over two thousand years old.

Made in Wuhan, Hubei Province

101 mm x 46 mm

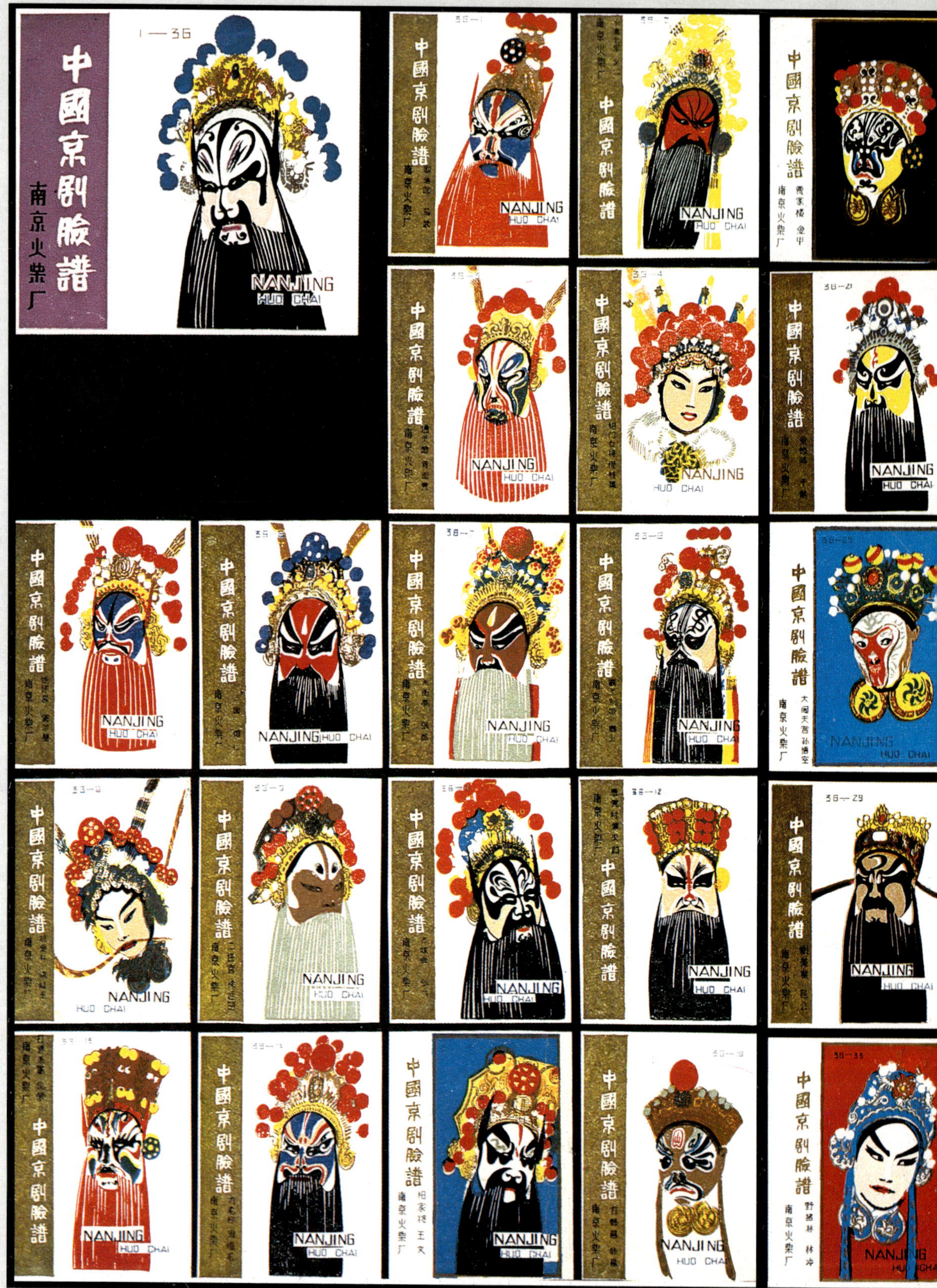
1—36
中國京劇臉譜
南京火柴厂
NANJING
HUO CHAI
大闹天宫 孙悟空
野猪林 林冲
相家楼 王文

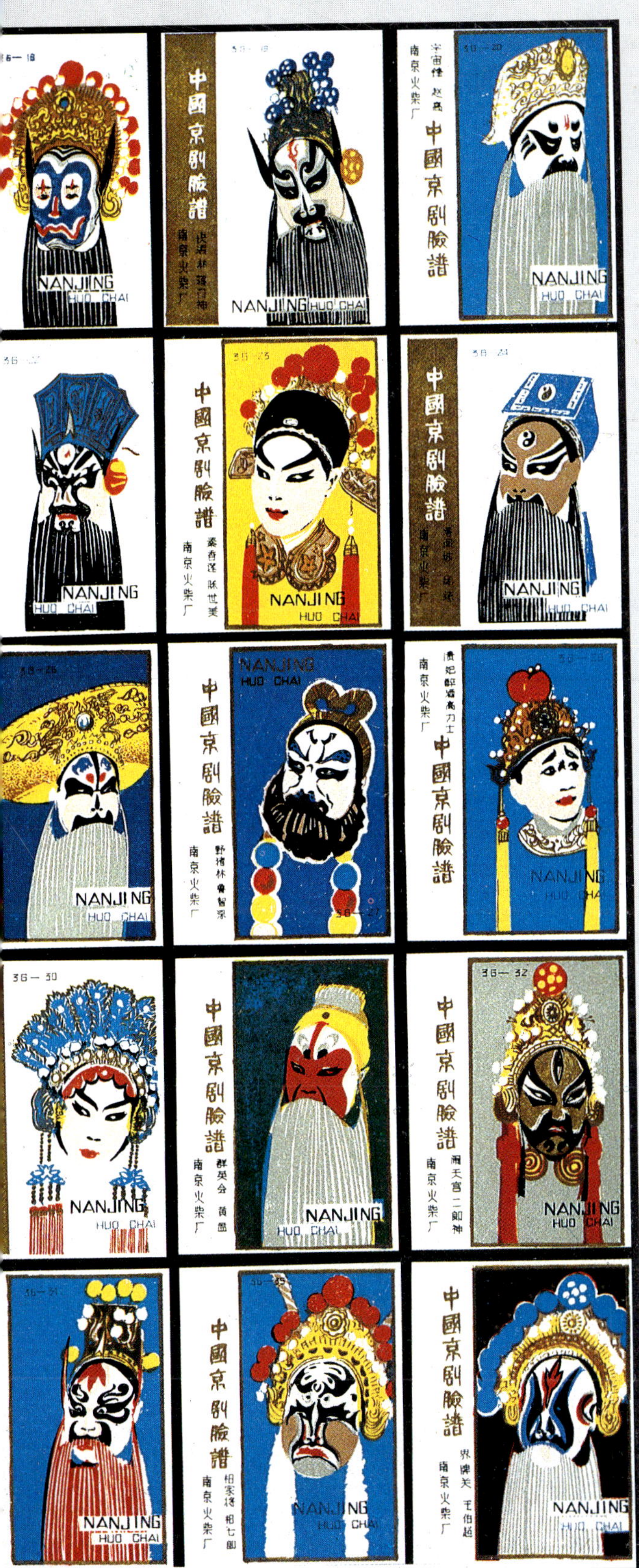

Stage Masks

Stage masks are used in traditional Chinese operas to create a sense of exaggeration. Each mask, designed to embody a symbolic meaning, reflects the temperament and idiosyncracies of the different characters.

The thirty-six stage masks here portray the different characters in traditional Chinese operas.

Made in Nanjing, Jiangsu Province

70 mm x 63 mm, 48 mm x 36 mm

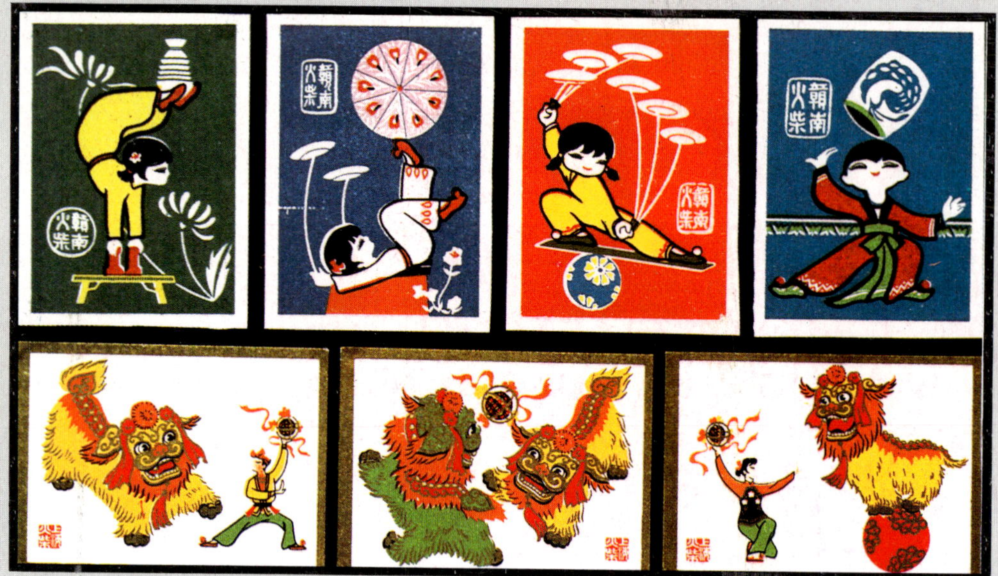

Acrobatics

Chinese acrobatics began in the 20th century B.C. and has continuously developed into a unique art form with a distinctive national style over the centuries.

Above: balancing bowls; juggling an umbrella with the feet; plate spinning; jar tricks; and lion dance.

Below: wire walking; exercises with a long-handle sword; diabolo play; small springboard stunts; traditional-style conjuring; and balancing on a bicycle.

Made in Ganzhou, Jiangxi Province; Shanghai; and Tianjin

49 mm x 36 mm, 49 mm x 35 mm, 105 mm x 53 mm

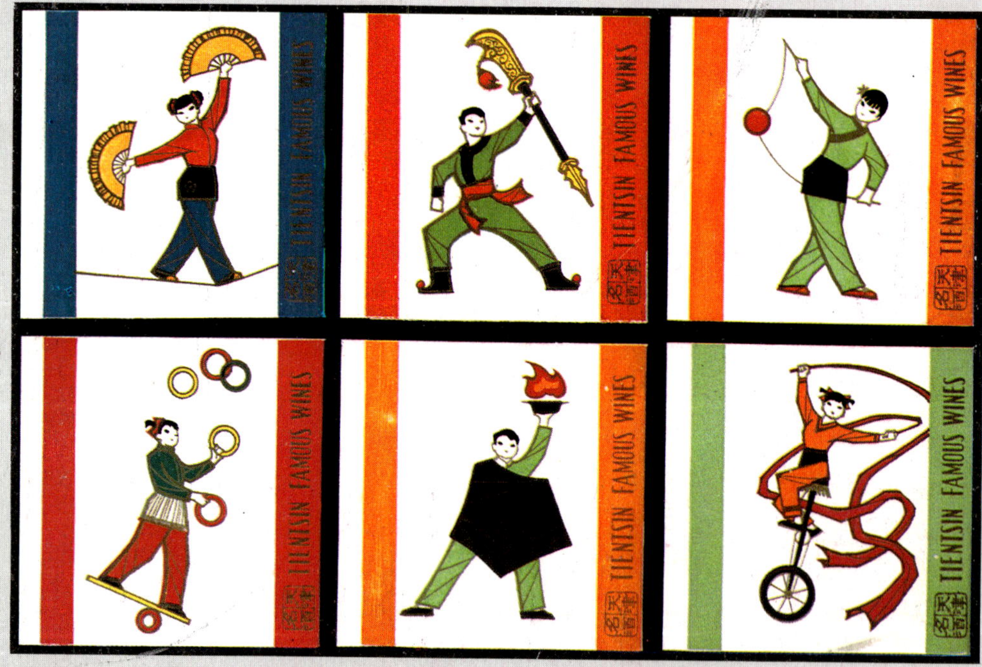

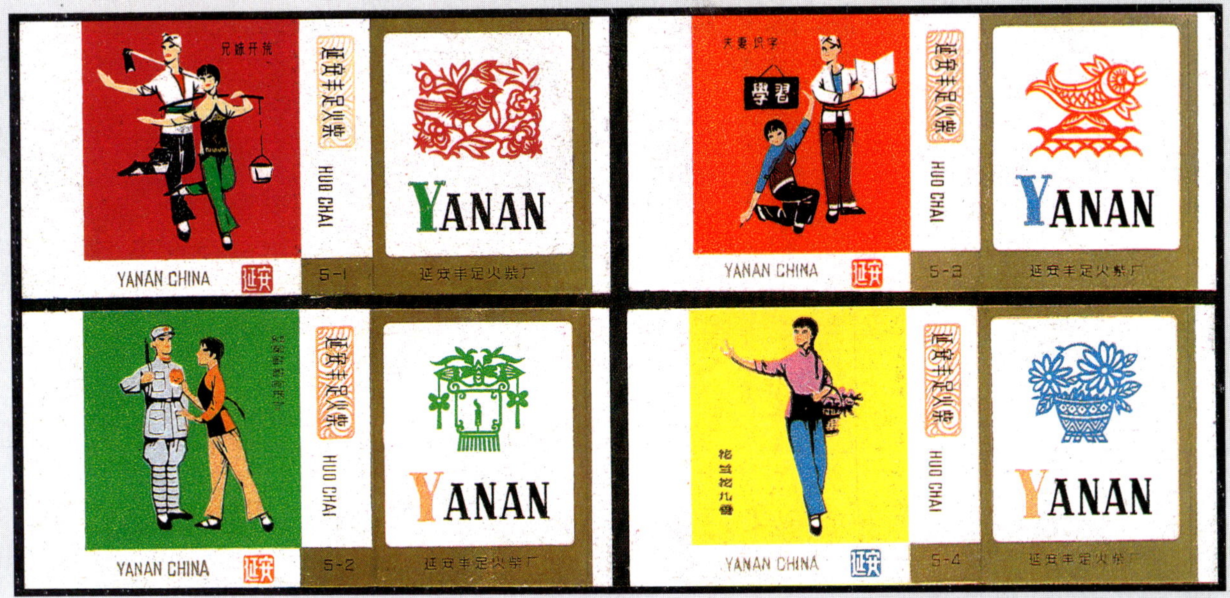

Yangge Opera

New Yangge operas emerged in the Yan'an area of Shaanxi Province along with the pop songs of the early 1940s.

From left, top: *Brother and Sister Together Open Up Waste Land* and *Husband and Wife Learn to Read*. From left, bottom: *The Red Army Brother Is Home* and *The Baskets Are Full of Fragrant Flowers*.

Made in Yan'an, Shaanxi Province

101 mm x 46 mm

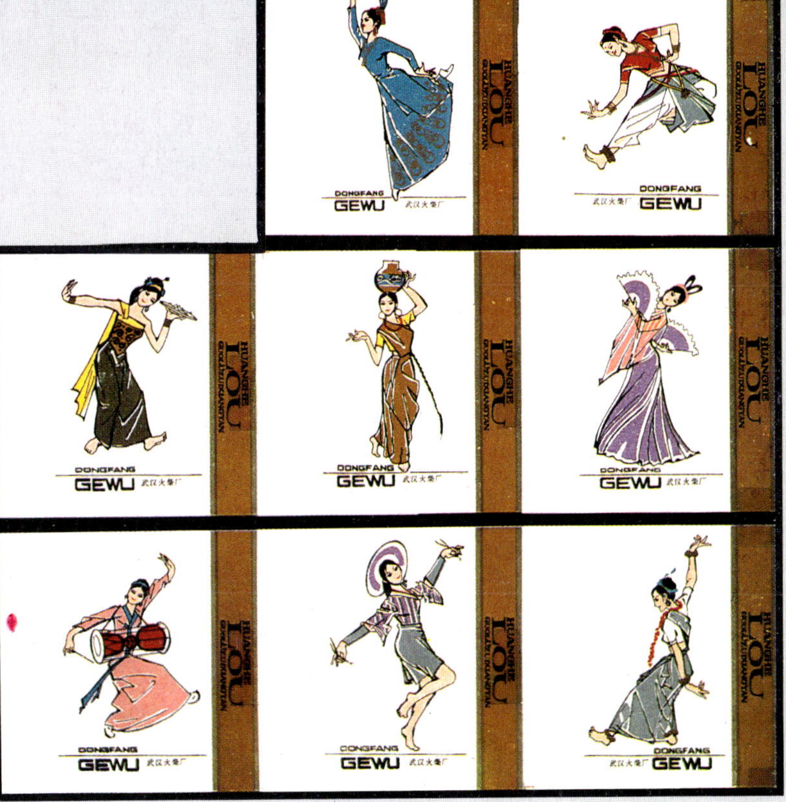

Oriental Dances

This set includes folk dances of different Asian countries. From left, top to bottom: Peacock Dance, Foot Bell Dance, Plate Dance, Jar Dance, Fan Dance, Drum Dance, Rice Transplanter's Dance, and Foot Bell Dance.

Made in Wuhan, Hubei Province

74 mm x 45 mm

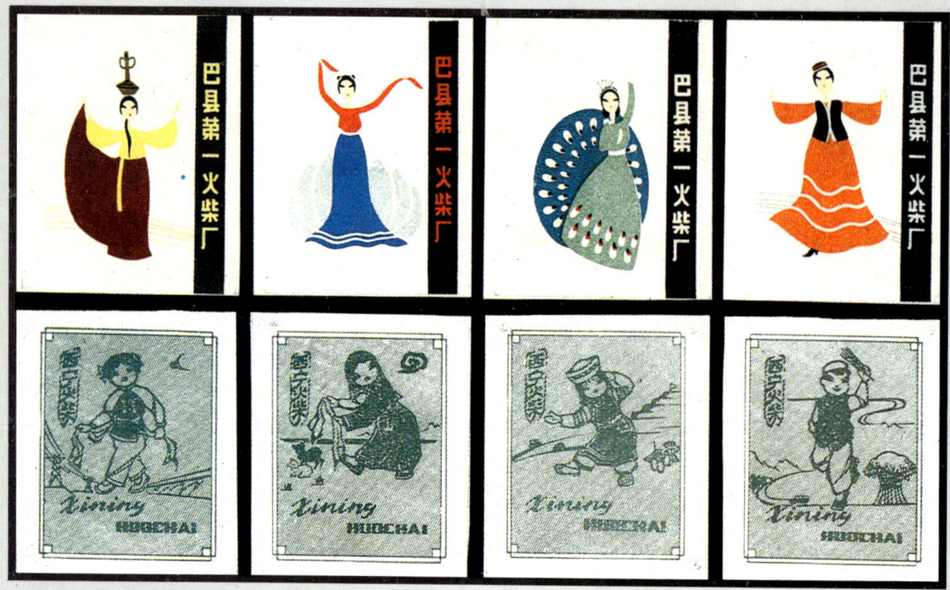

Folk Dances

Chinese folk dances are simultaneously colourful and distinctive of national customs.

Clockwise: Jar Dance of the Korean nationality, Lotus Dance of the Han nationality, Peacock Dance of the Dai nationality, Cup Dance of the Mongolian nationality, Flower Dance of the Hui nationality, Solo Dance of the Salar nationality, Hada Dance of the Tibetan nationality, and Yangge Dance of the Han nationality.

Made in Baxian, Sichuan Province; and Xining, Qinghai Province

44 mm x 34 mm, 42 mm x 35 mm

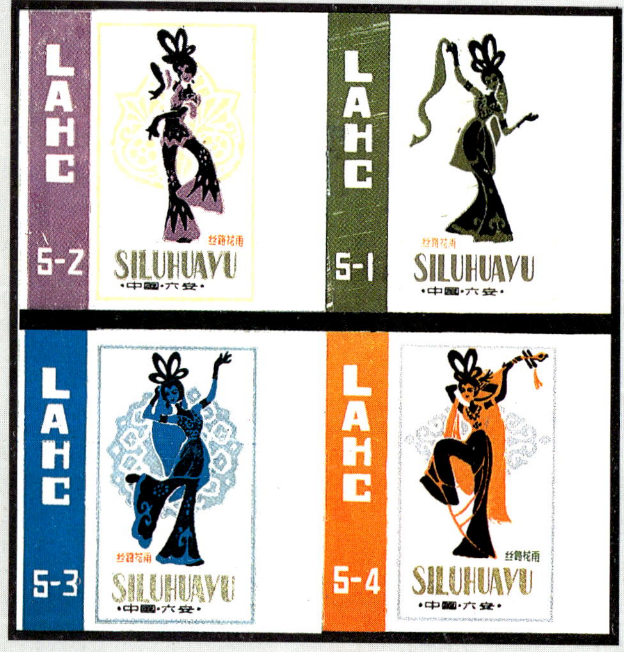

Along the Silk Road

Along the Silk Road is a dance drama set in the background of the ancient Silk Road. It depicts friendly exchanges between the people of China and other countries, reproducing the customs of that time. This set of covers presents some of the stage photos of Yingniang, the protagonist in the drama.

Made in Liu'an, Anhui Province

101 mm x 55 mm

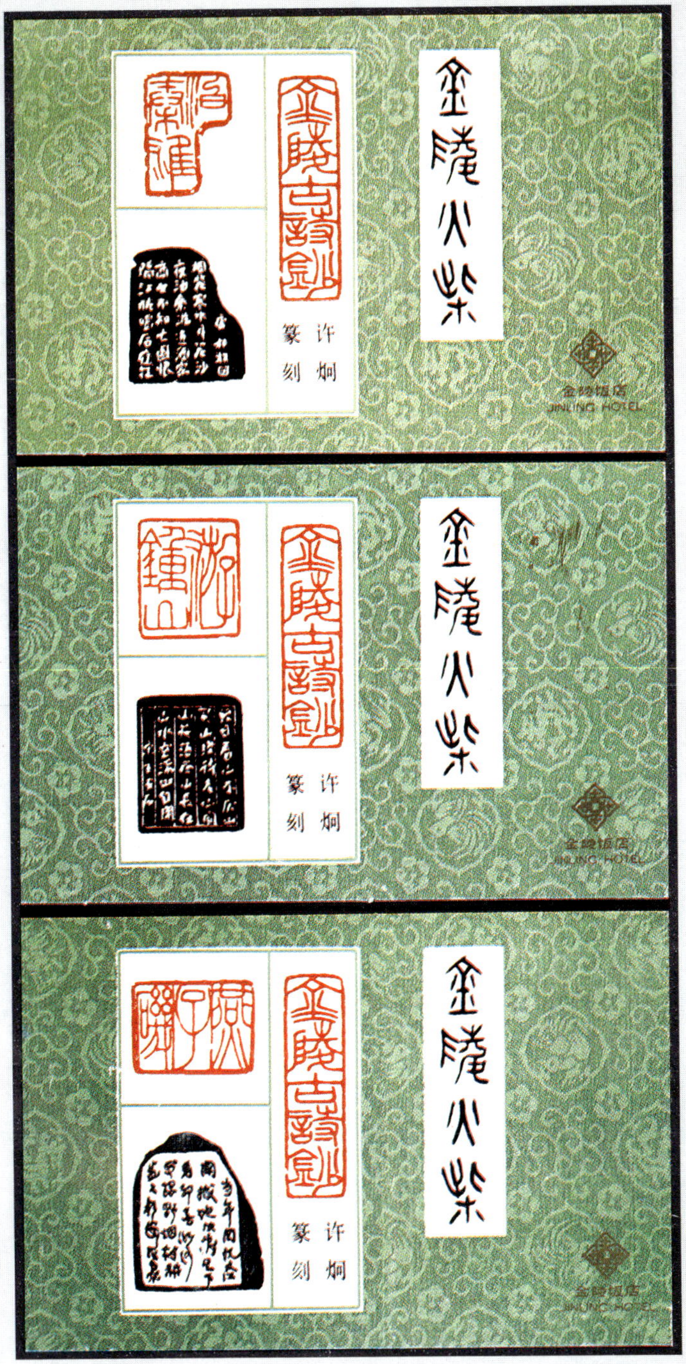

Nanjing Classical Poems Engraved in Seals

Seal engraving is a traditional Chinese art form. Reverse characters are engraved on stone or metal surfaces and then printed on paper for general appreciation.

This group presents a few poems composed by ancient Chinese poets.

From top to bottom: *Mooring at the Qinhuai River, Visiting Mount Zhongshan,* and *Yanzi Hill.*

Made in Nanjing, Jiangsu Province

125 mm x 83 mm

Engraved Seals

Engraved seals are divided into intaglio and relief. The artistic value of these seals is judged mainly by their calligraphic style, quality of wording and cutting.

All the seals included here, except for the first one, are engraved in intaglio. The words are: Cascade in Goose Hill, Sunset at Dongtai, Flopping Fish on the South China Sea, and A Heavenly Steed Soaring Across the Skies.

Made in Liuzhou, Guangxi Zhuang Autonomous Region

44 mm x 35 mm

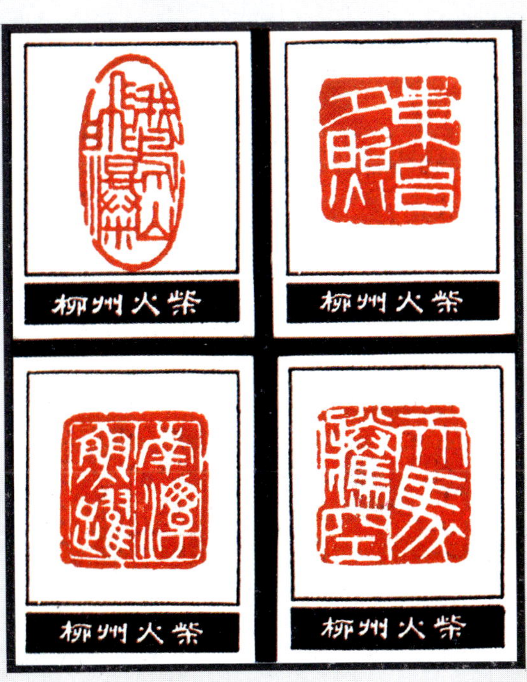

Calligraphy

Calligraphy is a traditional Chinese art form. Over three thousand years of development, this art was continuously enriched. Many different schools, styles and calligraphers emerged.

This set presents four eminent calligraphers, who belonged to the four most representative schools of calligraphy in ancient China.

From top to bottom: Wang Xizhi (321—379), Yan Zhenqing (709—785), Liu Gongquan (778—865), and Ouyang Xun (557—641).

Made in Beijing
102 mm x 56 mm

Brick Sculptures of the Han Dynasty

Brick sculptures are unearthed mainly from the tombs of the Eastern Han Dynasty (25—220). These sculptures, cut in bas relief, generally tell a story or describe an event in life.

Clockwise: Driving a Cart, Fish Dance, Striking a Bell, and Pitching Arrows into a Pot (an ancient game).

Made in Shanghai 99 mm x 50 mm

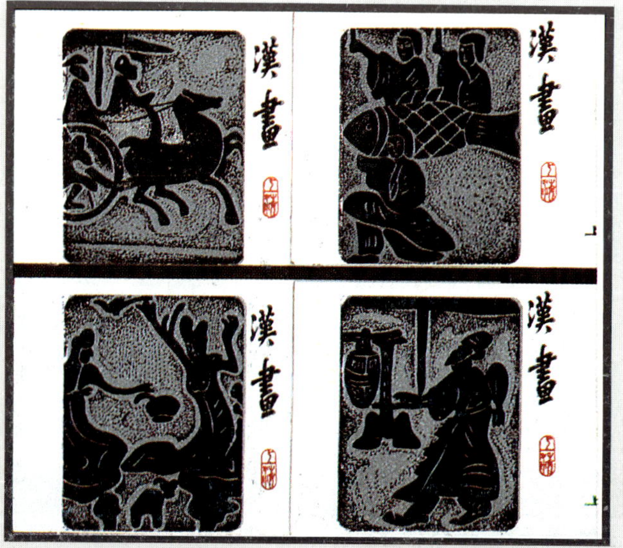

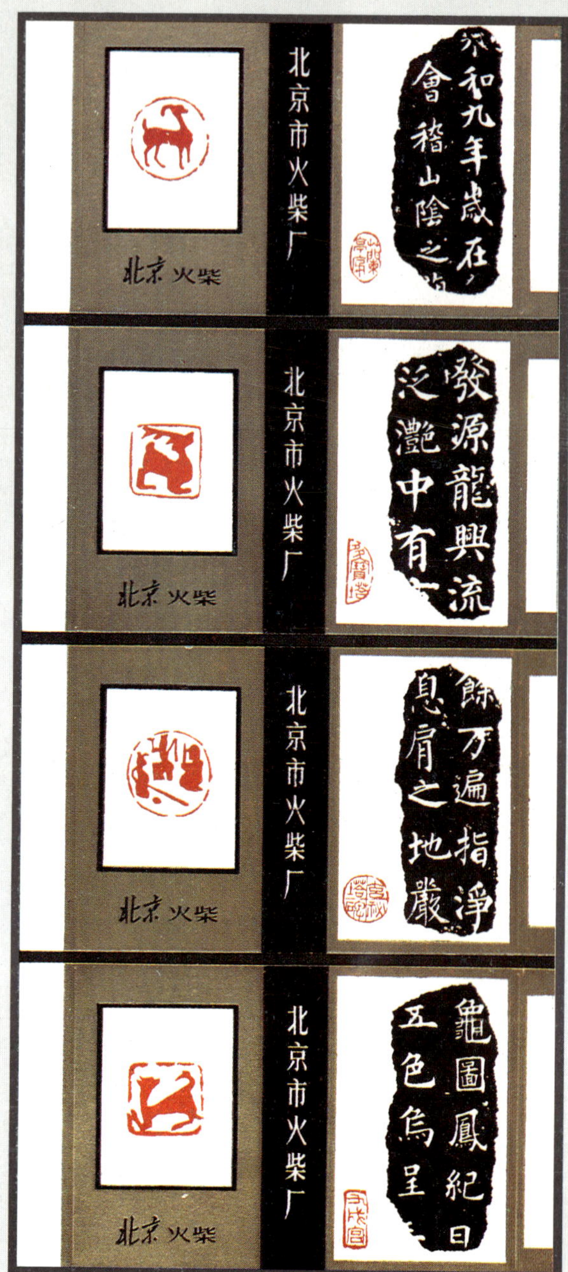

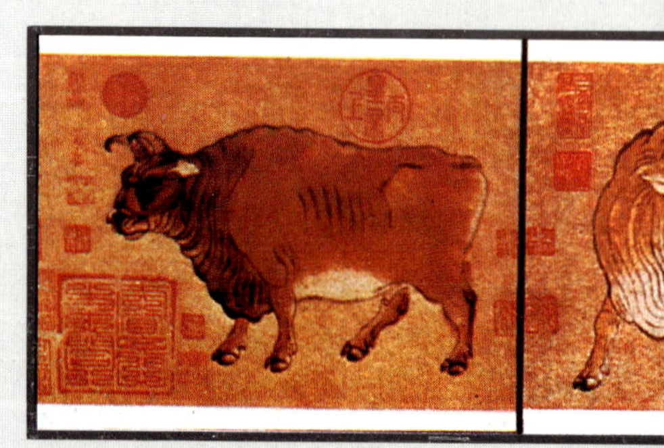

Jinling Painting

Jinling, called Jianye in ancient times, is the present-day city of Nanjing. Numerous men of letters and distinguished scholars in the past left an enormous legacy of poems and paintings on their visits to the place.

This set presents a four-piece collage entitled *Summer Scene at Jianye.*

Made in Nanjing, Jiangsu Province

125 mm x 82 mm

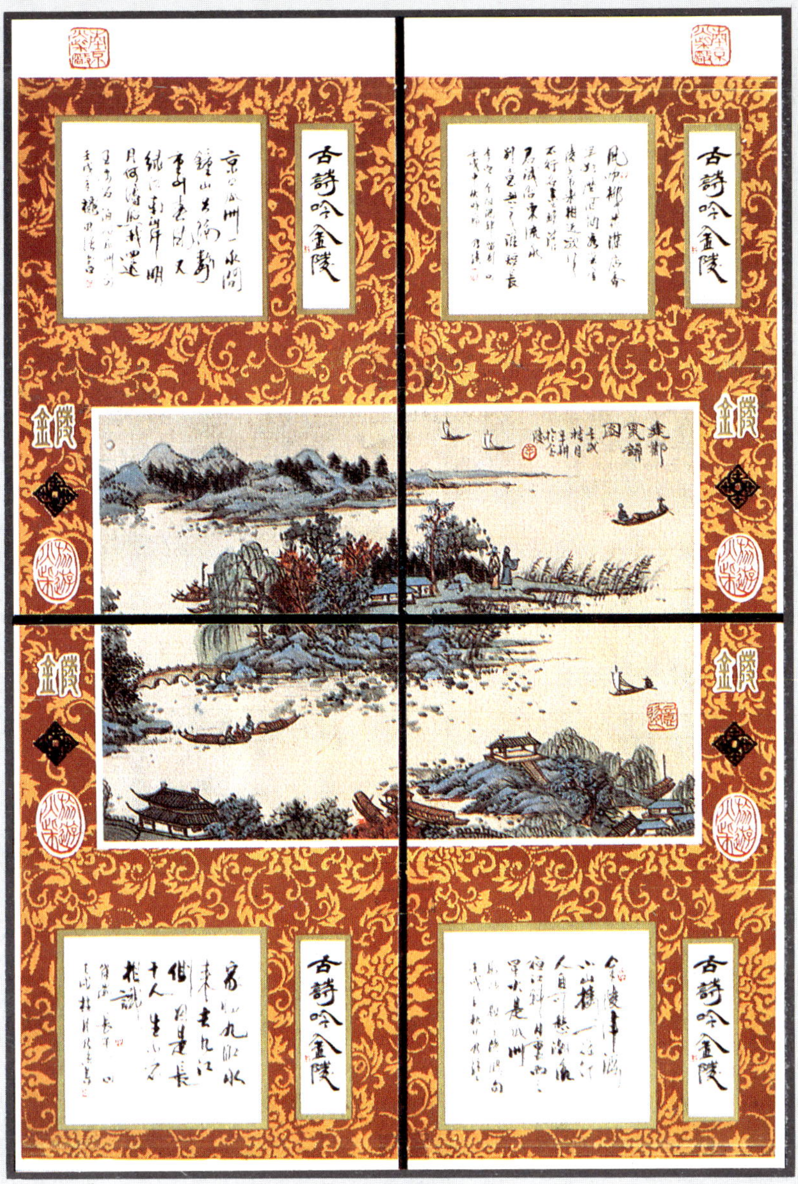

Five-Ox Painting

The five-ox painting composed by the Tang Dynasty painter Han Huang (723—787) is a *piece de resistance* handed down over the centuries. The painting, which is 20.8 cm high and 139.8 cm long, portrays five oxen. All are extremely life-like.

The five-ox painting presented here is a five-piece collage.

Made in Shanghai

104 mm x 52 mm

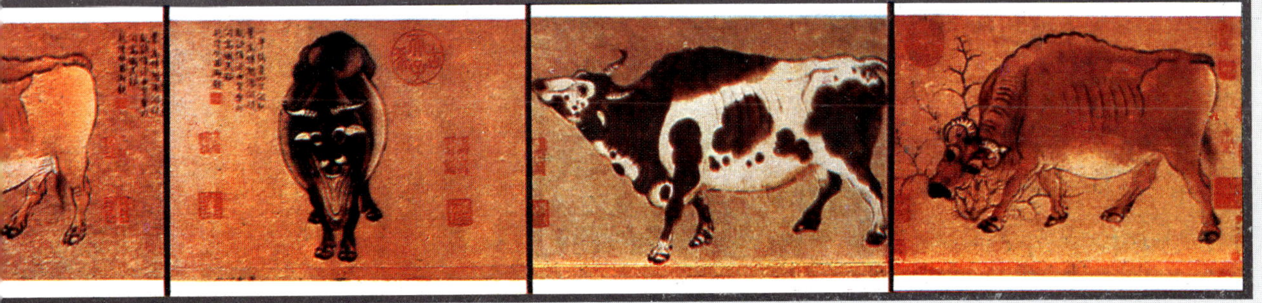

Traditional Chinese Painting

Traditional Chinese painting generally concerns such content as human figures, landscape, birds and flowers. Painting styles include free-sketch and meticulous styles, both of which are expressed in a myriad of techniques. Traditional Chinese painting stresses form in order to bring out the spirit of the subject matter.

This set of covers includes paintings by such modern Chinese painters as Xu Beihong, Wu Zuoren, Li Kuchan, Li Keran and Huang Yongyu.

Made in Nanjing, Jiangsu Province

115 mm x 53 mm

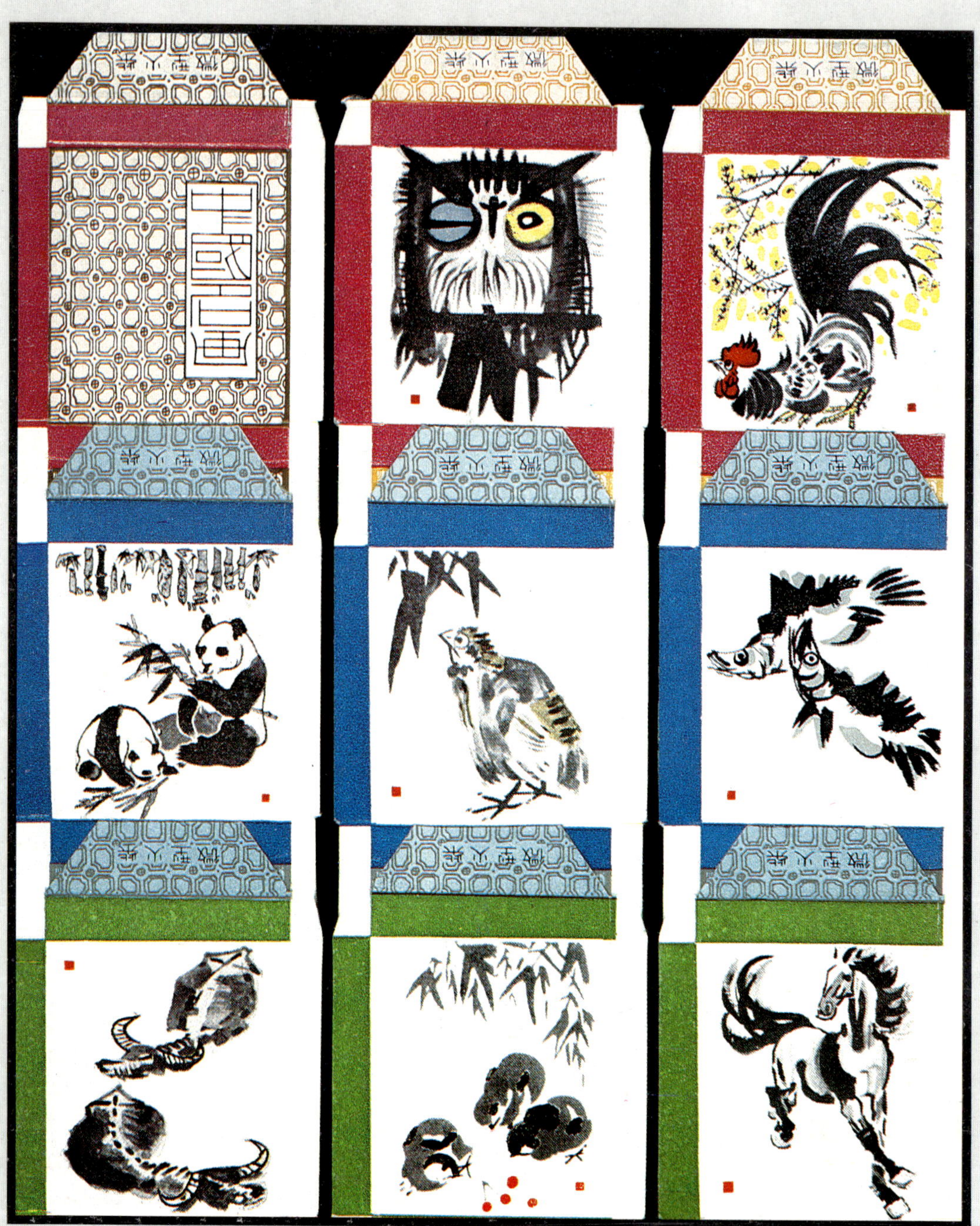

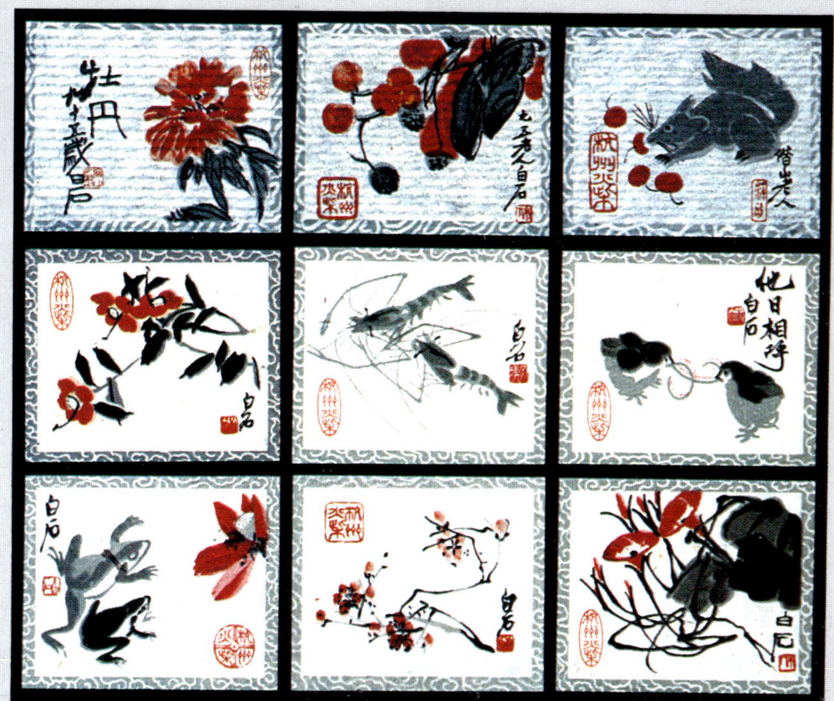

Paintings by Qi Baishi

An outstanding painter in modern Chinese history, Qi Baishi (1863—1957) is noted for his unique painting style. His paintings, which are composed in either free-sketch or meticulous style, use both the sharp black and white contrasts of ink and a profusion of red and violet colours.

This set includes nine of Qi Baishi's paintings.

Made in Hangzhou, Zhejiang Province

43 mm x 34 mm

Paintings by Xu Beihong

A famous Chinese painter and art educator, Xu Beihong (1894—1953) was well versed in both oil and traditional Chinese paintings. His influence has been felt in art circles both in China and abroad. His paintings, such as human portraits, landscapes, birds and flowers are extremely life-like, but he was best known for his paintings of horses.

Made in Fuzhou, Fujian Province

43 mm x 34 mm

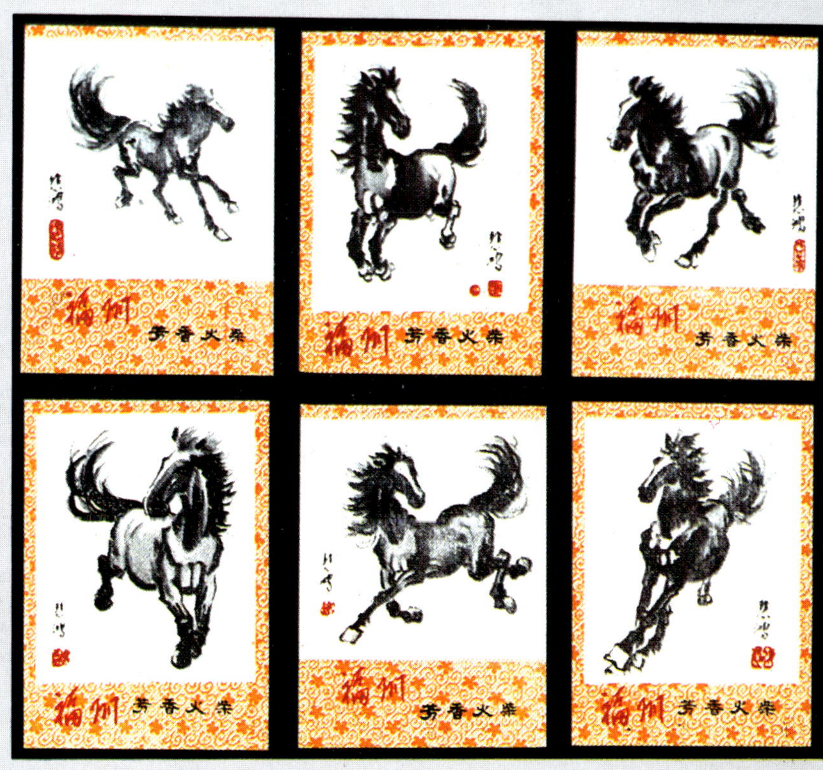

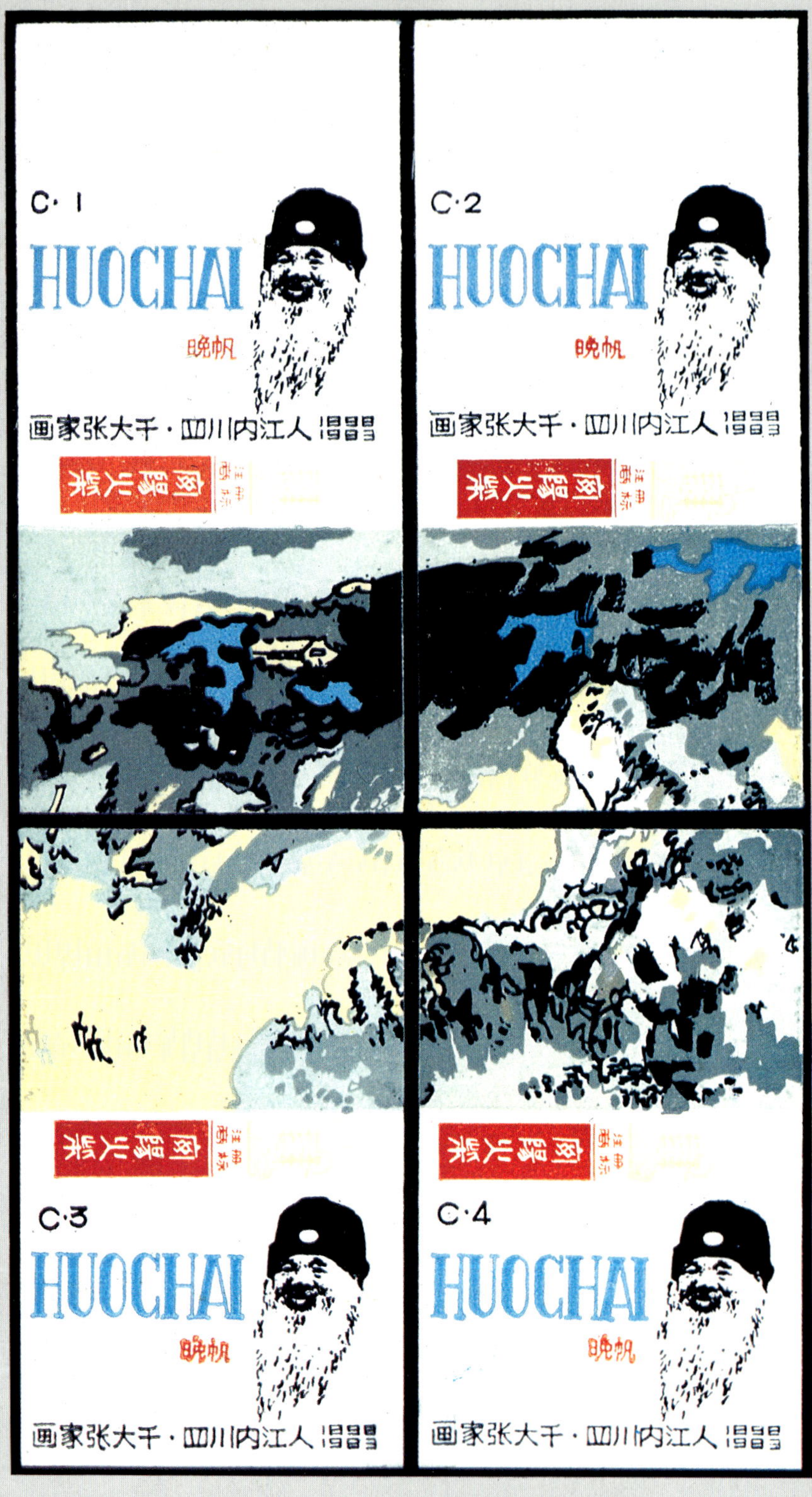

Paintings by Zhang Daqian

Zhang Daqian (1899—1983) was an outstanding Chinese painter who excelled in landscape paintings, portrait paintings, and bird-and-flower paintings. All his paintings are tinged with a touch of classical simplicity, gracefulness, lucidity and are at the same time full of variations. In his late years, he adopted European painting techniques, perfecting his colour-splashed landscape paintings.

This set presents one of Zhang Daqian's four-piece collage landscape paintings entitled *Sails at Dusk*.

Made in Anyang, Henan Province

101 mm x 50 mm

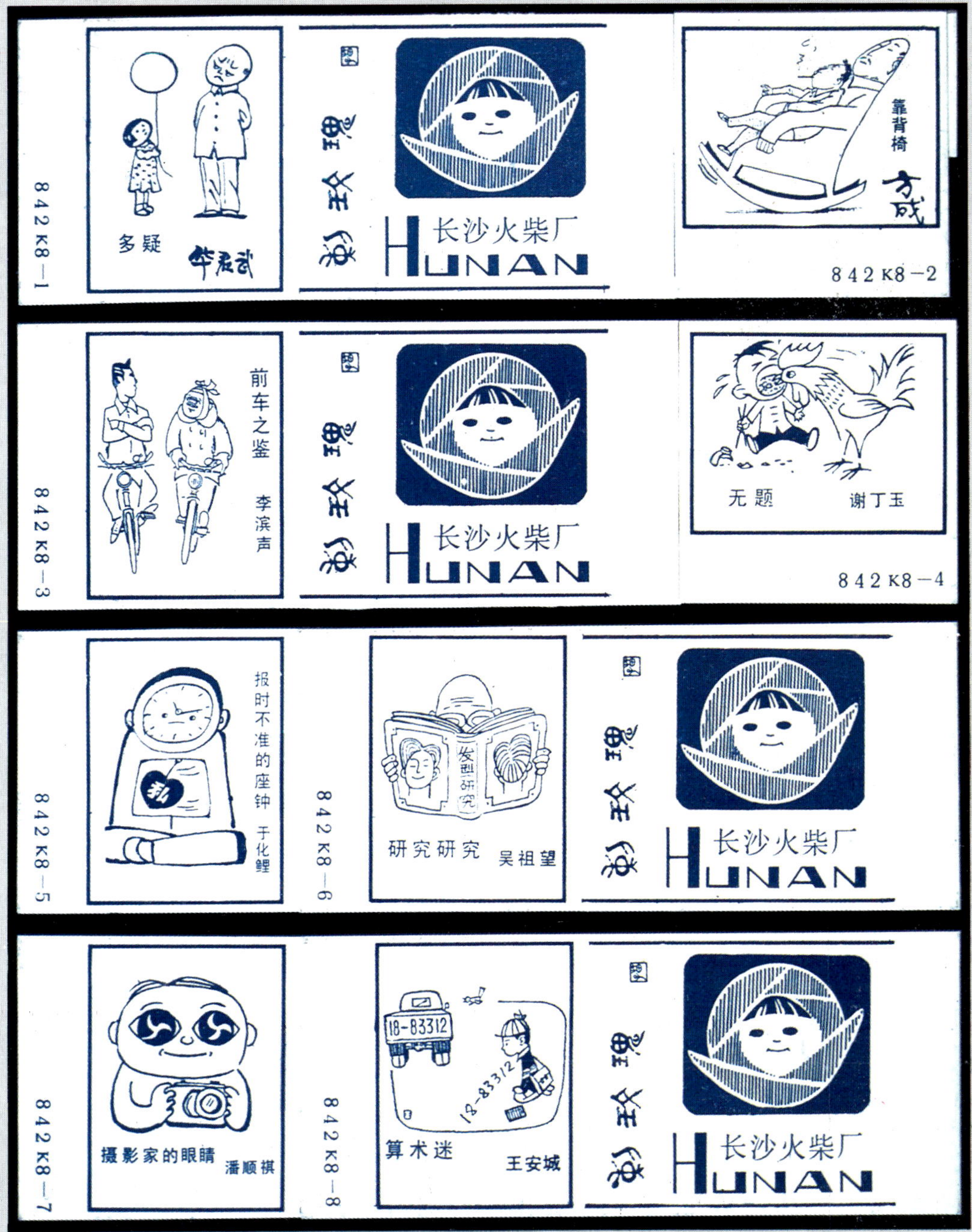

Thorny Roses—a Collection of Cartoons

In cartoons, the artist generally employs devices such as exaggeration, analogy, symbolization and parable to create a sense of humour and satire in a concise and vivid style.

This set contains eight cartoons selected from the works of such contemporary Chinese cartoonists as Hua Junwu, Fang Cheng, and Li Binsheng.

Made in Changsha, Hunan Province
103 mm x 43 mm

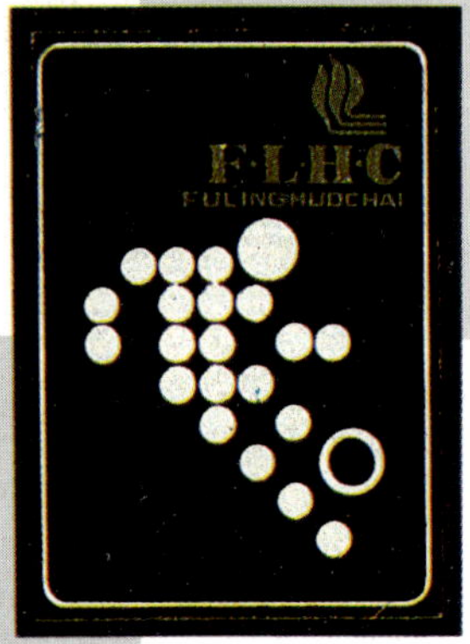

Sports

For the last three decades, sports in China have developed rapidly and made definite achievements. China has reversed its backward position in the sports world to become an athletic power in Asia and among advanced nations. In the past few years, Chinese athletes have dared to compete with formidable opponents and made great strides in many events, demonstrating the superb potential and prospects of Chinese athletes.

This section gives a general overview on the historical development and the present situation of Chinese physical culture in some important sports fields. The following matchbox covers show succinct composition, bright colours and a strong sense of motion.

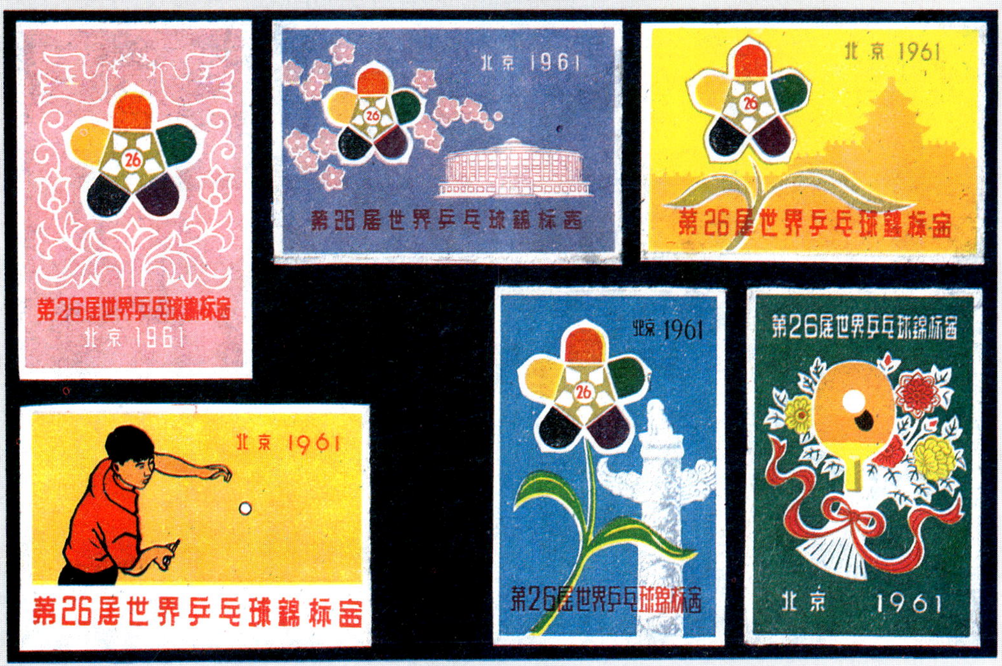

The 26th World Table Tennis Championships

In the 26th World Table Tennis Championships held in 1961, Chinese players won many titles. From then on, China has held the leading position in world table tennis. This group of matchbox covers is designed for the commemoration of the event.

Made in Beijing

51 mm x 35 mm

Vigorous Women's Volleyball

With energetic spirit, the Chinese women's volleyball team has carried off three championship titles of the Third World Cup Women's Volleyball Tournaments, the Ninth World Women's Volleyball Championships, and the 23rd Olympic Games in succession.

This group of matchbox covers is designed to co mmemorate the three championships secured by the women's volleyball team.

Made in Kunming, Yunnan Province

43 mm x 32 mm

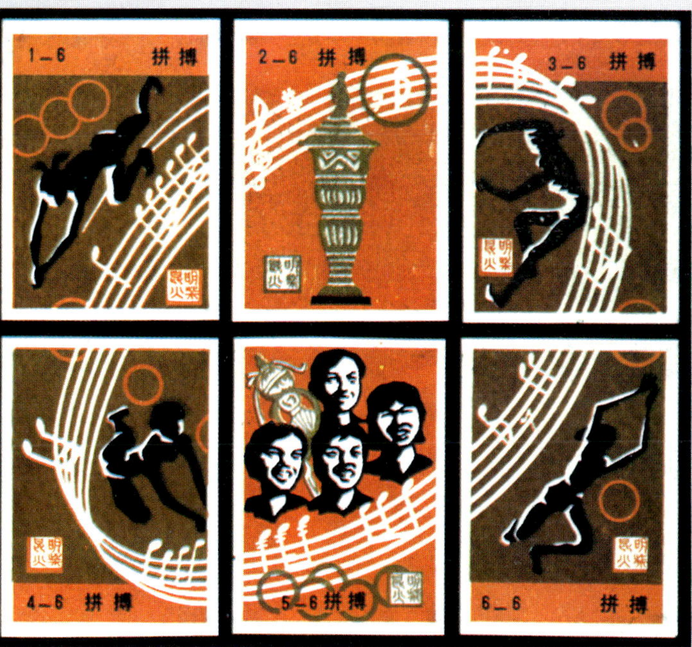

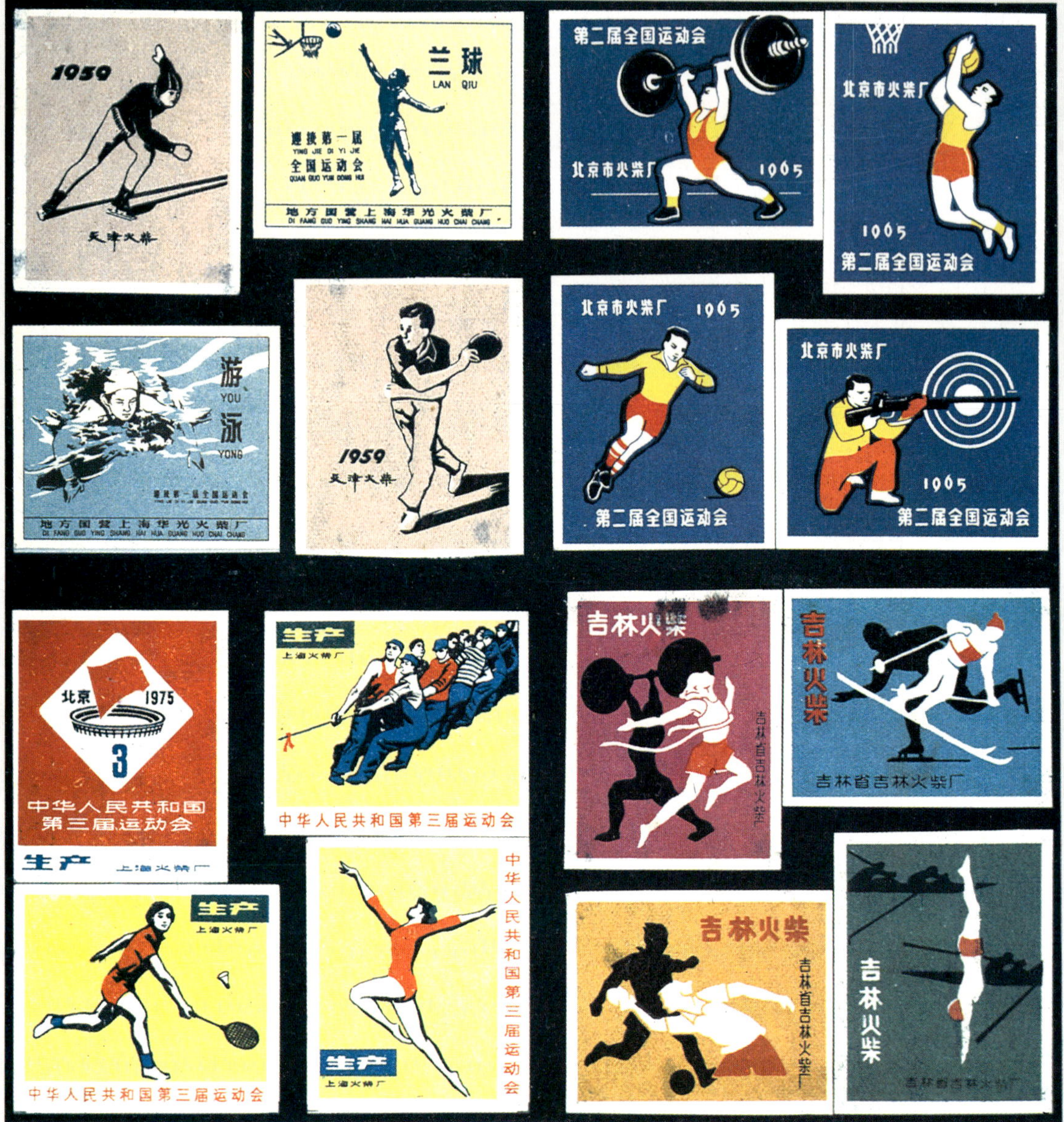

National Games

The Chinese government calls on its citizens to: "Promote physical culture and build up the people's health." The national mass sports activities and the five national games have effectively fostered the development of sports and raised the levels of competition, laying a solid foundation for China's athletic achievements of the 80s.

The two groups of matchbox covers on these two pages are designed to commemorate the five national games.

Made in Beijing; Shanghai; and Jilin, Jilin Province

43 mm x 36 mm, 43 mm x 35 mm, 42 mm x 34 mm, 42 mm x 33 mm, 105 mm x 52 mm

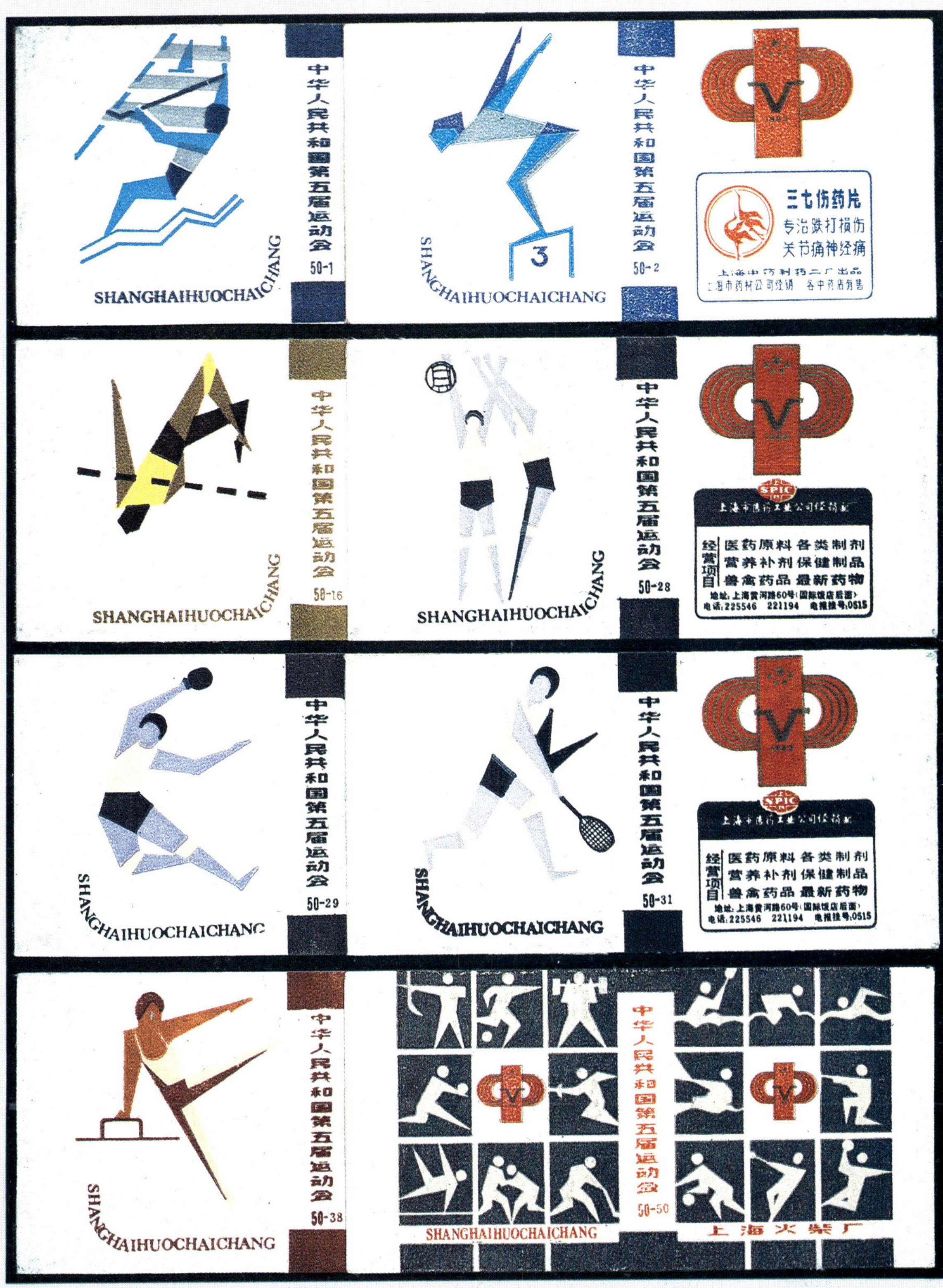
中华人民共和国第五届运动会
50-1
SHANGHAIHUOCHAICHANG
中华人民共和国第五届运动会
50-2
SHANGHAIHUOCHAICHANG
三七伤药片
专治跌打损伤
关节痛神经痛
中华人民共和国第五届运动会
50-16
SHANGHAIHUOCHAICHANG
中华人民共和国第五届运动会
50-28
SHANGHAIHUOCHAICHANG
SPIC
经营项目
医药原料 各类制剂
营养补剂 保健制品
兽禽药品 最新药物
地址：上海黄河路60号（国际饭店后面）
电话：225546 221194
中华人民共和国第五届运动会
50-29
SHANGHAIHUOCHAICHANG
中华人民共和国第五届运动会
50-31
SHANGHAIHUOCHAICHANG
SPIC
经营项目
医药原料 各类制剂
营养补剂 保健制品
兽禽药品 最新药物
地址：上海黄河路60号（国际饭店后面）
电话：225546 221194
中华人民共和国第五届运动会
50-38
SHANGHAIHUOCHAICHANG
中华人民共和国第五届运动会
50-50
SHANGHAIHUOCHAICHANG
上海火柴厂

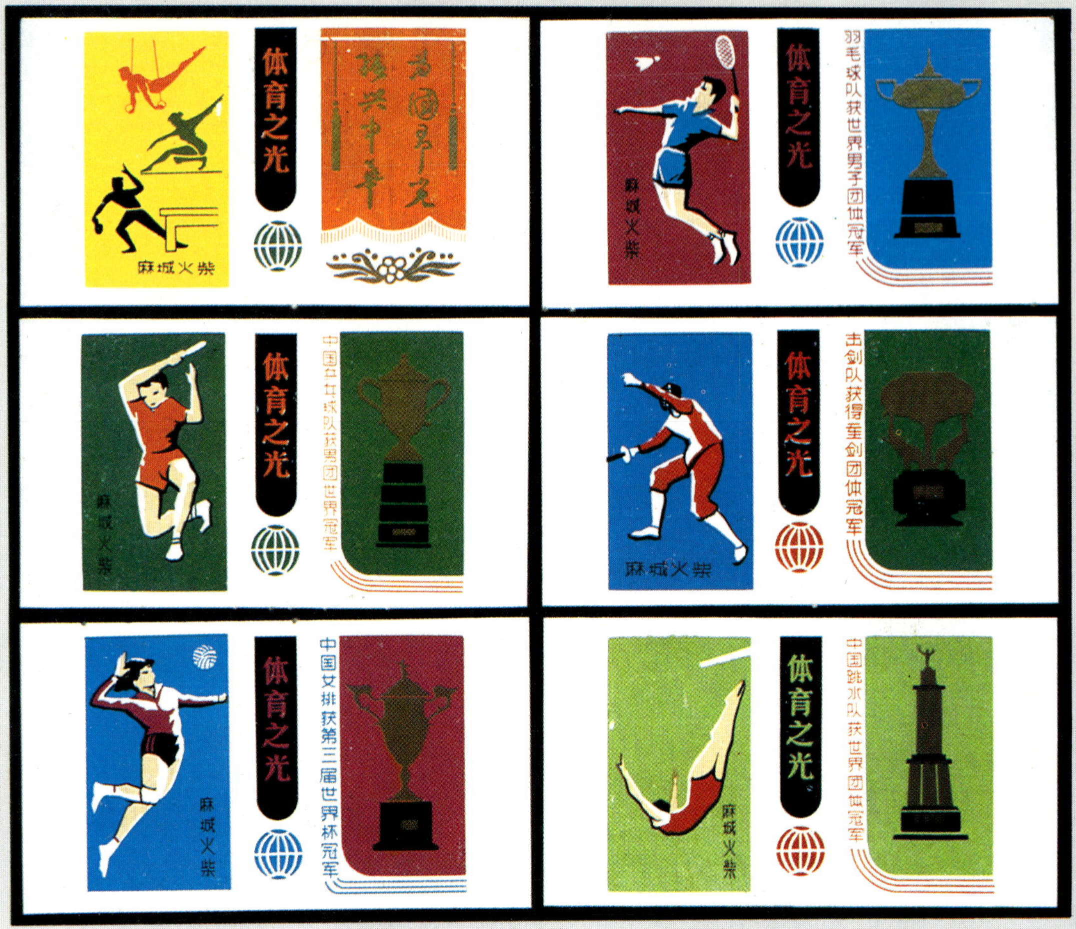

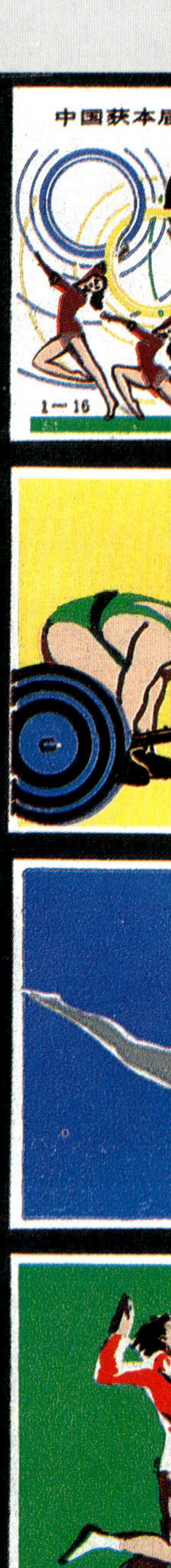

Honours for Chinese Sportsmen

This group introduces to the achievements made by Chinese athletes in recent international competitions. They have won honours for China in gymnastics, badminton, table tennis, fencing, volleyball and diving.

Made in Macheng, Hubei Province

83 mm x 45 mm

The 23rd Olympic Games

In 1984, Chinese athletes took part in the 23rd Olympic Games held in Los Angeles, U.S.A. and won fifteen gold medals in shooting, weightlifting, gymnastics, women's diving, women's foil and women's volleyball. This group of covers co mmemorates the 15 gold medals.

Made in Suzhou, Jiangsu Province
105 mm x 54 mm

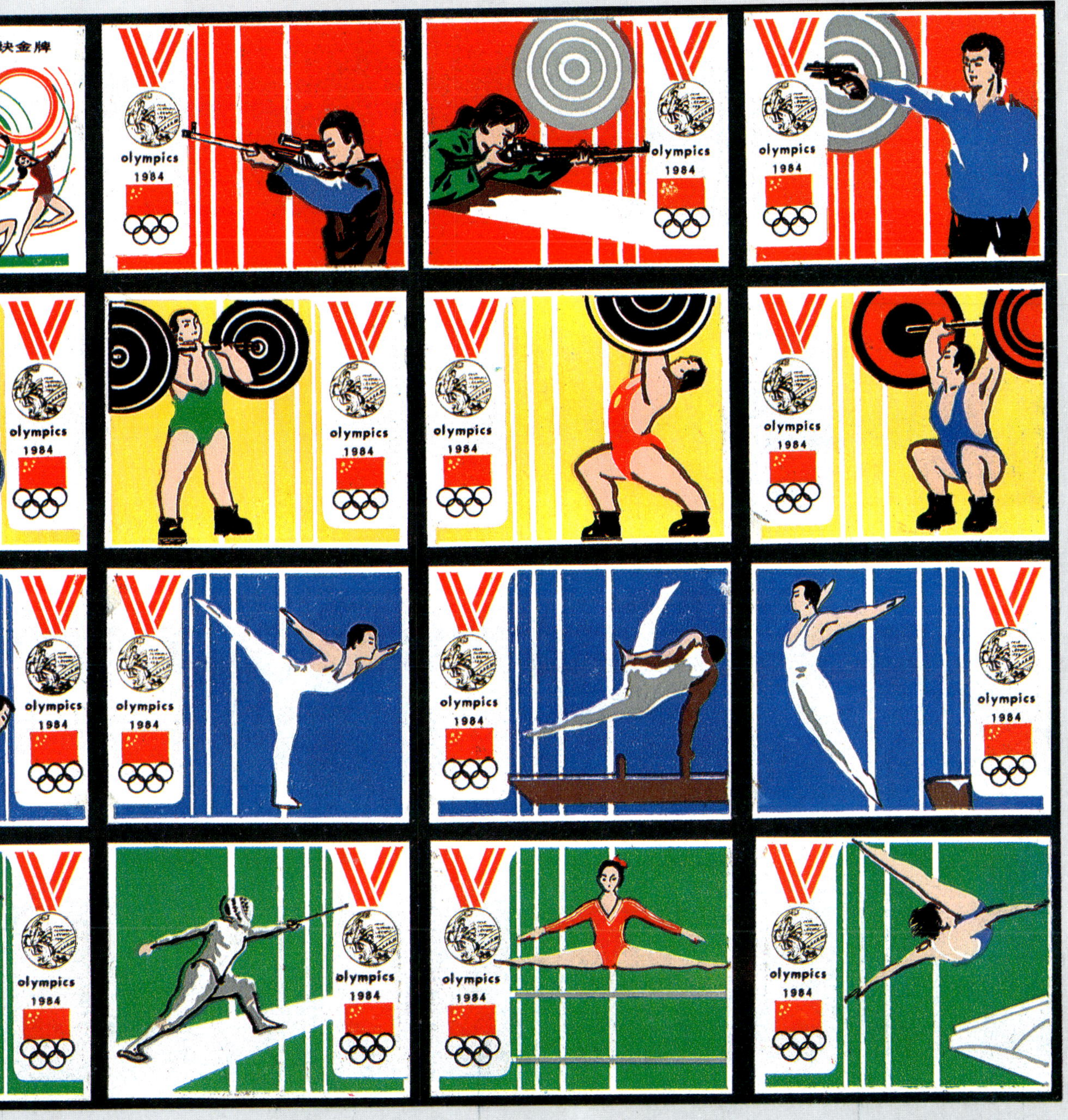

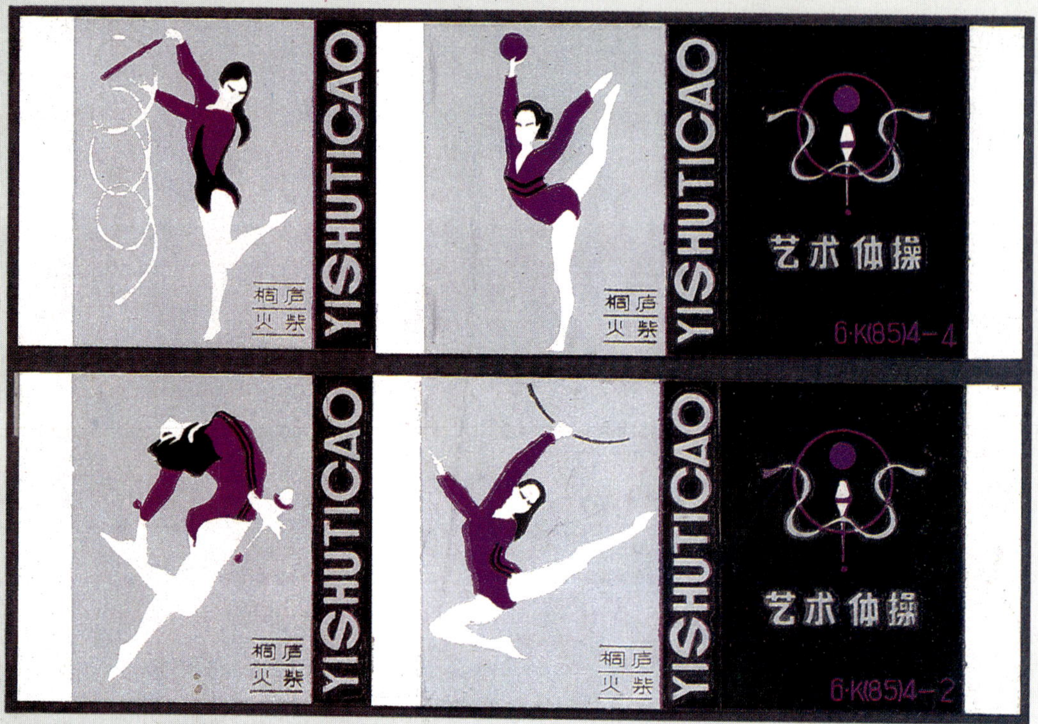

Callisthenics

Callisthenics comes from floor exercises and sports acrobatics with individual and collective performances. Its apparatus includes hoops, balls, clubs and ribbons. Its graceful and vigorous movements take on many and varied formations.

Made in Tonglu, Zhejiang Province
89 mm x 44 mm

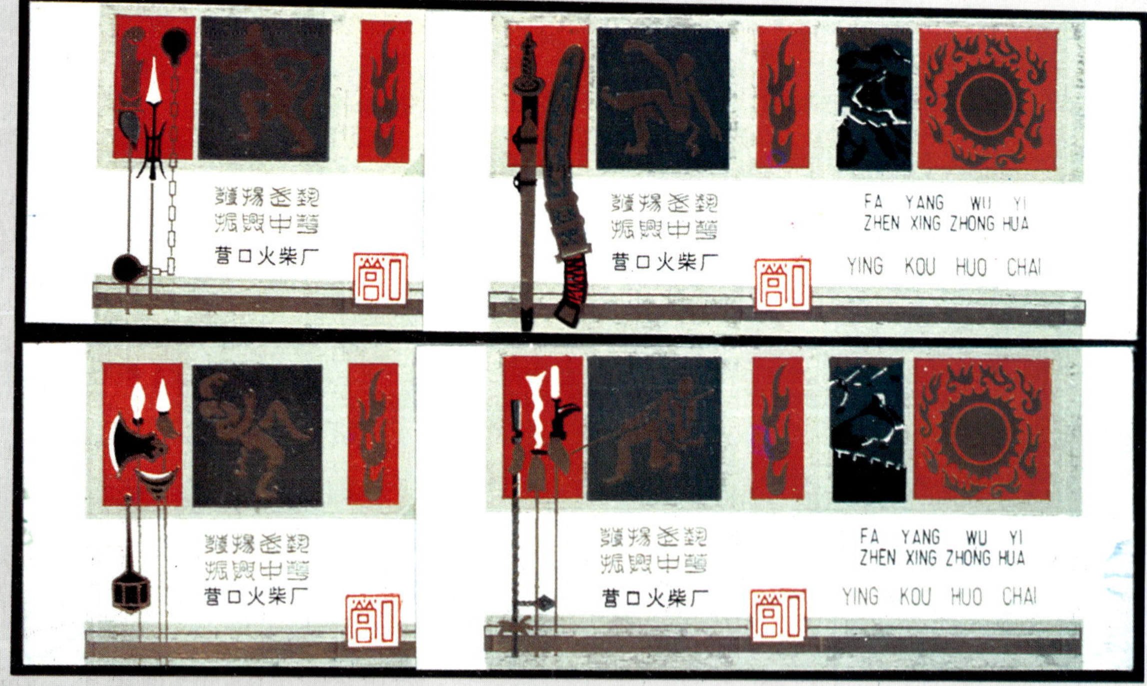

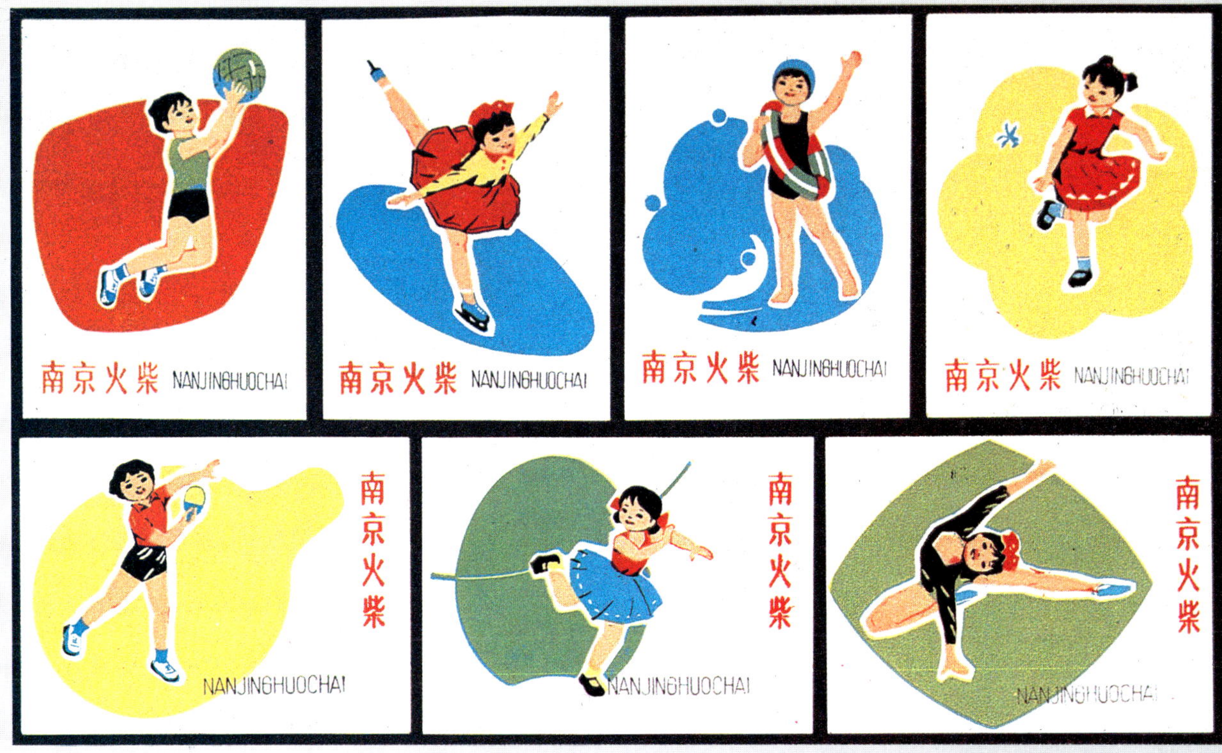

Children's Sports

These covers depict children's sports and games, including shuttlecock kicking (upper right) and rubber band skipping (lower middle), both of which are primary students' favourites.

Made in Nanjing, Jiangsu Province

49 mm x 36 mm

Martial Arts

Wushu, or martial arts, is a traditional Chinese sports event, possessing the two functions of strengthening health and defence. Its different schools came from different locales. It is divided into two major types of exercises: barehanded and with weapons. The sparring techniques include several hundred set movements. Weapons include broadsword, spear, sword, halberd and dozens of others.

This set shows the scenes of *wushu* exercises, barehanded or with weapons.

Made in Yingkou, Liaoning Province

105 mm x 46 mm

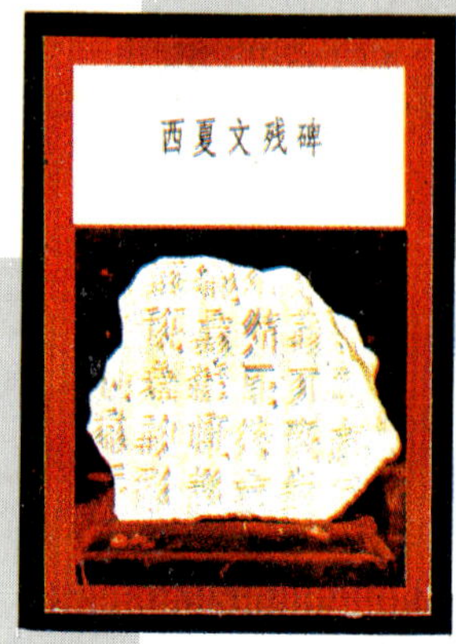

Cultural Relics

China is an old civilized country with a five-thousand-year history and an impressive ancient culture. There are countless unearthed cultural relics, many of them rare treasures both in China and in the world.

The archaeological finds shown in this section includes painted pottery of remote antiquity, ancient bronze wares, stone carvings, murals and gold and silver vessels of past dynasties. The exquisite workmanship of these relics demonstrates the highly developed technology of ancient peoples. For instance, the huge scale and rich contents of the Qin Shi Huang Mausoleum, along with the pottery warriors and horses, and the frescoes of the Mogao Grottoes, are rarely seen anywhere in the world.

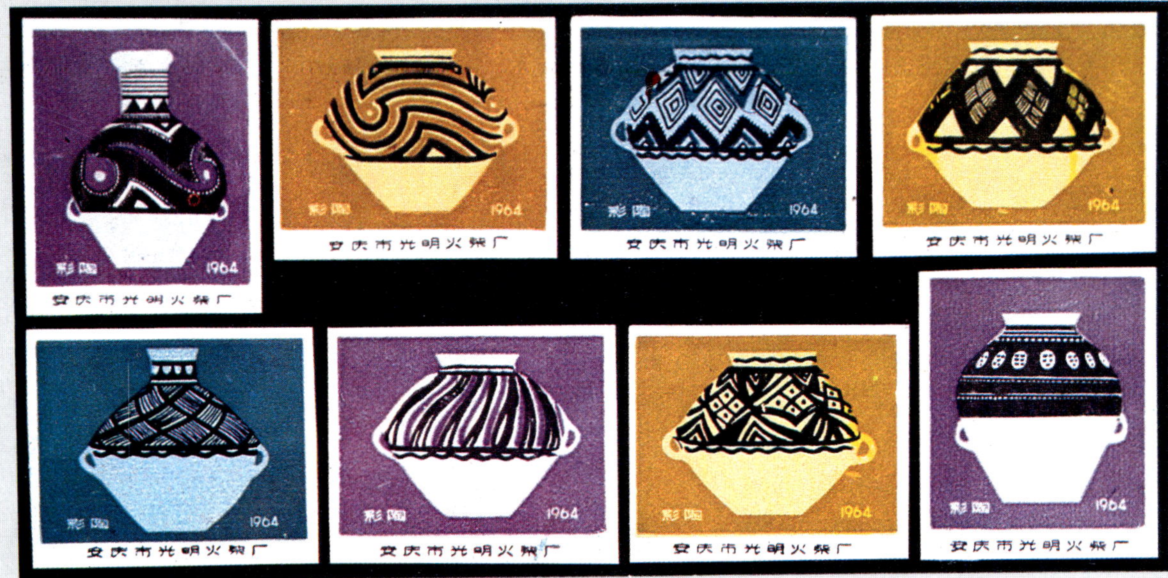

Painted Pottery

Painted pottery was made as early as the Neolithic Age by applying black and red pigments to clay moulds and then baking them in a fire. Its brightly coloured patterns are generally animals, plants and geometric figures. Great numbers of painted earthenware whose pigment remains intact have been unearthed in the Central Plain and Northwest regions of China.

Made in Anqing, Anhui Province; and Wuxi, Sichuan Province

44 mm x 35 mm,
40 mm x 30 mm

Ceramics

In the late Neolithic Age, the progenitors of the Chinese people produced exquisitely crafted pottery vessels (upper left). With the application of porcelain glaze in the 17th century, the production of Chinese ceramics entered a new era.

This group of covers presents nine pottery vessels of different historical periods after the Neolithic Age.

Made in Nanjing, Jiangsu Province

53 mm x 35 mm

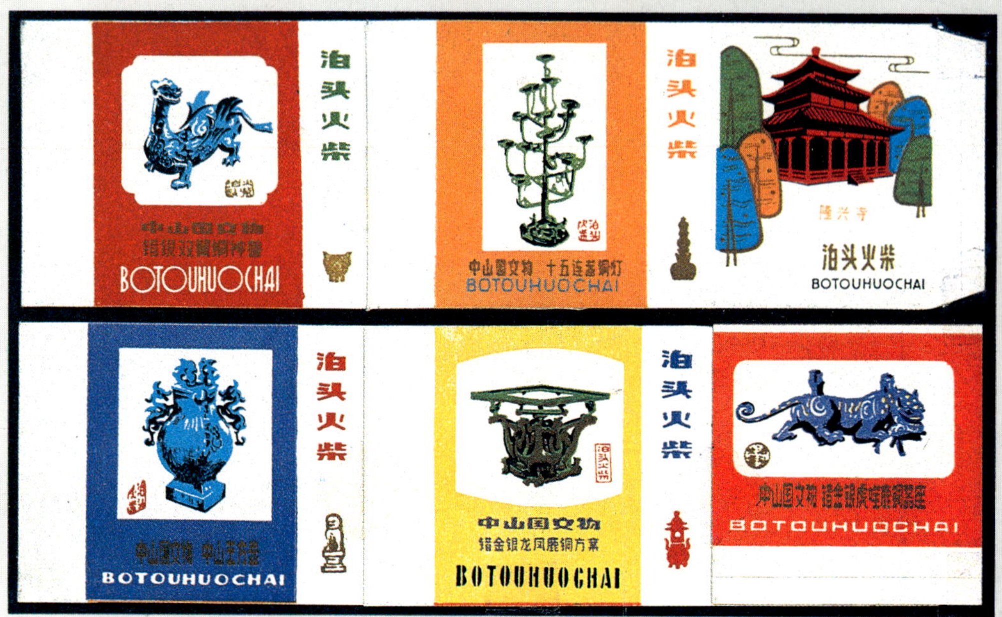

Cultural Relics of Zhongshan State

Situated in today's Hebei Province, Zhongshan State was established by an ethnic group of North China before the Christian era. In 1974, 19,000 pieces of cultural relics , many of them unknown to the outside world, were excavated from the tomb of the Zhongshan King. This set displays six masterpieces selected from the finds: winged bronze mythical beast inlaid with silver (upper left), a series of fifteen connected bronze lamps (upper middle), a square bronze kettle with inscriptions (lower left), a dragon-phoenix-deer bronze table inlaid with gold and silver (lower middle), and a silver-inlaid bronze tiger-swallowing-deer pedestal.

Made in Botou, Hebei Province
105 mm x 47 mm

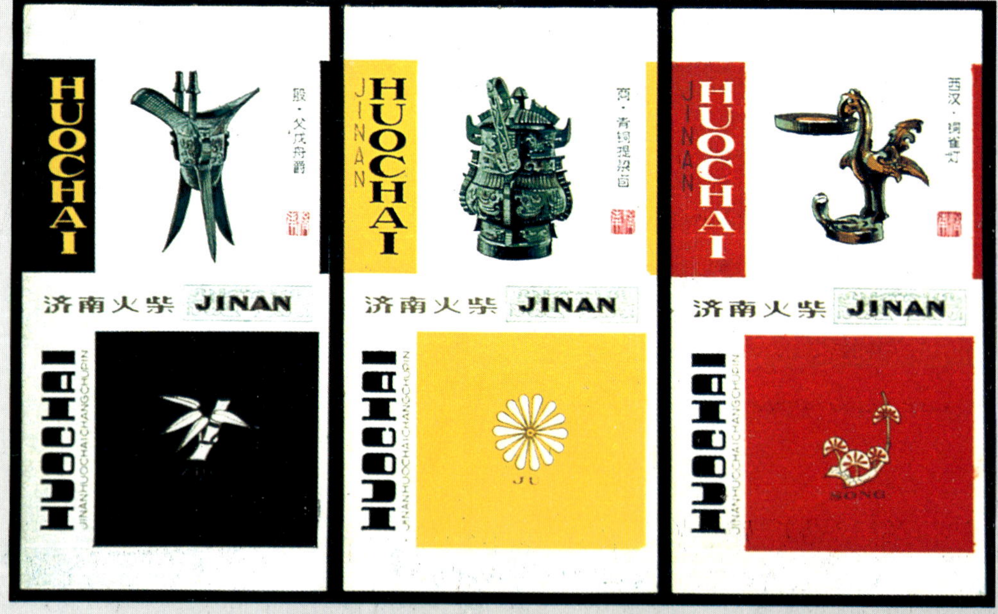

Figurines Buried with the Dead

After the transformation of Chinese social structure from a slave society to a feudal society, pottery, wooden, or stone figurines instead of human beings were buried with the dead. In the later stages of feudal society, they were displaced by paper funerary objects. This group of matchbox covers includes, top to bottom: child, robed figurine, warrior and folk entertainer.

Made in Yingkou, Liaoning Province

97 mm x 52 mm

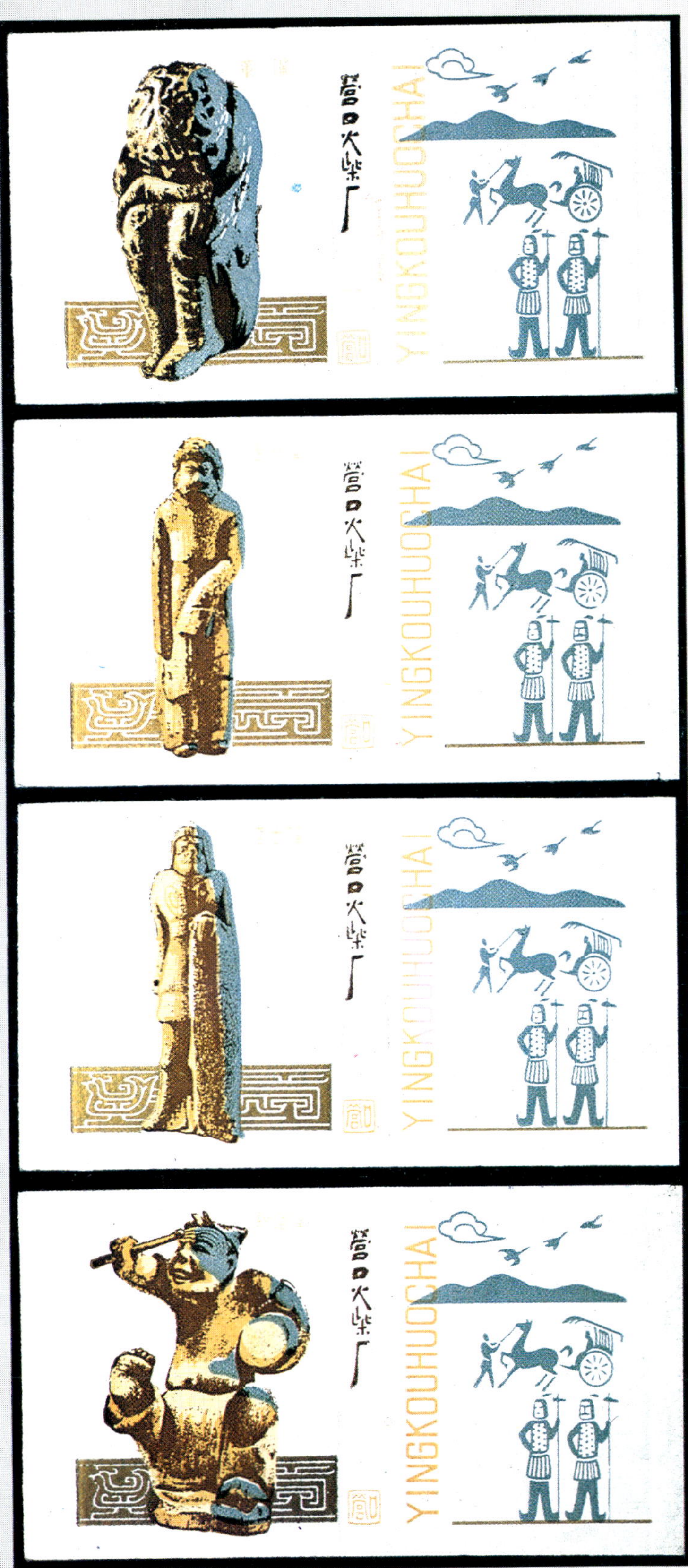

Bronzeware

The three pieces of bronzeware in this group of covers are daily-used articles of pre-Christian era. Exquisitely crafted with beautiful shapes, they demonstrate the ancient Chinese achievements in metallurgy. From left to right: Fu Wu boat-shaped wine vessel of the 12th century B.C., wine container of the 16th century B.C., and sparrow-shaped lamp of the 2nd century B.C.

Made in Jinan, Shandong Province

102 mm x 55 mm

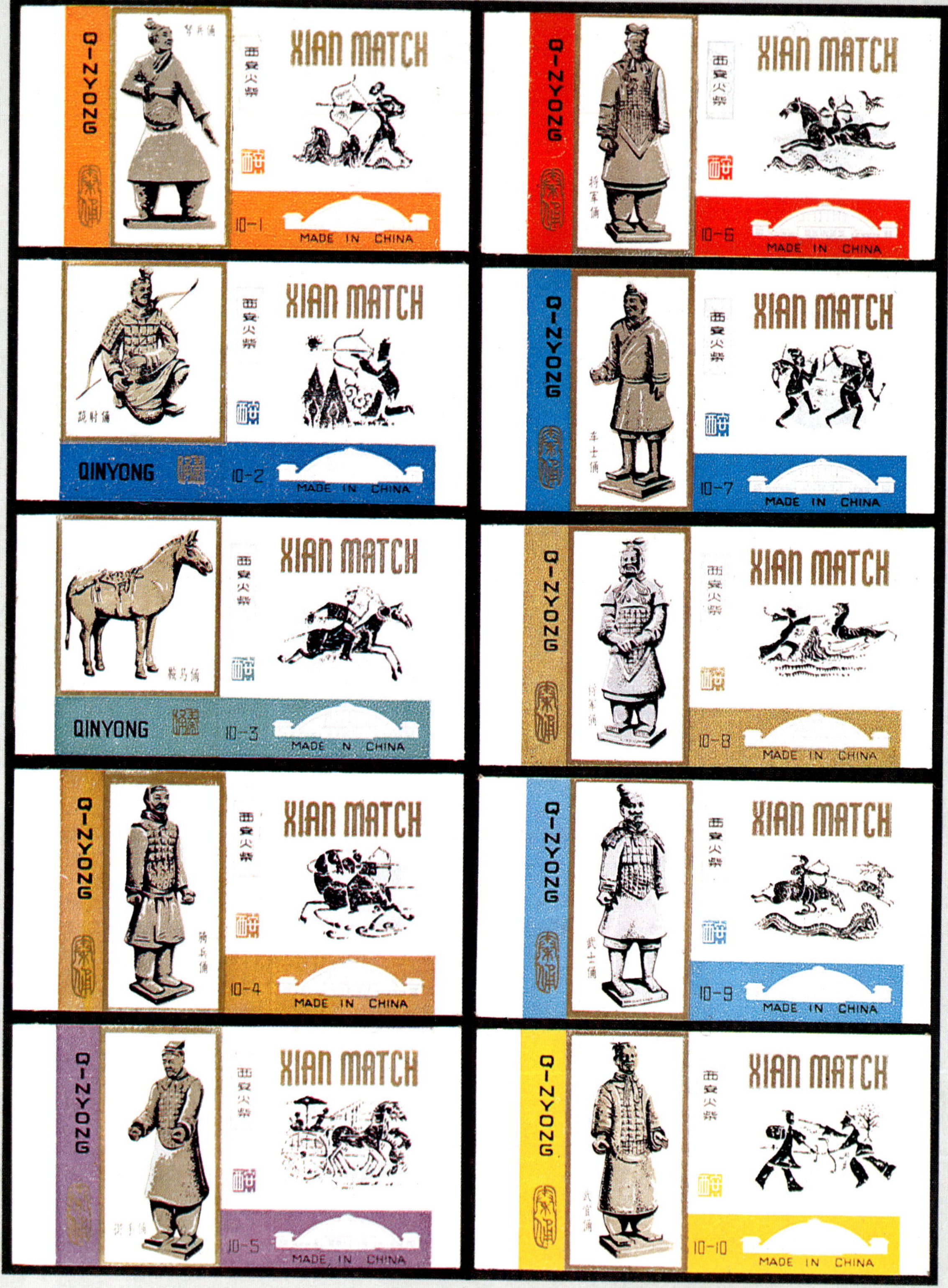
QI-NYONG
弩兵俑
西安火柴
XIAN MATCH
10-1
MADE IN CHINA
QI-NYONG
将军俑
西安火柴
XIAN MATCH
10-6
MADE IN CHINA
跪射俑
西安火柴
XIAN MATCH
QINYONG
10-2
MADE IN CHINA
QI-NYONG
车士俑
西安火柴
XIAN MATCH
10-7
MADE IN CHINA
鞍马俑
西安火柴
XIAN MATCH
QINYONG
10-3
MADE N CHINA
QI-NYONG
将军俑
西安火柴
XIAN MATCH
10-8
MADE IN CHINA
QI-NYONG
骑兵俑
西安火柴
XIAN MATCH
10-4
MADE IN CHINA
QI-NYONG
武士俑
西安火柴
XIAN MATCH
10-9
MADE IN CHINA
QI-NYONG
驭手俑
西安火柴
XIAN MATCH
10-5
MADE IN CHINA
QI-NYONG
武官俑
西安火柴
XIAN MATCH
10-10
MADE IN CHINA

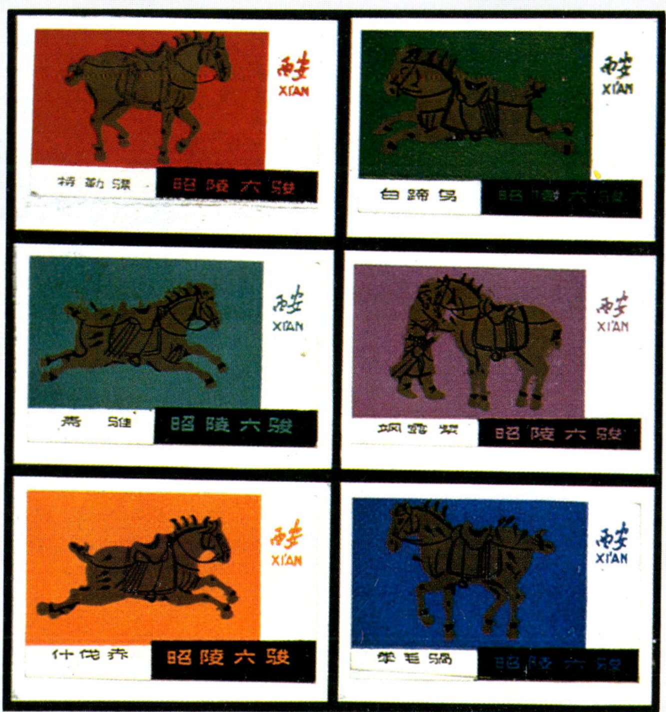

The Six Steeds of the Zhaoling Mausoleum

The six steeds were carved in relief on six pieces of stone in front of the tomb of Emperor Taizong of the Tang Dynasty. They were his six favourite horses. From left, top to bottom: Te Le Steed, white-hoofed steed, piebald horse, purple steed, red Shi Fa steed, and Quan Mao piebald horse. Two steeds, the purple steed and the Quan Mao piebald horse, were stolen in 1914 and are now in Philadelphia, U.S.A.

Made in Xi'an, Shaanxi Province
42 mm x 26 mm

Pottery Warriors and Horses in Qin Shi Huang Mausoleum

Qin Shi Huang (First Emperor of the Qin Dynasty) ordered the construction of a huge mausoleum for himself. Situated in the east of Lintong County, Shaanxi Province, and covering more than twenty thousand square metres, the tomb is surrounded by four figurine pits. In 1974, 6,000 life-size pottery warriors, 30 pottery horses and 8 chariots were excavated from Pit 1, arrayed in battle formation.

Made in Xi'an, Shaanxi Province
101 mm x 52 mm

Wadang

Wadang refers to the tile for water drainage from the eaves of ancient Chinese architecture. The tile is often decorated with patterns and words. The eaves tiles here are relics of the pre-Christian era.

Made in Anqing, Anhui Province
42 mm x 35 mm

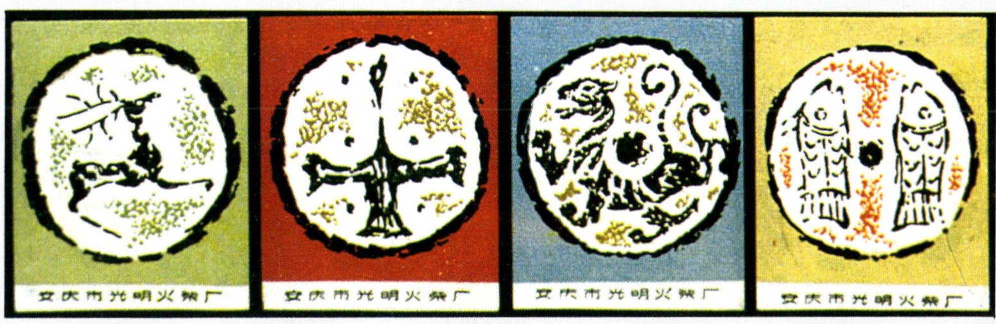

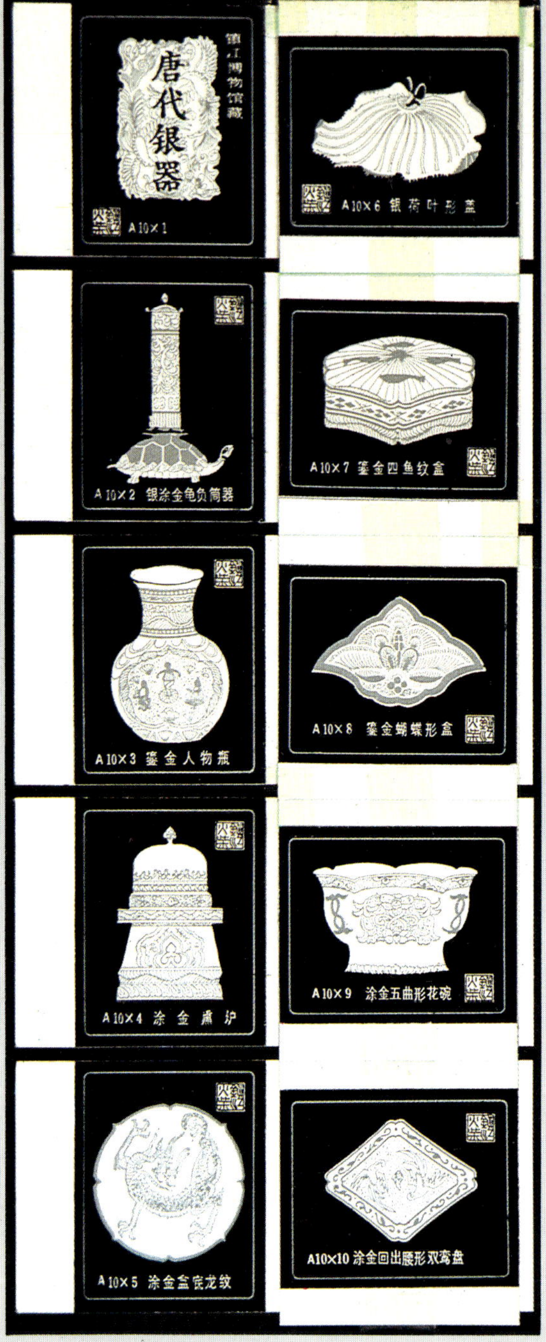

Silver Vessels of the Tang Dynasty

This group of covers presents the silver vessels of the Tang Dynasty (618—907). From top to bottom, left column: patterns of the silver vessels; silver tortoise-carrying-cylinder vessel with gold-plating; gilded vase with human design; gold-coated incense burner; and gilded basin with dragon design. From top to bottom, right column: silver lid in the shape of lotus leaf; gilded basin with fish pattern; gilded butterfly-shaped basin; gilded curved bowl with flower patterns; and gilded double-phoenix plate.

Made in Zhenjiang, Jiangsu Province

100 mm x 47 mm

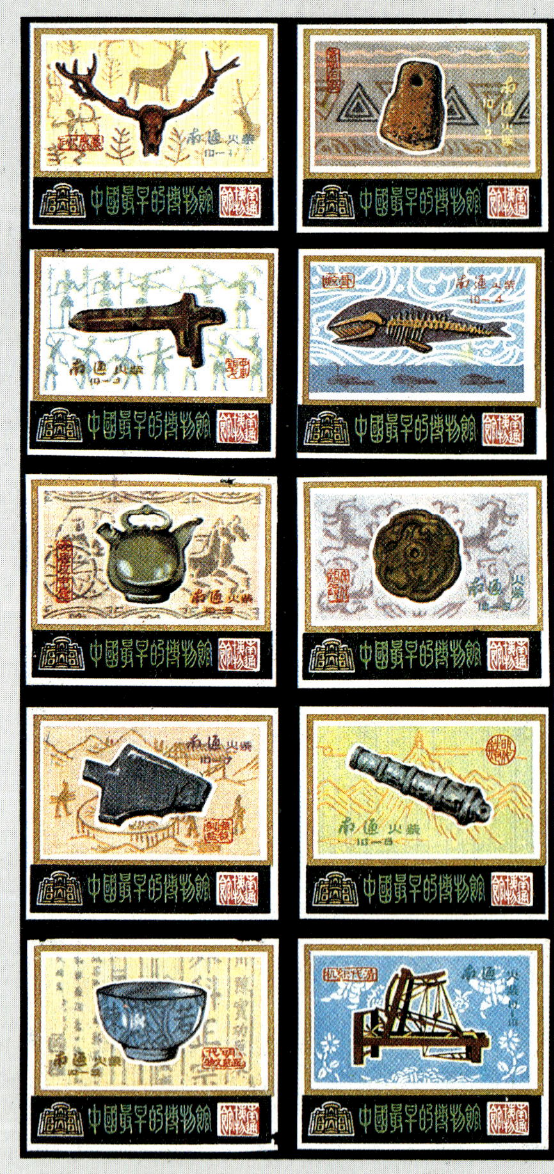

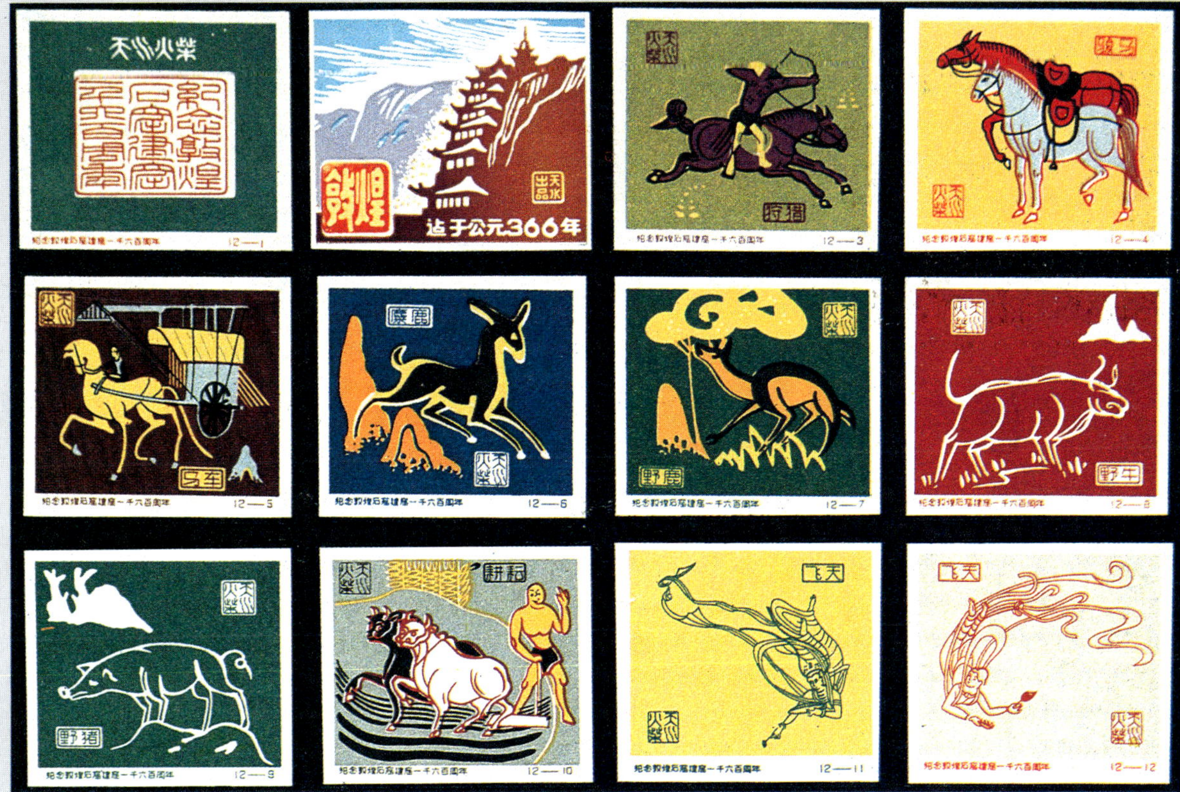

Cultural Relics in Nantong Museum

The Nantong Museum of Jiangsu Province is the earliest of its kind in China to preserve cultural relics. The ten covers in this group present representative cultural relics of past dynasties in the museum's collection. From top to bottom, left column: fossils of David's deer, bronze dagger-axe of the Western Zhou Dynasty (10th century B.C.), leather pot produced around the 7th century, salt-making, medicinal relics of the 15th century; from top to bottom, right column: Qingdun stone implements, whale skeleton, bronze mirror from the 10th century, iron canon from the 15th century, and loom from the 18th century.

Made in Nantong, Jiangsu Province
42 mm x 35 mm

Dunhuang Grottoes

Situated east of Dunhuang County, Gansu Province, and measuring two kilometres from north to south, the Dunhuang Grottoes were first carved in A.D. 366. In this largest treasure of Buddhist art in the world, there are 492 caves containing a total of 45,000-square-metre murals and 2,400 coloured Buddhist statues.

This group of covers was designed to celebrate the 1,600th anniversary of the initial construction of the Dunhuang Grottoes. The pictures are selected from images in the grottoes' murals. From left, top to bottom: title signet, exterior view of the grottoes, hunting, steed, horse-drawn chariot, David's deer, wild deer, wild ox, wild boar, ploughing, and flying Apsaras.

Made in Tianshui, Gansu Province
40 mm x 35 mm

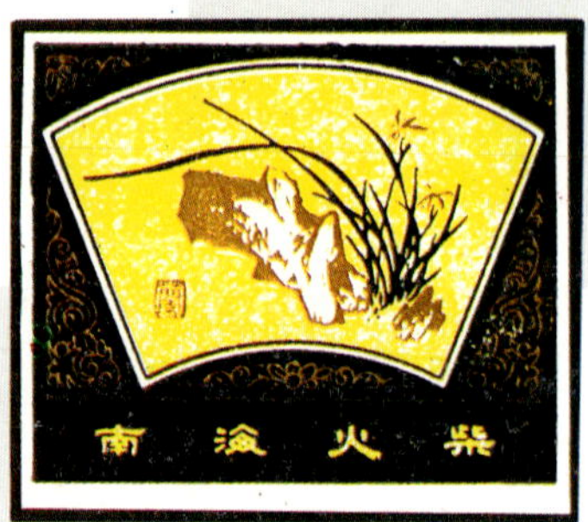

VII.
Folk Crafts and Folk Decorative Motifs

Chinese folk crafts and decorative designs are a component part of traditional Chinese art and are closely related to the people's material and spiritual life. They are aesthetically pleasing as well as practical.

This section focuses first on those arts and crafts used on a daily basis and, second, those used for decoration. The pictures show detailed traditional patterns used in the decorative function of Chinese folk handicrafts. Because of differences in history, geography, economy, culture, and national customs, handicrafts also differ in aesthetic standards.

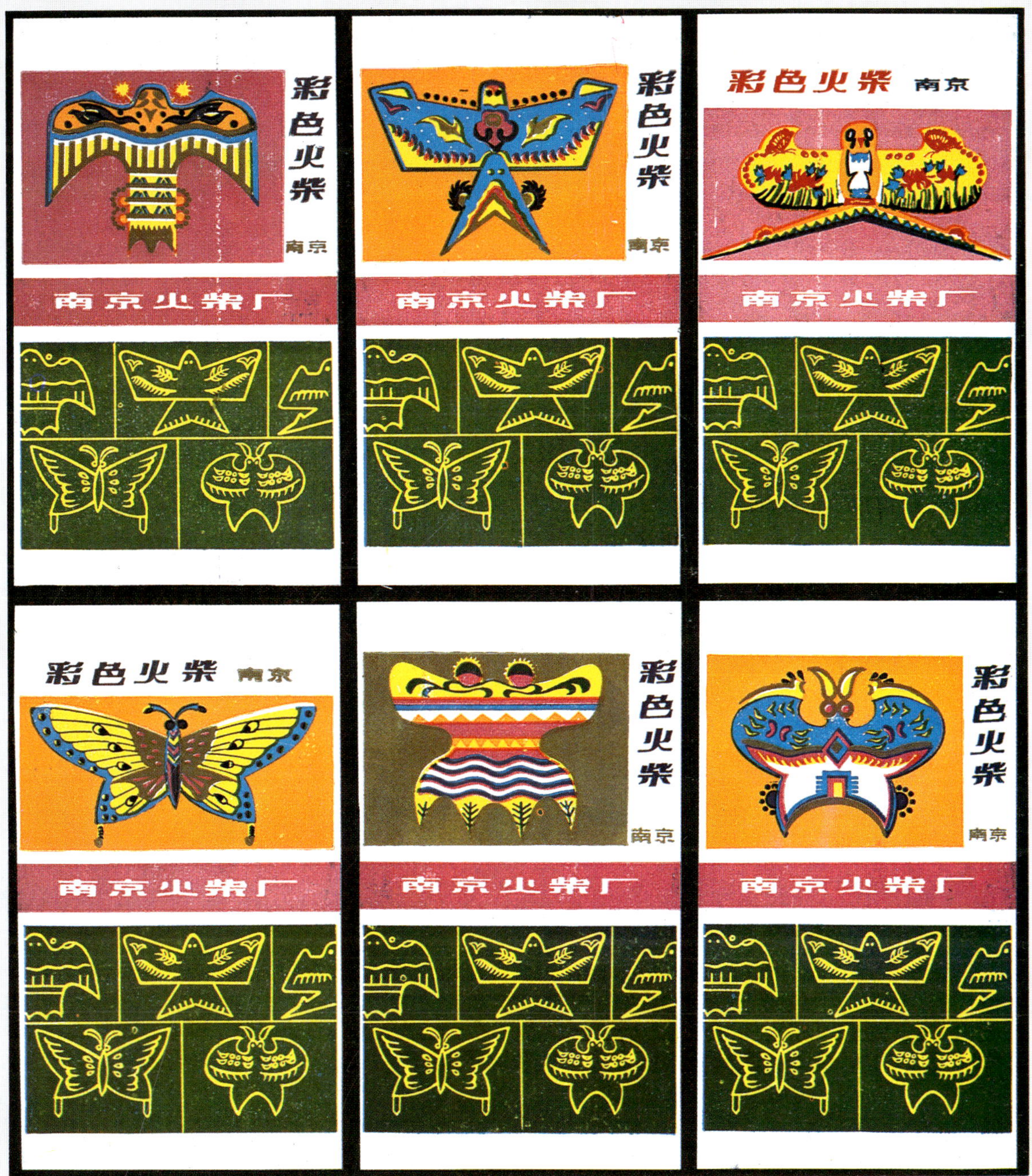

Kites

Divided into two types: "hard wing" and "soft wing," the Chinese kite has a 2,500-year history. It is famous both at home and abroad for its distinctive shapes and bright colours. This group presents six kites of different shapes.

Made in Nanjing, Jiangsu Province

93 mm x 54 mm

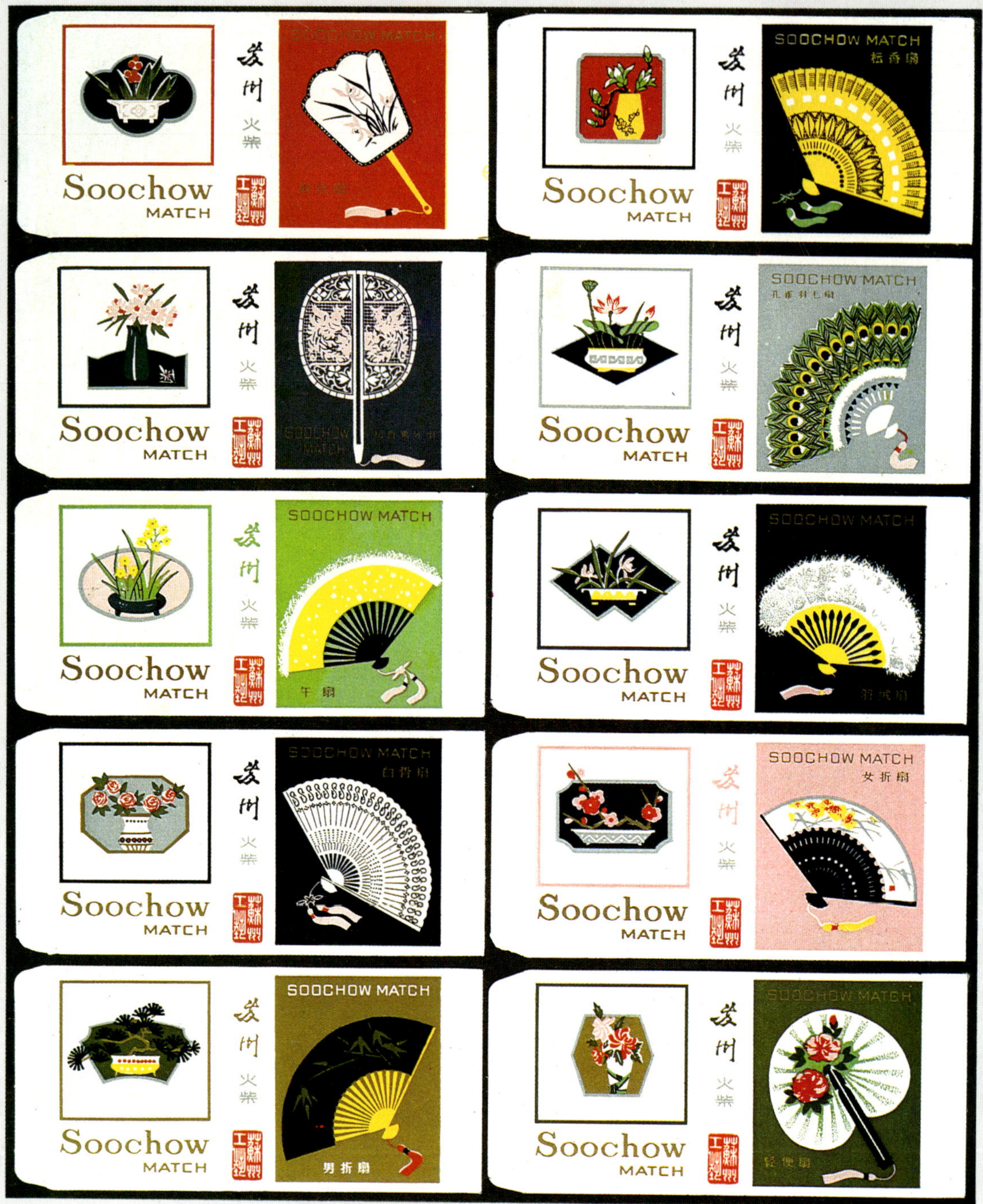

Fans

The Chinese fan is exquisitely made in various styles. The drawings on the fan coverings and the sculpture and burnt decorations on the fan ribs are attractive and delicate.

This group introduces different types of Suzhou fans. From top to bottom, left column: silk palace fan, sandalwood and ivory fan, dance fan, white-bone fan, men's folding fan; from top to bottom, right column: sandalwood fan, peacock feather fan, feather fan, women's folding fan, convenient fan.

Made in Suzhou, Jiangsu Province
117 mm x 54 mm

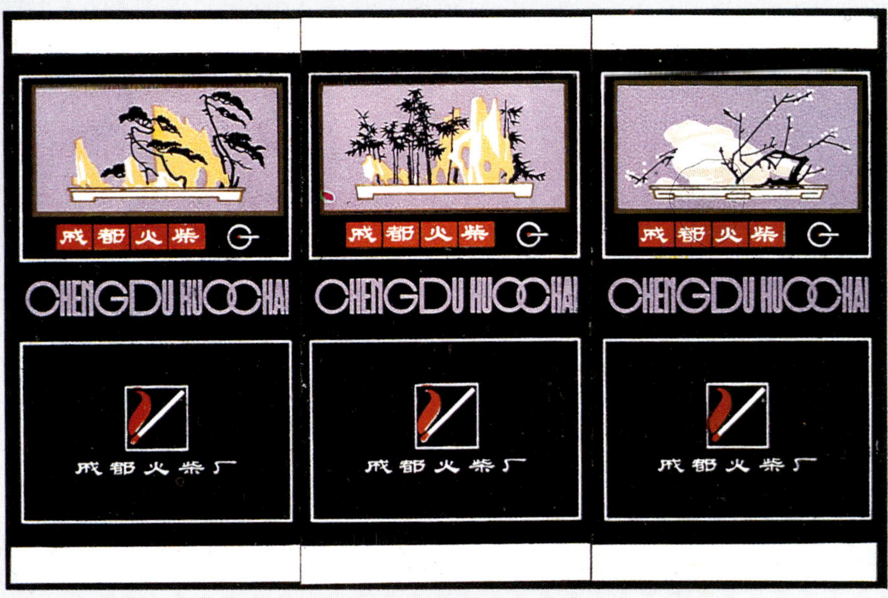

Potted Plants: Three Friends of the Cold

Pine, bamboo and plum are characterized by resistance to cold. Chinese people describe these plants as "Three Friends of the Cold" and compare them to people of integrity.

From left to right: pine, bamboo and plum.

Made in Chengdu, Sichuan Province

88 mm x 46 mm

Plum, Orchid, Bamboo and Chrysanthemum

Plum, orchid, bamboo and chrysanthemum are likened to "Four Gentlemen" by Chinese scholars in successive dynasties. Plum is resistant to cold weather, chrysanthemum is resistant to frost, bamboo is upright and orchid is fragrant.

Made in Shanghai; and Suzhou, Jiangsu Province

42 mm x 33 mm, 41 mm x 34 mm

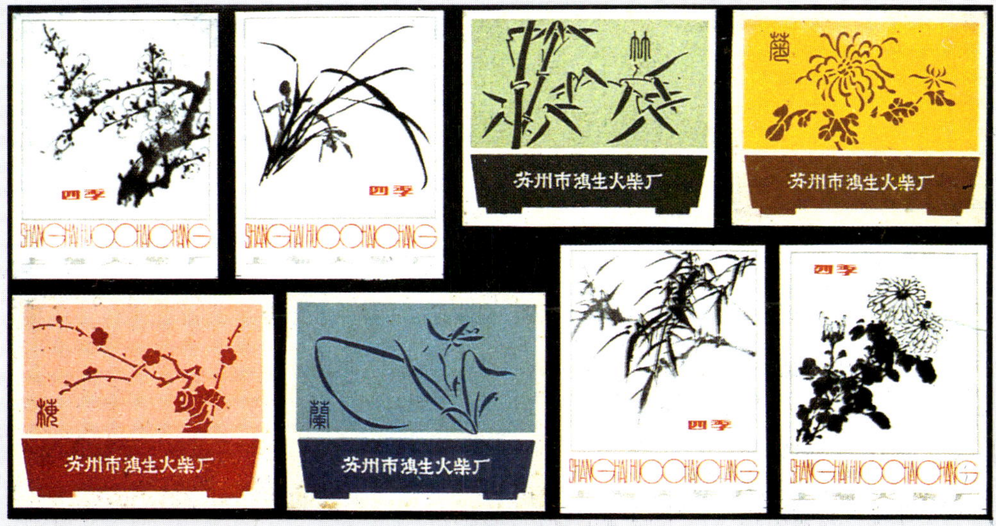

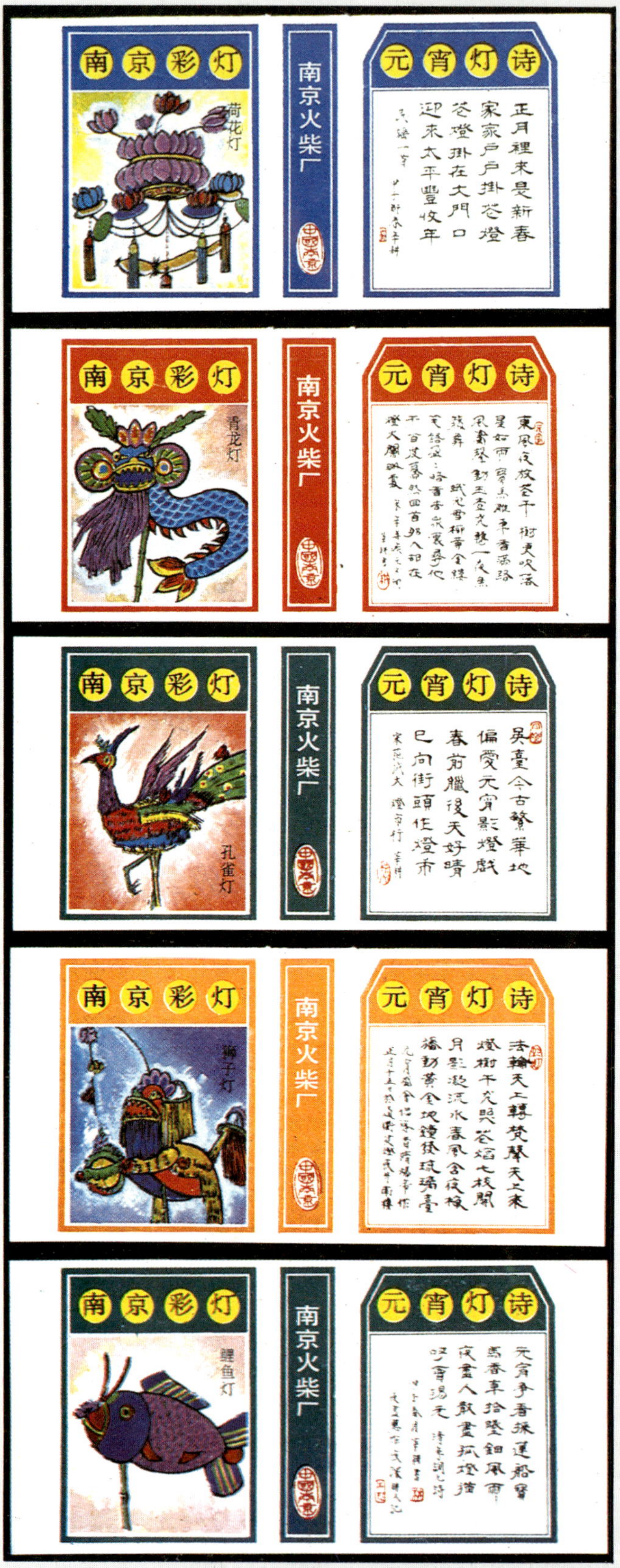

The Coloured Lantern

The coloured lantern is a typical Chinese handicraft. Its frame of bamboo or wood sticks is covered with silk or paper and then decorated with paintings of animals, flowers and human figures. During festivals, large numbers of these lanterns are suspend-

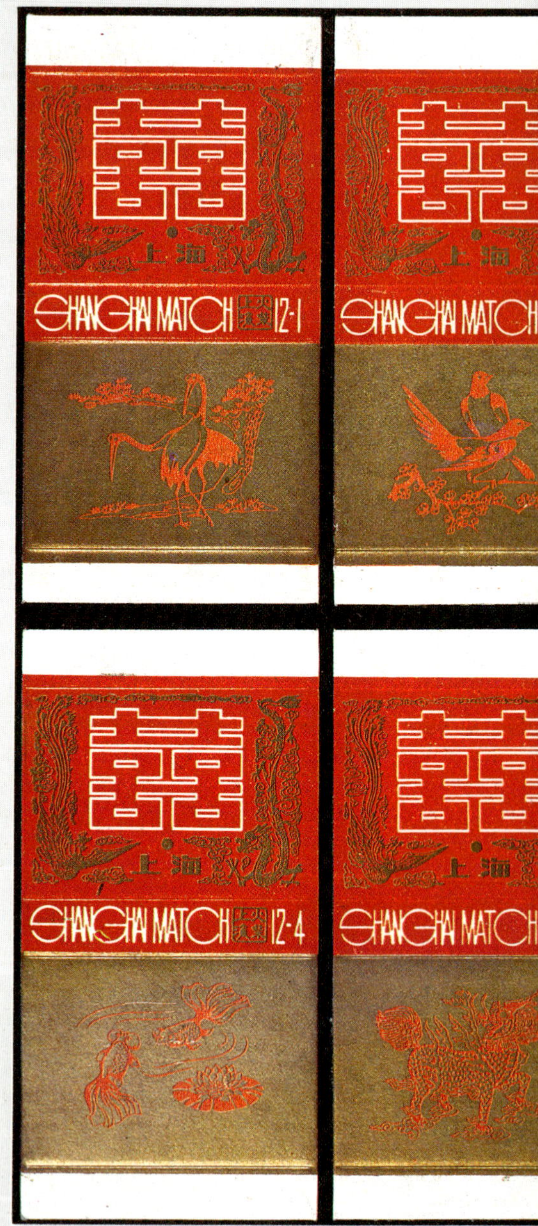

ed and inscribed with entertaining lantern poems and riddles. This group of matchbox covers presents the painted lanterns of Nanjing. From top to bottom: lotus lantern, green dragon lantern, peacock lantern, lion lantern and carp lantern.

Made in Nanjing, Jiangsu Province
97 mm x 46 mm

Patterns Formed by the Character for Double Happiness

The character for double happiness implies joy and happiness. This group supplements the character for double happiness with related patterns which amplify the auspicious implications of the character.

Made in Shanghai
102 mm x 52 mm

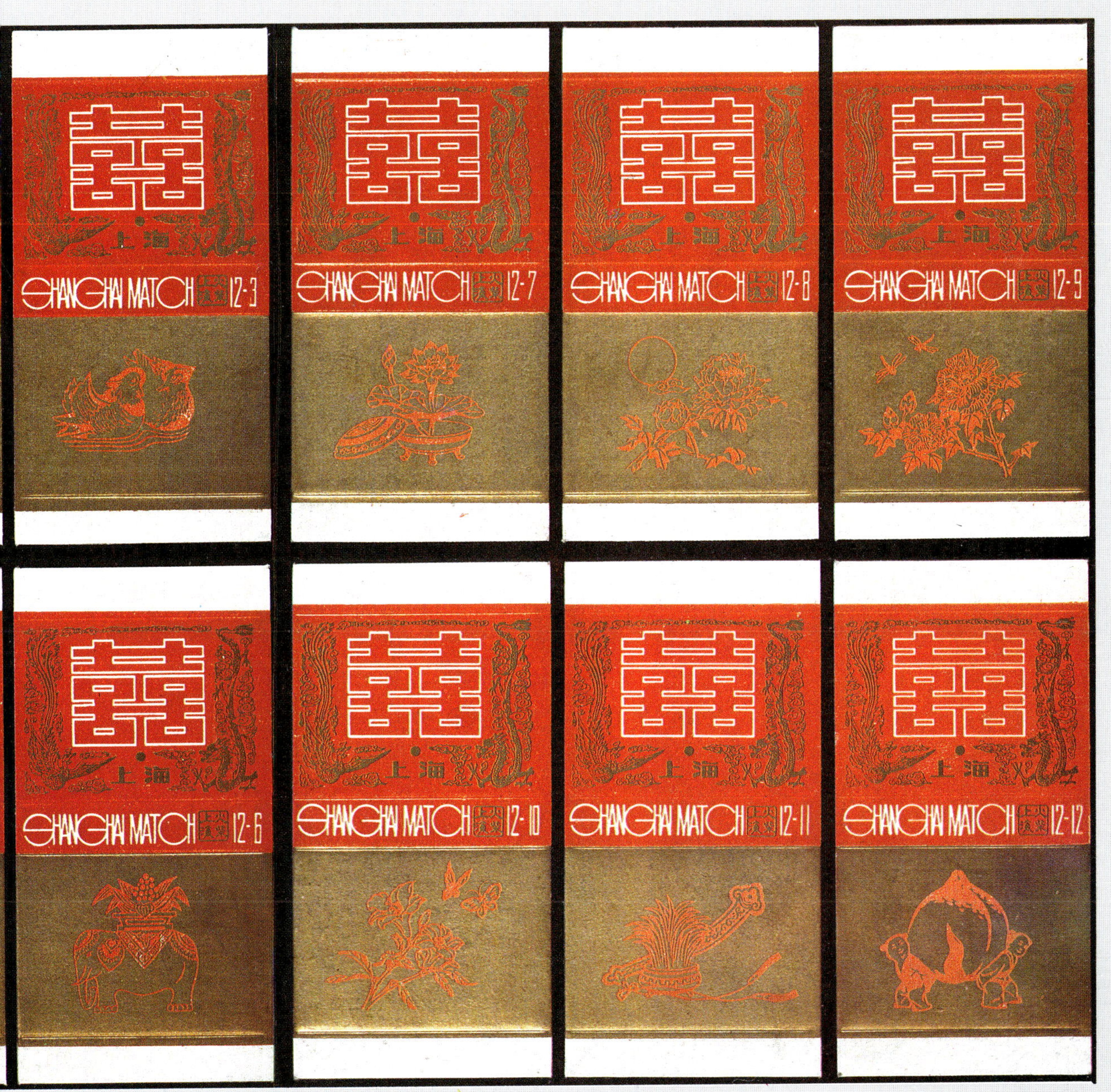

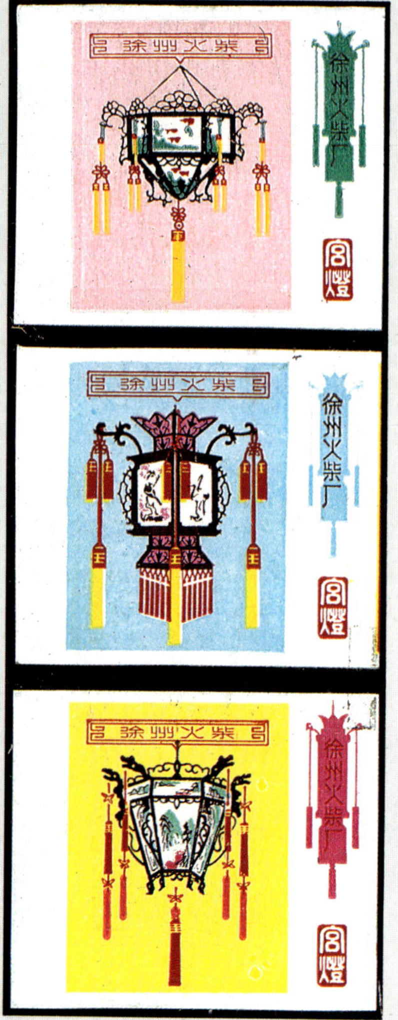

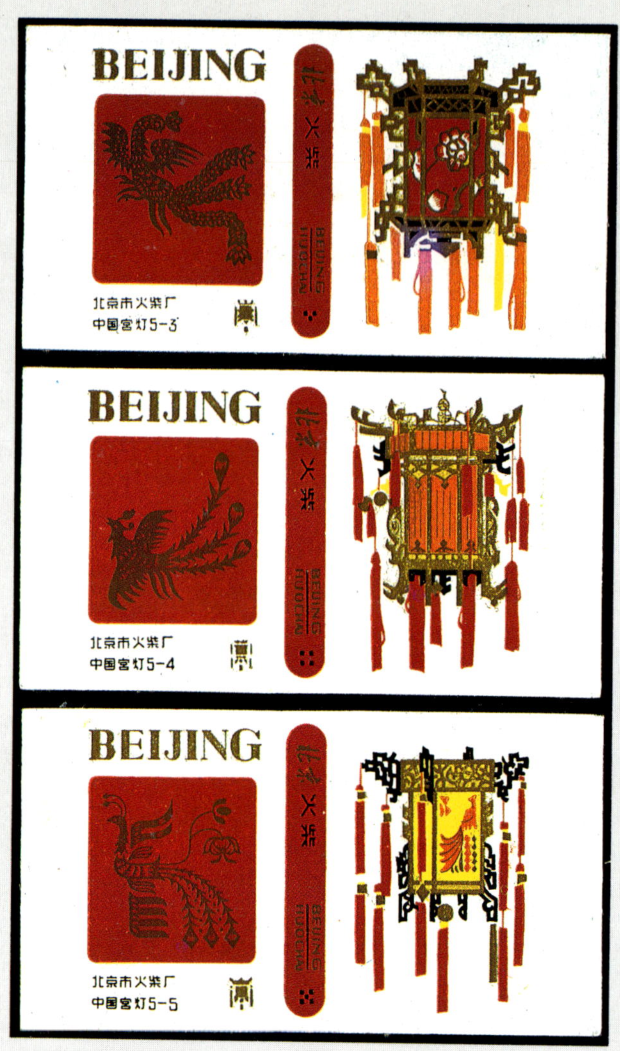

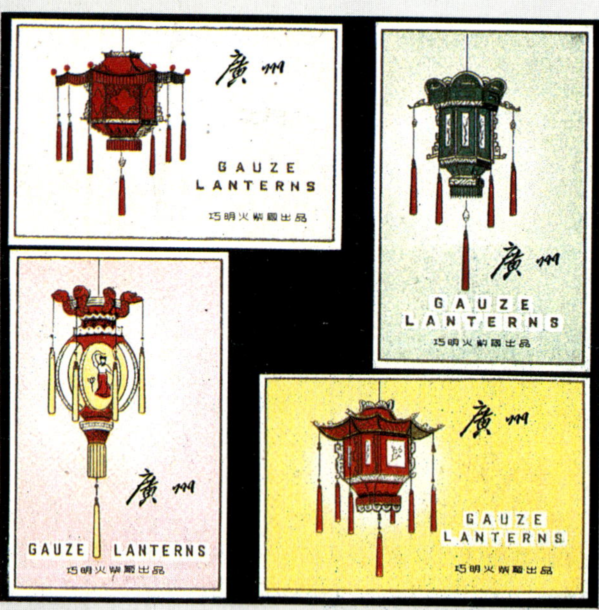

Palace Lantern

An old Chinese handicraft, the palace lantern is used for lighting and architectural decoration. The lantern is made from wood and bamboo and inlaid with bronze, gauze and glass. Decorated with landscape, figure and flower-and-bird paintings, and tassels, palace lantern is sumptuous and beautiful.

Made in Xuzhou, Jiangsu Province; Beijing; and Guangzhou, Guangdong Province

97 mm x 46 mm, 103 mm x 55 mm, 52 mm x 34 mm

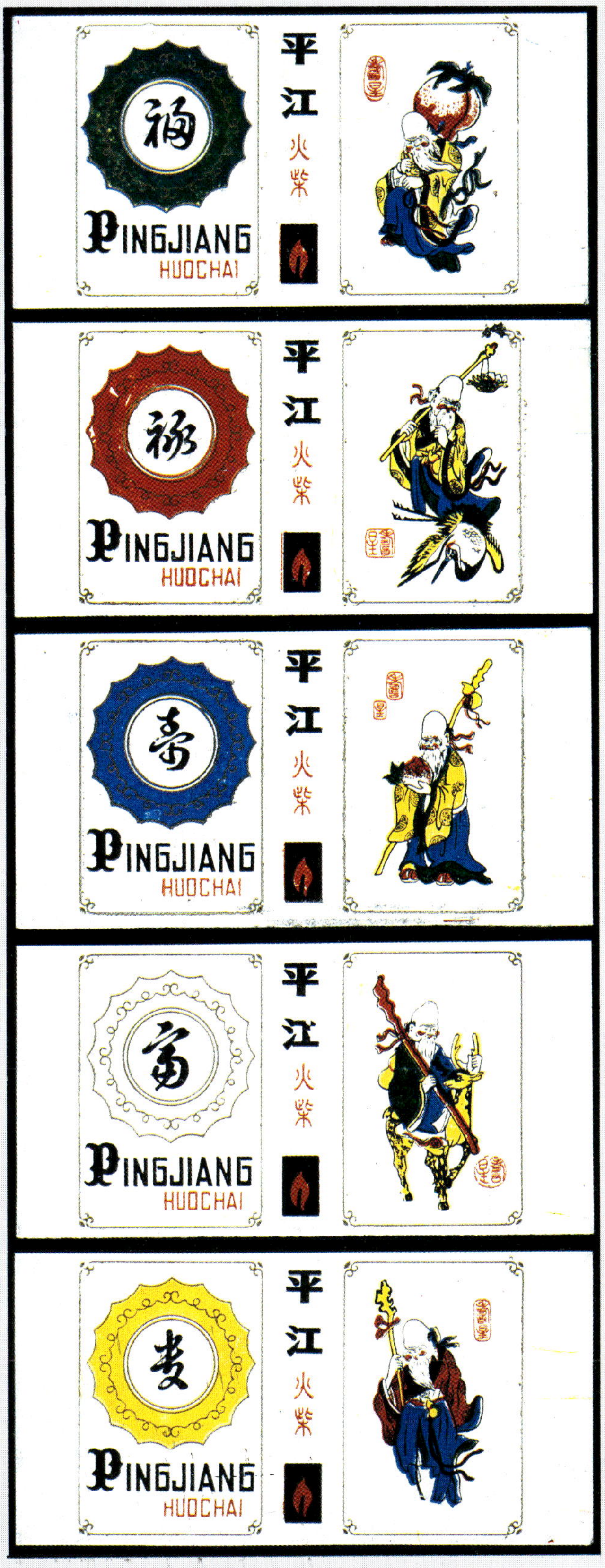

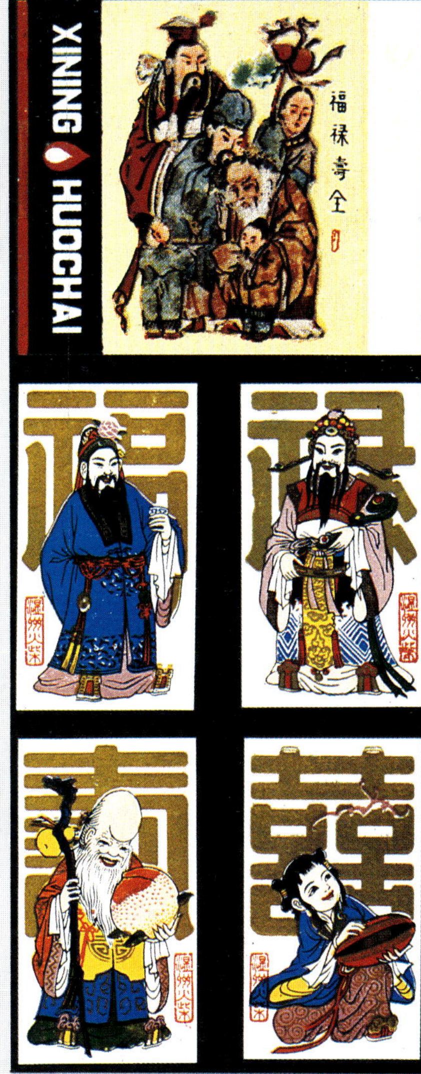

Patterns of Auspicious Characters

Fu (luck), Lu (fame), Shou (longevity), Fu (wealth) and Gui (high rank) are five Chinese characters implying auspiciousness. On festive occasions, birthdays and other joyous days, people would write them in bold form and hang them on walls to create a colourful atmosphere and attract good luck.

Made in Pingjiang, Hubei Province; Xining, Qinghai Province; and Wenzhou, Zhejiang Province

91 mm x 45 mm, 101 mm x 48 mm, 44 mm x 25 mm

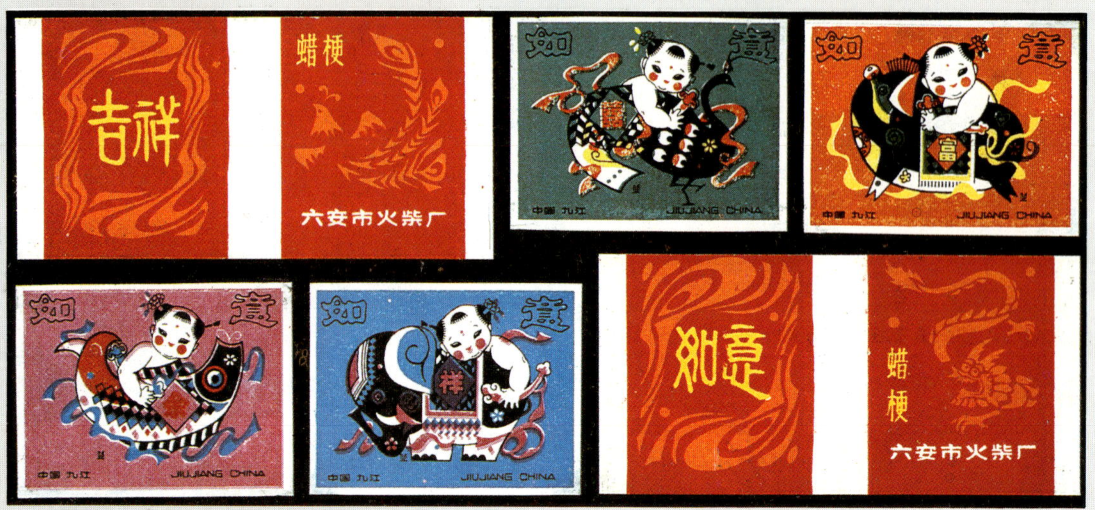

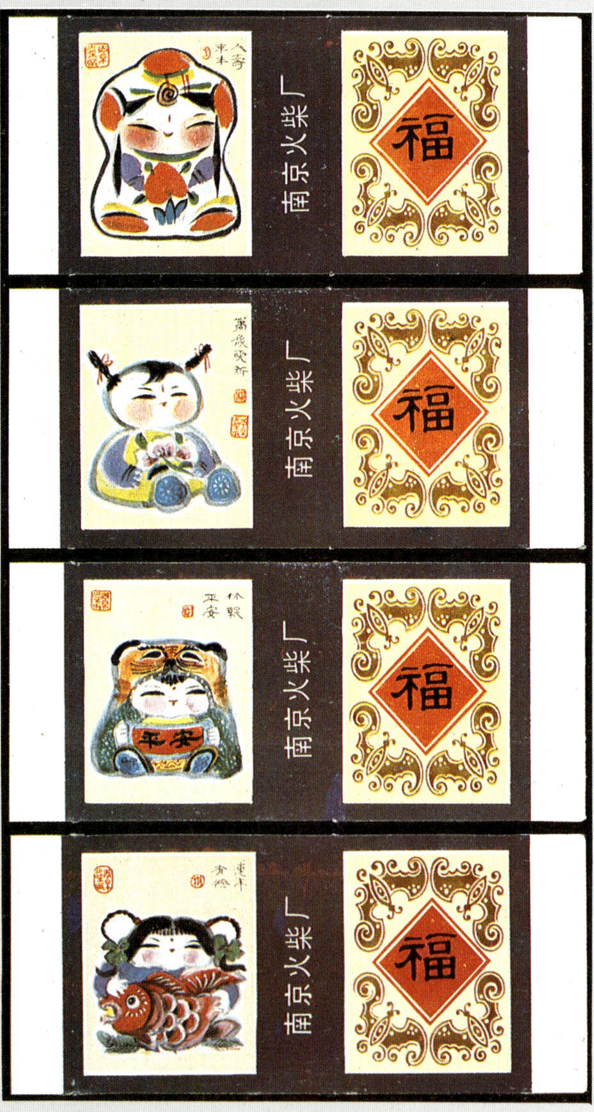

Patterns of Good Wishes

Each matchbox cover in this group exhibits the method of New Year pictures and expresses certain meanings. For example, the chicken symbolizes auspiciousness, the elephant, luck, the pig, wealth, and the fish, plenty. All the symbols signify people's hopes for a better life.

Made in Liu'an, Anhui Province; and Jiujiang, Jiangxi Province

80 mm x 39 mm, 46 mm x 35 mm

Clay Dolls

Clay dolls are handicraft products produced in the Wuxi area of Jiangsu Province. Some of their vivid and lifelike facial characteristics are exaggerated to appear charmingly naive.

All the dolls here imply meanings. From top to bottom: longevity and good harvest; freshness and gaiety; firecrackers scaring away demons and bringing harmony to the New Year; and abundance every year.

Made in Nanjing, Jiangsu Province

109 mm x 47 mm

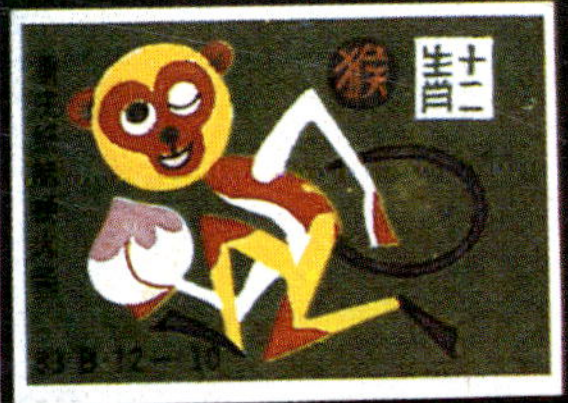

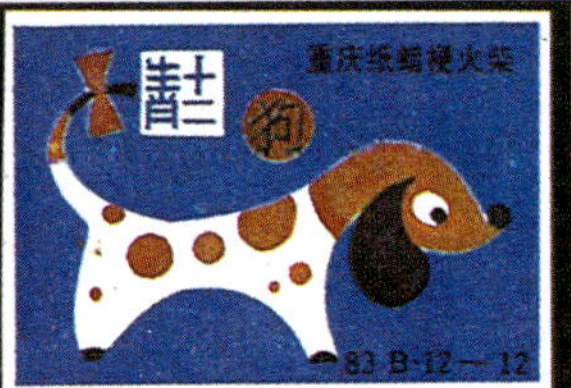

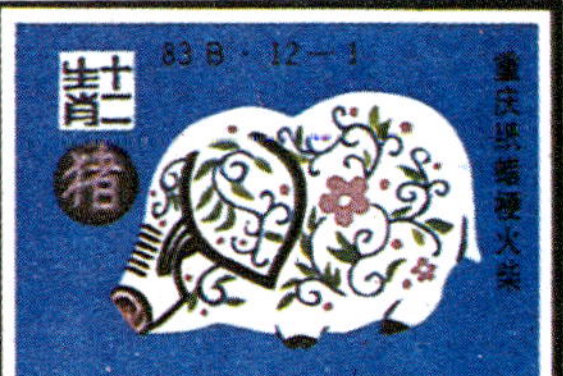

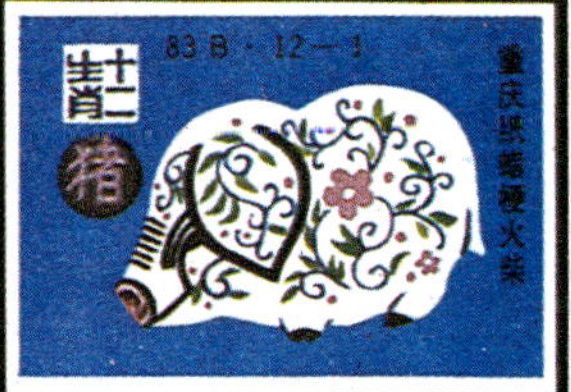

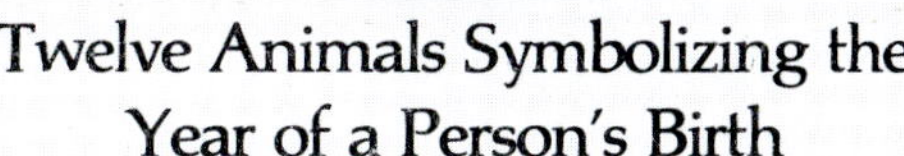

Twelve Animals Symbolizing the Year of a Person's Birth

In ancient China, the years were designated by the Ten Heavenly Stems and the Twelve Earthly Branches, each of which represented a different animal, and each person is symbolized by the corresponding animal symbolizing the year of the person's birth.

Made in Chongqing, Sichuan Province
41 mm x 28 mm

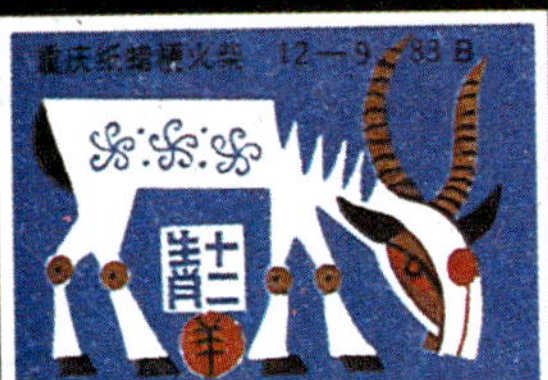

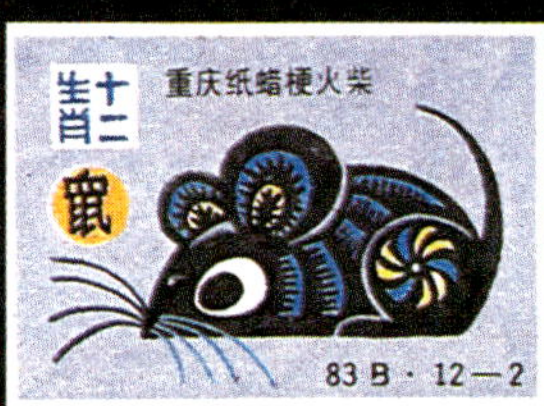

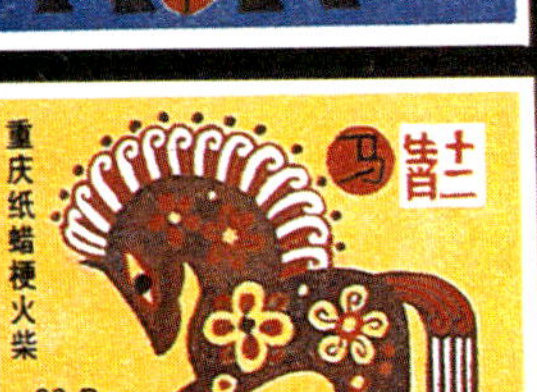

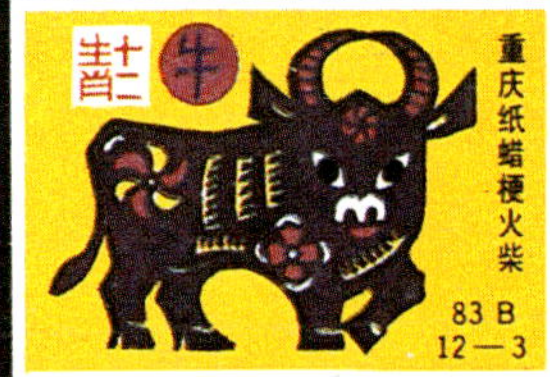

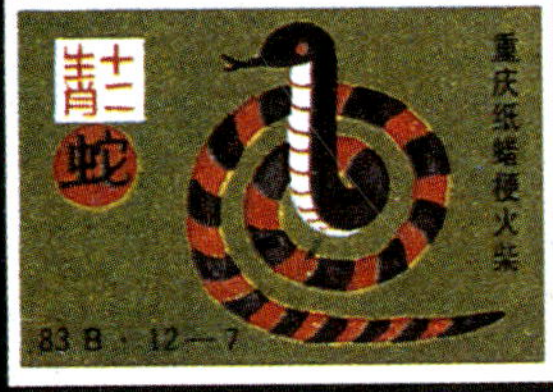

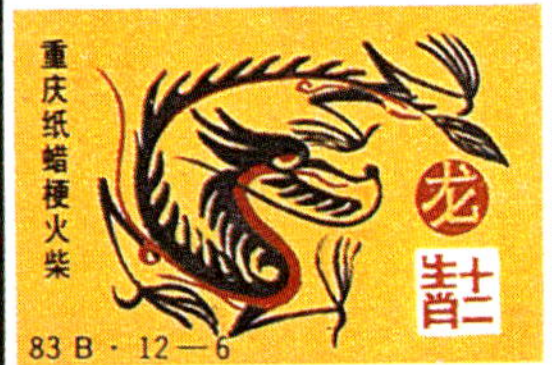

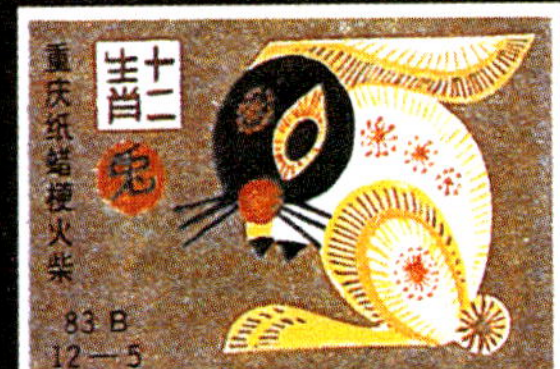

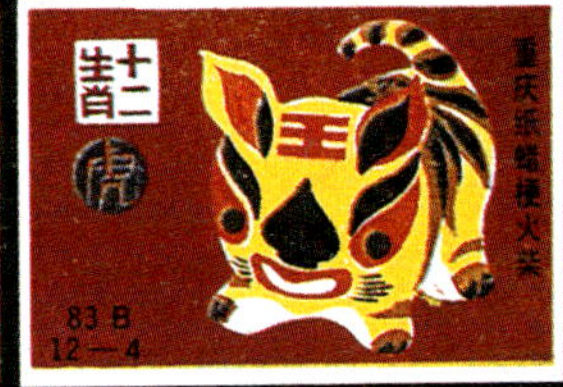

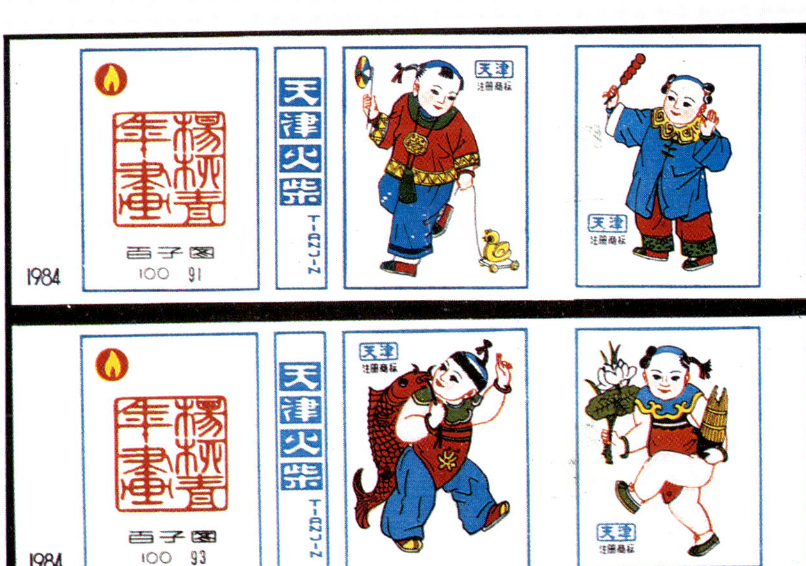

One-Hundred-Children Picture

"One hundred children," implying a growing family, is often the theme of traditional Chinese New Year pictures. This group of covers follows the design of the Yangliuqing New Year pictures of Tianjin.

Made in Tianjin
101 mm x 46 mm

The Flying Apsaras

In the Buddhist art of Dunhuang Caves, Gansu Province, the flying apsaras is a fairy maiden who plays musical instruments and dances in the air. Her image is widely used as a pattern on various traditional handicraft articles.

Made in Qinhuangdao, Hebei Province; and Wuhu, Anhui Province

98 mm x 46 mm, 42 mm x 26 mm

Paper-Cutting

The traditional Chinese craft of paper-cutting requires only a pair of scissors to cut paper into complex designs. The paper can then be pasted on windows and walls or presented to friends as a gift.

This group of matchbox covers shows paper-cuttings of flowers. The flower patterns contain four Chinese characters which mean "a hundred flowers will blossom."

Made in Qimen, Anhui Province

103 mm x 46 mm

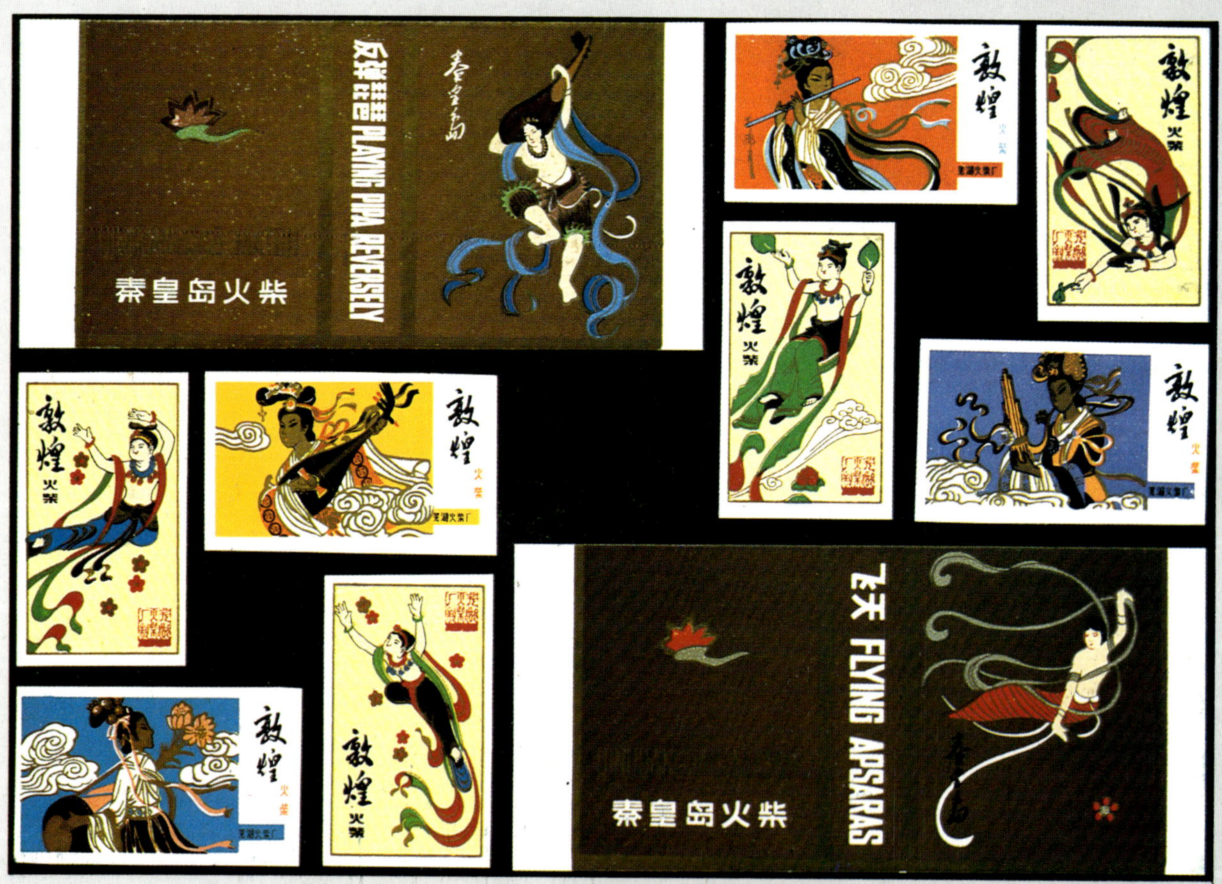

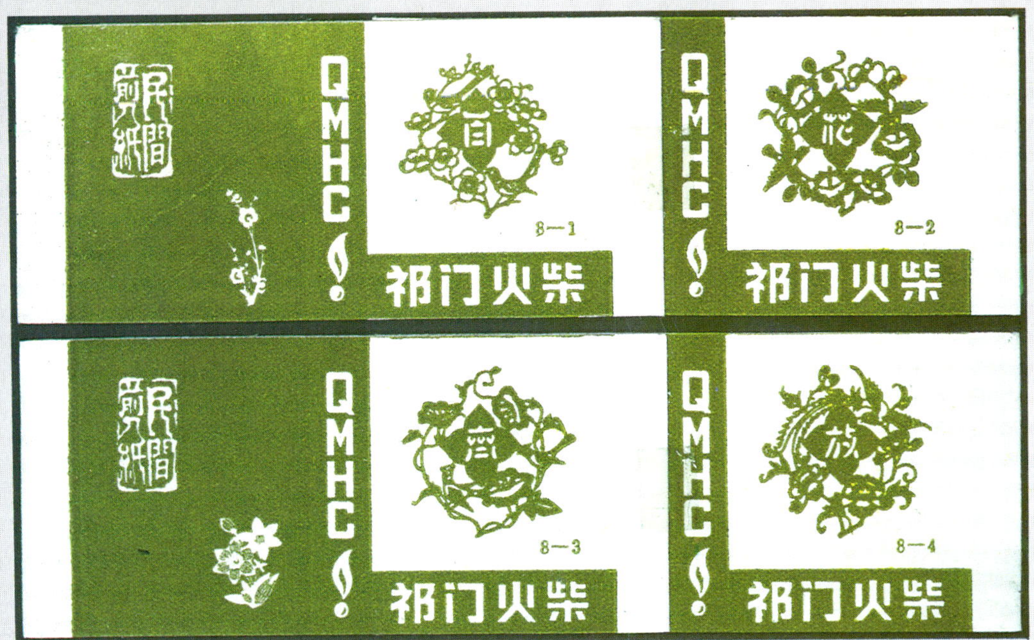

Dragon-and-Phoenix Pattern

In the Chinese mythology, the dragon and the phoenix are mythical beast and bird, symbolizing auspiciousness, luck, wealth and beauty. In feudal society, they were also symbols of imperial power.

Made in Tianjin; and Anyang, Henan Province

100 mm x 46 mm, 93 mm x 53 mm

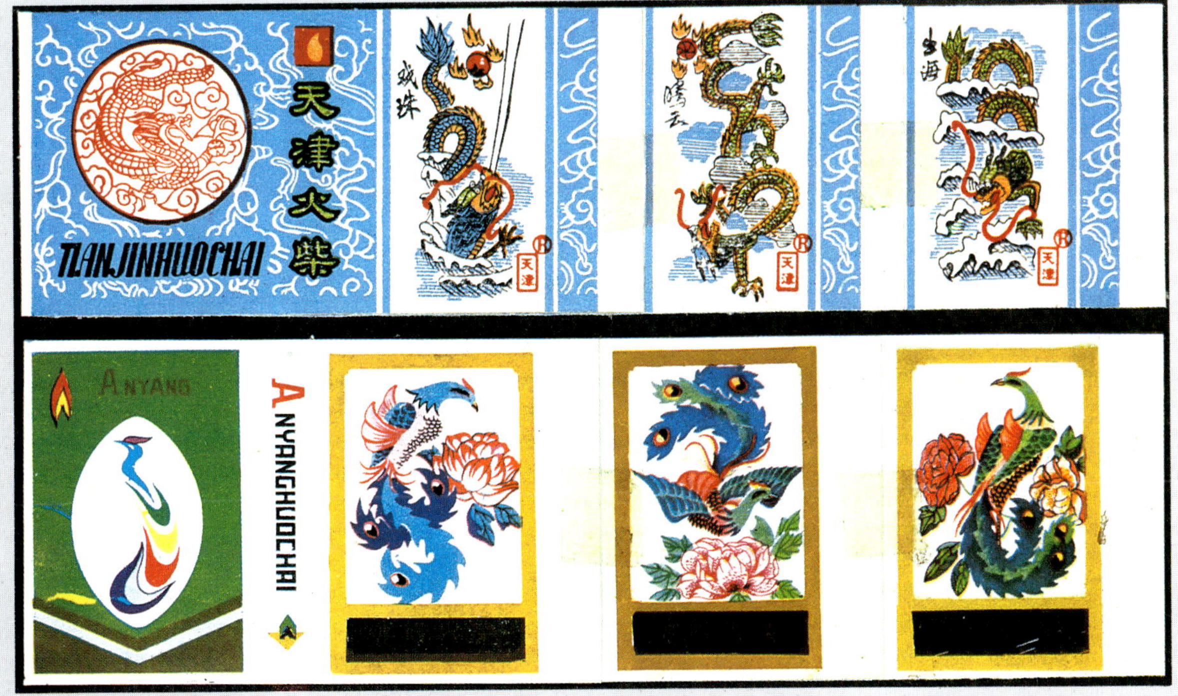

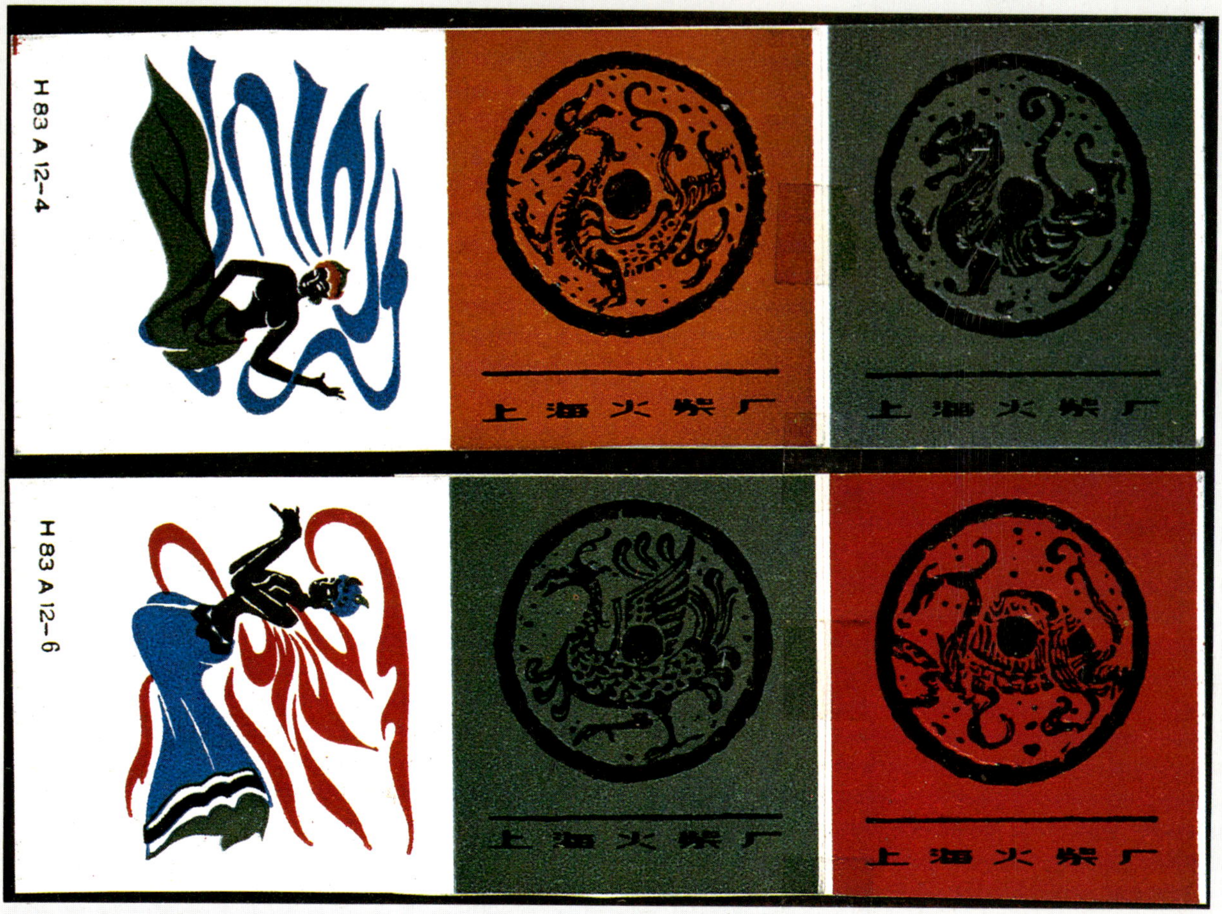

Eaves-Tile Patterns

The patterns consist of green dragon (upper left), white tiger (upper right), rosefinch (lower left) and tortoise and snake (lower right). These represent respectively the east, the west, the south and the north.

Made in Shanghai

106 mm x 53 mm

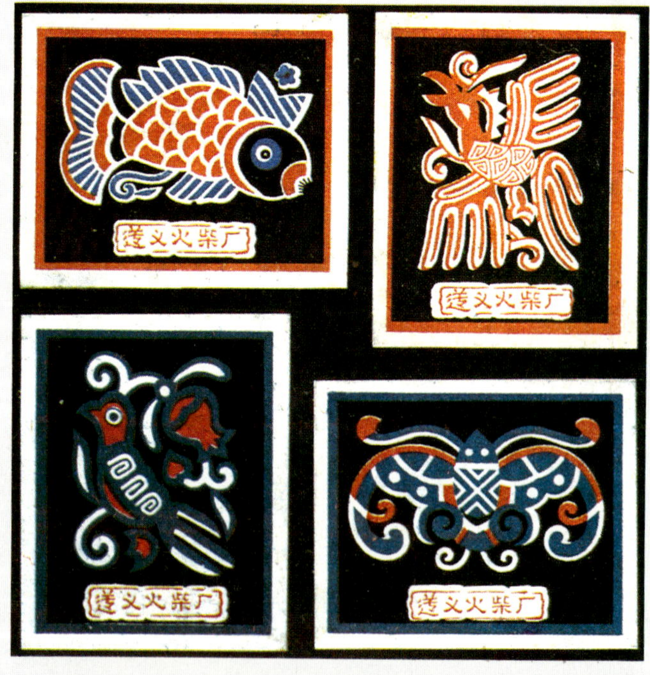

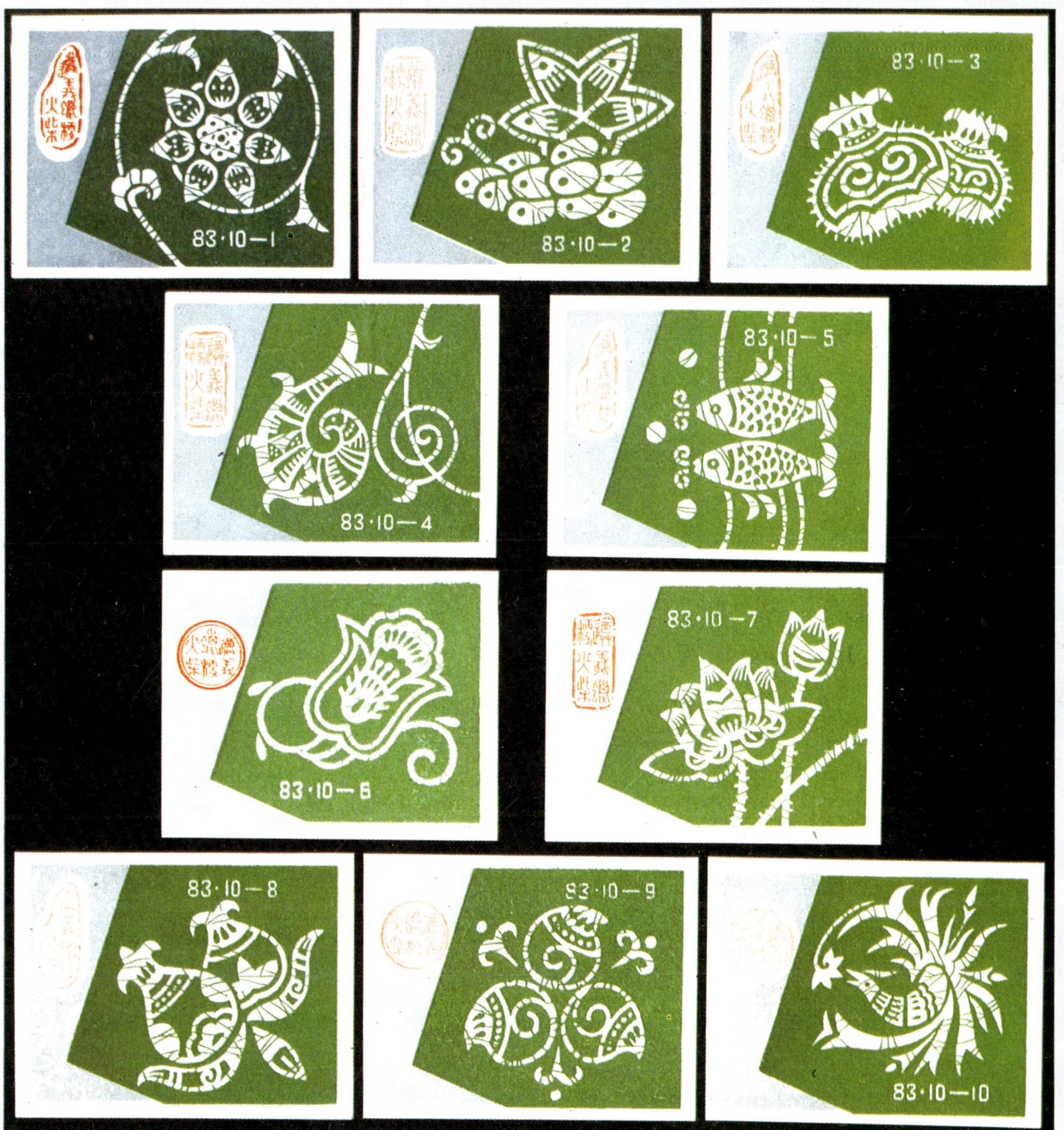

Wax Printing or Batik

Popular with minority nationalities in the southwestern areas of China, wax printing is a technology of printing and dying. The process consists of drawing patterns with wax on white cloth. The cloth is then dyed in blue. When the wax is peeled away, the blue cloth is printed with white patterns.

Made in Zunyi, Guizhou Province

44 mm x 33 mm, 43 mm x 35 mm

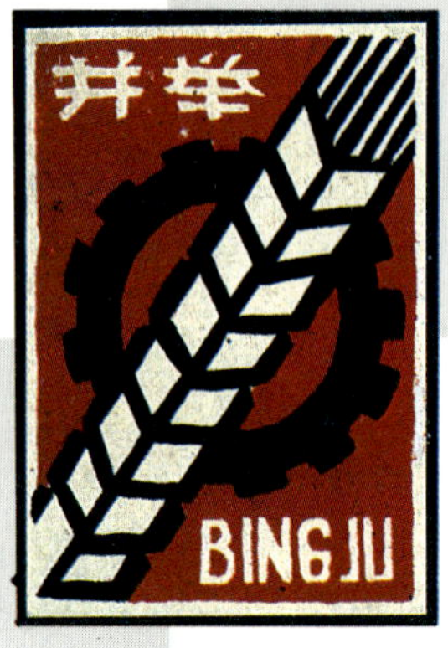

Industry and Agriculture

For more than three decades after the founding of New China, unprecedented achievements have been made in industry, agriculture, science, technology and national defence. People's lives have also been greatly improved.

This section of the book is intended to introduce the achievements of the Chinese socialist construction, especially industry and agriculture. Though these pictures are confined to a small space, one can feel the pulse of Chinese industry and smell the earthy aroma of the Chinese countryside which has assumed a new form after tremendous changes. To strengthen the visual effect of these matchbox covers, the designers used vivid artistic images and distinctive national forms that enable people to comprehend the meaning instantly and spark the imagination.

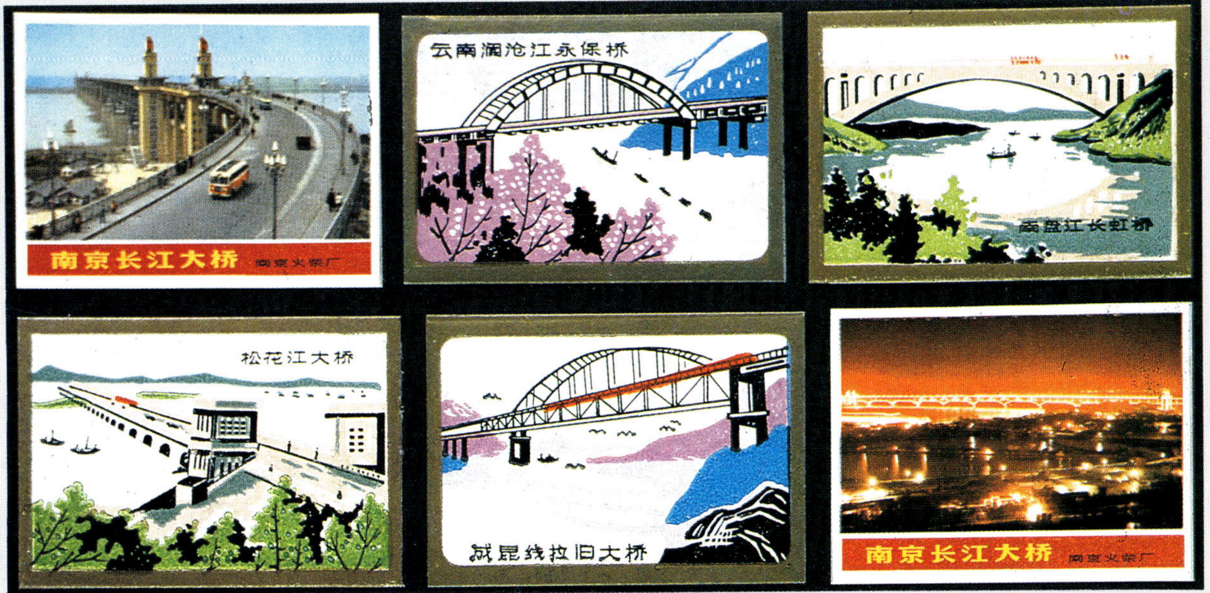

Bridge Construction

Bridge construction has a quite long history in China. As early as 257 B.C., pontoon bridges were thrown across the thrashing waves of the Yellow River. Since that time, the technology of bridge construction has advanced enormously. Many well-known bridges have been built in China. In the technology of contemporary bridge construction, China ranks among the most advanced countries in the world.

This group of covers shows some of the bridges constructed in China during the last twenty years. Clockwise: Nanjing Yangtze River Bridge, Yongbao Bridge over the Lancang River, Changhong Bridge over the Nanpan River, view of Nanjing Yangtze River Bridge at night, Lajiu Bridge on the Chengdu-Kunming Railway, and Songhua River Bridge.

Made in Nanjing, Jiangsu Province; and Anyang, Henan Province

50 mm x 36 mm, 51 mm x 35 mm

China's Printing Industry

Printing is one of the great inventions of ancient China, although it was very backward during the long feudal period. In the past few decades, however, printing industry has developed quickly. It is now capable not only of doing careful printing jobs, but of manufacturing printing machinery. Shown here are three printing machines produced in Shanghai.

Made in Shanghai

40 mm x 32 mm

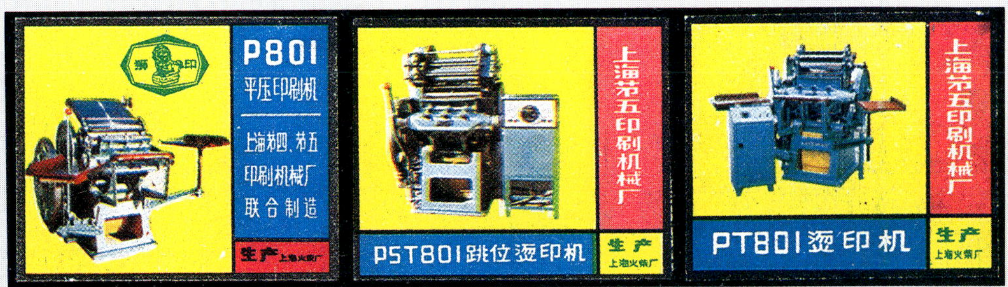

Communication and Transportation

These covers contain motifs of China's communication and transportation, which have developed rapidly along with the rapid growth of industry, agriculture and science.

Made in Jinan, Shandong Province

95 mm x 58 mm

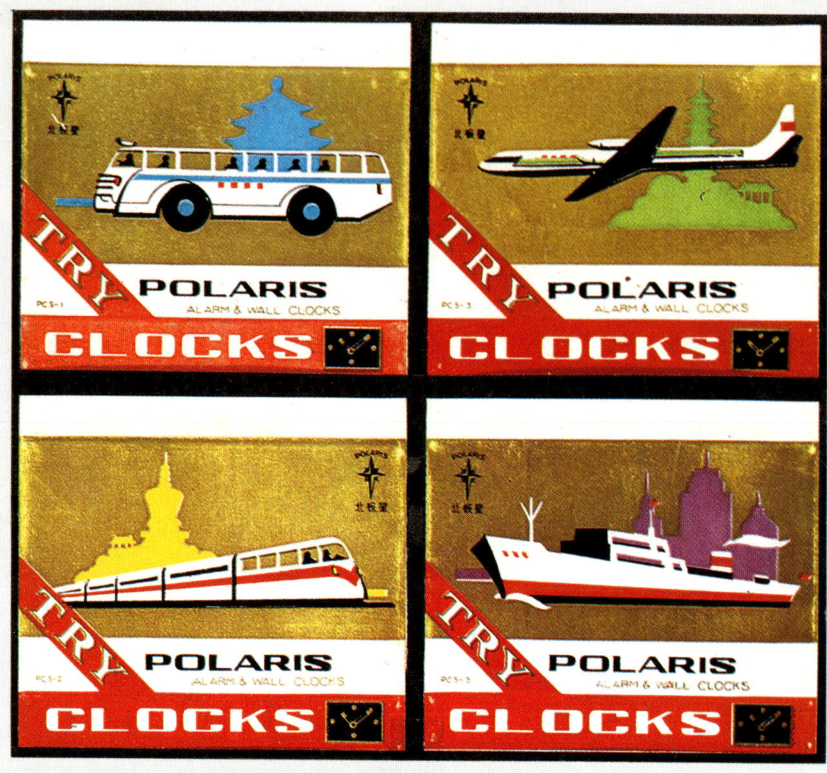

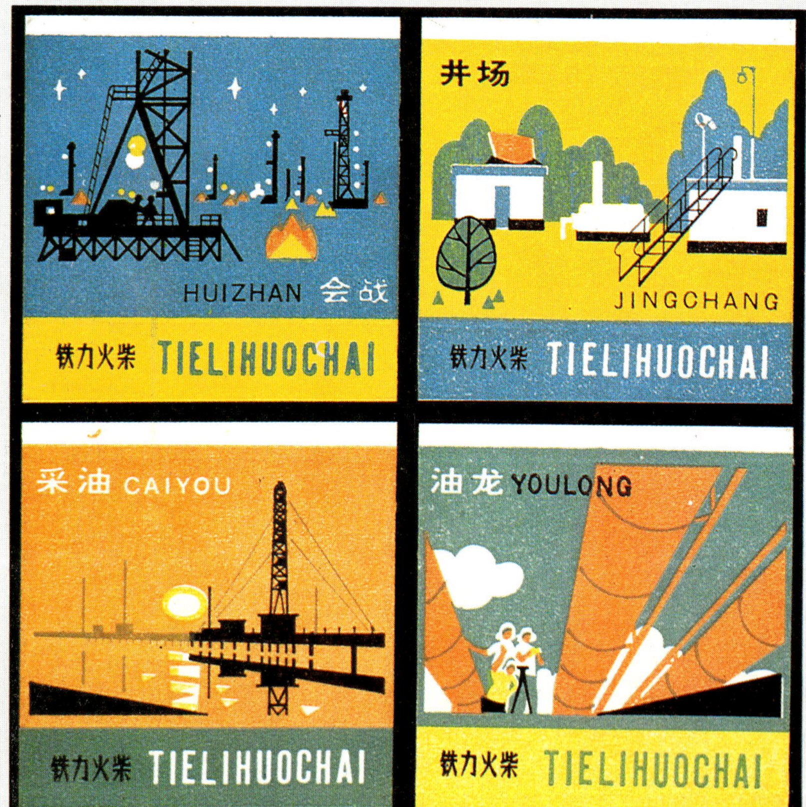

The Oil Industry

Since the 1960's, when Daqing Oilfield was established, several high-yield oilfields have been built in China. At present, China is self-sufficient in oil and capable of exporting it as well.

Made in Tieli, Heilongjiang Province

101 mm x 50 mm

Ten Big Buildings

In celebration of the 10th anniversary of the founding of the People's Republic of China, the building workers of Beijing completed ten magnificent structures in only one year, demonstrating the high potential of Chinese architecture. From top to bottom, left column: the Great Hall of the People, Museum of Chinese History, Cultural Palace of Nationalities, Overseas Chinese Hotel, Exhibition Hall of Agriculture; from top to bottom, right column: the Monument to the People's Heroes, Military Museum of the Chinese Revolution, Hotel of Nationalities, Worker's Stadium, and Beijing Railway Station.

Made in Beijing

49 mm x 33 mm

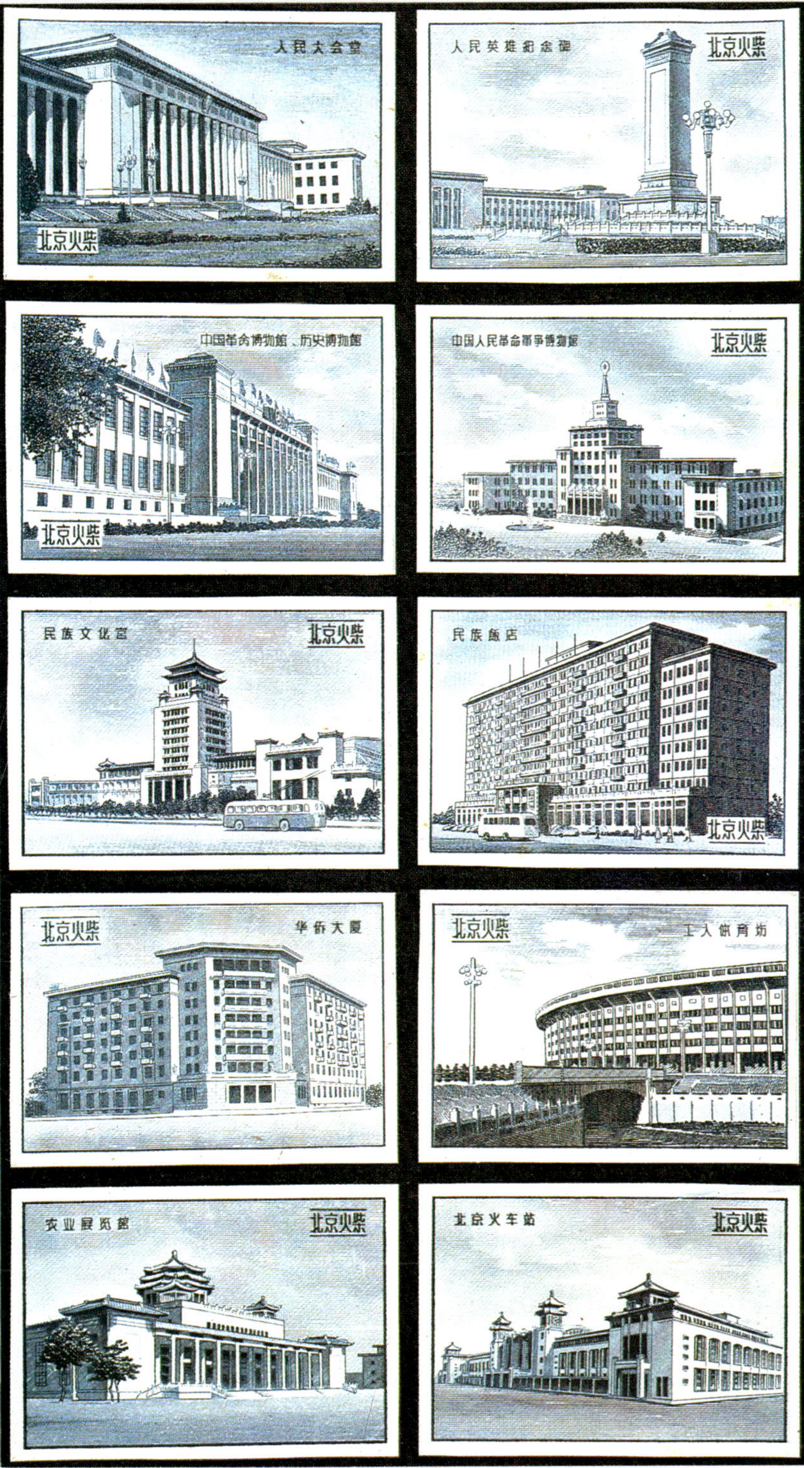

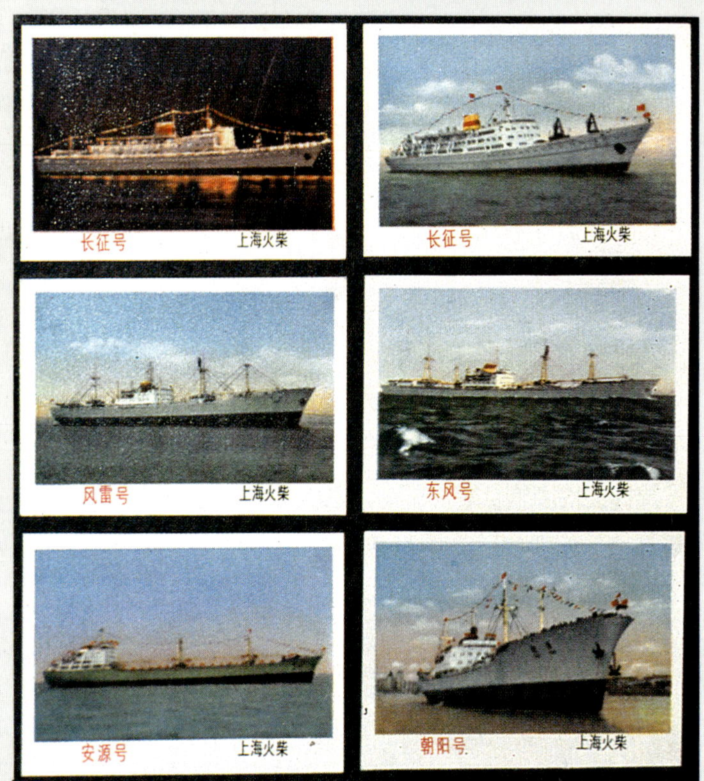

The Shipbuilding Industry

The modern shipbuilding industry hardly existed in China before the 1950's. Now China produces large ships like those shown here to meet domestic and foreign needs.

Made in Shanghai

50 mm x 35 mm

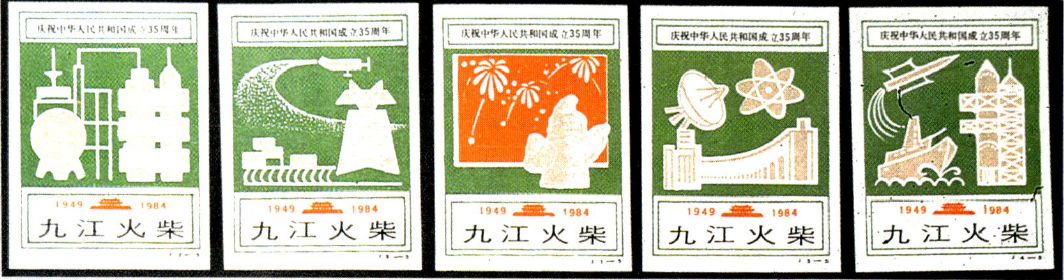

China's Achievements in Construction

The new look of industrial and scientific development in China is displayed in this group of covers designed to celebrate the 35th anniversary of the founding of New China. The piece in the middle shows festive fireworks in Beijing's Tiananmen Square.

Made in Jiujiang, Jiangxi Province

44 mm x 34 mm

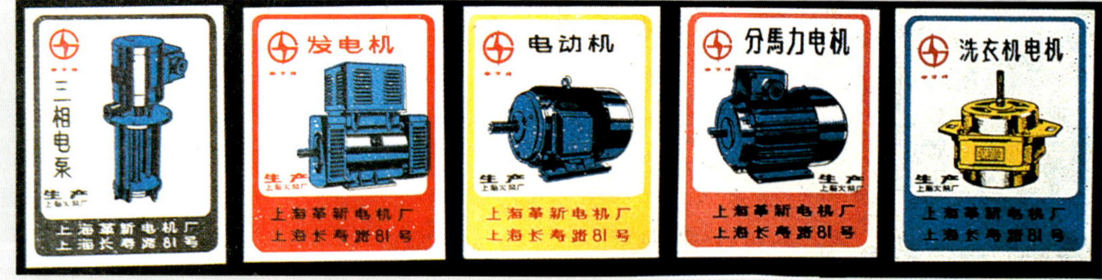

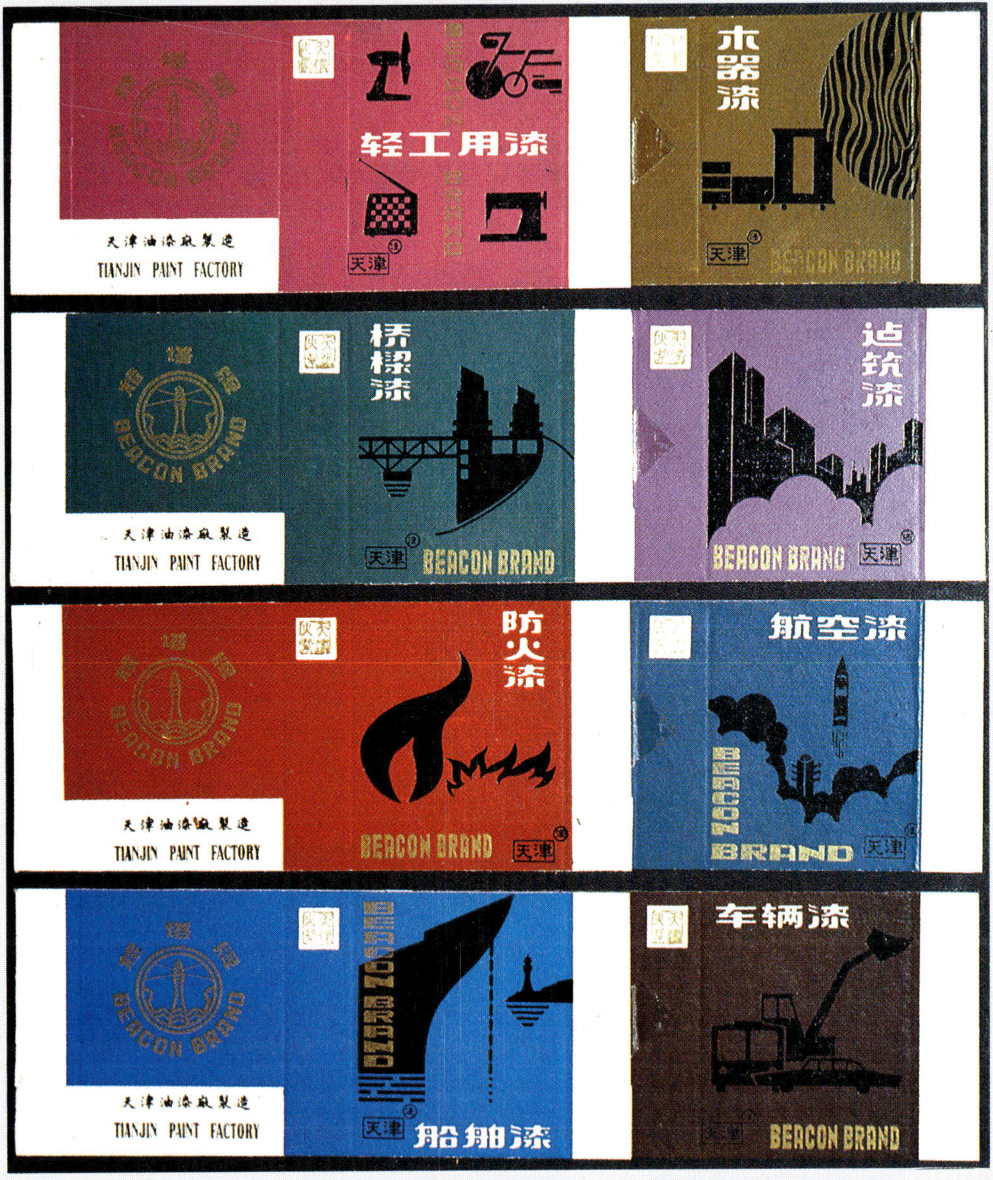

Electrical Machinery

This group shows the products of Shanghai's Gexin Electrical Machinery Plant. From left: three-phase electric pump, generator, electric motor, fractional horsepower motor, and washing-machine generator.

Made in Shanghai

41 mm x 33 mm

The Paint Industry

China's paint industry stagnated at the artisan level for a very long time. After the rise of industrial construction, production of industrial paint has been increasing.

This set of matchbox covers displays different kinds of paint for different uses.

Made in Tianjin

107 mm x 45 mm

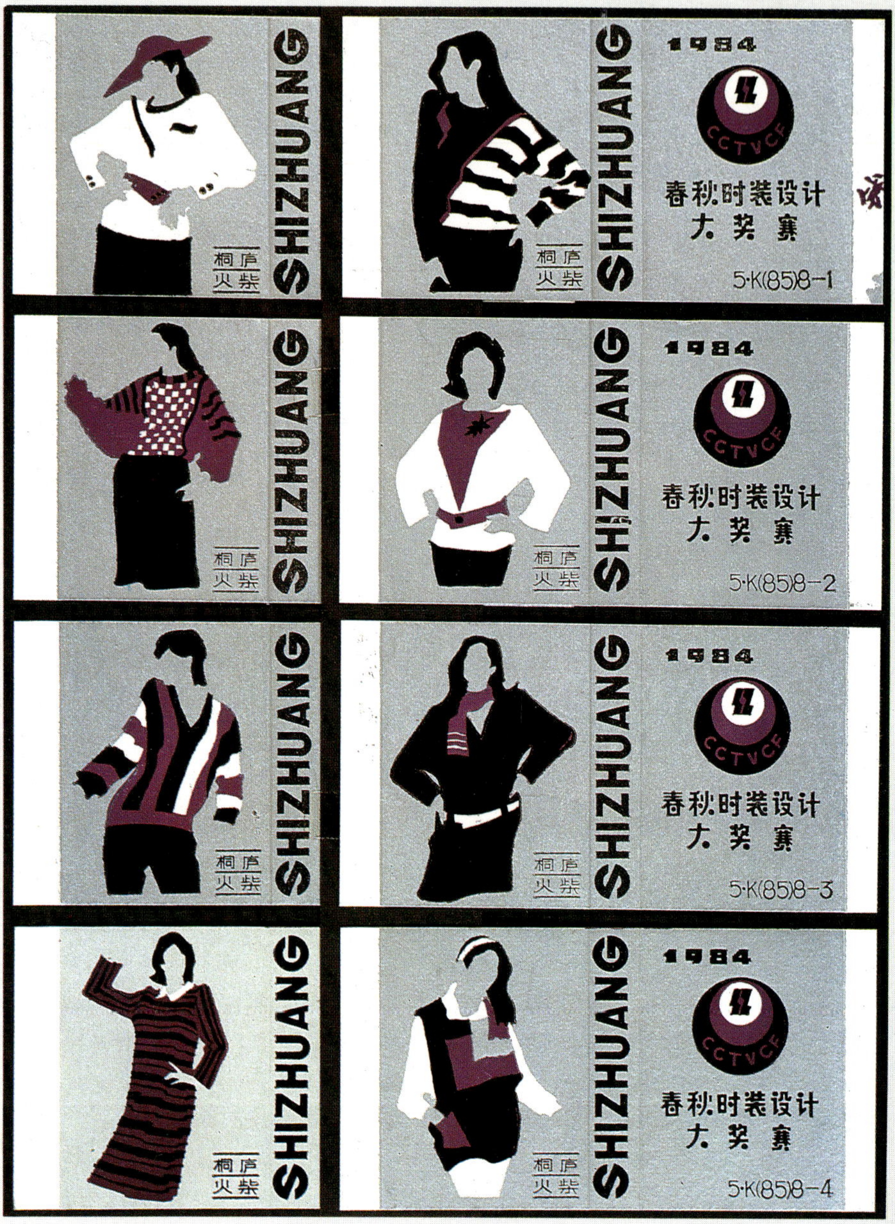

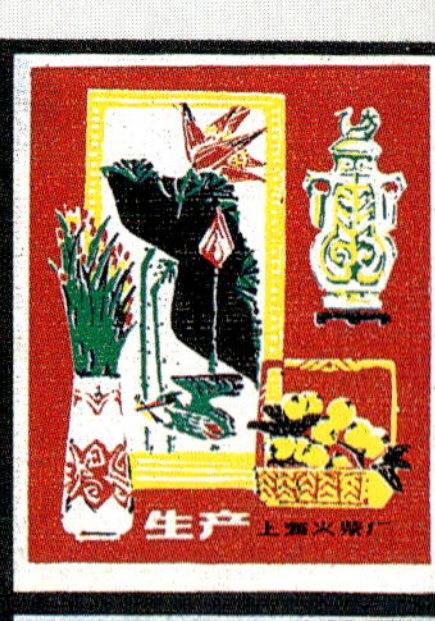

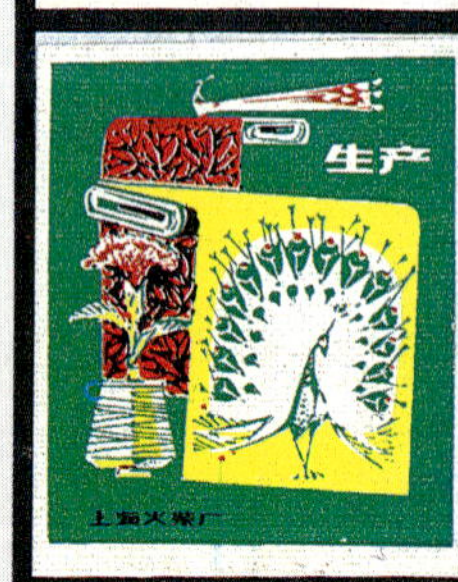

Clothing

This group of covers carries designs from the spring and autumn fashion shows organized by CCTV in 1984. Here we can see Chinese clothing becoming beautiful and diversified.

Made in Tonglu, Zhejiang Province

86 mm x 44 mm

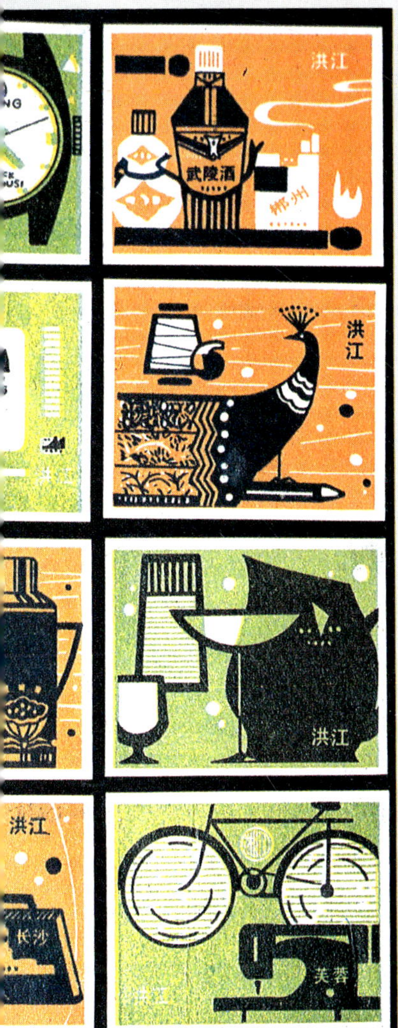

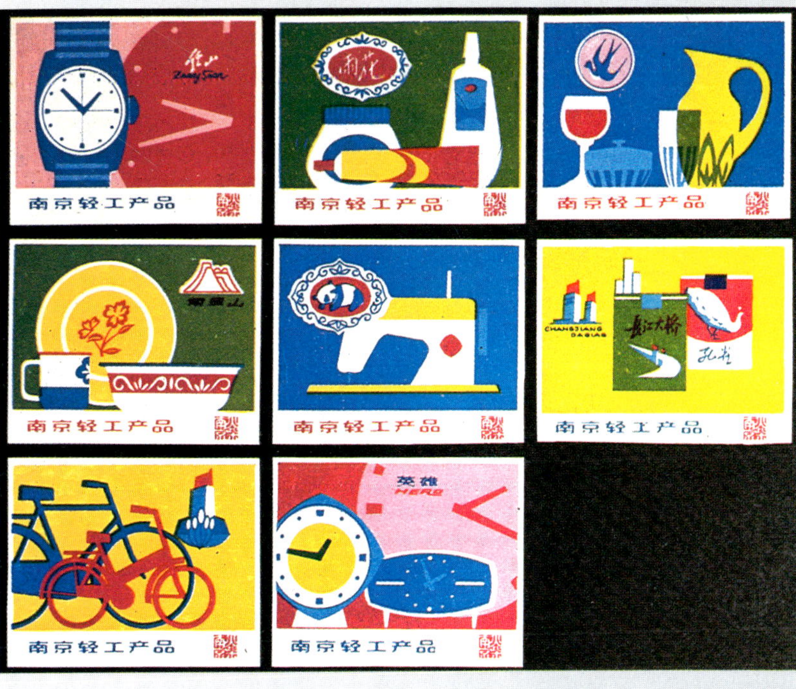

Products of Light Industry

This four groups demonstrate the great variety of products for daily necessities. The design of each group has distinctive characteristics.

Made in Hongjiang, Hunan Province; Shanghai; and Nanjing, Jiangsu Province

42 mm x 35 mm, 40 mm x 33 mm, 45 mm x 36 mm, 41 mm x 33 mm

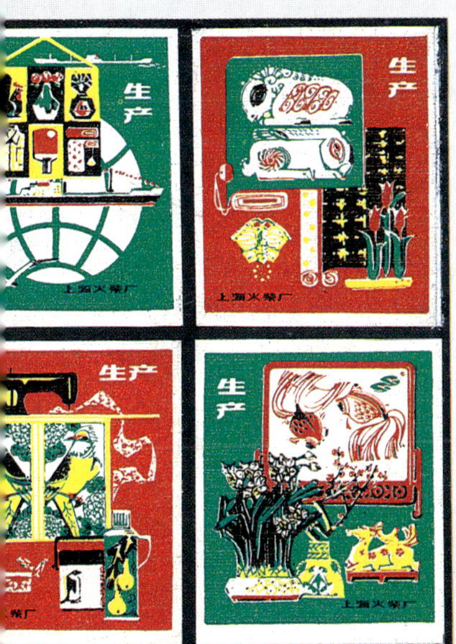

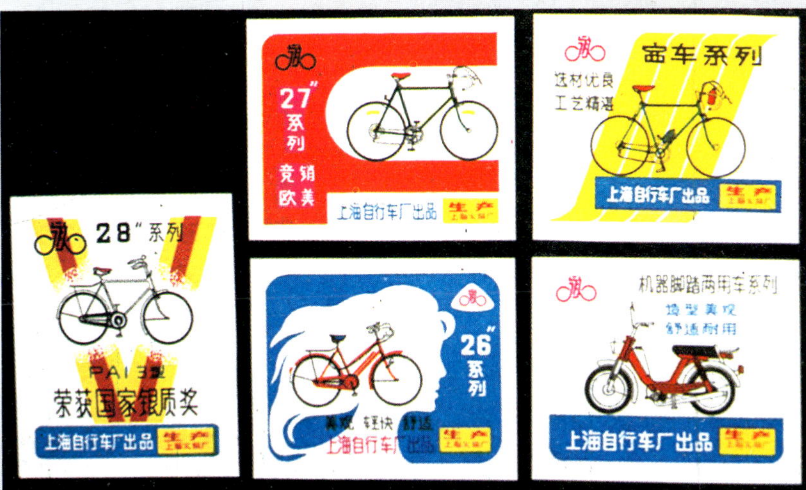

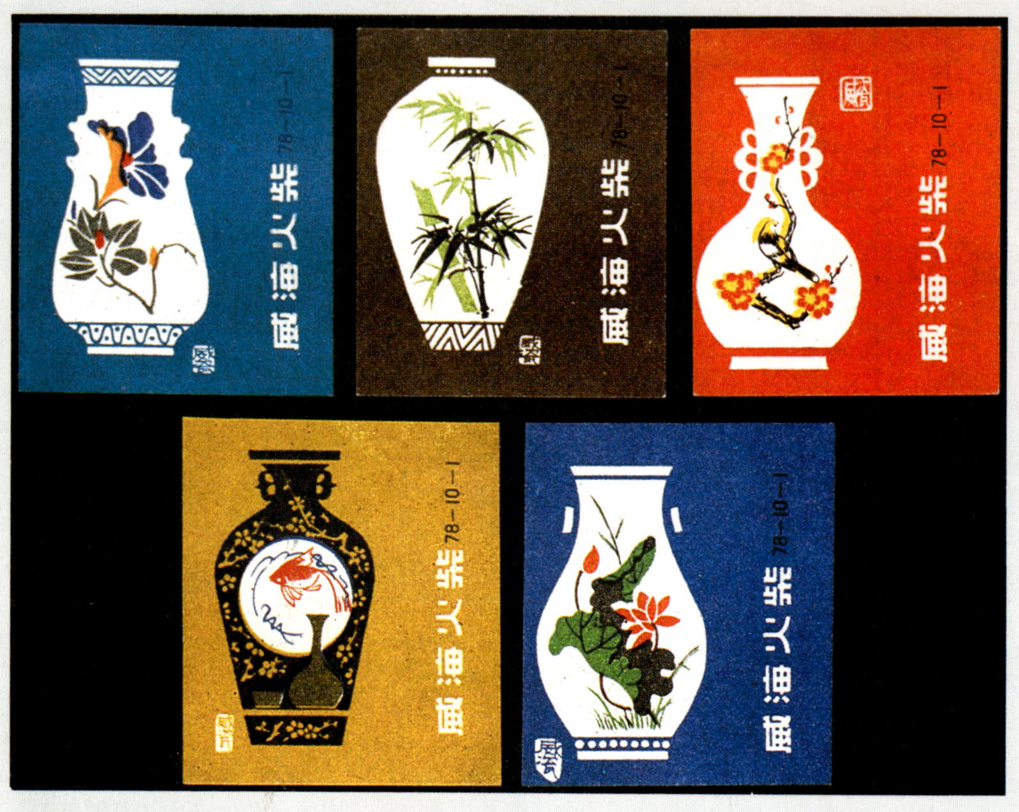

The Ceramic Industry

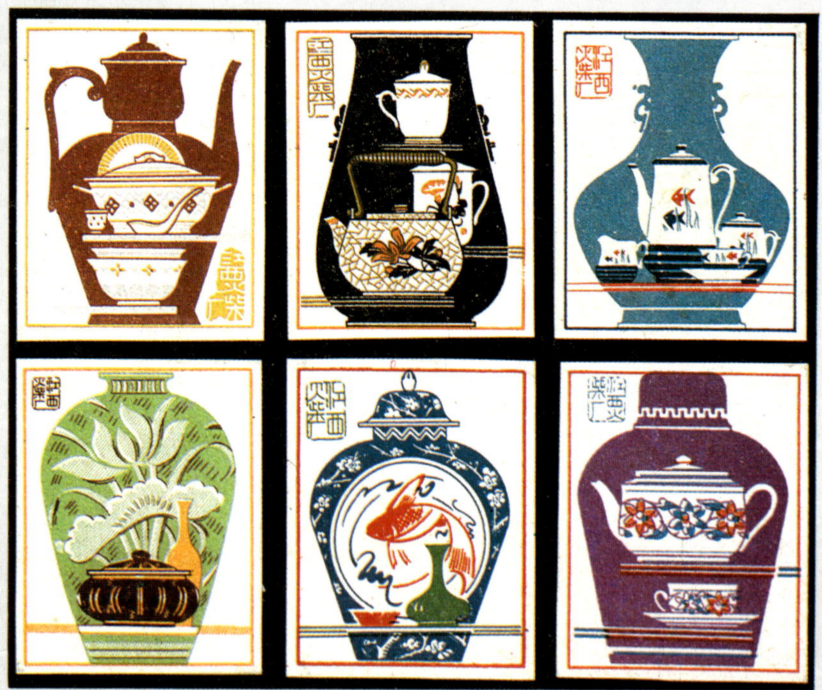

Noted as a "Nation of Porcelain," China exports a large quantity of porcelain including Jingdezhen Porcelain which is known both at home and abroad for being "thin as paper and white as jade."

These two groups of matchbox covers show the unique compositions in the patterns of the ceramics.

Made in Weihai, Shandong Province; and Nanchang, Jiangxi Province

43 mm x 37 mm, 42 mm x 34 mm

The Lingnan Area

Abundant in products, the Lingnan area (Guangdong and the greater part of Guangxi) has the climate of a subtropical zone. The group of covers here briefly introduces its natural conditions, local products and agricultural production. Clockwise: picking coconuts, making palm-leaf fans, cutting sugarcane, transporting vegetables, fishing, and harvesting papaya.

Made in Guangzhou, Guangdong Province

54 mm x 35 mm

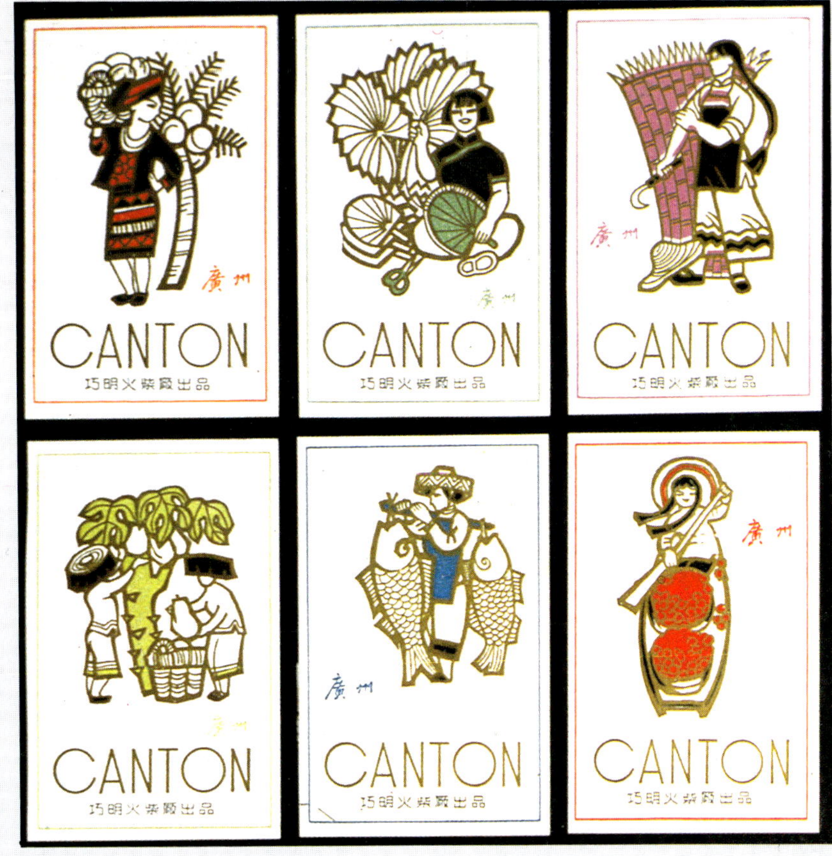

New Countryside

The agricultural activities in the new countryside of south China are shown here. Clockwise: transporting fertilizer, pumping water, harvesting fruit, harvesting wheat, transplanting rice seedlings, and fishing.

Made in Nanjing, Jiangsu Province

49 mm x 36 mm

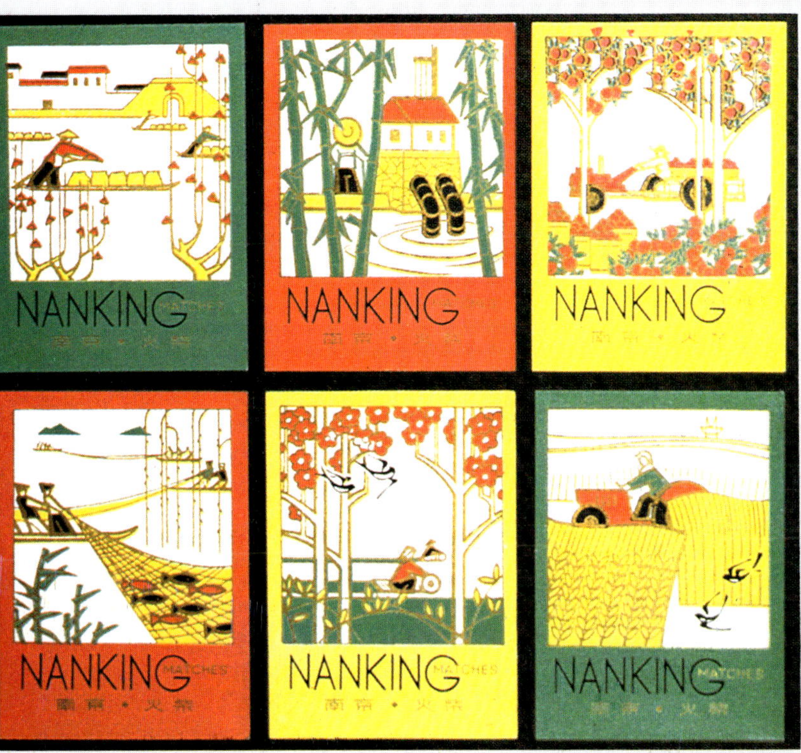

Water Conservation

Water conservation is the key to developing agriculture. Since the founding of New China, many water conservation works have been built to make the farmland more resistant to natural calamities.

This group of covers shows the construction of water conservation in Hebei Province. Clockwise: Haihe Sluice Gate, Guanting Reservoir, the Pioneer Bridge over the Grand Canal, Gangnan Reservoir, and a key water control project on the Haihe River.

Made in Botou, Hebei Province
105 mm x 56 mm

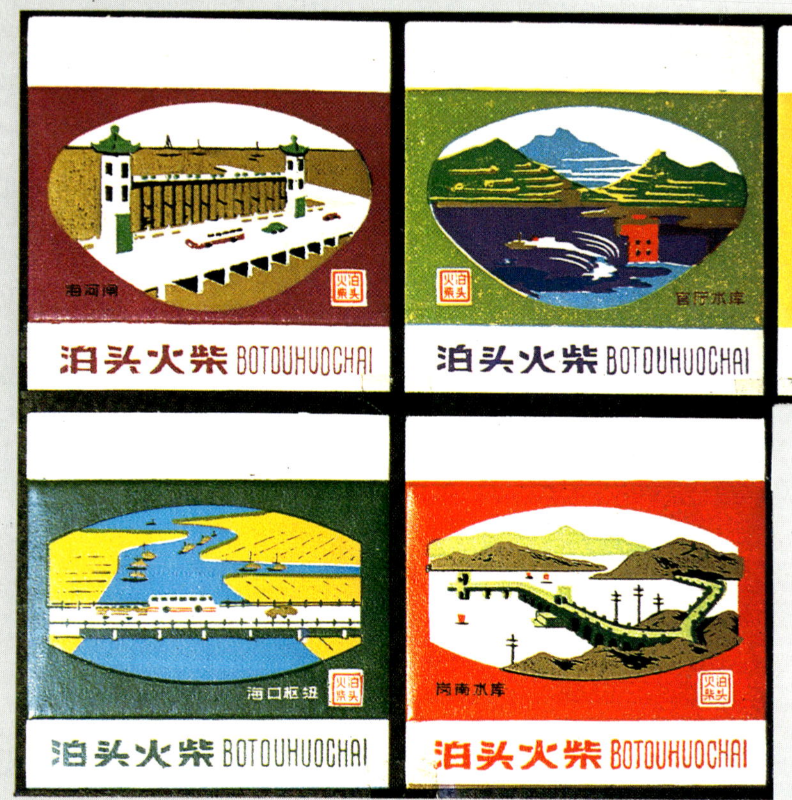

Desire for a Bumper Harvest

"An abundant harvest of all food crops" and "the thriving of all domestic animals" have been the desire of Chinese peasants since ancient times. During the Spring Festival, every household puts up poems and New Year's pictures to express their hope for bumper harvests. This group of covers combines the Spring Festival couplets with the New Year pictures.

Made in Liu'an, Anhui Province
45 mm x 36 mm

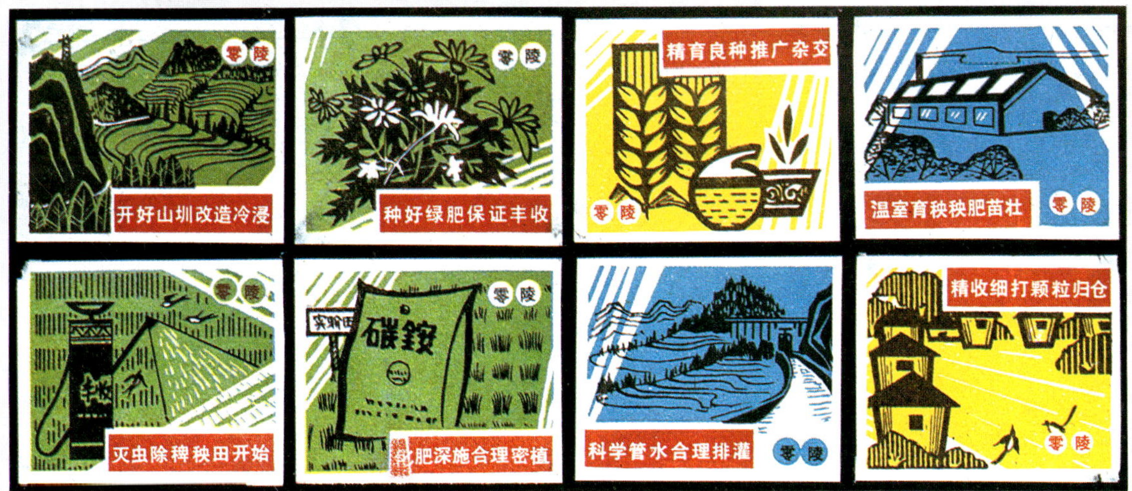

Scientific Farming

Clockwise: opening up mountain valleys and transforming the low-yield fields; planting the green manure crop to guarantee a good harvest; raising the improved variety and spreading hybrid crops; nursing young plants in hot-houses; careful harvesting and transporting every grain to the granary; scientific and rational irrigation; deep fertilizing and rational close planting; and eliminating insect pests to ensure the fast growth of rice seedlings.

Made in Linlin, Hunan Province
42 mm x 34 mm

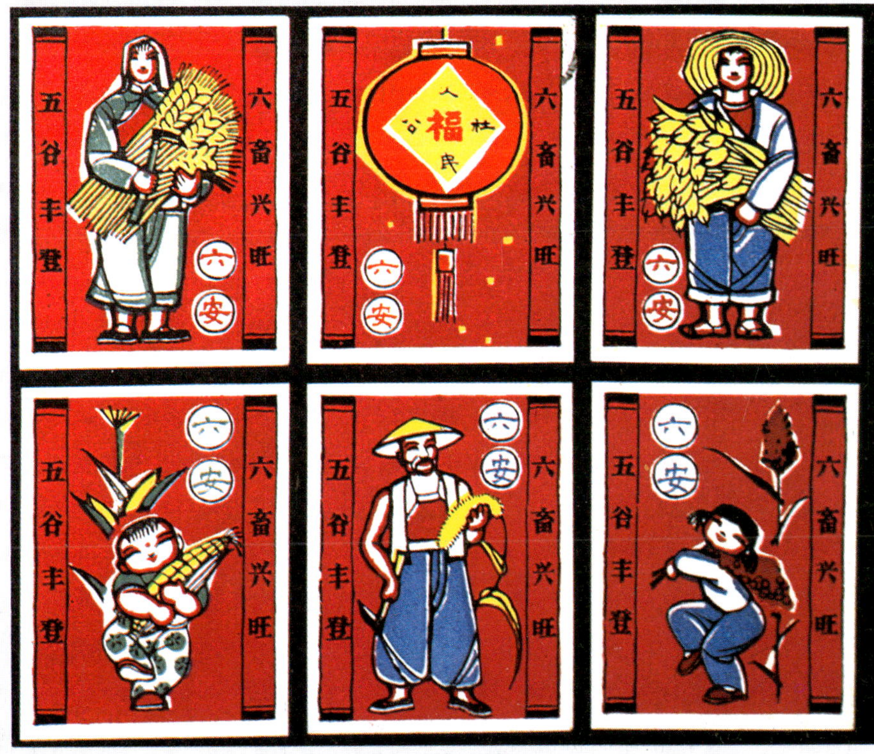

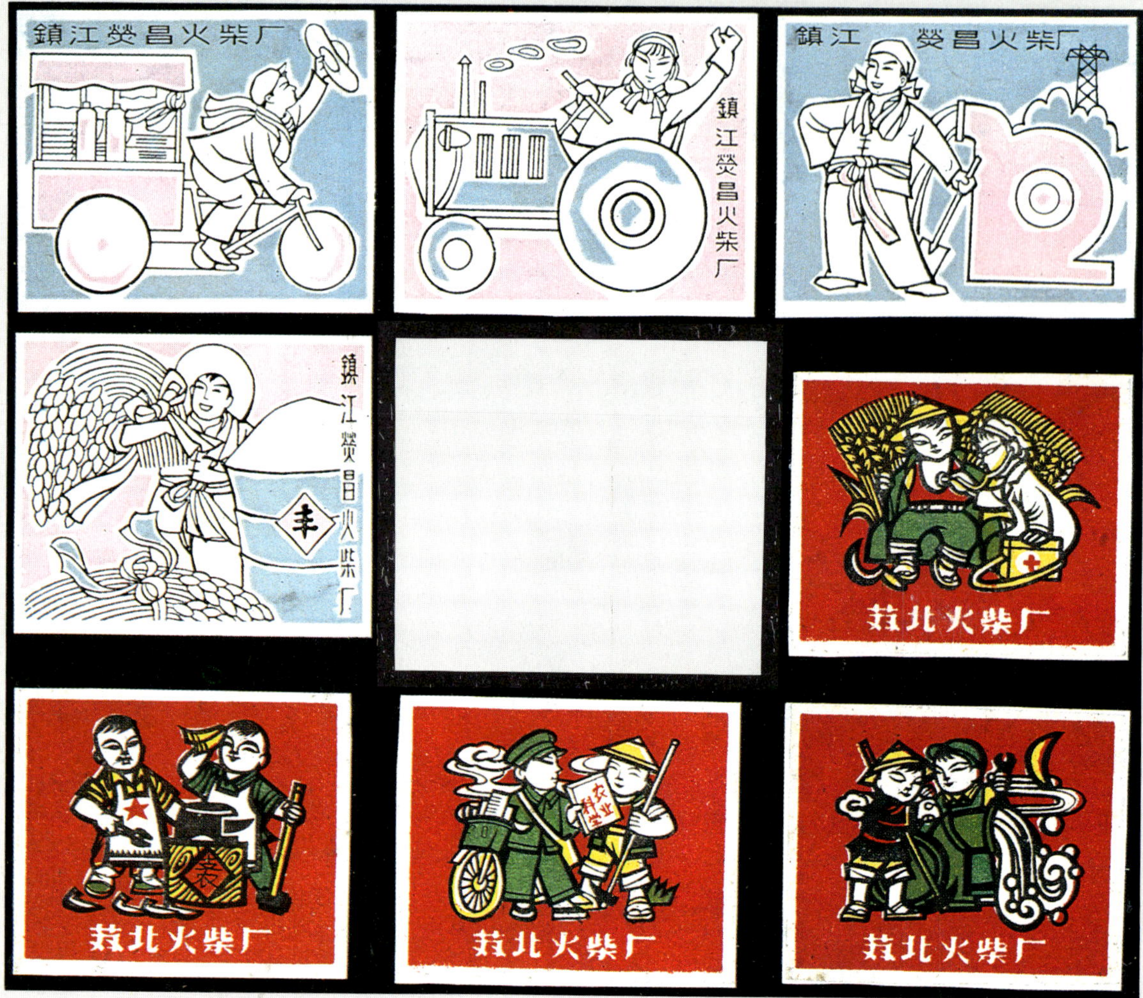

Supporting Agricultural Production

These two groups of covers show the scenes supporting agricultural production from all areas of China. Their goal is to produce a bumper harvest.

Made in Zhenjiang and Yangzhou, Jiangsu Province

46 mm x 37 mm, 43 mm x 35 mm

Five Flourishing Trades

Chinese agriculture is guided by a policy of overall development of agriculture, forestry, animal husbandry, sideline and fishery. Agriculture is thought to be the key factor. The two groups of covers here show the flourishing five trades in paper-cuttings, an art form with a strong rural flavour.

Made in Shanghai; and Liu'an, Anhui Province

42 mm x 34 mm, 44 mm x 36 mm

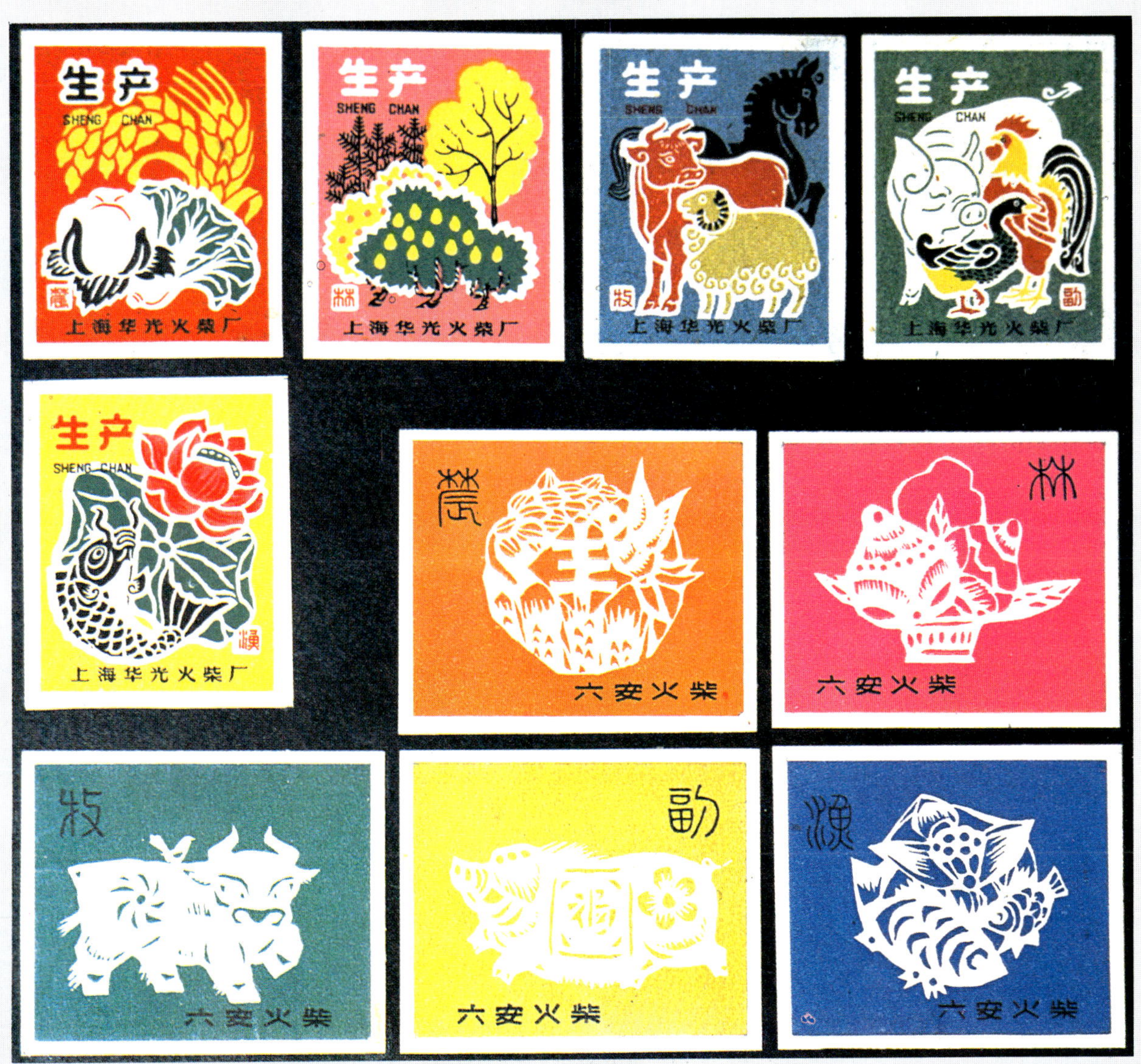

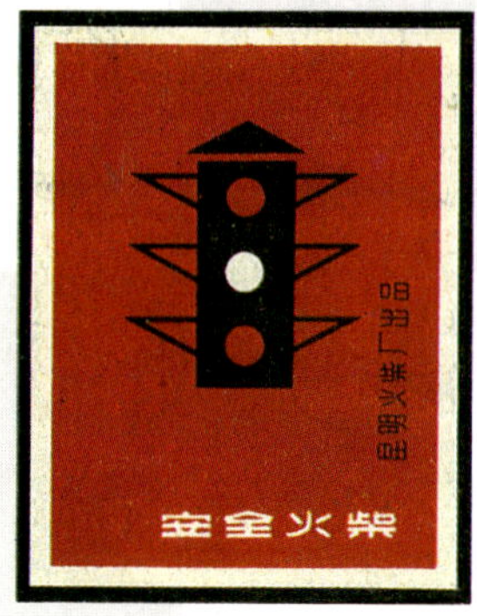

General Knowledge

This section of matchbox covers concerns general knowledge about people's work and lives. Through vivid images on matchboxes the artist conveys the facts. By means of interesting games and riddles, these matchbox covers convey both entertainment and factual information.

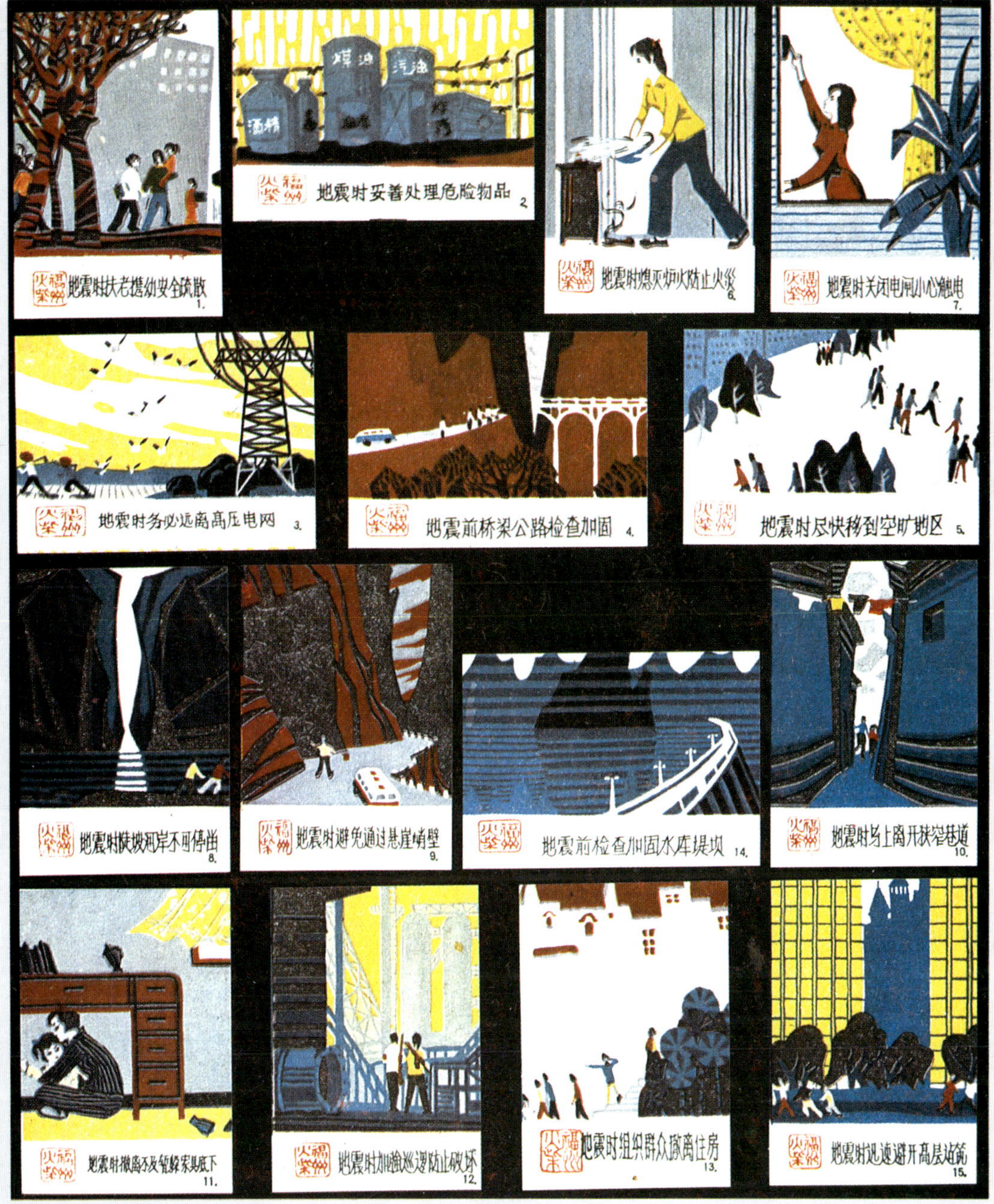

Basic Knowledge of Earthquakes

Since earthquakes cause great damage to humans, it is necessary to gain knowledge on how to prevent casualties in earthquakes.

This group of pictures demonstrates means to avoid damage: Examining and reinforcing bridges and dykes before an earthquake; switching off lights; extinguishing stove fire; discarding dangerous articles; and avoiding buildings, river slopes, precipitous cliffs and high-tension lines.

Made in Fuzhou, Fujian Province
50 mm x 35 mm

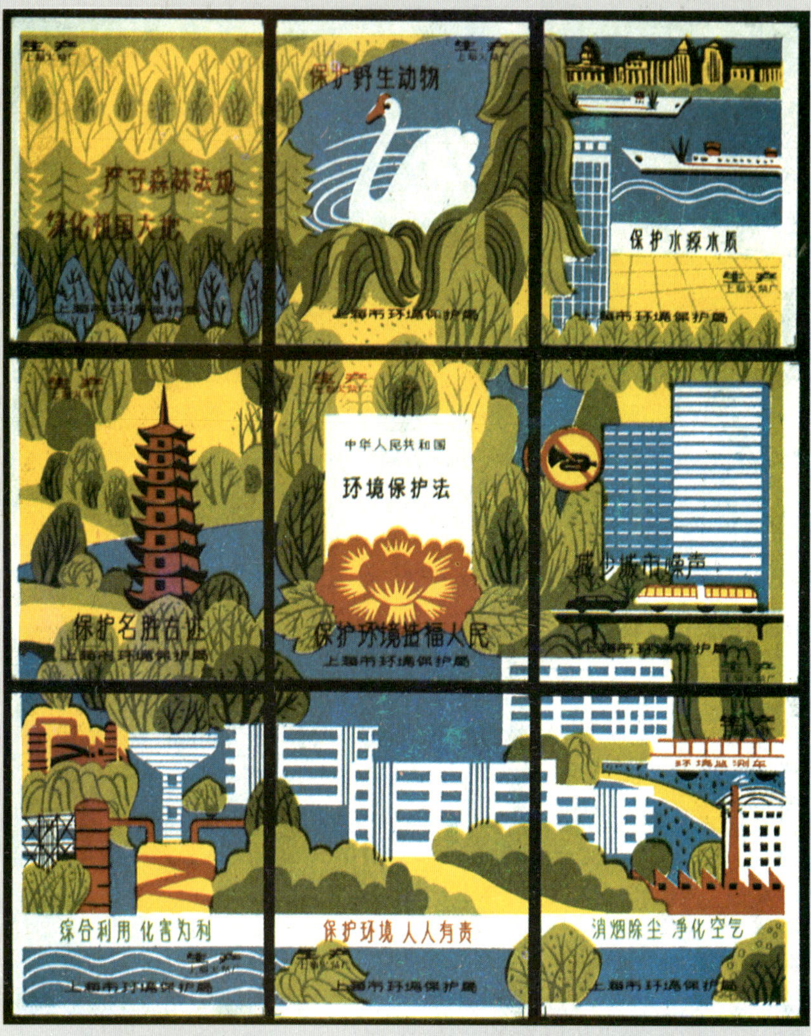

Environmental Protection

People have paid attention to protecting and harnessing natural resources so that the environment in which they live can be protected against contamination and damage. To this purpose, the Chinese government has promulgated *The Environmental Protection Law* to remind people of the importance of forests, wild animals, water resource and quality. There is interest in the decrease and even the elimination of noise, smoke and dust in the cities, and further, a comprehensive administration of the natural environment.

Made in Shanghai
42 mm x 34 mm

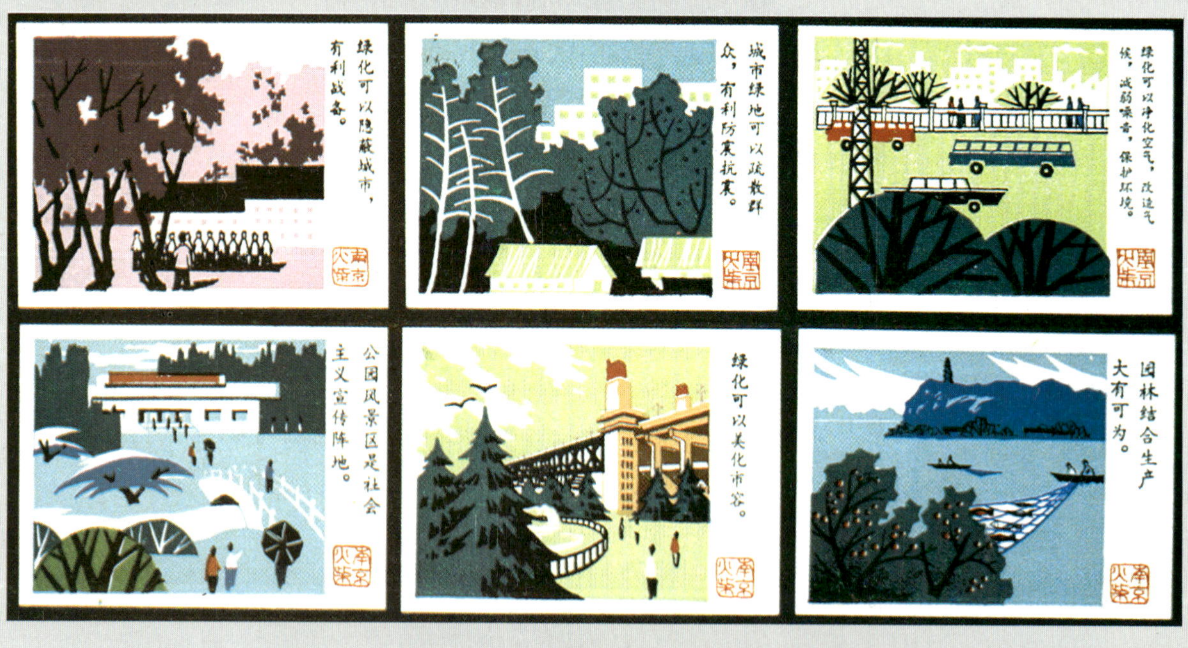

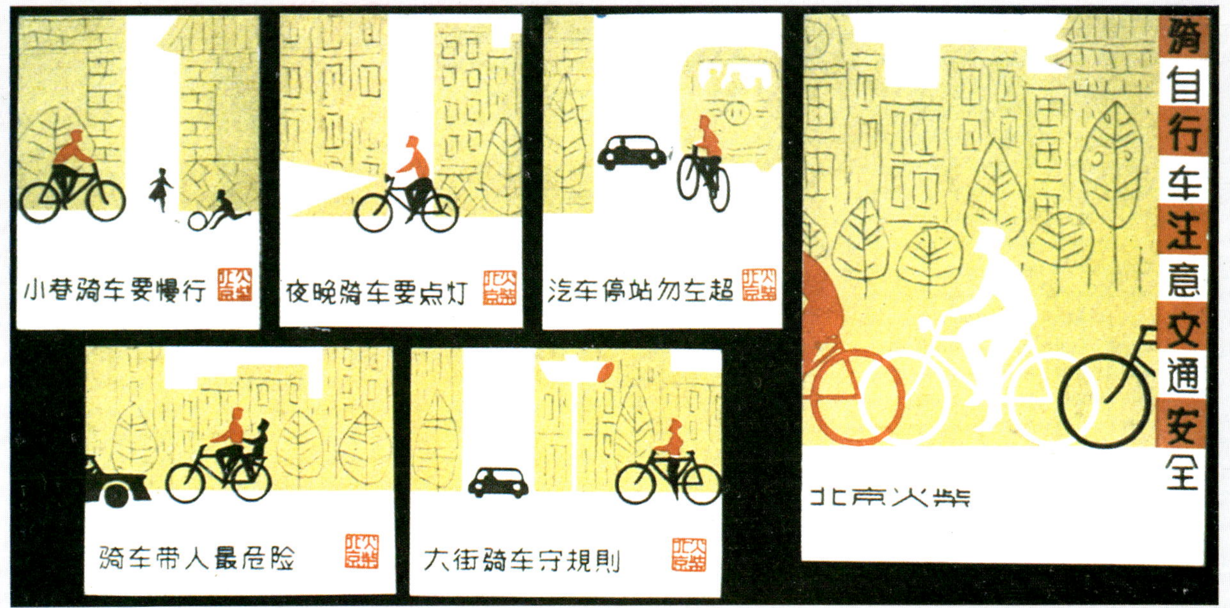

Traffic Safety

China is noted as the "kingdom of bicycles." Beijing alone has six million. The matchbox covers here exhort bicyclists and pedestrians to pay attention to traffic signals and walk on zebra-crossing.

Made in Beijing; and Hangzhou, Zhejiang Province

76 mm x 58 mm, 44 mm x 34 mm, 42 mm x 34 mm

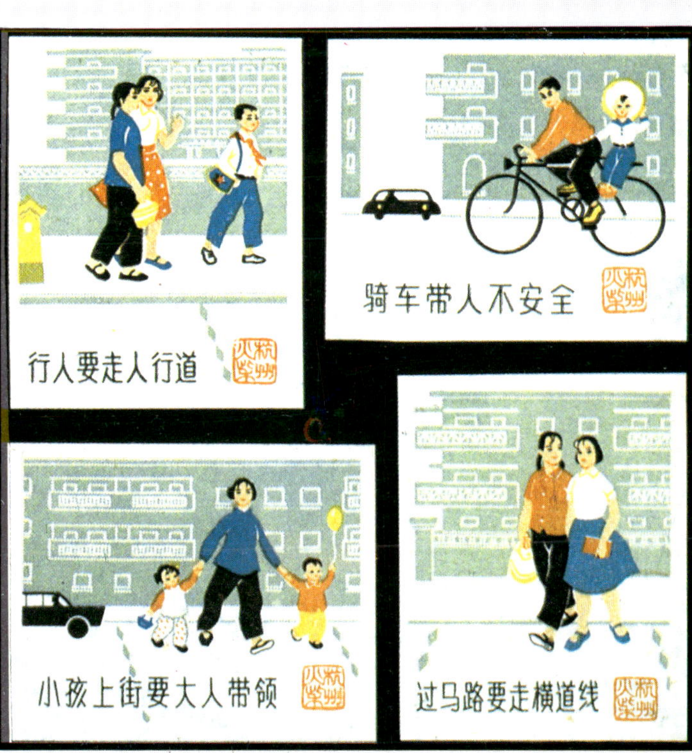

Forestation

Planting trees, grass and flowers is an important means of beautifying the natural surroundings and purifying the air. This group of matchbox covers shows its advantages.

Made in Nanjing, Jiangsu Province

50 mm x 37 mm

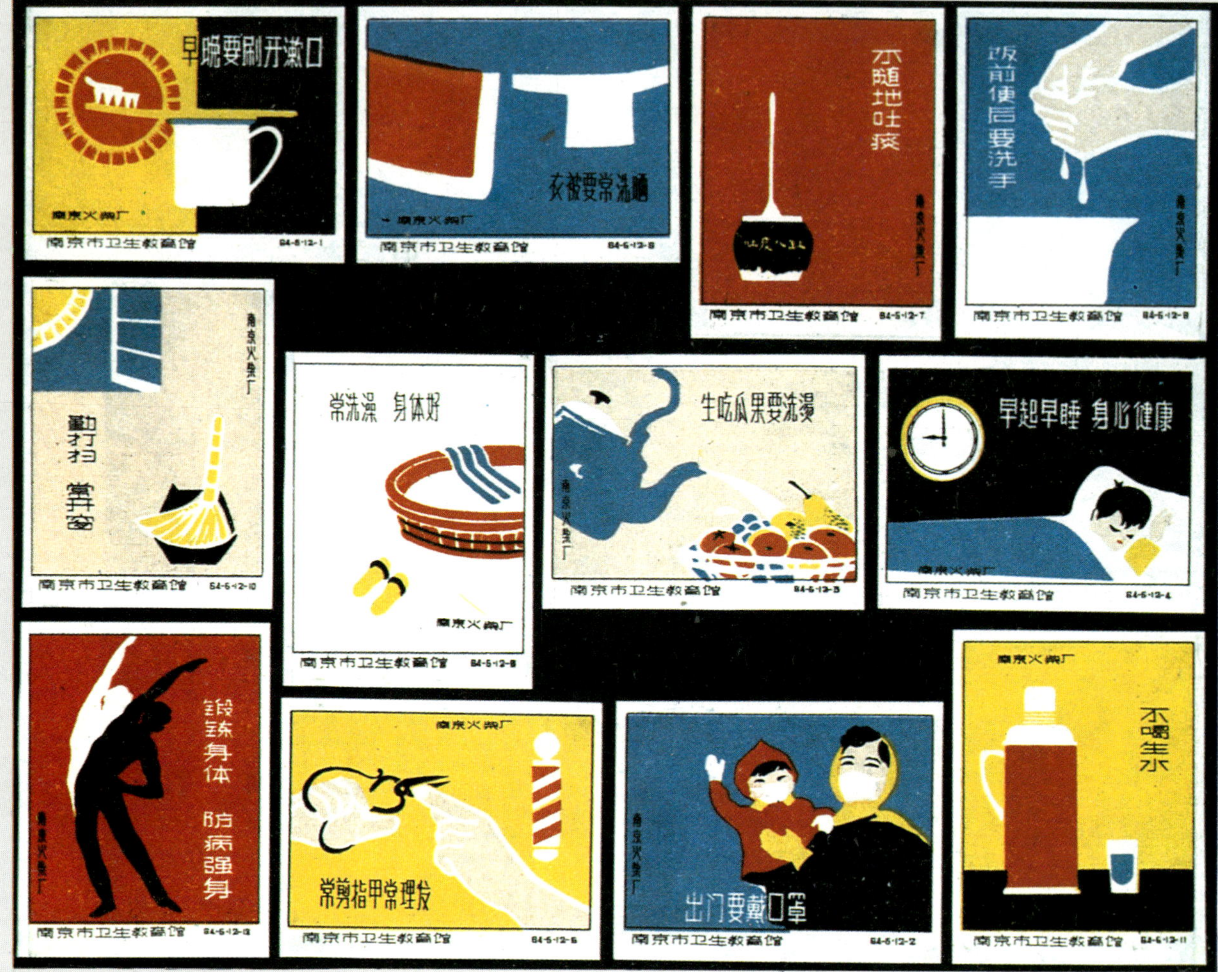

Hygiene and Health Protection

These matchbox covers teach people to pay attention to hygiene and to build physical strength in their daily lives.

Made in Nanjing, Jiangsu Province

43 mm x 34 mm

A Corner of Kitchen

Presenting an aspect of the Chinese kitchen, this set shows how housewives use liquified petroleum gas for cooking.

Made in Qingdao, Shandong Province

106 mm x 57 mm

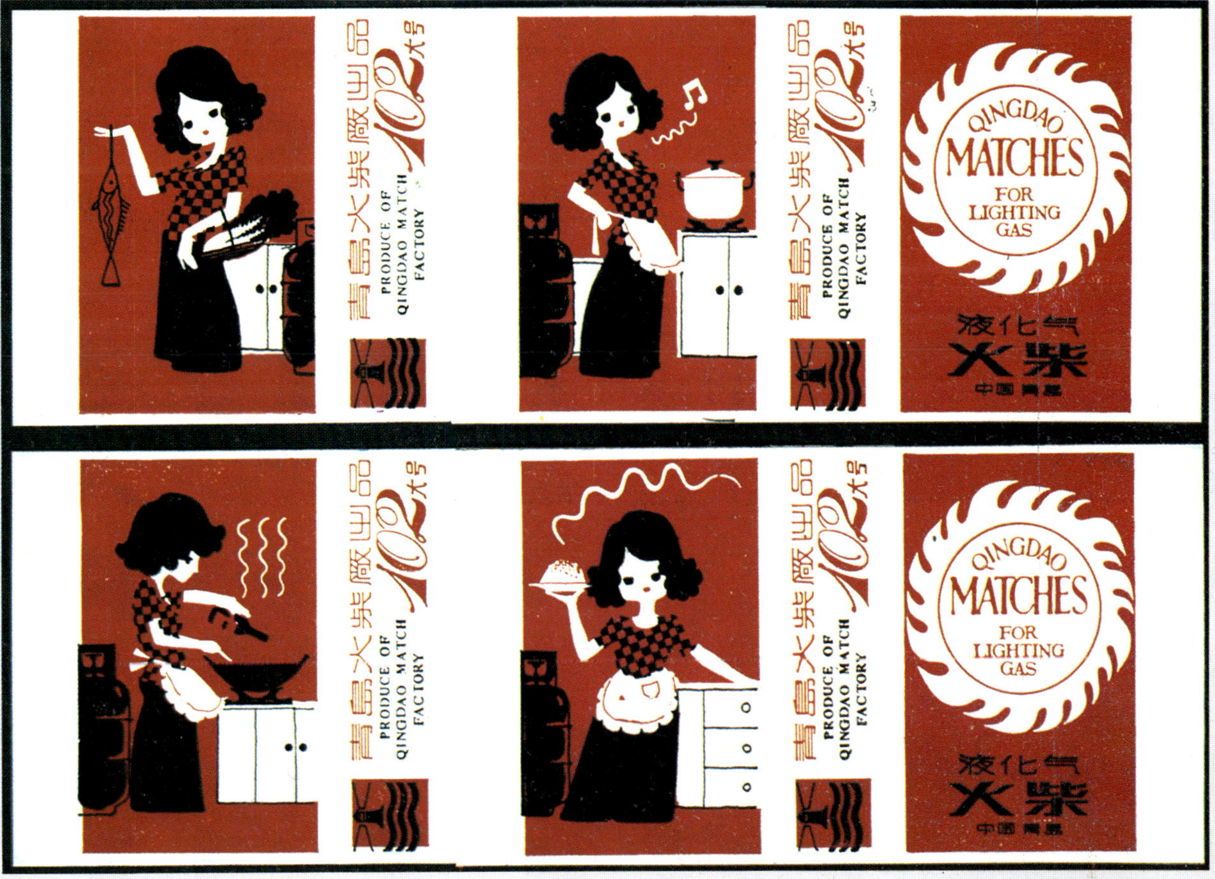

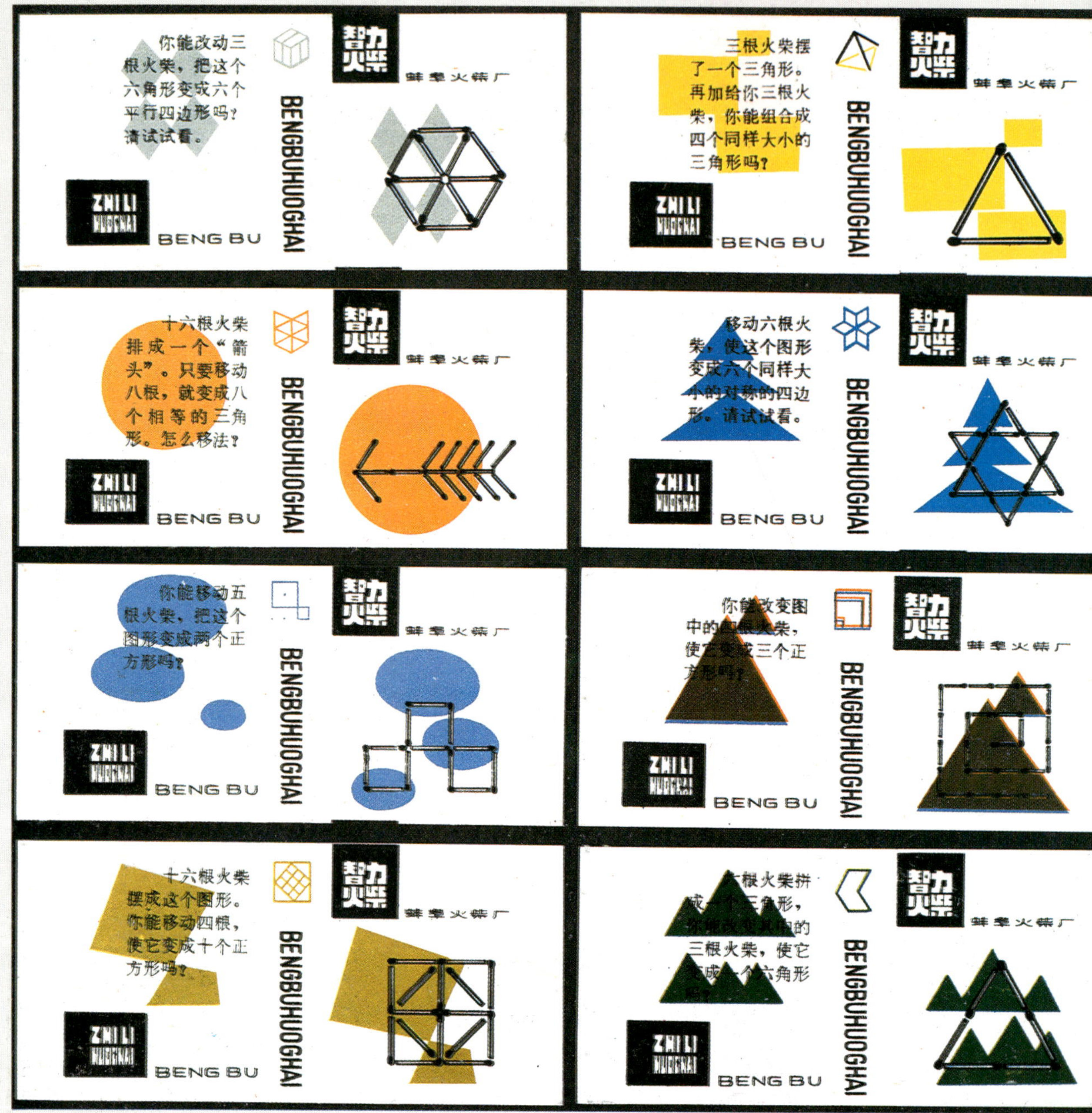

Match Games

Riddles are the subject matter in this group of matchbox covers.

Reading from left on the first row: If you move three matches can you get six parallelograms? Add three more matches and form four identical triangles. Move only three matches and turn the picture upside down. Move three matches again and make the area of the new picture five-ninths of the original one.

Reading from left on the second row: Move eight matches and get eight identical triangles. Move six matches and get six identical sy mmetrical quadrilaterals. Move six matches again and get three lozenges. Move four

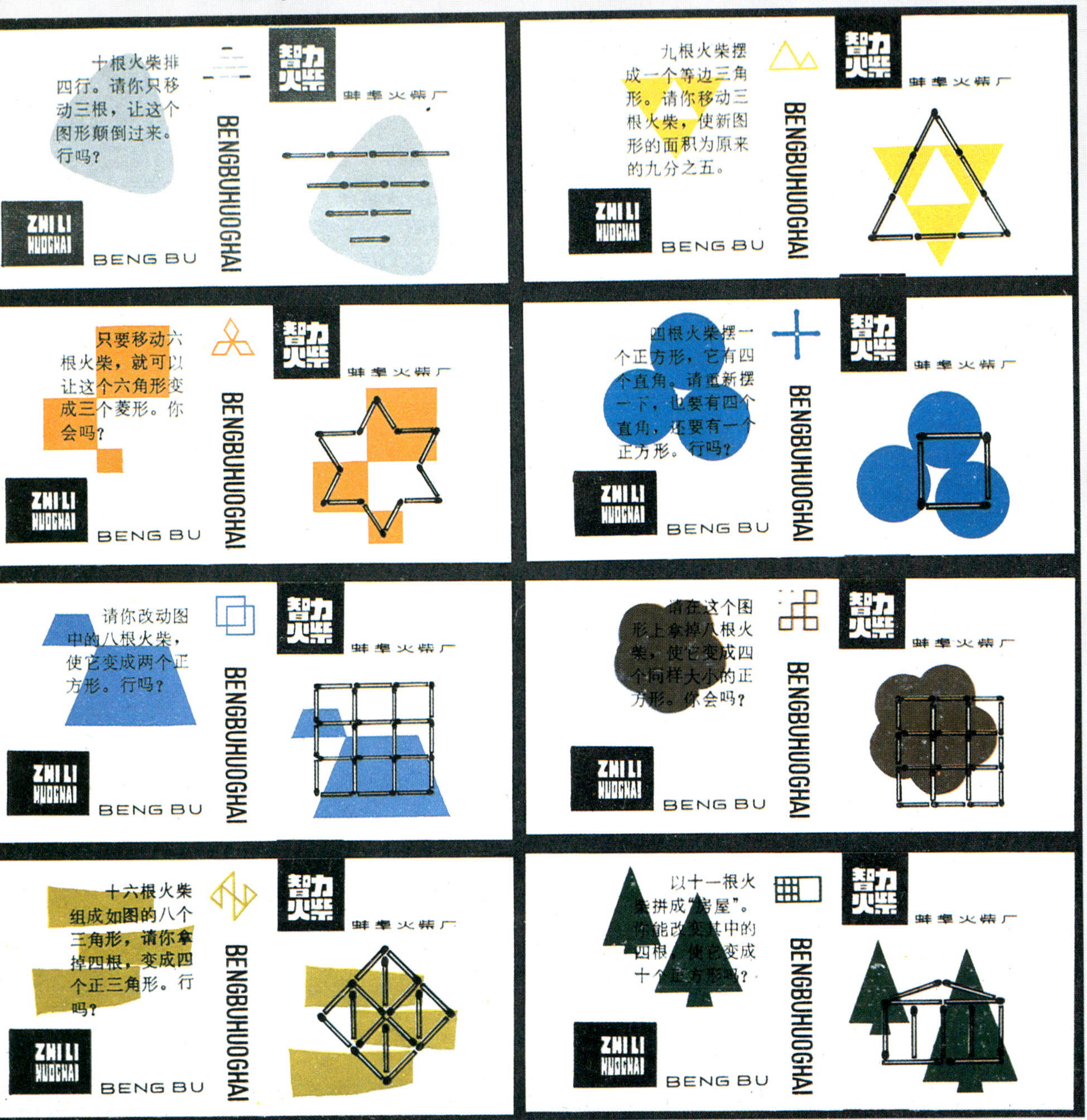

matches and get a square with four right angles.

Reading from left on the third row: Move five matches and get two squares. Move four matches and get three squares. Move eight matches and get two squares. Remove eight matches and get four identical squares.

Reading from left on the fourth row: Move four matches and get ten squares. Move three matches and get a hexagon. Remove four matches and get four triangles. Shift four matches and get ten squares.

Made in Bengbu, Anhui Province

101 mm x 46 mm

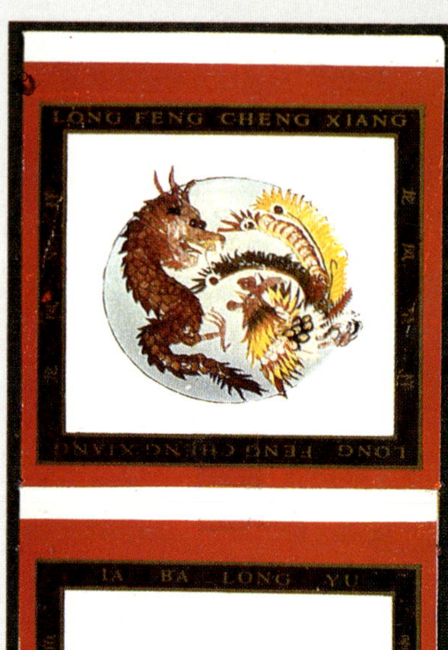

Chinese Cooking

Chinese cooking enjoys a high reputation both at home and abroad. Its famous dishes include Guangdong, Jiangsu, Sichuan and Shandong cooking. Chinese cooks are particular about colour, odour, flavour and shape. These two sets introduce some well-known menus and cakes of the Jiangsu kind.

Made in Nanjing, Jiangsu Province

123 mm x 55 mm, 93 mm x 62 mm

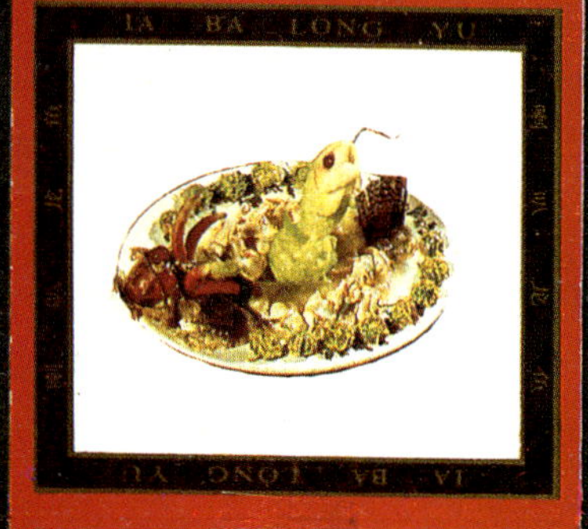

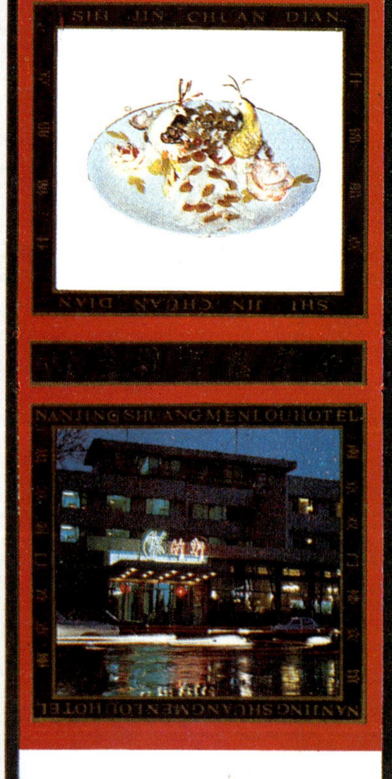

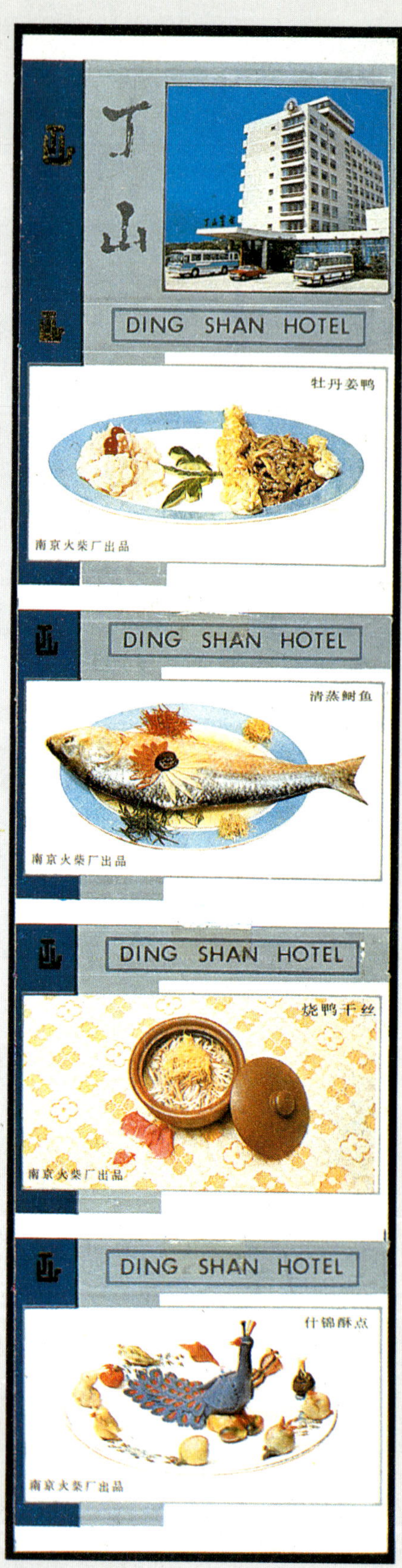

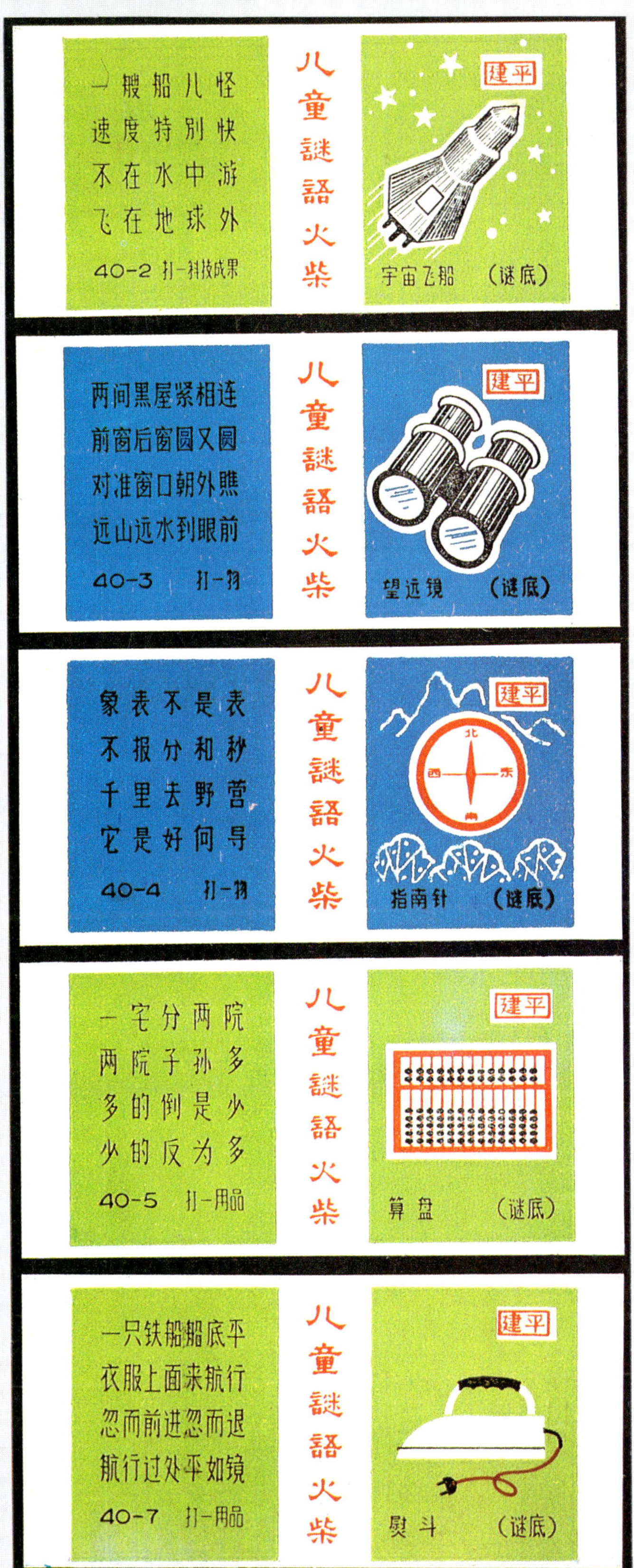

Children's Riddles

Life-like and easy to understand, the riddles on this ingeniously designed set of matchbox covers can stimulate children's thought and develop their intelligence. For example, the riddle of the second matchbox says: "Two dark rooms are closely connected, front windows and back windows are closely connected, look out of the windows to the mountains and rivers in the distance. How can we see that far?" The answer to the riddle is that the picture is a telescope.

Made in Jianping, Hebei Province

97 mm x 45 mm

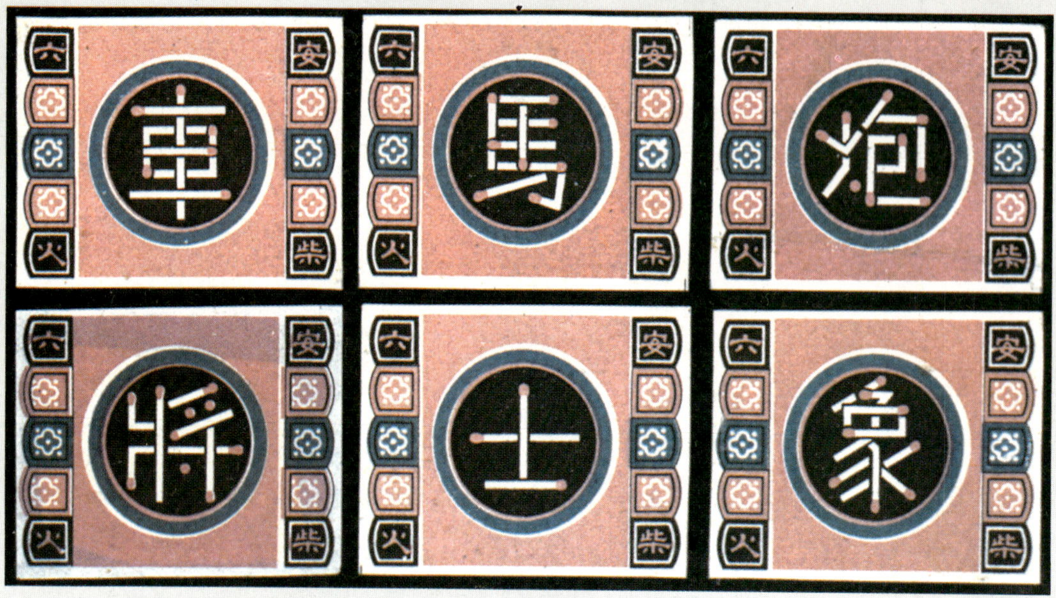

The Chinese Chess

Chinese chess is the topic of this group of covers. It is played by two people with sixteen pieces on each side. A collection of this set of matchbox covers is equal to a set of Chinese chess. The pieces shown here are the Chariot, Horse and Cannon (upper), Commander, Bodyguard and Elephant (lower).

Made in Liu'an, Anhui Province
43 mm x 34 mm

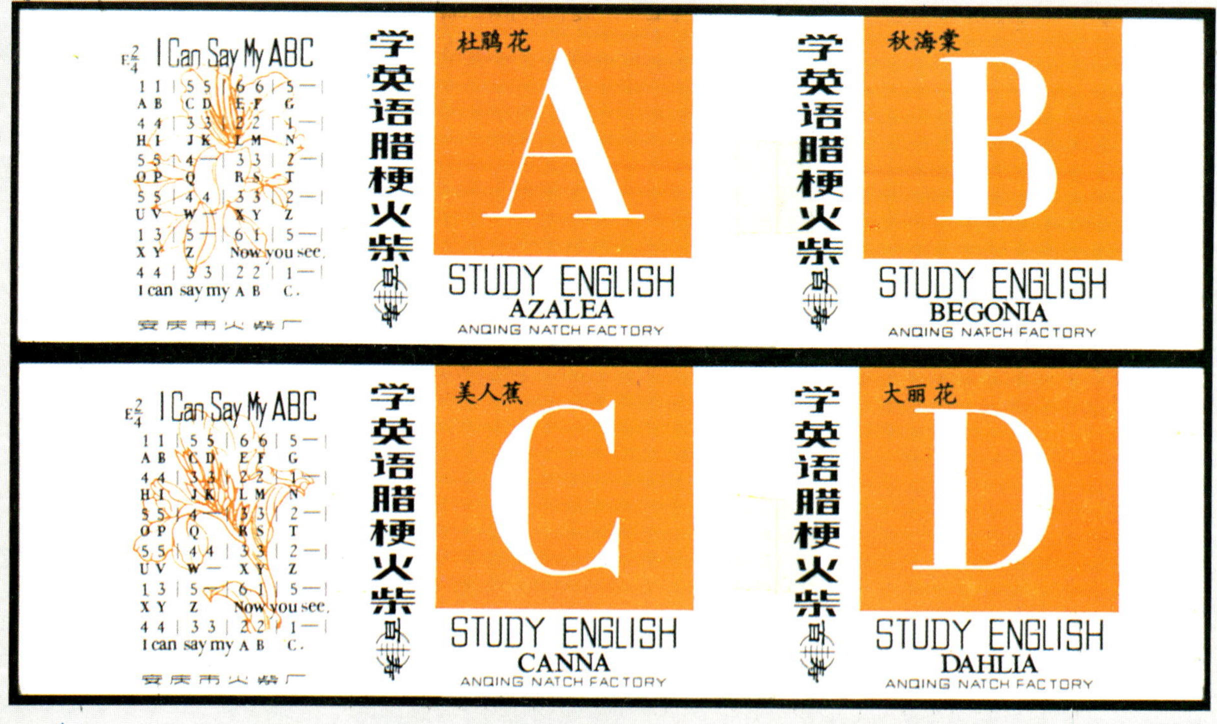

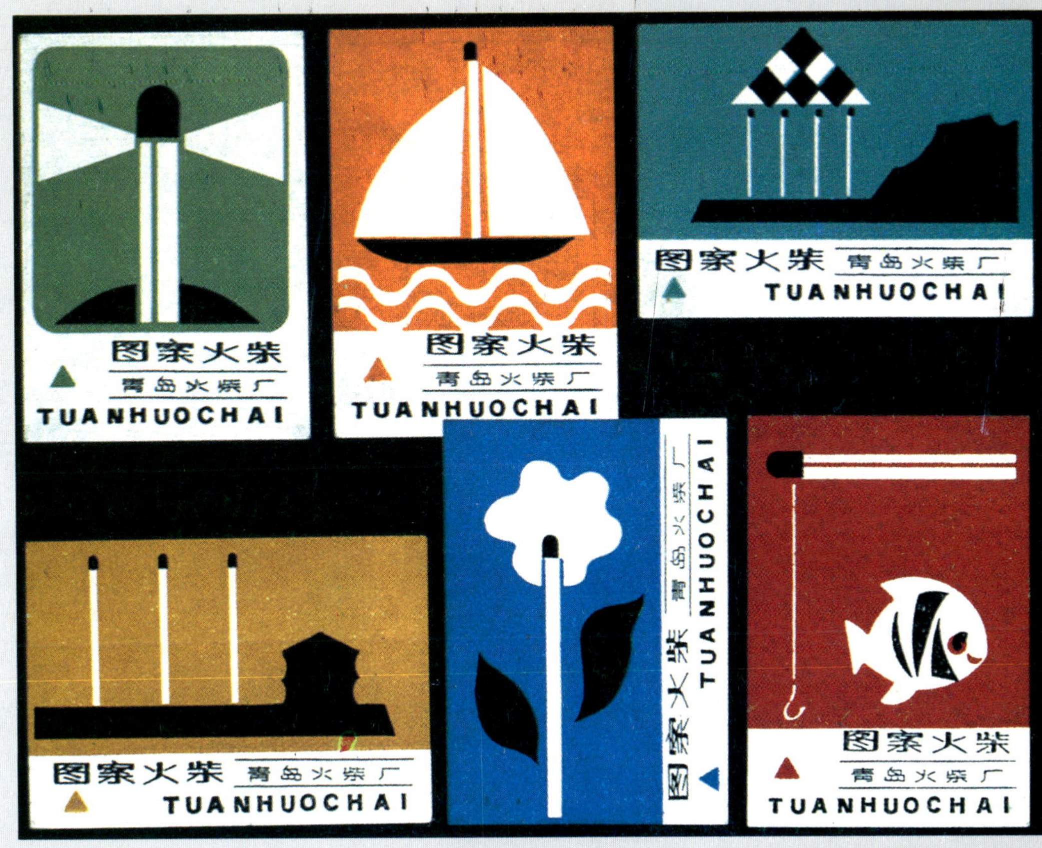

Seascapes

Seaside views commonly seen in Qingdao such as beacons, boat sails and bathing beach, are seen in these covers.

Made in Qingdao, Shandong Province

49 mm x 35 mm

Learning English

This group of matchbox covers presents a set of four English vocabulary cards with names of flowers in English and Chinese.

Made in Anqing, Anhui Province

108 mm x 46 mm

中国火柴盒贴集锦
编辑　周大光
供稿　季之光
撰文　吴之实
*
外文出版社出版
（中国北京百万庄路24号）
二二〇七工厂印刷
中国国际图书贸易总公司
（中国国际书店）发行
北京399信箱
1989年（16开）第一版
（英）
ISBN 7-119-00390-9／J·202（外）
03600
84-E-671P

35

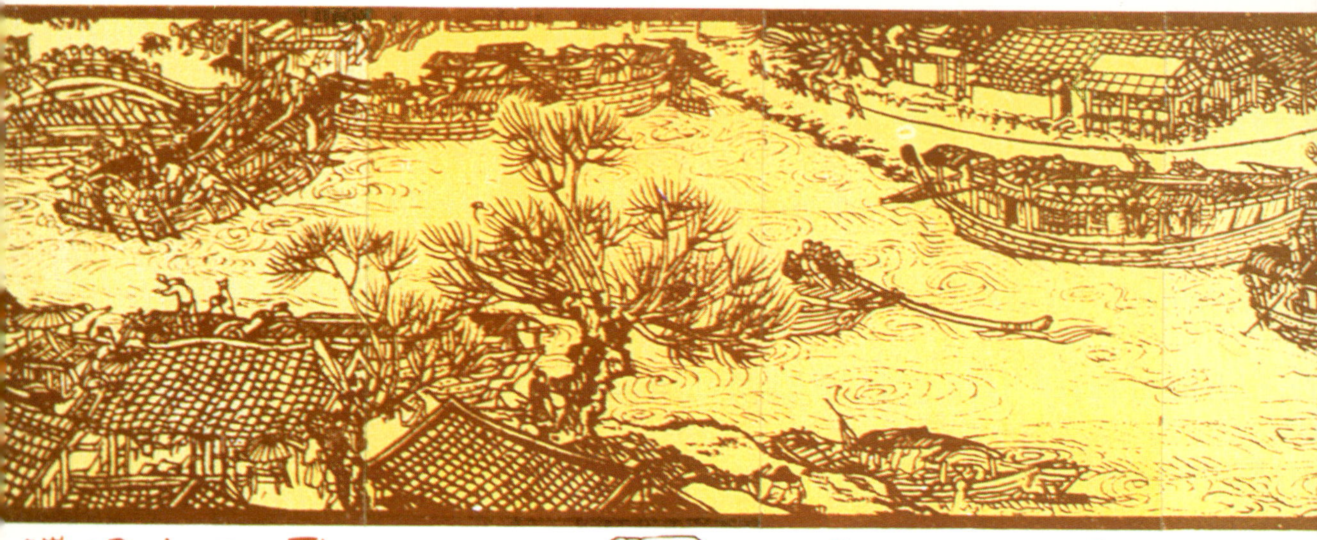

清明上河圖  清明上河圖

Riverside Scene at Qingming Festival

Riverside Scene at Qingming Festival was painted by the 12th-century artist Zhang Zeduan. Measuring 525 cm in length and 25.5 cm in height, the painting depicts the prosperous scene at Bianjing in present-day Kaifeng, Henan Province, capital of the Northern Song Dynasty. The painting, acclaimed as a highly realistic piece of art work, describes over 700 people, 90-plus heads of livestock, over 100 rooms and 20-odd boats.

Made in Kaifeng, Henan Province
159 mm x 52 mm

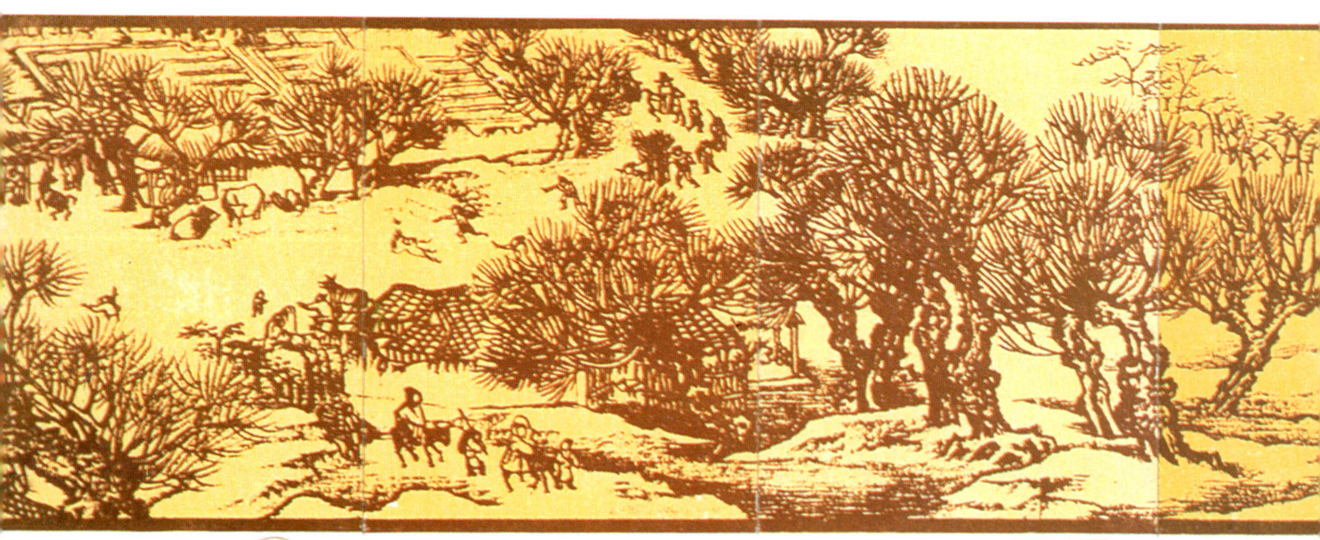

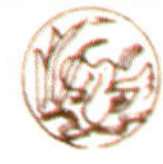 清明上河圖 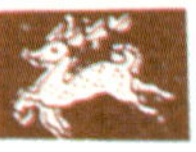 清明

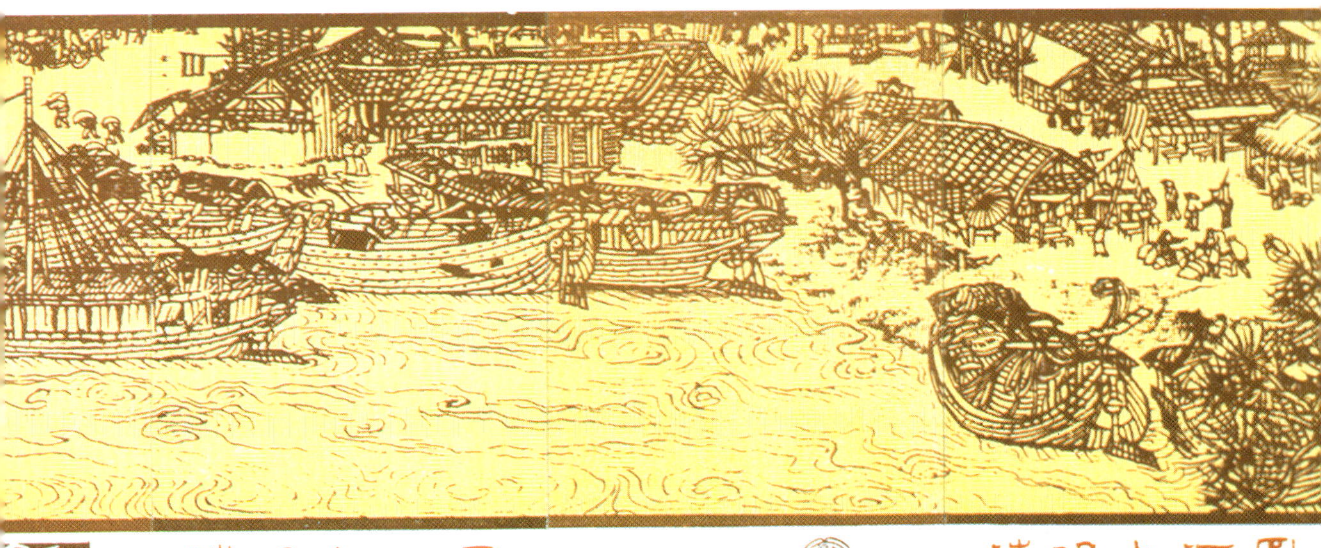

清明上河圖 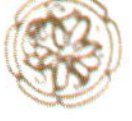 清明上河圖

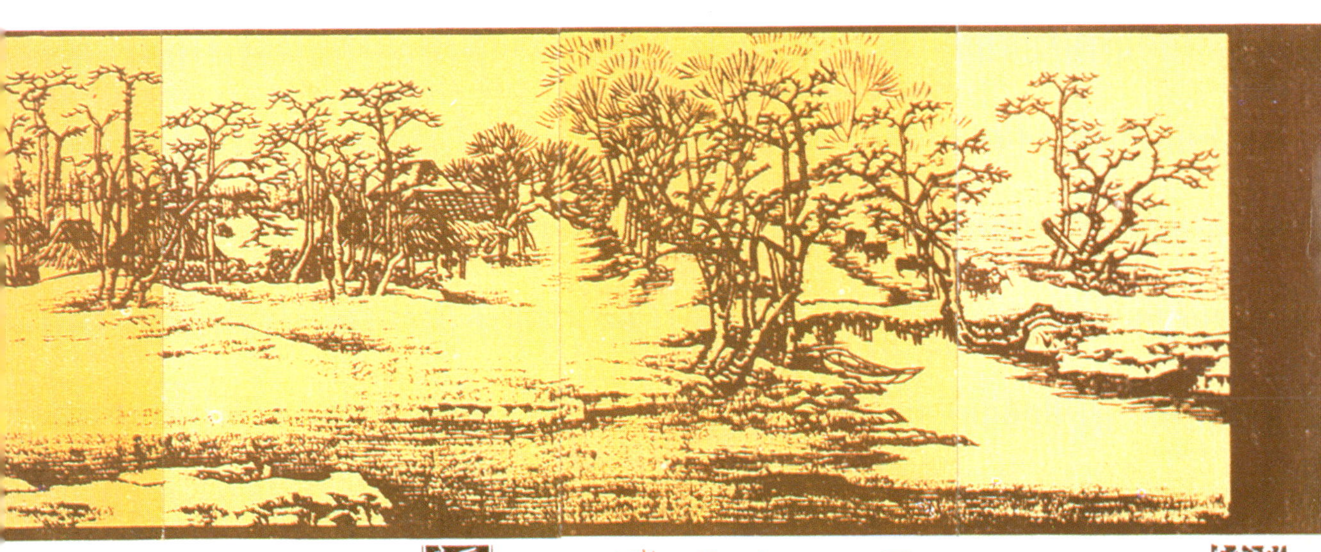

河圖 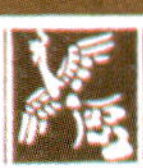 清明上河圖 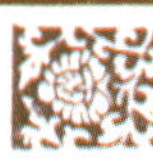